"A feast of feminism and history . . . Fascinates readers, and informs and entertains along the way." — *Roanoke Times*

"The perfect book for anyone interested in Anne Boleyn. Highly readable, interesting and thought-provoking." — **The Anne Boleyn Files**

"Susan Bordo's *Boleyn* did the impossible — it made me excited to read about the Tudors again while reminding me to approach history and historical fiction with curiosity and a questioning mind." — *Historical Fiction Notebook*

"Engrossing . . . blending biography, cultural history and literary analysis with a creative writer's knack for narrative and detail." — *Louisville LEO Weekly*

"A fascinating and accessible study of Anne Boleyn's history and popular myth." — *Shelf Awareness*

"The University of Kentucky humanities chair does a superb job of separating fact from fiction in contemporary accounts of Boleyn's life, before deftly deconstructing the myriad and contradictory portraits of her that have arisen in the centuries since her death . . . This engaging portrait culminates with an intriguing exploration of Boleyn's recent reemergence in pop culture." — *Publishers Weekly*

"A great read for Boleyn fans and fanatics alike." — *Kirkus Reviews*

"Beautiful, intelligent and true." — **Geneviève Bujold, actress, *Anne of the Thousand Days***

"Strong and discerning." — **Natalie Dormer, actress, *The Tudors***

"In *The Creation of Anne Boleyn,* we watch Anne Boleyn the woman transform into Anne Boleyn the legend — a fascinating journey. Susan Bordo covers Anne's historical footprints and her afterlife in art, fiction, poetry, theater and cinema, each change reflecting the concerns of a different era. Meticulous, thoughtful, persuasive — and fun."

— Margaret George, author of *The Autobiography of Henry VIII* and *Elizabeth I*

"By turns sassy and serious, playful and profound, Susan Bordo cuts through the layers of legend, fantasy, and untruth that history and culture have attached to Anne Boleyn, while proving that the facts about that iconic queen are every bit as intriguing as the fictions."

— Caroline Weber, author of *Queen of Fashion: What Marie Antoinette Wore to the Revolution*

"In this rigorously argued yet deliciously readable book, Susan Bordo bursts through the dead weight of cultural stereotypes and historical clichés to disentangle the fictions that we have created from the fascinating, elusive woman that Henry VIII tried — unsuccessfully — to erase from historical memory. This is a book that has long been needed to set the record straight, and Bordo knocked it out of the park."

— Robin Maxwell, national best-selling author of *The Secret Diary of Anne Boleyn* and *Mademoiselle Boleyn*

"*The Creation of Anne Boleyn* is a refreshing, iconoclastic and moving look at one of history's most intriguing women. It is rare to find a book that rouses one to scholarly glee, feminist indignation and empathetic tears, but this is such a book."

— Dr. Suzannah Lipscomb, author of *1536: The Year That Changed Henry VIII*

The Creation of Anne Boleyn

Books by Susan Bordo

The Flight to Objectivity: Essays on Cartesianism and Culture

Twilight Zones: The Hidden Life of Cultural Images from Plato to O. J.

The Male Body: A New Look at Men in Public and in Private

Unbearable Weight: Feminism, Western Culture, and the Body

*The Creation of Anne Boleyn: A New Look at
England's Most Notorious Queen*

The Creation
of Anne Boleyn

A New Look at England's
Most Notorious Queen

SUSAN BORDO

Mariner Books
Houghton Mifflin Harcourt
BOSTON • NEW YORK

First Mariner Books edition 2014

Copyright © 2013 by Susan Bordo

www.hmhco.com

Library of Congress Cataloging-in-Publication Data
Bordo, Susan, date.
The creation of Anne Boleyn : a new look at England's most notorious queen / Susan Bordo.
pages cm
Includes bibliographical references and index.
ISBN 978-0-547-32818-8   ISBN 978-0-547-83438-2 (pbk.)
1. Anne Boleyn, Queen, consort of Henry VIII, King of England,
1507–1536 — Influence. 2. Henry VIII, King of England, 1491–1547 — Marriage.
3. Great Britain — History — Henry VIII, 1509–1547. I. Title.
DA333.B6B67 2013
942.05'2092 — dc23   2012039119

Book design by Brian Moore

Printed in the United States of America
DOC 10 9 8 7 6 5 4 3 2 1

For Cassie Regina

Contents

The Erasure of Anne Boleyn and the Creation of "Anne Boleyn"

F OR ANNE, THE ARREST was sudden and inexplicable. At the end of April 1536, the king, by all outward appearances, was planning a trip with her to Calais on May 4, just after the May Day celebrations. She had no idea that at the same time the trip was being organized, the Privy Council had been informed of planned judicial proceedings against her, on charges of adultery and treason. Her husband was a genius at keeping his true intentions hidden. He had it down to an art: the arm round the shoulder, the intimate conversations, the warm gestures of affection and reassurance. And then, without warning, abandonment — or worse. It had happened with his longtime counselor and second Lord Chancellor, Thomas Wolsey, who saw him ride off one morning with promises of a friendly conversation that never happened. More famously, it had happened with Thomas More, whose intellect Henry had once valued above any other man's and whose conscience he had pledged to honor, then punished with death. This time, however, Henry's turnabout was not only fatal but also unprecedented. For the first time in English history, a queen was about to be executed. And, if Henry had gotten his way, written out of his memory — and history.

Even before the execution, Henry had begun the business of attempting to erase Anne Boleyn's life and death from the recorded legacy of his reign. On May 18, the day before Anne's execution, Thomas

Cromwell, aware of rumors that people were beginning to question the justice of the verdict and concerned that foreign ambassadors might write home sympathetic accounts of Anne's last moments, ordered William Kingston, constable of the Tower of London, to "have strange-rys conveyed yowt of the Towre."[1] Kingston carried out the order and assured Cromwell that only a "reasonable number" of witnesses would be there, to testify that justice had been done.[2] In fact, by the time of the execution, delayed still further due to the late arrival of the execu-tioner from Calais, there were more than a thousand spectators. For unknown reasons and despite Cromwell's orders, the Tower gates had been left open, and Londoners and "strangerys" alike streamed in.

As Anne prepared for her death, distraught over the delays, which she feared would weaken her resolve to bravely face the executioner, Henry was spending much of his time at Chelsea, visiting his future bride Jane Seymour and making plans for their wedding. He was eager to remarry as quickly as possible. But first he had to eradicate Anne. Even before the call sounded her death, dozens of carpenters, stone-masons, and seamstresses had been hard and hastily at work at Hamp-ton Court, instructed to remove all signs of Anne's queenship: her ini-tials, her emblems, her mottoes, and the numerous carved, entwined H's and A's strewn throughout the walls and ceiling of the Great Hall. Similar activities were going on at other royal residences. Henry was determined to start afresh with his new wife. Sometimes, the altera-tions were easy. Anne's leopard emblem became Jane's panther with clever adjustments to the head and tail. Various inscriptions to "Queen Anne" could be painted over and replaced with "Queen Jane." He got rid of her portraits. He (apparently) destroyed her letters. But the task of erasing Anne was an enormous one, since even before they were married, Henry had aggressively enthroned her symbolically in every nook and cranny of his official residences. Not surprisingly, especially since Henry wanted it done with such speed, many H's and A's were overlooked by Henry's revisionist workmen. Today, even the guides who provide information to visitors at Hampton Court are not sure how many there are.

Researching this book has been a lot like standing in the middle of that Great Hall at Hampton Court, squinting my eyes, trying to find unnoticed or "escaped" bits of Anne, dwarfed but still discernible within the monuments of created myths, legends, and images. In part because of Henry's purge, very little exists in Anne's own words or indisputably depicts what she did or said. Although seventeen of his love letters to her escaped the revision, having been stolen earlier and spirited away to the Vatican, only two letters that may be from Anne to Henry remain, and one is almost certainly inauthentic. Beyond these and some inscriptions in prayer books, most of our information about Anne's personality and behavior is secondhand: George Cavendish's "biography" of Cardinal Wolsey, which credits Anne with Wolsey's downfall; the gossipy, malicious reports of Eustace Chapuys and other foreign ambassadors to their home rulers, Constable Kingston's descriptions of her behavior in the Tower, and various "eyewitness" accounts of what she said and did at her trial and execution. Since Henry destroyed all the portraits he could lay his hands on, it's even difficult to determine what Anne actually looked like. Later artistic depictions, all of them copies and only a few believed to be copies of originals done from actual sittings, are wildly inconsistent with one another, from the shape of her face to the color of her hair, and her looks, as described by her contemporaries, range from deformed to "not bad-looking" to "rivaling Venus." Whether or not these portraits are actually of Anne is a source of constant debate among historians and art historians.

You might expect Anne to be resuscitated today at the various historical sites associated with Henry's reign, but, in fact, she's not very prominent there either. In the gift shops, thimbles, small chocolates, and tiny soaps "commemorate" Henry's wives democratically. Everything is in sets of six, each wife given equal billing among the tiny trinkets, as though they were members of a harem. The "and his six" view of the wives is everywhere in Britain. Yet despite the "all wives are equal" spin of Hampton Court and the Tower of London, and despite the absence of Anne's own voice and image among the relics of the period, she is undoubtedly the most famous of Henry's wives. Ask any random person who Katherine of Aragon, Anne of Cleves, Katherine Howard, or Katherine Parr were, and you probably won't even get an attempt to scan stored mental information. The name "Jane Seymour" will probably register as the apparently ageless actress well-known for

Lifetime movies and ads for heart-shaped jewelry. But Anne Boleyn, at the very least, is remembered as "the one who had her head chopped off."[3]

Henry may have tried to erase her, but Anne Boleyn looms large in our cultural imagination. Everyone has some tidbit of Anne mythology to pull out: "She slept with hundreds of men, didn't she?" (I heard that one from a classical scholar.) "She had six fingers — or was it three nipples?" (From a French-literature expert.) "She had sex with her own brother." (From anyone who has learned their history at the foot of Philippa Gregory.) She has been the focus of numerous biographies, several movies, and a glut of historical fiction — *Murder Most Royal, The Secret Diary of Anne Boleyn, The Lady in the Tower, The Other Boleyn Girl, Mademoiselle Boleyn, A Lady Raised High, The Concubine, Brief Gaudy Hour* — which, thanks to Showtime's *The Tudors*, have multiplied over the last several years. (By a 2012 count on Amazon, more than fifty biographies, novelizations, or studies were published in the preceding five years alone; and that's without considering electronic editions, reprints of Henry's love letters, or Tudor books within which Anne is a central, though not main, focus.) Anne has also become a thriving commercial concern (Halloween costumes, sweatshirts, coffee cups, magnets, bumper stickers). Internet sites are devoted to her, and feminist art deconstructs her demise.

My own obsession with Anne began early in 2007, with an e-mail from England sent by a young journalist looking for a feminist to co-author a book with him. The book was to be about famous women and their pursuit of pleasure, in defiance of the rules and restrictions of their cultures. In the original plan, Anne Boleyn was to be one of many, from Cleopatra to Queen Latifah. Uncommitted but curious, I started casually reading about Anne. And found I couldn't stop. It was a total gorge. I consumed Boleyn voraciously, sometimes several books a week, one after another, as if I were chain-smoking. I rented movies and documentaries, read all the popular histories, delved into all the scholarly debates, and discovered the thriving industry in Tudor fiction. I gobbled them like candy. My lust for Boleyniana was right up there with Cherry Ames, Student Nurse (fourth grade), James Bond (college), Sylvia Plath bios (graduate school), and O. J. Simpson and JonBenét Ramsey (pop culture critic). And in the end, she became the only woman on our list whom I wanted to write about, and researching her life and how it has been represented has consumed me for the past six years.

Why is Anne Boleyn so fascinating? Maybe we don't have to go any further than the obvious: The story of her rise and fall is as elementally satisfying — and scriptwise, not very different from — a Lifetime movie: a long-suffering, postmenopausal wife; an unfaithful husband and a clandestine affair with a younger, sexier woman; a moment of glory for the mistress; then lust turned to loathing, plotting, and murder as the cycle comes full circle. As Irene Goodman writes, "Anne's life was not just an important historical event. It was also the stuff of juicy tabloid stories... It has sex, adultery, pregnancy, scandal, divorce, royalty, glitterati, religious quarrels, and larger-than-life personalities. If Anne lived today, she would have been the subject of lurid tabloid headlines: RANDY KING DUMPS HAG FOR TROPHY WIFE."[4]

But Anne hasn't always been seen as a skanky schemer. For supporters of Katherine of Aragon, she was worse: a coldhearted murderess. For Catholic propagandists such as Nicholas Sander, she was a six-fingered, jaundiced-looking erotomaniac who slept with butlers, chaplains, and half of the French court. For Elizabethan admirers, she was the unsung heroine of the Protestant Reformation. For the Romantics, particularly in painting, she was the hapless victim of a king's tyranny — a view that gets taken up in the earliest film versions of Anne, Ernst Lubitsch's silent *Anna Boleyn* and Alexander Korda's *The Private Life of Henry VIII*. In postwar movies and on television, Anne has been animated by the rebellious spirit of the sixties (*Anne of the Thousand Days*), the "mean girl" and "power feminist" celebration of female aggression and competitiveness of the nineties (*The Other Boleyn Girl*), and the third-wave feminism of a new generation of Anne worshippers, inspired by Natalie Dormer's brainy seductress of *The Tudors* to see in Anne a woman too smart, sexy, and strong for her own time, unfairly vilified for her defiance of sixteenth-century norms of wifely obedience and silence. Henry may have tried to write his second wife out of history, but "Anne Boleyn" has been too strong for him, in the many guises she has assumed over the centuries.

One goal of this book is to follow the cultural career of these mutating Annes, from the poisonous *putain* created by the Spanish ambassador Eustace Chapuys — a highly biased portrayal that became history for many later writers — to the radically revisioned Anne of the Internet generation. I'm not such a postmodernist, however, that I'm content to just write a history of competing narratives. I'm fascinated by their twists and turns, but even more fascinated by the real Anne, who has not been *quite* as disappeared as Henry wanted. Like Marilyn Monroe in our own time, she is an enigma who is hard to keep one's hands off of; just as men dreamed of possessing her in the flesh, writers can't resist the desire to solve the mysteries of how she came to be, to reign, to perish. I'm no exception. I have my own theories, and I won't hide them. There are so many big questions that remain unanswered that this book would be very unsatisfying if I did not attempt to address them.

Perhaps the biggest question concerns Henry more than Anne herself. *How could he do it?* The execution of a queen was extreme and shocking, even to Anne's enemies. They may have believed Anne guilty of adultery and treason — and Henry may have too — but even so, it still does not explain Anne's *execution*. Eleanor of Aquitaine had been banished for the same crimes. Why did Anne have to die? The answer, I believe, is psychological as well as political; to find it, we have to venture — with caution, for his was an era that lived largely by roles rather than by introspection — into Henry's psyche.

Another unsolved mystery is the relationship itself, which began with such powerful attraction, at least on Henry's part, and created such havoc in the realm. It is often assumed that Anne, in encouraging Henry's pursuit, was motivated solely by personal (or perhaps familial) ambition, while Henry was bewitched by her sexual allure. This scenario is a sociobiologist's dream relationship — woman falls for power and protection, man for the promise of fertility — but ignores how long and at what expense the two hung in there in order to mesh their genes. We know that Henry was intent on finding a new wife to secure the male heir that Katherine, through their seventeen-year marriage, had failed to produce. But why Anne Boleyn? She wasn't the most beautiful woman at court. She wasn't royalty and thus able to serve in solidifying foreign relations. She wasn't a popular choice (to put it mildly) among Henry's advisers. Yet he pursued her for six years, sending old friends to the scaffold and splitting his kingdom down the middle to achieve legitimacy for the marriage. Surely he could have found a less divisive baby maker among the royalty of Europe?

One enduring answer to the mystery of Henry's pursuit of Anne portrays her as a medieval Circe, with Henry as her hapless, hormone-driven man toy. This image, besides asking us to believe something outlandish about Henry, is an all too familiar female stereotype. Even the slight evidence we have tells us that Anne's appeal was more com-plicated than that of a medieval codpiece teaser. We know, from re-corded remarks, that she had a dark, sardonic sense of humor that stayed with her right to the end. We know that she *wasn't* the great beauty, in her day, that Merle Oberon, Geneviève Bujold, Natalie Dor-mer, and Natalie Portman are in ours, and that her fertility signals were weak: Her "dukkys" were quite small, and her complexion was sallow. We know that there was something piquantly "French" about her. Just what that means — today as well as then — is somewhat elusive, but in Anne's case, it seems to have had a lot to do with her sense of fashion, her excellent dancing skills, and her gracefulness, which according to courtier and poet Lancelot de Carles, made her seem less like "an Eng-lishwoman" than "a Frenchwoman born."[5]

Anne the stylish consort is a familiar image. What is less generally familiar, outside of some limited scholarly circles, is Anne the free-thinking, reformist intellectual. Both courts at which she spent her teenage years were dominated by some of the most independent, in-fluential women in Europe. Anne spent fifteen months or so in the household of the sophisticated and politically powerful Archduchess Margaret of Austria, regent of the Netherlands, and then seven years in France, where she came into contact with Marguerite de Navarre, the sister of Francis I. Marguerite was visited by the most famous re-formist thinkers of the day and was a kind of shadow queen at Fran-cis's court; Queen Claude had the babies, but Marguerite, who is sometimes called "the mother of the Renaissance," ran the intellectual and artistic side of things. Anne spent most of her formative years at Francis's court and was clearly influenced by Marguerite's evangelical-ism — which in those days meant a deep belief in the importance of a "personal" (rather than a church-mediated) relationship to God, with daily prayer and Bible study as its centerpiece.[6]

It's also possible that Marguerite taught Anne, by example, that a woman's place extended beyond her husband's bed and that this, iron-ically, was part of her appeal for Henry. For traditionalists at court, Anne's having any say in Henry's political affairs would have been outrageously presumptuous, particularly since Anne was not of royal blood. Henry, however, had been educated alongside his two sisters and was extremely close to his mother; there's no evidence that he saw Anne's "interference," so long as it supported his own aims, as anything other than proof of her queenly potential. In fact, in the six-year-long battle for the divorce, they seem much more like coconspirators than manipulating female and hapless swain. Henry, whose intellect was, in fact, more restless than his hormones (compared to, say, the rapacious Francis), and who was already chafing at the bit of any authority other than his own, may have imagined Anne as someone with whom he could shape a kingdom.

These are pieces of Anne's life that are like those entwined H's and A's that Henry's revisionist architects didn't see. But while Henry's workmen were blinded by haste, we have had centuries to find the missing pieces. Sometimes our failure to see has been the result of po-litical animosity, misogyny, or religious vendetta. Others have wanted to tell a good story and found the facts got in the way. Still others have been too trusting of the conclusions of others. And others didn't know where or how to look when the trail wandered outside the boundaries of their discipline, time period, or areas of specialization. The Great Hall at Hampton Court is thus for me not just a reminder of Henry's efforts to erase Anne, but also a metaphor for how later generations have perpetuated that erasure.

This book is *not*, however, a "corrective" biography of Anne that traces her life from birth to death, chronicling all the central events. For that, we already have Eric Ives's magnum opus, *The Life and Death of Anne Boleyn*, as well as several other excellent biographies. Anyone who wants to find a full narrative of Boleyn's life should consult those sources. Nor do I enter into specialized scholarly debates, found only in academic journals. What you *will* find here, in the first part of the book, is some cultural detective work into what I see as the soft spots — the missing pieces, the too-readily-accepted images, the biases, the absence of some key cultural context — in the existing literature, along with some theories of my own, based on the six years of research I've conducted for this book. Although not meant to be straight "history," I have organized it chronologically and have attempted to provide enough historical detail to create a coherent backstory. That section, called Queen, Interrupted, concludes with Boleyn's death.

The second part, Recipes for "Anne Boleyn," and the third, An Anne for All Seasons, comprise a cultural history not of her life, but of how she has been imagined and represented over the centuries since her death, from the earliest attackers and defenders, to the most recent novels, biographies, plays, films, television shows, and websites. Readers whose image of Anne has been shaped by the recent media depictions and novels may be surprised at the variety of "Annes" who have strutted through history; I know I was. My annoyance with popular stereotypes was one reason why I started this book; I expected it to be a critical exposé of how thoroughly maligned and mishandled she has been throughout the centuries. But the truth is not so simple. Anne has been less the perpetual victim of the same old sexist stereotyping than she has been a shape-shifting trickster whose very incompleteness in the historical record has stirred the imaginations of different agendas, different generations, and different cultural moments to lay claim to their "own" Boleyn. In cutting her life so short and then ruthlessly disposing of the body of evidence of her "real" existence, Henry made it possible for her to live a hundred different lives, forever.

PART I

Queen, Interrupted

1

Why You Shouldn't Believe Everything You've Heard About Anne Boleyn

"FOR WEEKS ANNE, like the goddess of the chase, had pursued her rival. She bullied Henry; she wheedled; she threatened; and most devastatingly, she cried. Her arrows pierced his heart and hardened his judgement. It was how she had destroyed Wolsey. Now she would remove Katherine."[1]

Is this a quotation from Philippa Gregory's novel *The Other Boleyn Girl*, with its desperate, vengeful Anne? Or perhaps a fragment from Catholic propagandist Nicholas Sander's famously vitriolic portrait of Anne in *The Rise and Growth of the Anglican Schism*? Directions from the shooting script of an episode from the first season of *The Tudors* television series? No, the description was written by one of the twentieth century's most respected and admired historians of the Tudor era, and it comes from a book that is advertised as "biography" and lauded, on the back cover, as "a masterful work of history."

There's no doubting David Starkey's expertise or his ability to juice up the dry bones of the historical record with the narrative drive and color of a novel. It's one of the main reasons his books like *Six Wives*

(2004) are so popular; people enjoy them. They are less likely to recognize, though (it's obscured by that label of authority: "historian"), that Starkey is creating a dramatic fantasy of what Anne thought, said, and did — and an equally creative fantasy about the impact her actions had on Henry. Starkey doesn't have any proof that Anne bullied or shed tears in order to get her way with Henry; and his theory that the hardening of Henry's character was due to Anne's manipulation is just that — a theory. The idea that it was Anne who engineered Wolsey's fall is speculation. The evidence for the portrait he paints — and it *is* a painting, though he presents it as documentary — would never pass muster in a modern court of law, for it is slender to begin with and is nestled in the gossip and hearsay of some highly biased sources. As such, Starkey might have legitimately presented it as a case that can be made. Instead, he delivers Anne's motivation, moral character, and effect on Henry to us as though it were established fact.

Starkey is hardly alone in mixing fact and fantasy in his accounts of the life and death of Anne Boleyn. Not everyone tells the same story. But few historians or biographers acknowledge just how much of what they are doing *is* storytelling. It's unavoidable, of course, for writers not to string facts together along some sort of narrative thread that, inevitably, has a point of view. But when it comes to Anne Boleyn, the narrative threads are more like lawyers' briefs that argue for her sinfulness or saintliness while (like any good lawyer's argument) cloaked in the grammar of "fact." In the old days, the arguments were up-front: Paul Friedmann, in his 1884 biography, boldly states: "Anne was not good. She was incredibly vain, ambitious, unscrupulous, coarse, fierce, and relentless."[2] James Froude, who followed in 1891 with a pro-Protestant defense of Henry's divorce proceedings, did not extend his sympathies to Anne, although she was much more devotedly anticlerical than Henry: "Henry was, on the whole, right; the general cause for which he was contending was a good cause . . . [but] [h]e had stained the purity of his action by intermingling with it a weak passion for a foolish and bad woman, and bitterly he had to suffer for his mistake."[3] Henry William Herbert charged Anne with responsibility for every death that occurred during the years she was Henry's consort; with her ascension in Henry's eyes, "Wolsey's downfall was dated . . . [and] likewise may be dated the death-sentence of the venerable Fisher, bishop of Rochester, and of the excellent Sir Thomas More; for they had both given opinions adverse to the divorce, and although they continued to hold office, and even apparently to enjoy the royal favor, they were both inscribed on the black-list of the revengeful mistress, who never rested from her ill offices toward them, until their heads had fallen."[4] More current prosecutors rely more on rhetoric than bald statements such as these. Starkey, for example, never actually accuses Anne of murder, but he certainly paints her as capable of it. Here he describes Anne's reaction to Henry's beheading of Thomas More, which has left her craving the blood of Katherine and her daughter, Mary, too:

> Anne undoubtedly rejoiced . . . But she wanted other, yet more distinguished victims . . . Would she get her way in this too?[5]

Throughout *Six Wives*, rhetorical flourishes such as these and the constant use of hunting metaphors paint a portrait of Anne as an evil huntress worthy of Greek mythology — or perhaps a vampire novel: "Anne's first target was Wolsey,"[6] "Anne had Mary in her sights,"[7] "Anne had her own quarry, too: Wolsey,"[8] "The hunting down of another of her old enemies offered some compensation,"[9] etc.

Although, as we'll see, it has been challenged by other narratives, this view of Anne as ruthless predator is one of the oldest and most enduring in our cultural stockpile of Anne Boleyn images. As recently as March 2012, journalist and novelist Vanora Bennett, having traipsed through a variety of contradictory perspectives on Anne in a piece devoted to the swelling of contemporary interest in Anne, cautions against sympathy for her.

> She was vindictive. It wasn't enough for her to persuade Henry to arrest her archenemy Cardinal Wolsey: it had to be her ex-admirer Henry Percy who made the arrest. Nor was it enough to usurp the position of Henry's first wife; Anne also mercilessly bullied the little Princess Mary, who never saw her mother again . . . She harangued Henry about his flirtations with other women, blaming him for her miscarriages. She alienated her powerful uncle and protector, the

Duke of Norfolk, by speaking to him in words that, according to one biographer, "shouldn't be used to a dog." And she fell out with Cromwell over foreign policy — whether England should be allied to France (her choice) or the Holy Roman Emperor (his) — something that was more his business than hers . . . No one was sorry to see her go.[10]

Let me say up front that I do not believe Anne Boleyn was the helpless innocent that some of her later defenders made her out to be. But Bennett, like many of Anne's detractors, goes way too far. Can it possibly be that Henry VIII, who began his reign executing his father's ministers, later declared himself the Supreme Head on Earth of the Church of England, and was miserably cruel to Princess Mary even after Anne's death, became a pathetic wimp under the spell of this all-powerful temptress? I won't begin, at this point in the book, to document all the factual errors and unjustified conclusions in this Anne-blaming, Henry-exonerating account. For now, I simply ask: Where did this view of Anne come from and how did it become so familiar, so accepted, that not only a journalist such as Bennett but also a respected historian such as David Starkey can treat it as established fact? The answer to that, it turns out, casts doubt on virtually all that we have taken to be certain about Anne's brief reign.

Eustace Chapuys was just thirty years old when, in 1529, he was sent to replace Don Inigo de Mendoza as the ambassador of Emperor Charles V at the court of Henry VIII. Mendoza was known to be "hot-tempered" and "indiscreet,"[11] and Chapuys, a legal scholar and humanist enthusiast, was thought to be a better choice for Henry's court. He was an erudite and clever diplomat, and devoted to those whom he loved and the causes he believed in. Queen Katherine fell into both categories, for the emperor was Katherine's nephew, and Chapuys was fiercely pro-Catholic. He also hated all things French and later in his life would threaten to disinherit a niece who planned to marry a Frenchman.[12] It's difficult to imagine someone who would be less disposed to the dissolution of Henry's marriage to Katherine and more opposed to the marriage of Henry and Anne Boleyn, who was both sympathetic to reformist ideas and "more French than a Frenchwoman born." And indeed, from his first dispatch home in 1529, in which he fervently wished that "[m]ay God remedy" the king's affection for "La Bolaing,"[13] to his delight, in May 1536, over "the fall and ruin of the concubine," Chapuys was Anne's sworn enemy and Katherine and Mary's most passionate defender.[14]

Chapuys hated Anne with a passion that he didn't even try to disguise, disgustedly referring to her in his official communications as "the concubine" and "that whore"—or, with polite disdain, "The Lady." Accordingly, Elizabeth was "the little bastard." He accused Anne of plotting to murder Katherine and Mary—without a shred of proof beyond a few reported outbursts of Anne's—and was the first to advance the argument that she was responsible for Henry's "corruption." ("[I]t is this Anne," Chapuys wrote, "who has put [Henry] in this perverse and wicked temper."[15]) His biases are very clear. Yet, unfortunately, his lengthy, anecdote-filled letters home also offer the single most continuous portrait of the sixteen crisis-ridden years in which he served in his position, and despite his undisguised hatred of Anne—not to mention the fact that he did not view himself as writing history but skillfully adjudicating between Henry and Charles—biographers have relied on him heavily in their attempts to create a coherent narrative about the divorce from Katherine, the role of Anne Boleyn, and her relationship with Henry.

It's easy to see why. History abhors a vacuum. Chapuys clearly loved to write, he did so often, and he had a taste for juicy detail. The frustrating fact is that without Chapuys and Cavendish—Wolsey's secretary and later "biographer," whose *The Life of Cardinal Wolsey* is the basis for the narrative that Anne hated Wolsey for breaking up an earlier romance—it would probably be impossible to construct a "story" at all in the sense in which popular histories require, in which events can simply be "reported" without the kind of constant qualification, caution, posing of questions, that authors fear will bore readers. If we were to acknowledge that the "history" of Anne Boleyn is largely written by the poisonous pen of hostile sources, the entire edifice of pop Tudor history would become quite shaky. Instead, it has been fortified by a foundation of titillating, crowd-pleasing mythology. Chapuys was not the sole architect of this mythology, but he was the first, the most respected, and the most influential. The fact is that it is Eustace Chapuys, Anne's sworn enemy, who has most shaped our image of her. He has done so not directly, but via the historians and novelists who have accepted his reports as "biased" but accurate, and hardened them, over time, into history.

Most nonhistorians, before Showtime's *The Tudors* introduced him to popular audiences, had never even heard of Chapuys. He plays virtually no role in previous media depictions of the reign of Henry VIII — or novelistic fictionalizations — and those audiences who came to know him through *The Tudors* got to know him largely as a warm, devoted friend of Katherine of Aragon and later, Princess Mary. In one scene, he does tacitly encourage an assassination attempt on Anne's life, but the extent of his involvement in the court intrigues that led to Anne's downfall is vastly underplayed, and most scenes feature him lavishing fatherly love and comfort on the abandoned and bereft queen and her daughter. The contrast the show draws is clear: On the one hand, we have warm, caring, ever-faithful Chapuys; on the other, narcissistic, fickle, ruthless Henry. Thanks largely to this sympathetic portrayal of Chapuys as Katherine's comfort and Mary's gentle confidant, he has gathered lots of fans. When I posted a piece on the Internet that was critical of his account of the failure of Anne and Henry's marriage, I was amazed to find readers leaping to his defense: "I love Anne immensely and I know that Chapuys was not fair to her many times, but I hold a very special place in my heart for that man"[16]; "As a researcher I just really appreciate his letters and reports, they're fantastic. I can't blame him for how he felt about Anne and his support of Mary and his visiting Katherine at the end of her life is so moving"[17]; "I must admit to having a real affection for Chapuys as often when I'm trying to find something in the archives I'll find what I'm looking for in his very detailed reports, bless that man! What would we do without him?!"[18]; "He always seemed like a kind and gentle man to me."[19]

He always seemed like a kind and gentle man to me. The enmeshment of fact and fiction, of the real and the imagined in our collective history of the Tudors, could not be more succinctly captured. And it doesn't begin with pop culture. Chapuys himself played a huge role in creating the collective fantasy of "virtuous, patient Katherine" versus "self-seeking, impatient Anne." When you closely examine events, it's clear that Katherine was as self-interested and stubborn a player as any other in the drama. She was, after all, the daughter of Queen Isabella and raised with a sense of royal privilege and entitlement from the day of her birth. She also believed, as Henry did about his own kingship, that her position was a manifestation of God's will. When Henry proposed divorce, she was emotionally shattered, but also fiercely resistant and full of righteous indignation — and stayed so right up until her death in 1536. She simply wouldn't let go, impervious even to the disastrous consequences for her beloved Catholic Church, as Henry's position became more and more oppositional. When Cardinal Lorenzo Campeggio proposed the solution that she take the veil, giving Henry his freedom to remarry without putting Mary's inheritance in question, she flatly refused, although it was, as historian David Loades puts it, a "simple and plausible" way to resolve things.[20]

> Katherine knew, as well as Henry did, that she would never bear him another child. She also knew, although she may not have sympathized with, his burning desire for a son. She was a deeply pious woman, and the religious life had appealed to her in the past. There would have been no question of dishonour, and no need to defend her daughter's rights.[21]

Katherine not only refused the nunnery solution, insisting that "she intended to live and die in the state of matrimony, to which God had called her: that she would always remain of that opinion, and that she would never change it" but she also startled Campeggio with the intensity of her fervor; they could tear her "limb from limb," she told him, and if she were then brought back to life she "would prefer to die over again, rather than change."[22] Why was Katherine so fixed in her position? In part, because she was an orthodox Catholic (as opposed to Henry's more pragmatic variety), and she firmly believed in the authority of the pope who had earlier given dispensation for their marriage. In part, because she truly did believe she had been called by God to be queen of England. And in part, I believe, because she was too humiliated, her queenly pride too wounded, to simply creep away. The only way to restore any sense of dignity was to show the world —

and Henry—that her argument was the righteous one. In this effort, the "steely determination" that Loades calls her "chief characteristic" was as strong and singular as Henry's.[23] Events might have played out very differently if she had been more invested in the "bigger picture" and less fixated on her own rights. At one point, in fact, Pope Clement VII, fearing that Katherine's obstinacy would "be the cause of the destruction of the spiritualities," told Henry's ambassadors that he wished "for the wealth of Christendom" that "the Queen were in her grave."[24]

This picture of Katherine will come as a surprise to those who have learned about Henry VIII's "great matter" from popular history, where typically it's not Katherine who appears as the stubborn, willful, female power player in the drama, but Anne Boleyn. Katherine's earliest biographers, Agnes and Elizabeth Strickland, write: "Sustained by her own innate grandeur of soul, her piety, and lofty rectitude, [Katherine] passed through all her bitter trials without calumny succeeding in fixing a spot on her name."[25] Although the Stricklands' male contemporaries found much to fault in their "feminine" view of history, they did not disagree about Katherine. "I know of no woman," wrote Henry William Herbert in 1856, "recorded in veritable history, or portrayed in romance, who approaches so nearly to perfection. So far as it is permitted to us to see her character, without or within, there was no speck to mar the loveliness, no shadow to dim the perfection, of her faultless, Christian womanhood. If anything mortal could be perfect, that mortal thing, so far as man may judge, was Katherine of Aragon."[26] This sanctified picture, from which qualities such as Katherine's stubbornness and self-righteousness have been removed, has remained pretty much intact, with few exceptions,[27] up through the present day and Showtime's *The Tudors*. And it comes straight from Chapuys, who took every opportunity to contrast "the people's" hatred of Anne with their great love of Katherine. When Henry had Katherine removed from court,

> All the neighborhood assembled to see her and pay her honor; and
> it is incredible what affection has been shown to her along the whole
> route. Notwithstanding that it has been forbidden on pain of death to

call her Queen, they shouted it out at the top of their voices, wishing her joy, repose, and prosperity, and confusion to her enemies. They begged her with hot tears to set them to work and employ them in her service, as they were ready to die for the love of her.[28]

The contrast is almost Hollywood-ready: the sullen, disrespectful observers of Anne's procession; the cheering throngs, ready to die for their true queen as she was led away from her rightful throne. And there is undoubtedly some truth in it. Katherine was extremely beloved and Anne was the Other Woman, so she certainly had strikes against her. But "the people" didn't record or publish their sentiments themselves, and virtually every report of their virulent animosity toward Anne is open to question. When Venetian diplomat Francesco Sanuto writes that "it is said" that a mob of seven to eight thousand women attempted to seize and kill Anne (she escaped by boat), it sounds implausible, especially since he is the only diplomat to mention it, and it's odd that none of the mob was apprehended or punished (Sanuto says it's because they were women — which certainly didn't stop Henry in other cases.[29]) Similarly, the routine depiction of Anne's coronation procession as attended by throngs of resentful, sullen townspeople who refused to remove their hats for her seems to be based on an anonymous account whose details of Anne's dress alone are a giveaway that the description was written with a poison pen.

> Though it was customary to kneel, uncover, and cry "God save the King, God save the Queen," whenever they appeared in public, no one in London or the suburbs, not even women and children, did so on this occasion. One of the Queen's servants told the mayor to command the people to make the customary shouts, and was answered that he could not command people's hearts, and that even the King could not make them do so . . . [The queen's] dress was covered with tongues pierced with nails, to show the treatment which those who spoke against her might expect. Her car was so low that the ears of the last mule appeared to those who stood behind to belong to her. The letters H. A. were painted in several places, for Henry and Anne, but were laughed at by many. The crown became her very ill, and a wart disfigured her very much. She wore a violet velvet mantle, with a high

ruff of gold thread and pearls, which concealed a swelling she has, resembling goître."[30]

I'll discuss the wart and the goiter, which pop up regularly in descriptions of Anne penned by her enemies, in the next chapter. The most insidious claims, though, are not nearly so transparently fantastical as a king's consort with severe disfigurements or a dress pierced with nails, but come from those whose hostility to Anne rests on the "monstrosity" of her character rather than her looks. In this, later defenders of "the faith" such as Nicholas Sander, as we'll see, played a large role. But by then — 1585 — the battle lines between Catholic and Protestant were more clearly drawn than in 1530, and the polemical nature of *The Rise and Growth of the Anglican Schism* is pretty transparent. Chapuys, in contrast, writing when the conflict over church authority was still muddied by the domestic scandal of the divorce proceedings, has not been seen as a propagandist, but as a not-quite-objective recorder of events. Yet anyone who does read his letters objectively can see that he was the founding father of anti-Anne propaganda. His aim: to convince (and reassure) Charles that Katherine's rival was so full of "iniquity and detestable wickedness"[31] that Henry was sure to eventually see through her and get rid of her, while at the same time scaring and inciting Charles with talk of Anne's "importunate and malignant cravings"[32] that "will not be satisfied until she sees the end of both the mother and the daughter."[33]

How accurate were Chapuys' reports? It's almost impossible to say because he is often the sole reporter of events. But what is clear is that his interests were served by painting the worst picture possible of Anne and that he worked hard to construct it. He had an informal network of "conservative" (i.e., pro-Rome, pro-Katherine, pro-Imperial) nobles who would meet with him secretly to convey the latest anti-Anne gossip, which he then relayed to the emperor as "word from a trustworthy source." And although there is no evidence that he played a direct role in the plot to charge Anne with treason, he "carefully watched all courtly signs of rejection leading up to her fall and exerted small pushes of encouragement, particularly with Cromwell"[34] and declared it "wonderful" when she was arrested.[35] Chapuys was even willing to foment war between England and Spain if that was the only way to get Anne out of the picture and (as he saw it) keep Katherine and Mary out of harm's way and restore relations between Henry and Rome.

"Englishmen, high and low . . ." he wrote to Charles, "would wish Your Majesty to send here an army with which to destroy the poisonous influence of the Lady [Anne] and her adherents, and make a new reformation of all this kingdom . . . the moment this accursed Anne sets her foot firmly in the stirrup she will try to do the Queen all the harm she possibly can, and the Princess also. . . . Indeed, I hear she has lately boasted that she will make of the Princess a maid of honour in her Royal household, that she may perhaps give her too much dinner on some occasion, or marry her to some varlet, which would be an irreparable evil."[36]

Chapuys' hostility toward Anne is obvious in every communication from the very start of his service. Even more strikingly, until Chapuys' arrival, the *Letters and Papers, Foreign and Domestic, of the Reign of Henry VIII* contain no negative personal reports about Anne, except for a not very flattering description of her physical appearance by Francesco Sanuto, Venetian ambassador to France, in 1532. As soon as Chapuys arrived, "Madam Anne" became "the concubine," and everything that the pro-Katherine forces saw as dishonorable in Henry's behavior became the fault of Anne's "perverse and malicious nature."[37] "It is she who now rules over, and governs the nation; the King dares not contradict her," he wrote to Charles in November of 1535 — an extraordinary (and unbelievable) statement that paints the formidable Henry as nothing more than a pussy-whipped hubby.[38] In particular, Chapuys saw Anne's continual goading as the cause of Henry's shabby treatment of Princess Mary. Anne undoubtedly was unsettled by Mary, whose insistence on her status as princess threatened Elizabeth's claims to succession. And Henry truly did treat his first daughter terribly, refusing to let her see her mother even when Katherine was dying, and turning the coldest of shoulders to his once-beloved child when she would not acknowledge his marriage to Anne. But Mary was as unbudgeable and self-righteous as her mother, and she and Henry remained locked in a contest of wills long after Anne was dead. Yet for Chapuys, every action against Mary was Anne's fault alone, as she steered the king away from his affection for the princess and plotted Mary's ruin. Chapuys could even turn evidence of Anne's good nature into a demonstration of her scheming nature. When Anne (not the king, who, as reported by the French ambassador to Chapuys, refused to speak to Mary) made overtures of friendship to Mary, Chapuys suggested to Charles that it was a ruse to enable Anne to "execute her wicked will . . . with less suspicion under color of friendship."[39]

The idea that Anne was plotting to murder both Katherine and Mary was a special obsession of Chapuys'. In 1534 he wrote to Charles that:

> Nobody doubts here that one of these days some treacherous act will befall [Katherine] . . . the King's mistress has been heard to say that she will never rest until he has had her put out of the way . . . These are, indeed, monstrous things, and not easily to be believed, and yet such is the King's obstinacy, and the wickedness of this accursed woman (Anne), that everything may be apprehended.[40]

Later that year, after a planned meeting between Henry and Francis had been postponed, Chapuys told Charles it was because Henry was afraid to leave Anne alone in England.

> A gentleman worthy of credit has this day sent me word that the Queen's [sic] mistress has said more than once, and with great assurance, that the very moment the King crosses over [to France] to hold his interview with king Francis, and she remains governess of the kingdom, she will certainly cause the death of the said Princess by the sword or otherwise. And upon Rochefort, her brother, saying that by doing so she might offend the King, she answered him that she cared not if she did, even if she were to be burnt or flayed alive in consequence.[41]

Just who the "gentleman worthy of credit" was is never revealed, as is almost always the case with Chapuys' reports (in another, he writes that "A gentleman told me yesterday that the earl of Northumberland told him that he knew for certain that [Anne] had determined to poison the Princess"[42]). It's always "a trustworthy source" or "a gentleman" or "central gentlemen" or "a certain personage" whom Chapuys credits his information to. But Katherine's supporters did not ask for references, and Chapuys, spreading these tales around court and encouraging Katherine and Mary's suspicions of Anne, was able to generate an atmosphere of hostility toward Anne.

"The more ill used [Katherine and Mary] could appear," writes Loades, "the more indignant their many supporters would become, and the more opprobrium would be heaped on the Queen, since everyone, for good reasons, was anxious to avoid blaming Henry. And so the myth of 'that goggle-eyed whore Nan Bullen,' promoting heresies and driving a besotted king to further tyranny and brutality, took root in the popular imagination."[43]

It's a shockingly short trip from the popular imagination to the official historical record. Both of Anne's early biographers, Paul Friedmann (1884) and James A. Froude (1891), despite acknowledging that "Chapuis . . . may have exaggerated" (Friedmann) and that "Chapuys was not scrupulous about truth" (Froude) go on to give his stories credit.[44] Froude is circumspect and ambiguous, saying that Chapuys' account "shows the reputation which Anne had earned for herself, and which in part she deserves."[45] (Which part, one wants to know, but Froude doesn't say.) Friedmann, astonishingly, goes even further: "There can be no doubt that [Chapuys'] account [that Anne was planning to murder Mary] is substantially true."[46] No doubt? The plot to murder Katherine had, by Friedmann's times, been disproved, when the symptoms that Katherine's physician claimed showed poison (a suspicion he immediately reported to Chapuys) were declared by medical authorities to be indicative of cancer. You would think that would be enough to cast at least a shadow of doubt on "the plot to murder Mary." Albert Pollard is similarly hyperbolic in his assessment of Anne: "The new Queen's jealous malignity passed all bounds"; he then goes on to quote Chapuys on how deeply "the people" resented Anne's treatment of Mary.[47]

It is Chapuys, too, who is largely responsible for our ideas about the decline of Anne and Henry's relationship. In a letter of September 3, 1533 — just a few days before Elizabeth was born — he reports how Anne, "very jealous of the King, and not without legitimate cause, made use of certain words which he (the King) very much disliked, telling her that she must shut her eyes and endure as those who were better than herself had done, and that she ought to know that he could at any time lower her as much as he had raised her."[48] This speech has made its way into virtually every later biography, historical fiction, and film, probably due to its foreboding nature in light of later events and because it signals such a startling turnaround in Henry's treatment of Anne. But as irresistibly drama friendly as it is, there's little corroboration for it. Chapuys never explains the "not without legitimate cause" nor how he happened to be present at this argument (if indeed he was). His real purpose in "reporting" the incident (which even he admitted was "love quarrels") is revealed at the end of the letter, when he adds that "those who know the King's nature and temper consider the above events as of good omen and a sign that the King will soon begin to think of recalling the Queen [Katherine]."[49] Chapuys was always working this angle with Charles and, when he could, orchestrating anti-Anne sentiment and activity around Henry's court.

Nowadays we would regard someone like Chapuys as a noncredible witness by virtue of his hostility, and his reports little more than hearsay. The most responsible historians, such as Eric Ives and David Loades, take Chapuys' insistence that Anne was out to murder Katherine and Mary with a large dose of skepticism. They acknowledge that perhaps Anne said such things — although we have no corroborating evidence. Even so, they read more like the incautious, emotional outburst of a frustrated, furious (and then pregnant) woman whose own daughter's rights were at stake than a real plan to commit murder. If Anne actually had such a plan in mind, why on earth would she announce it at court, especially in earshot of those who might report it to Chapuys, whom she knew to be her adversary?

I came to my research for this book not only as a cultural historian, but as a skeptical reader of texts. As such, I was amazed to discover the degree of reliance on Chapuys for information about Anne's character and behavior — along with an almost total lack of cautionary qualification, or even clarity, when presenting his version of events. True, Starkey (for example) usually puts quotation marks around Chapuys' exact words and notes that "Chapuys reported" or "Chapuys discovered" such and such. However, those quotations are so smoothly incorporated into Starkey's own narrative — Chapuys' voice blends seamlessly with Starkey's — that the reader is given no reason to be skeptical of their construction of events. Here, for example, again from the popular *Six Wives*, he describes Anne's reaction to Henry's installation of himself as "Supreme Head on Earth of the Church of England":

> When [Anne] heard the news, Chapuys discovered, "[she] made such demonstrations of joy as if she had actually gained Paradise."[50]

How are we to take the phrase "Chapuys discovered"? It sounds less like the offering of one observer's impressions than the reporting of established fact. "Discoveries" unearth what is *there*, after all. And with Anne so vividly "hunting" and "stalking" her prey throughout Starkey's narrative, a not-very-historically-informed reader — that would be most of Starkey's readers, as he is not interested in courting the academics but rather the general audience — probably doesn't even notice that Starkey's predatory Anne is largely based on Chapuys' dispatches.

Starkey is hardly alone here. It's virtually standard operating procedure for historians to warn the reader, in an introduction or the beginning of a chapter, about Chapuys' biases and tendencies to believe the most vicious court gossip about Anne, and then go on to use him liberally and without qualification all the same. Sometimes there is a barely noticeable hedge, as in the popular histories of Alison Weir:

> If Chapuys is to be believed — and it was a constant theme in his dispatches — Anne had "never ceased, day and night, plotting against" Mary, and had relentlessly, but fruitlessly, urged Henry to have his daughter and her mother executed for their defiance under the provisions of the Act of Supremacy of 1534. The ambassador heard that she had repeatedly threatened that, if the King were to go abroad and leave her as regent, she would have Mary starved to death, "even if she were burned alive for it after."[51]

But *is* Chapuys to be believed? Barely six pages earlier, Weir warns that for generations historians have relied "perhaps too trustingly" on Chapuys' diplomatic reports.[52] Weir acknowledges that he hated Anne, was a "crusader in the cause of Katherine and Mary,"[53] was "unable to view affairs from any other viewpoint,"[54] and often repeated gossip or rumor (which swirled a great deal around court) as fact. Yet she herself takes many of his reports at face value—for example, his claim that Anne had repeatedly urged Henry to send Katherine and Mary to the scaffold (we only have Chapuys' word on this). And, when it helps to fill out her own narrative, Weir does not hesitate to rely on Chapuys' descriptions of what Henry did and felt.

> In 1536, a disillusioned Henry told Chapuys in confidence that his wife had been "corrupted" in France, and that he had only realized this after their marriage.[55]

It's easy for the reader to overlook the fact that Weir only "knows" that Henry was "disillusioned" about Anne's "corruption" because Chapuys says so. Conveniently for Chapuys (and Weir), Henry told him this "in confidence," so there's no way of fact-checking. And even if Chapuys was being truthful, there's a good possibility that *Henry's* information was not trustworthy. This was a period, very near to Anne's fall, when outlandish rumors and malicious plotting swirled unchecked in court, and Henry's paranoid imagination seemed inflamed beyond concern for proof; in another letter written during this period, Chapuys reports that Henry told him that "upwards of 100 gentlemen have had criminal connexion"[56] with Anne. These bits and pieces of lurid gossip have to be read skeptically.

Instead, the slippage that turned this unsubstantiated report into the grammar of fact has gathered steam. In her more recent biography of Anne's sister, Mary, Weir cites what she now calls Henry's "revelation" that Anne had been corrupted in France as *evidence* that Anne had, in fact, been sexually active at the French court. If this is so, then why don't we have more documentation about her scandalous behavior there? Weir's explanation: "Evidently Anne was discreet and clever enough to ensure that barely a soul knew of these early falls from grace."[57] In other words, Anne Boleyn's "corruption" in France, told to Chapuys "in confidence" and (because Anne was so very discreet and clever) witnessed by no one, is uncorroborated from beginning to end.

Multiply this slippage by a hundred of its like and you can see why you shouldn't believe everything you've heard about Anne Boleyn.

2

Why Anne?

WHEN HENRY BEGAN divorce proceedings in 1527, many (including the pope) saw Henry's seemingly sudden qualms about the legitimacy of his first marriage, based on a passage in Leviticus declaring it to be an "impurity" if a "man shall take his brother's wife," to be a ruse, putting a pious spin on what was really just lust.[1] In 1510, Pope Julius II had granted Henry dispensation to marry Katherine despite the consanguinity of their relations. Now Henry wanted that dispensation declared invalid. It seemed all too conveniently timed. In 1526, Henry began to wear a provocative new motto on his jousting costume: *"Declare je nos"* (Declare I dare not), with a heart engulfed in flames embroidered about the words. The woman who had set his heart ablaze was Anne Boleyn. By 1527, he was writing her letters describing being "stricken with the dart of love" for more than a year.[2] The signature of these letters was sometimes accompanied by a tiny heart. The manly king — thirty-six years old, vigorous, physically imposing, brilliant, and charismatic — had become a trembling schoolboy passing notes to an imperious crush.

It's unlikely that many at court, in 1526, saw marriage on the horizon. Anne was not the daughter of royalty; although her mother, Elizabeth Howard, came from an illustrious family, her father, Thomas Boleyn, the son of an alderman, had achieved a place at court by virtue of his skills as a courtier and linguist. Anne's older sister, Mary, thought by many to be the prettier of the two, had already been courted and discarded by the king. And the still youthful Henry had indulged in other infatuations over the years. But a year later, it was clear that Anne was hovering in the background of the divorce proceedings, as Henry's longtime adviser and Lord Chancellor, Thomas Wolsey, anxiously assured the pope that he would stake his own soul that the king's "conscience is grievously offended" by living in a marriage that was contrary to God's law and that his "desire is grounded in justice" rather than displeasure with the queen or "undue love to a gentlewoman of not so excellent qualities."[3] Covering all his bases, though, Wolsey then went on to praise Anne for the "purity of her life, her constant virginity, her maidenly and womanly pudicity, her soberness, chasteness, meekness, humility, wisdom, descent of right noble and high through regal blood, education in all good and laudable [qualities] and manners, aptness to procreation of children with her other infinite good qualities, more to be regarded and esteemed than the only progeny."[4] Except for the good education, these are not exactly the qualities that we associate with Anne Boleyn. Tudor statesmen and diplomats, much like politicians today, were bald-faced spinmeisters, and at this point, Wolsey was spinning madly for Henry.

It's true, though, that Henry had been thinking about a divorce from his first wife long before Anne Boleyn entered the picture. During the first four years of their marriage — from 1510 to 1514 — Katherine had given birth to three stillborn infants — one girl and two boys — and a boy who lived for less than two months. It was beginning to look as though the couple's chances of producing a healthy child were grim. By as early as August of 1514, it was rumored in Rome "that the King of England means to repudiate his present wife, the daughter of the King of Spain and his brother's widow, because he is unable to have children by her, and intends to marry a daughter of the French Duke of Bourbon."[5] But then, in 1516, Princess Mary was born, and Henry's hopes were revived. "We are both young; if it was a daughter this time, by the Grace of God the sons will follow," he is reported to have said.[6] But the next child was stillborn, and Henry began wondering once again whether he had offended God by marrying his brother's wife. Leviticus declares that such a union will be childless, which Henry and Katherine were not, but Henry, whose religious conscience was always filtered through his dynastic concerns, didn't see Mary as "counting." It wasn't so much that, as a woman, she was seen as unfit to rule, but, as a woman, she would have another "ruler" herself—her husband—and this raised dangerous possibilities for the continuance of Tudor supremacy. If she married a foreign prince, English autonomy could be threatened; if she married an English subject, internal dissension could result. Only a male heir would keep the Tudor reign intact and secure.

It's not clear why there isn't any mention of other pregnancies after the last stillbirth. The official word was that Katherine was "of such an age" that pregnancy was no longer possible—which is believable by 1525, when she was forty, but seems unlikely in 1519. Katherine had no trouble conceiving before then, and in 1519 she was only thirty-four. Her stillbirths, in an age when shutting the queen up in a hot, dark room for a month was the extent of "prenatal care" and when more children died than lived through infancy, are not remarkable. When he later appealed to the pope for the divorce, Wolsey referred to "certain diseases in the Queen defying all remedy" that prevented the king from living with her "as his wife."[7] Wolsey would not say what those "diseases" were, but the truth may be that Henry had stopped having regular sex with her long before she actually entered menopause. Katherine was eight years older than he was, which probably was exciting when he first married her, as Henry was then virtually a boy and, as the precious "spare" heir, had been sheltered like a princess after Arthur died. But by 1520 he was "in the flower of his age,"[8] while Katherine, at thirty-five, was middle-aged by the standards of the time. Also, in 1519 Henry had gotten decisive proof that a male child was possible with a woman other than Katherine when his mistress, Elizabeth Blount, had a boy.

Why did Henry, if he had given up on the marriage by 1520, hang on with Katherine for seven more years? There is widespread historical belief that about this time Henry began a four-year-long affair with Mary Boleyn, Anne's older sister, and possibly this affair took the pressure off his marriage to satisfy his sexual and emotional needs. But Katherine was also not someone to discard lightly. Just as her marriages to Arthur and then Henry were intended to solidify relations with Spain, a divorce would destabilize them. And Katherine was extremely popular with the English people. Regal, dignified, and unfalteringly virtuous in all her daily habits (which involved much time at prayer), she was everything a queen was supposed to be; Venetian ambassador Ludovico Falieri describes her as "more beloved by the Islanders than any queen that has ever reigned."[9] Henry was aware of this, and he probably also knew, as others did not, how proud and stubborn she could be.

But then Anne entered the picture. We don't know for certain when he first became attracted to her or what the circumstances were, in large part because the available sources only begin to speculate about her when the king's interest was publicly known, and by the time that happened, in 1527, people were more interested in the divorce and scandal of it all than how it had begun. All later accounts of Henry and Anne's meeting are retrospective. George Cavendish, Wolsey's gentleman usher, writes (thirty-five years after the event) that "the King's love began to take place" when, after her return from France, Anne was made one of Katherine's ladies-in-waiting, "among whome, for her excellent gesture and behaviour, she did excel all other; in so much that the Kinge began to grow enamoured with her; which was not known to any person, ne scantly to her owne person."[10] Agnes Strickland, citing Gregorio Leti, whose seventeenth-century *Life of Elizabeth I* includes many colorful but uncorroborated anecdotes, relates that:

> [T]he first time Henry saw her [Anne] after her return to England . . . [was] in her father's garden at Hever, where . . . admiring her beauty and graceful demeanor he entered into conversation with her; when he was so much charmed with her sprightly wit, that on his return to Westminster he told Wolsey, "that he had been discoursing with a young lady who had the wit of an angel, and was worthy of a crown."[11]

Cavendish and Strickland/Leti disagree sharply on Wolsey's reaction. Strickland, citing Leti, describes Wolsey as so eager to get power in his own hands that he was "glad to see the king engrossed in the intoxication of a love affair" and delighted that it was Anne, whom he had first recommended to be one of Katherine's ladies.[12] But Leti was a devoted Elizabethan Protestant and harsh critic of Wolsey. Cavendish, in contrast, was Wolsey's faithful admirer and servant, and presents Wolsey as only "acting on the King's devised commandment" in breaking up Anne's relationship with Henry Percy so that Henry could get his hands on her.[13] Wolsey's interference, according to Cavendish, "greatly offended" Anne, who "promis[ed] if it ever lay in her power, she would work much displeasure to the Cardinal" (which, according to Cavendish, "she did in deede" by goading Henry to turn against Wolsey).[14] Cavendish goes on to show that he clearly belongs to the "greedy Anne/patient Katherine" school of thought: "After [Anne] knewe the kings pleasure, and the bottom of his secret stomacke, then she began to look very haughty and stoute [arrogant], lacking no manner of jewells, or rich apparel, that might be gotten for money," while Katherine accepted all this "in good parte," showing "no kinde or sparke of grudge or displeasure."[15]

With historical sources leaving no clear record, the imaginations of biographers, novelists, and screenwriters have followed their own fantasies — or those that they felt would appeal to audiences. Many of them, in one way or another, have Henry being struck by the thunderbolt of love at first sight. William Hepworth Dixon, in his 1874 pro-Protestant biography of Anne, describes Henry as "taken by a word and smile. A face so innocently arch, a wit so rapid and so bright, a mien so modest yet so gay, were new to him. The King was tiring of such beauties as Elizabeth Blount; mere lumps of rosy flesh, without the sparkle of a living soul . . . He fell so swiftly and completely that the outside world imagined he was won by magic arts."[16] In *Anne of the Thousand Days*, Henry sees Anne dancing at court, is immediately smitten, and instructs Wolsey to "unmatch" Anne and Percy, and then send her packing back to Hever. Henry then takes off himself (on a "hunting" trip, as he tells Wolsey) for Hever, where he tells Anne that he will have her "even if it breaks the earth in two like an apple and flings the halves into the void."[17] In the movie *The Other Boleyn Girl*, Henry picks Anne (Natalie Portman) out of the Boleyn family lineup with nary a glance at Mary (Scarlett Johansson); he takes up with Mary first only because Anne humiliates him by being a more expert rider than he. *The Tudors* has Anne and Henry locking eyes in the tower of Château Vert, where Henry, as the shooting script tells us, "comes face to face with his destiny — with a sharp intake of breath, like an arrow through his heart. A very beautiful, 18-year-old young woman with jet-black hair and dark, expressive, exquisite eyes looks back at him."[18] Later, after the dancing begins, "he stares at Anne as if suddenly rendered incapable of speech . . . 'Who are you?' he asks, when the steps of the dance bring them eye to eye. And she whispers back, 'Anne Boleyn.'"[19]

Anne Boleyn did make her debut at court at the Château Vert pageant, an extravagant affair complete with a triple-turreted, shining green minicastle created especially for the occasion. The pageant was supposed to be a celebration of courtly love. The players, both male and female, each represented one of the chivalric ideals — Nobleness, Loyalty, Gentleness, Attendance, Constancy, Honor, and so forth. (Anne was Perseverance — very apt, as it later turned out.) But the eight female players, masked and dressed in white and yellow satin with headdresses of gold, made little beyond a pretense of maidenly resistance when eight dashing masked courtiers, announced by a cannon blast and led by the king, stormed the castle with dates, oranges, and "other fruits made for pleasure," and carried the damsels off for a night of dancing. When the dancing was over, the masks were removed and all sat down to a lavish banquet.

We do not know which lady the king carried off from the Château Vert to be his first partner for that night's dancing, but it was unlikely to have been Anne, and it certainly wouldn't have happened as depicted in *The Tudors*. Anyone who has even the slightest actual knowledge of Tudor history is aware that the Anne who could turn men to jelly at first sight is a myth — or perhaps more accurately, a reflection of the limits of twentieth-century conceptions of attraction, fixated as they are on the surface of the body. It's hard for us to imagine a woman for whom a king would split the earth in two who is anything less than ravishing. But in her own time, Anne's looks were not rated among her greatest assets. "Reasonably good-looking," pronounced John Barlow, one of Anne's favorite clerics.[20] "Not one of the handsomest women in the world," reported the Venetian diplomat, Francesco Sanuto: "[S]he is of middling stature, swarthy complexion, long neck, wide mouth, bosom not much raised, and in fact has nothing but the English King's great appetite, and her eyes, which are black and beautiful, and take great effect on those who served the Queen when she was on the throne."[21]

Sanuto was not a fan, but George Wyatt, grandson of one of Anne's early admirers, the poet Thomas Wyatt, was. In 1623, he gave his nephew a manuscript that he had apparently written some twenty-five years earlier, in which, drawing on the reports of relatives and friends who had known Anne, he writes that although Anne was a "rare and admirable beauty," she was not without flaws: Her coloring was "not so whitely" as was then esteemed and she had several "small moles . . . upon certain parts of her body."[22] Wyatt also writes that "[t]here was found, indeed, upon the side of her nail upon one of her fingers, some little show of a nail, which was yet so small, by the report of those that have seen her, as the workmaster seemed to leave it an occasion of greater grace to her hand, which, with the tip of one of her other fingers might be, and was usually by her hidden without any least blemish to it."[23]

None of Anne's "flaws," in our multiracial, post–Cindy Crawford age, seems particularly significant. Some, such as Anne's olive skin, boyish physique, and wide mouth—not to mention the well-placed moles—could put her in contention for *America's Next Top Model*. But in Anne's own time, beauty spots were not yet a fashion accessory, and even so slight a deformity as a "little show" of extra nail, despite Wyatt's courtly spin, could raise questions about Satan's influence on Anne's conception. Snow-white skin, which women (including Anne's famous daughter, Elizabeth I) would try to simulate using makeup, was a requisite of English beauty and remained so for hundreds of years, overdetermined by racial, class, and moral meanings distinguishing the leisured classes from their "coarse and brown inferiors" and thought to be the outward manifestation of a "fair and unspotted soul."[24] And fair hair, which Anne's predecessors (both legal and extramarital) apparently enjoyed, reigned in the Tudor hierarchy of beauty. Both the Virgin Mary and Venus (most famously in Botticelli's

1486 painting) were always pictured as blondes. So were all the heroines of the literature of courtly love, from Iseult to Guinevere: "Gallant knights, poets and troubadours celebrated their love of blondes
with much eager serenading" and "felicitous poems and romantic
tales bursting with golden-haired heroines poured from the pens of
passionate lovers."[25] Light-haired women were also considered to be
more "cheerful and submissive" (very desirable). Within a century or
so, the generous, sweet, needing-to-be-rescued blonde heroine would
become an essential ingredient of every successful fairy tale.

"Look for a woman with a good figure and with a small head; Hair
that is blond but not from henna; whose eyebrows are spaced apart,
long and arched in a peak; who is nice and plump in the buttocks,"
advised fourteenth-century poet and priest Juan Ruiz. "A Lady's hair
should be fine and fair, in the similitude now of gold, now of honey,
and now of the shining rays of the sun,"[26] wrote another courtier in
1548.[27] Today, evolutionary psychologists would argue that these preferences are hardwired into male brain circuitry, as both fair skin and
curvaceous bodies signal youth, health, and a high estrogen load. If
so, "swarthy," slender Anne Boleyn was a perverse choice for Henry to
make in his attempt to secure an heir.[28] Her moles were an even bigger
problem, because birthmarks were often seen as ominous signs. The
medievals, whose notions about the human body often lingered into
the Renaissance, believed that a mother's imagination while pregnant
could rupture the skin, and they read birthmarks the way later generations would decipher bumps on the skull. A mole on the throat (where
several observers report Anne's to have been) predicted a violent death.
One on the upper lip meant good fortune for a man — but debauchery
for a woman. If it was just above the left side of her mouth, "vanity and
pride, and an unlawful offspring to provide for."[29] Fifteenth-century
witch hunter Lambert Daneau saw moles as witch's marks. Daneau
and other "witch-prickers" would stick pins in the moles to find the
bedeviled ones; when the suspect registered no pain (hard to imagine),
it indicated Satan's handiwork.[30]

Notions such as these explain how Anne's moles could morph, in
the hands of Catholic propagandist Nicholas Sander, writing half a
century after Anne's death, into a third nipple. Sander, who probably

never saw Anne dressed, let alone naked (he was a small child when she was executed — but he was exiled by Elizabeth I), is responsible for most of the mythology surrounding Anne's body, including her notorious sixth finger. In his book, *Schismatis Anglicani (The Rise and Growth of the Anglican Schism),* written expressly to provide a counterhistory to John Foxe's *Book of Martyrs* (among whom Anne is numbered), Sander wallows in descriptions of Anne's body as the gateway that lured the lusting, ensnared Henry through the doors of heresy. But amazingly, Sander saw no contradiction in claiming that this desirable body was also marked with the outward manifestations of her league with Satan.

> Anne Boleyn was rather tall of stature, with black hair and an oval face of sallow complexion, as if troubled with jaundice. She had a projecting tooth under the upper lip, and on her right hand, six fingers. There was a large wen under her chin, and therefore to hide its ugliness, she wore a high dress covering her throat. In this she was followed by the ladies of the court, who also wore high dresses, having before been in the habit of leaving their necks and the upper portion of their person uncovered.[31]

This mythology was clearly ideologically motivated (more about the Catholic/Protestant culture wars in a later chapter). Such pronounced deformities as described by Sander would certainly have eliminated Anne as a lady-in-waiting, much less as a candidate for queen. Sander, moreover, was not well-informed about female fashion. High necks were not yet in vogue while Anne was alive, and a "large wen" would not have been hidden by the delicate ropes of pearls or the decorative "B" that she wore around her neck. The wen probably was inspired by the anonymous manuscript describing Anne's coronation that attributed a "disfiguring wart" and a neck swelling "resembling goître" to her.[32] The sixth finger seems likely to have been an exaggeration of the vestigial nail that Wyatt describes, and this explains Wyatt's mention of it, as his book was, by his own admission, "not without an intent to have opposed Saunders [Sander]," whom he calls "the Romish fable-framer."[33] The point of his book (entitled *Extracts from the Life of the Virtuous Christian and Renowned Queen Anne Boleigne*), he tells the reader, is to dispel the "black mists of malice . . . instructed to cover and overshadow [Anne Boleyn's] glory with their most black and venomous untruths."[34] So he was hardly an impartial reporter himself. But despite his biases, Wyatt's own sources are far more respectable than Sander's, especially when it comes to descriptions of Anne's physical appearance. Based on notes taken when he was young, gathered from Anne Gainsford, one of Anne's personal attendants, as well as relatives of his who were "well acquainted with the persons that most this concerneth," his corrections of Sander's descriptions of Anne's imperfections sound highly plausible, as Wyatt doesn't insist that Anne was a beauty without flaws, but acknowledges the nail, moles, and "not so whitely" complexion.[35]

The wens, goiters, and projecting tooth have all faded from the popular imagination. But that sixth finger just won't let go. By the nineteenth century, it had become a "fact" that even today many people remember as among the first things they learned about Anne.[36] At the beginning of every public lecture I ask my audiences what they know about Anne Boleyn; invariably, several attendees shout out, "She had six fingers!" Internet sites devoted to "fascinating facts" still list Anne's six fingers (sometimes multiplying them to six on *each* hand). A girls'-magazine feature giving inspiration for girls to "love their bodies" presents Anne and her extra finger (and the extra nipple) as a role model.[37] At least one well-known portrait, once hanging in Ludlow Castle and now privately owned, prominently features Anne with six fingers on each hand. One of the more imaginative histories cites her "malformed hand" as the reason she was kept out of sight in France until a suitable husband could be contracted.[38] When an art installation opened in 2011 with a full-size Anne among the creations, the wax figure had an extra finger. Anne's sixth finger is even mentioned in the movie *Steel Magnolias* when the women in Truvy's beauty shop banter through the bathroom door about an article in a woman's magazine. The bottom line, however: Anne did not have six fingers. Since Anne's death, the bodies buried in the chapel of St. Peter ad Vincula have been exhumed and none of the skeletons have shown evidence of a sixth finger. Of course, there are those who claim Anne's body is actually not among them. But skeletal remains aside, if the living Anne actually had a sixth finger, would the eagle-eyed Chapuys have failed to report it? Anne's liabilities were a favorite topic of his gossipy letters home; yet a sixth finger is not mentioned in one of them (or in any other court letters or papers prior to Sander).

Beyond the dark hair and eyes, the olive skin, the small moles, and the likelihood of a tiny extra nail on her little finger, we know very little with certainty about what Anne looked like. Before her execution, as we've seen, Henry, determined to wipe the slate clean, had any original portraits of Anne that he could find destroyed. Those that remain are almost all later copies and interpretations, and are quite inconsistent with one another. Some are thought to be of Jane Seymour or some other woman rather than Anne, while other portraits not identified as Anne — the beautiful Sommersby portrait thought to be of Jane Grey, for example — have been argued to actually be Anne. Historians and art historians have gone back and forth on the identity of the various sitters in many "Anne" portraits, with agreement on only a few. One is a tiny miniature in a locket ring worn by Elizabeth I, which was found among her belongings after her death. The existence of the ring, which bears the image of Elizabeth on one side and her mother on the other, is haunting, but, being so small, it tells us little about what Anne looked like. Also indisputably authentic is a medal, badly damaged but recently restored by sculptor Lucy Churchill, which shares features with a portrait of Anne, by an unknown artist circa 1533–36, that is on permanent display at the National Portrait Gallery. This portrait, often referred to as "the NPG portrait," has provided the model for many later depictions on book covers, magnets, and postcards, where it has been variously glamorized or distorted, depending on the artist's inclinations.

The NPG portrait is as reliable an indication as we have of what Anne looked like. But even this portrait cannot be taken "literally." Historian Lacey Baldwin Smith has written that "Tudor portraits bear about as much resemblance to their subjects as elephants to prunes."[39] A slight exaggeration, maybe. But it is true that portraits often bore the mark of "symbolic iconizing" — the translation of a belief or argument about the person's character into visual imagery — more than the attempt to mirror features with photographic precision. Hans Holbein's famous sketch of Henry (the painting itself was destroyed in a fire) clearly served this function, with the king posed to emphasize his power, authority, and resoluteness: legs spread and firmly planted, broad shoulders—and a very visible codpiece. Since generations of later artists were content with small variations on the Holbein paradigm, we have the sense that we know what Henry looked like. But actually, what we have is an icon that has settled into a recognizable shape over the centuries.

There is no icon of Anne comparable to that of Holbein's Henry, and in its place, we have created our own. It varies a bit from generation to generation, but she always has a beauty that stands out in the crowd by whatever standards appeal to the writers or directors who have cast her. Merle Oberon, Alexander Korda's Anne, was considered an "exotic beauty" at the time and later became his wife. Geneviève Bujold was picked out by Hal Wallis without benefit of a screen test; she was a little-known Canadian actress at the time when he saw her in her first role and immediately recognized that "this is my Anne." Although most Annes have followed the historical record in depicting her with dark hair, one of the most recent Annes, Miranda Raison, the first actress to play Anne in Howard Brenton's play *Anne Boleyn*, is a decidedly contemporary-looking blonde.[40] But perhaps the most stunning Anne of all is *The Tudors'* Natalie Dormer: exquisite, sensual, curvaceous in her push-up gowns. She gives a brilliant performance, but the only indisputable correspondence to the historical Anne is her dark hair (dyed for the role) and a few fetching facial moles.

⚘ What Color Was Anne Boleyn's Hair?

Asked in the twentieth or twenty-first centuries about Anne Boleyn's hair color, most people would answer "black"—or, perhaps, "very dark brown." With the exception of Geneviève Bujold, whose hair was distinctly chestnut hued, the best-known actresses who have played Anne—Merle Oberon, Dorothy Tutin, Natalie Portman, Natalie Dormer—have black or dark brown hair, and modern portraits and cartoons follow the prototype of Anne as a "raven-haired temptress." Yet the portraits and representations that have been judged to bear the closest resemblance to the historical Anne—including the

National Portrait Gallery painting—show her with auburn hair. This isn't incompatible with the many descriptions of her as "dark"—for in an aesthetic and religious world that divided things into "light" and "dark," you wouldn't have to have jet-black hair to be in the "dark" category.

In fact, there are only two descriptions of Anne from (roughly) her own time that associate Anne with the color "black": One is from the Catholic propagandist Nicholas Sander, who was clearly out to make Anne sound as witchlike as possible. The other is Cardinal Wolsey's private nickname—"the night crow"—a metaphor that may or may not have also been physically descriptive. All other sources describe her simply as "dark" or "brunette." "Brunette" translates to "brown" for us, but may have had a much broader referent then, covering many hues of darkish hair. It's not clear that the medievals even had a term for dark red hair; "auburn," for example, originally meant whitish! And "black" could refer to colors, but in their deepest, darkest hues.

It provides some perspective on our own visual stereotypes of Anne to learn that raven-haired Anne—Sander aside—is largely a twentieth-century invention. Not that other eras are more historically reliable than ours. The Romantics almost always depicted her as fair —the visual counterpart to their view of Anne as victim rather than vixen. This lasts well into the early twentieth century, as in this descrip-tion from Reginald Drew's 1912 novel: "She was radiant and dimpled, and her beautiful face, pink-hued and lily white, rippled with laughter and bubbled with vivacity. She had sparkling eyes, wavy, golden-brown hair which framed her face like a picture, and which her coif could not either confine or conceal."[41] Ernst Lubitsch's Anne, Henny Porten, is fair (1920). And Jessie Armstrong's Anne, in My Friend Anne (1935), could be Mary Pickford (whose style was already out-of-date in the thirties, but perhaps for that reason could represent "old-fashioned" beauty). In the thirties, "blonde" was already becoming, with Mae West and Jean Harlow, the mark of the vamp. But it hadn't happened yet. For the late nineteenth and early twentieth centuries, the old as-sociations of fair hair with innocence and purity still held. Today, it's surprising (and annoying, for those who care about historical accu-racy) when a blonde Anne pops up, but it doesn't signify much other than the loosening, in our postmodern age, of "moral" associations with hair color.

The most tenacious historical inaccuracy, actually, has not been in depictions of Anne, but of Katherine. She — unlike Anne — was indeed golden-haired. But she was Spanish, and our stunted racial imagination has therefore almost invariably given her dark hair (Irene Papas in *Anne of the Thousand Days*, Maria Doyle Kennedy in *The Tudors*, Ana Torrent in *The Other Boleyn Girl* — the outstanding exception: Annette Crosbie's Katherine in the 1970 BBC production of *The Six Wives of Henry VIII*). Racial stereotyping, it seems, trumps gender ideology. Or maybe it's more accurate to say that racial profiling collaborates creatively with gender ideology. "Our" Anne-the-seductress, still wearing the collective imprinting of Sander, is raven-haired. But since she has morphed into a great beauty, too, we've rejected the historical consensus (from sympathizers as well as detractors) that her skin was "not so whitely as desired."[42] Surely that better describes Katherine, the unglamorous Spanish discard! So Anne becomes Snow White in coloring, while Spanish Katherine, who was, in fact, the fairer skinned of the two, becomes the "swarthy" wife.

The bottom line: Fantasy, not fact, rules in the cultural imagination.

Among historians, it is generally recognized that the real Anne, however, although not deformed, was not a conventional beauty (by the standards of her own time). Yet dark-haired, olive-skinned Anne not only prevailed over the pale English roses, but seems to have done so defiantly. Ignoring the fashion for blondes, for example, Anne grew her dark hair so long that she could sit on it. Before marriage, young women were permitted to wear their hair loose (after, it had to be hidden under a hood; the exception was the queen, on those state occasions that required her to wear a crown). And then there were Anne's eyes. Eastern cultures foregrounded them for their sexual power. But proper English ladies did not brazenly issue a sexual invitation; they submitted, casting their eyes downward. Not Anne, apparently. Nearly every commentator mentions her eyes, not just "black and beautiful" (according to Sanuto, who was not a supporter), but also sexually artful. The French diplomat Lancelot de Carles, who later brought the news of her execution to France, was — being French — more lavish and precise in his description of Anne's "most attractive" eyes: "Which she knew well how to use with effect, Sometimes leaving them at rest, And at others, sending a message To carry the secret witness of the heart."[43] De Carles here describes a classic form of flirtation, which Anne may have explicitly learned as an "art" during her formative years at the French court or which may have simply come naturally to her personality. She was not afraid to "send a message" with her gaze, then provocatively turn away, inspiring pursuit. Thus, Anne challenged the Mary-fixated religious ideology of beauty by engaging in the more biologically potent use of the eyes to meet and invite. Thomas Wyatt, one of the first at court to develop an infatuation for Anne, probably had Anne in mind when, in one of his love poems, he describes his beloved's eyes as "sunbeams to turn with such vehemence, / To daze men's sight, as by their bright presence."[44]

Anne also seems to have had that elusive quality — "style" — which can never be quantified or permanently attached to specific body parts, hair color, or facial features, and which can transform a flat chest into a gracefully unencumbered torso and a birthmark into a beauty spot. "Style" cannot be defined. But in its presence, the rules of attraction are transformed. Style defies convention and calls the shots on what is considered beautiful. There are plenty of examples from our own time. Consider Audrey Hepburn, whose portrayal of Holly Golightly in *Breakfast at Tiffany's* turned teenage girls' gazes away from hourglass-shaped Sandra Dee and Annette Funicello, their bodies seemingly made for producing cute little babies, toward a new vision of cool, long-limbed, not-made-for-the-kitchen beauty that has remained a dominant ideal through the present day. Think of Barbra Streisand, who, like some modern-day Nefertiti, proudly offered her "Jewish" profile in dramatic, high-fashion poses that shouted "F*** you" to Gidget — and the rhinoplasts. Think Michelle Obama, whose prominent jaw would disqualify her immediately among those who insist that symmetry and a delicate chin are biologically inscribed requisites for female appeal. People with "style" remind us that the body is not just a piece of inert matter that can be measured and molded. And beauty, far from being cast in an unchanging, Platonic (or sociobiological) mold, is the human body moving through history, accepting or challenging the rules of its time and place. Sometimes, the prevailing rules of beauty are ripe for changing.[45] Anne seems to have been among those who have changed the rules.

And perhaps it was more than sex and style . . .

Among the numerous historical romances that Anne has inspired, one was written specifically for young girls, *Doomed Queen Anne*. In it, late one night, a very young Anne overhears her parents discussing her future. "What of Nan?" she hears her mother ask. "I cannot imagine that we shall ever be able to find her a suitable husband. The poor child is so ill-favored! Dark as a gypsy, and that blemish upon her neck, the little bud of an extra finger . . ." "Ill-favored, true enough," her father replies, "but not dull-witted."[46] *Doomed Queen Anne* reminds us that even the most notorious concubine was once a young girl. And apparently, with an unusually "promising" quickness of mind, ready enough to be sent to be educated, at the minimum age allowable, to the court of the Archduchess Margaret of Austria, who was serving as regent for her thirteen-year-old nephew, Charles of Burgundy. There began the first term in what Eric Ives calls Anne's "European Education."[47] Anne had not been there very long when Margaret wrote to Anne's father that she found Anne "of such good address and so pleasing in her youthful age that I am more beholden to you for having sent her to me than you are to me."[48] From there, she was sent to France, where Francis's sister, Marguerite de Navarre, had turned the Valois court into a center of intellectual and artistic brilliance. The "king's respected counselor and confidante" since he took the throne in 1515, Marguerite filled the court with poets, philosophers, and the most provocative reformist intellectuals of the time.[49]

It's easy to forget, given the bloody schism that was to follow, that there was a time — roughly from 1510 to 1520 — when criticism of the abuses of the clergy was not yet seen as heretical but as an effluence of the new humanism, which was all the rage among the intellectual avant-garde and perhaps best represented at the time by the Dutch scholar Erasmus, whose *The Praise of Folly,* published in 1511 (Anne was ten), was a runaway best seller throughout Europe. *Folly* lampooned all manner of human hypocrisy and foolishness, but sunk serious barbs into the clergy, including popes, who "by their silence" over the abuses of the clergy "allow Christ to be forgotten, who enchain him by mercenary rules, adulterate His teaching by forced interpretations, and crucify Him afresh by their scandalous life!"[50] Eighteen years later, Erasmus's good friend Thomas More was burning Martin Luther's theses and other criticisms of the clergy (as well as those who espoused those views). But at the time *Folly* was published, Luther was still an unknown German professor, and criticism of the abuses of the existing Church did not imply repudiation of the central tenets of Catholicism. The new humanism was provocative, it was "radical," it was antiestablishment, and it was scorned by traditionalists, but it was not viewed as heretical. Thomas More, in fact, was one of its shining lights; its brightest center in England was Cambridge University, where Erasmus taught from 1509 to 1514.

Women, of course, were not allowed to study at Cambridge (or any other university). But that didn't mean none of them had access to the new humanism. Some parents — such as Thomas More — made sure their daughters were schooled in the classics and were aware of contemporary debates. Arguably, Marguerite de Navarre's salons, visited by the foremost thinkers of the day (including, most likely, Erasmus, who left England in 1514), provided informal tutoring (not described in that way at the time, of course) for the women at Francis's court, including Anne. David Starkey, in fact, describes Anne's time at the court as "her Oxford . . . which, in everything but Latin, gave her a training at least as good as [her brother] George's."[51] The training Anne received was not, however, limited to classical literature. In Marguerite's court, all the hot humanist topics of the day were debated, from the "Bible Question" (Did people need priests to interpret Scripture for them or should vernacular versions be widely available?) to the "Woman Question." (Could a woman be virtuous? If so, what kind of virtue was distinctively hers? Was her intelligence lesser than man's? Was she even of the same species as man?) These issues had occupied philosophers since the Greeks; the misogynist answers are well-known. But early in the fifteenth century, women had begun to add their own voices to the discussion, coming up with some very different ideas, most notable among them Christine de Pizan's *The Book of the City of Ladies,* which protested the "many evil and reproachful things about women and their behavior" in male treatises, their depiction of "the entire female sex, just as if it were a monstrosity in nature."[52]

The Tudors, collapsing the significant differences between Marguerite de Navarre and her libidinous brother, depicts Marguerite as a full-breasted, ostentatiously horny visitor to Henry's court, whom Henry obliges by servicing her for the night. Nothing could be further from an accurate picture of Marguerite, who was a religious mystic; her recommendation for overcoming the sexual double standard that allowed male aggression free rein while condemning women who transgressed was religious transcendence and union with God — for both sexes. Marguerite was also the promoter and protector of many of the main actors in the Evangelical movement, including Jacques Lefèvre d'Étaples, one of the founders of French humanism, and Bishop Guillaume Briçonnet, who along with other reformist clergy frequently preached at the French court. These reformist clergy, French historian Robert Knecht writes, "appealed strongly to the ladies, many of whom yearned to reach out to God more directly than through the traditional channels."[53]

How much of this did Anne absorb? Anne's early-nineteenth-century biographers attribute a great deal of influence on Anne to Marguerite. Elizabeth Benger, in 1821, after several pages of lavish praise for the "learned and ingenious" Marguerite, writes that it cannot "be doubted that Anne Boleyn derived incalculable advantage from her early intercourse with one of the most brilliant women of the age."[54] S. W. Singer, in his notes to Cavendish's *The Life of Cardinal Wolsey* (1825), acknowledges Anne's debt to Marguerite, from whom "she first learnt the grounds of the Protestant religion."[55] But then, with the mid-century publication of the *Letters and Papers, Foreign and Domestic, of the Reign of Henry VIII* and the *Spanish Chronicle,* both of them chock-full of Chapuys' and others' negative commentaries about Anne, any positive influences on her early life or acknowledgment that she may have been something other than a pretty schemer abruptly disappear from the histories. Neither Froude nor Friedmann mention Marguerite, except — in the case of Friedmann — to report her refusal to attend the meeting at Calais, held shortly before Anne and Henry were married, that was intended to introduce Anne in the role of queen-to-be to the French. (Marguerite was opposed to the divorce.) Pollard, who found Anne's hold over Henry to be a "puzzle," saw "no evidence" of any "mental accomplishments" besides her excellent French.[56] Her "fluency in the gospel," which Singer had attributed to her time with Marguerite, "had no nobler foundation than the facts that Anne's position drove her into hostility to the Roman jurisdiction, and that her family shared the envy of church goods, common to the nobility and gentry of the time. Her place in English history is due solely to the circumstances that she appealed to the less refined part of Henry's nature."[57]

Although later historians were to question this picture of Anne, a certain skepticism has remained about the possibility that her time at the French court could have involved anything more than learning to dance, play courtly games, and soak up the latest styles in French fashion. But, in her own mind at least, Anne felt a strong connection to Marguerite, and with only twelve ladies-in-waiting serving at Claude's court, it's not a stretch to imagine frequent contact between them or that Marguerite would have served as something of a role model for Anne. In 1535, she sent Marguerite a message saying that her "greatest wish, next to having a son, is to see you again."[58] She also seems to have held no grudge against Marguerite for not attending the 1532 meeting, writing that although every possible comfort had been provided for her, "there was no one thing which her grace so much desired . . . as the want of the said queen of Navarre's company, with whom to have conference, for more causes than were meet to be expressed, her grace is most desirous."[59] But perhaps more telling than these communications, which could be argued to be diplomatic rather than heartfelt, is Anne's personal library, which was full of evangelical tracts and Bibles translated into French by members of Marguerite's reformist circle. Among these was a Bible that she and Henry owned jointly; another was a tract whose introduction pairs Henry and Francis, Anne and

Marguerite. Marguerite, remember, was Francis's sister. The more obvious analogy would have been between Anne and Claude, his wife. But Claude was timid and retiring, and — like Katherine — led a life of queenly obedience. Anne, although she never developed an intellectual salon of her own, loved liberal discussion and debate. And it was perhaps from Marguerite that she learned that in such debate, a woman's ideas were as worthy as a man's.

Henry's attraction to Anne, in any case, seems to have been fueled not only by sexual attraction but by common enjoyments, compatible interests, intellectual stimulation, and shared political purpose. In our own time, this ideal of love is so familiar (if rarely experienced) that it's become a cliché of Internet dating sites, which compete with one another in their promises of going beyond the "superficial" (read: good looks) to help you find your perfect, life-sharing "match." But in Henry's time, people didn't expect to find such a match in one person.[60] In fact, the ideal itself would have baffled them. Plato had advocated a love that began with erotic attraction for a specific individual, but ideally transformed itself into the worship of Beauty itself. That was familiar, even if few people managed to attain it. Aristotle's ideal love was personal, but nonerotic: friendship, such as Henry had with Charles Brandon throughout his life. The medieval marriage, whose conventions were still largely in place in Henry VIII's time, was a working relationship, with intercourse added to ensure the procreation of legitimate children. Mistresses were for uncomplicated sex (and, for Henry, to produce some backup bastard heirs should the legitimate route fail). Queens were satellites to their husbands, arranged for dynastic purposes; if the couple was lucky, they might find affection and sexual satisfaction in the match, but it was certainly not required.

What *was* required of a queen was a training very different from the "education" that court women such as Anne received in France. Anne of France's *Lessons for My Daughter*, written around 1498 but first printed around 1520, lays out the requirements of behavior for a future queen very clearly. Anne, the daughter of Louis XI, had effectively governed France for seven years when her father died (Louis' thirteen-year-old heir, Charles, was put in Anne's custody); when her own daughter, Suzanne, was of marriageable age — and thought to be headed for union with a foreign prince — Anne wrote *Lessons* to ensure that Suzanne received "the treasure of her experience."[61] But it was clearly not her experience as a ruler in her own right — or as a writer — that Anne had in mind. In outlining the duties of a queen, she emphasized not only chastity and obedience, but also *silence*. Not that a queen should *never* speak; but when she does, it is not to be for the purpose of entertaining or debating, but to comfort, reassure, and serve others, particularly "lesser folk": "Speak to them graciously about their husbands, wives, children, and households, comfort them in their poverty, and admonish them to have patience because to those who are patient come gifts of charity, and from patience comes both the grace of God and the world; for this reason, spare neither your efforts nor your words, which in this situation are appropriate and beneficial."[62]

We don't know if Katherine was familiar with *Lessons for My Daughter*. But we *do* know that she was on intimate terms with Juan Luis Vives's *Education of a Christian Woman*, which had been written in 1523 expressly for Princess Mary, Katherine's daughter, to accompany her readings in the classics, the Church fathers, and — for recreation — the legends of the saints and tales about Griselda and other self-sacrificing women. Vives's book purports to offer instruction for all women, but was clearly written with Katherine's strict Catholicism as its model. In it, young girls, reminded that they are "the devil's instrument," are given strict instructions for how to protect themselves and their chastity from temptation.[63] The essence of the instruction: Do not read anything other than Scripture or philosophers of high moral worth and employ no artifice of any sort in the "vainglorious" pursuit of physical beauty (adornments, perfumes, and ointments) that would "despoil her soul of the splendor of virtue." For "she who rouses allurement in those who behold her does not possess true chastity."[64] Bland food was recommended, so as not to "inflame the body," and children's movements should be disciplined against "unseemly gesture" or a "proclivity to talkativeness."[65] And above all else, avoid the kind of witty conversation with men cultivated in court, which Vives viewed as a prelude to sexual abandon. Heterosexual conversation is so much the devil's tool that Vives advises that "it is not to be permitted that a young woman and a man should converse alone anywhere for any length of time, not even if they are brother and sister."[66] Indeed, it is "best to have as little contact with men as possible."[67] For married women, he prohibits interest in "dances, amusements, and banqueting," even on the day of their wedding: "There is no need of dancing and all that hubbub of drinking and uncontrolled and prolonged gaiety ... Marriage was permitted as a remedy for lust, and we have made of the wedding day an occasion for unbridled lust."[68] Once married, she should leave the home as little as possible, speak "only when it would be harmful to keep silent," and at home "administer everything according to the will and command of her husband."[69]

If this was more or less Katherine's conduct manual, Anne must have appeared as a lifesaving remedy, and not only to an heirless throne. While in the French court, she had perfected a very different set of rules of female comportment, described by Baldassare Castiglione in his 1528 *The Book of the Courtier* as the cultivation of "a certain pleasant affability" designed to please men without ever tipping over into an unseemly boldness.[70] In theory, it was a delightful ideal. In practice, it was a delicate and precarious balancing act, constantly walking the tightrope between "vivacity" and "modesty," "a little free talk" and "unseemly words," "prudishness" and "unbridled familiarity."[71] In fact, the entire set of requirements of courtly behavior for women was framed in terms of contradictions (or, more realistically, double binds) that required constant calculation and self-scrutiny. The court lady must never appear to be "vain or frivolous."[72] However, she must "have the good sense to discern what those garments are that enhance that which is the gift of nature. Thus, if she is a little more stout or thin than the medium, or fair or dark, let her seek help from dress, but as covertly as possible; and while keeping herself dainty and neat, let her always seem to give no thought or heed to it."[73] While never appearing to show off, she should also be full of "witticisms and pleasantries," "have knowledge of letters, music, painting, and know how to dance and make merry," and be able to play those musical instruments that highlight "the mild gentleness which so much adorns every act a woman does."[74]

The point of all this was to be entertaining to men — while projecting feminine delicacy. Since men were expected to be hale fellows, hearty drinkers, and sexual pursuers — the court was a real boys' club, particularly after the vigorous young Henry became king — "femininity" was a balancing act that required great skill and social intelligence. The pleasure of often boisterous, sexually aggressive men was the goal; but there were exacting sexual boundaries a woman was not permitted to violate. She should be physically desirable and could engage in flirtatious, even sexually provocative talk (and *should*, when to do otherwise would shame the men or mark her as a prude), but her social performance must never raise doubts about her virtue.[75] To guard against this, constant vigilance — in precarious tension with the "vivacity" expected of her — was required. Giuliano de' Medici (brother of Lorenzo): "She ought also to be more circumspect, and to take better heede that she give no occasion to bee ill reported of, and so behave her selfe, that she be not onely not spotted with any fault, but not so much as with suspition."[76]

Ultimately, Anne was to pay a high price for her own vivacity and flirtatiousness, which she could not simply turn off as if it were a faucet once the crown was on her head, and which her enemies used to raise suspicions about her fidelity to Henry. But in the beginning, it was likely her consummate skill in walking the tightrope between desirability and chastity that made her a standout in the English court. Enemies may have described this as manipulative, and, of course, it was; but it was conventionally manipulative — a game all court ladies were expected to play. The "chastity" part may not have been entirely an act either, despite the reputation spread by her enemies. In France, Anne was, after all, lady-in-waiting to Queen Claude, known for her virtue and religious devotion and high moral expectations of her ladies. But then, too, her husband, Francis, was a notorious womanizer, whose own Catholicism, apparently, had different rules than Claude's. Anne's years at the French court, divided between the expectations of Claude and the imperative to please men, were excellent training in walking the tightrope. Did Anne have sex with dozens of courtiers, as film and television portrayals would have us believe? That seems highly unlikely, as Claude would have undoubtedly kicked her out of court had there been even a hint of that. Did she bring back to England the provocative yet diffident confidence that French women are known for? It seems that she did.

Having been "finished" as a court lady, Anne's sense of propriety was very different from Katherine's. In France, Anne had learned that clever, provocative talk was an art, not a transgression. Katherine, raised much more strictly in Spain and with her royal status always in mind, had learned that it was a sin. Her everyday regimen was organized around goodness, duty, obedience, and silence. All that, of course, was what was expected of a good Tudor wife — especially of a queen. But Eros rebels at such conventions. Whatever their affection for each other, Henry and Katherine were not exactly vibrantly in tune. Neither one expected that, however, for neither "falling in love" nor "being in love" was the norm for Tudor marriage, particularly not for an arranged royal marriage. They probably were delighted to discover what appears to have been some real mutual attraction when they were young and Henry's inexperience matched Katherine's. Had Katherine been able to deliver a male heir, that — and Henry's mistresses — probably would have kept the marriage alive indefinitely. But they were not soul mates.

For one thing, Henry was never the same kind of Catholic as Katherine was. Henry's Catholicism was conventional, and in the end proved less precious to him than his own earthly ambitions. He and Anne thought nothing of writing little love notes to each other on a book of hours, exchanged between them in church like teenagers passing notes in class. Katherine would probably have regarded this as sacrilege. Her religiosity was deeply etched in her being and her daily habits. She spent hours in prayer every day and had been taught that dancing, singing, and hunting were inappropriate, if not sinful, for a woman to engage in. But these were among Henry's greatest pleasures. Initially raised to be the "spare" heir, Henry's childhood years had been fairly free. But when his brother Arthur died when Henry was eleven, his upbringing changed dramatically. His father was now focused obsessively on keeping Henry safe from harm, and the boy's chief care was given over to his grandmother, Lady Margaret Beaufort, every bit as pious as Katherine, and her closest adviser, John Fisher, Bishop of Rochester. They provided Henry with a broad and liberal education for his mind, but "cabined, cribbed, and confined" his body, which was powerfully endowed by nature: tall and broad chested, with strong legs and a restless vitality that immediately burst its chains the moment he became king, at the age of eighteen. Even at forty-two, he was still brimming with masculine energy. An adept horseman, jouster, and tennis player, Henry was also a splendid dancer — as was Anne ("Her gracefulness rivaled Venus," wrote the French chronicler Pierre de Bourdeilles Brantôme), whose personality and pleasures were better matched with Henry's than Katherine's were. Like Henry, she loved hunting, riding, and cards. Educated to be a court lady rather than a queen, she was far from silent and verbally jousted with the men around court. (Even Wolsey's man Cavendish, who rarely had anything good to say about her, admitted she had "a very good wit."[77]) She was also bold and not afraid to challenge the superstitious streak that Henry's grandmother had implanted in him. Elizabeth Benger relates an incident in which Anne was able to persuade Henry to visit a spot in Woodstock Forest, which had the reputation for being haunted. It was believed, in particular, that no king who entered would leave alive. Henry had been taught not to take chances with the gods or the fates. Yet Anne was able to convince him to ride through the forest, and to his relief and gratitude he exited in one piece. The anecdote may be apocryphal in detail, but in spirit it squares with what we know about Anne. It requires no stretch to see how she could come to represent youthful liberation to Henry, while Katherine's piety, although perfectly "normal" for a queen, may well have carried unpleasant memories of the stifling regime of his grandmother.

As a dedicated reformist, Anne was also perfectly in synch with Henry's growing hostility toward the papacy. Once in league with him in pursuit of the divorce, she more than supported Henry's efforts, supplying the reformist texts and arguments that gave Henry the justification he needed to enlarge his role as the spiritual leader of the nation, including William Tyndale's *The Obedience of a Christian Man*, which must have prickled Henry's sense of manliness as well as supported his resistance to the Church — and it suggests that opposing the Church could be very profitable as well. Tyndale complains that the monarchs of Christendom had become mere shadows, "having nothing to do in the world but when our holy father needeth help," and encourages them to take back "every farthing," "all manner of treasure," and "all the lands which they have gotten with their false prayers."[78] It was Anne who showed Henry this book, but it's easy to see that feminine brain-washing was hardly required for Henry to "get" that antipapal ideas were on the side of kings. As early as 1515, the youthful Henry, pro-nouncing on a dispute about the relative powers of ecclesiastical and state courts, declared that the king of England has no "superior but God only" and upheld the authority of "temporal jurisdiction" over Church decrees. This point of view, growing sharper every year that followed, was the cutting edge that ultimately cost Thomas More his head. More's fatal dispute with Henry was not over Anne, for Henry and Anne were already married by then, without the pope's approval; it was clear he no longer needed any official "permission" to make her his wife. But what Henry always needed — demanded — was recogni-tion, among his own subjects, of the greater justice of his own author-ity. More, who was as stubborn and egotistical as Henry when it came to what he thought was "right," wouldn't give it, and Henry couldn't let that go.

For a traditionalist such as Chapuys, of course, Anne's having any say at all in Henry's political affairs would have been outrageously pre-sumptuous, particularly since Anne was not of royal blood. Henry, however, at least at this point in his life, may not have had the same ideas about women and their proper place. Educated alongside his two sisters and extremely close to his mother, he may have had far less than the usual Tudor stock of misogynist ideas about women and their nat-ural inferiority. At various times during their marriage, Katherine had been entrusted with responsibilities that went far beyond the wifely, serving as a mediator between Henry and Spain, and a strong advocate — some even say instigator — of war with France. When Henry left for war, he constituted her as "Regent and Governess of England, Wales, and Ireland" and gave her sweeping powers to raise troops, make ap-pointments, issue warrants, and in general take charge of governing on the domestic front. The active role that Katherine took not only gives the lie to the conventional portrait of her as Henry's doormat, but also shows that those who later resented Anne's "interference" in political matters had ideological or personal reasons for their annoyance. Queens, especially well-educated queens such as Katherine, were not just shirt embroiderers or alms distributors. When their husbands were open to it, they often played an active role in international affairs.

Henry would later become less open to the political participation of his wives, warning Jane Seymour, for example, not to meddle and holding the example of her predecessor ominously over her head (so to speak). But there's no evidence that during the six years he pursued Anne he had any objection to her counsel. It has to be remembered that these were six years in which Henry spent far less time mooning about Anne than he did arguing, gathering forces, reviewing texts — his ego and his authority more on the line every year that passed. Initially, Henry had every expectation that the pope would quickly reverse the dispensation he had granted for the marriage to Katherine. But for complexly tangled political reasons, the pope was not about to give Henry the easy divorce he imagined, and Henry was drawn into battle with the papacy itself. It was long, fierce, and bloody, fracturing English loyalties, sending devoted papists such as Thomas More to the scaffold and ultimately resulting in a new Church of England with Henry as its head. Anyone who follows it closely can see that the autonomy and authority of kings ultimately became more of an issue for Henry than the divorce.[79]

"She is not of ordinary clay," Henry had once said to Wolsey, explaining his infatuation for Anne, a comment that most historians take to refer to Anne's unwillingness to engage in sex before marriage.[80] But perhaps Henry, tired of docile mistresses and a wife whose undeniable intelligence was cramped by obedience to role and religion, found Anne's independence and ingenuity of mind among those qualities that made her extraordinary. Certainly, he was more than willing — without any "wheedling" or "crying" — to accept the help she offered in strategizing for the divorce. Even David Starkey notes this. "In the divorce, Anne and Henry were one. They debated it and discussed it; they exchanged ideas and agents; they devised strategies and stratagems. And they did all this together." For Starkey, this made them "Macbeth and Lady Macbeth" — and Anne, "like Lady Macbeth, frequently took the initiative."[81] But this venomous, anti-Anne gloss on the partnership of Henry and Anne skips over the most unusual thing about it: that it *was* a partnership. And an unusually "modern" one that did not fit into any of the available cultural patterns. It took a woman "not of ordinary clay" to shatter the mold — and a king who was glad to see it in pieces. For the moment.

3

In Love (or Something Like It)

I N 2009, AS PART of an exhibit at the British Library marking the 500th anniversary of Henry's accession to the throne, a letter described by David Starkey as a piece of the most "explosive royal correspondence" in the history of England was displayed. For the general public, it created quite a stir. HENRY VIII REVEALS HIS SOFTER SIDE IN NEVER-BEFORE-SEEN GUSHING LOVE LETTER TO ANNE BOLEYN, read the *Daily Mail* headline on February 14, while Starkey made the most of it: "This marks the moment when British history changes . . . and the world turns upside down," he pronounced.[1]

Tudor scholars were already well aware of the existence of this letter, along with sixteen others, all undated, which were revealed, roughly fifty years after they were written, to be in the Vatican, presumably stolen from among Anne's possessions in order to make the case, should it be needed, that Henry's request for a divorce stemmed from erotic rather than theological considerations. The letter Starkey chose to exhibit, however, was not the most lust-filled — that title goes to one in which Henry pines to be in his "sweetheart's arms, whose pretty dukkys [breasts] I trust shortly to cusse [kiss]."[2] Instead, perhaps capitalizing on the success of *The Tudors,* Starkey chose Henry's response to a gift from Anne, which he interprets (as does the series) to be the moment when Henry finally receives a yes from Anne. Anne has sent Henry a trinket in the shape of a ship, on which a "solitary damsel" (so reads Henry's letter), adorned with a pendant diamond, is "tossed about."[3] Henry thanks Anne, not so much for the trinket but for the "interpretation and the too humble submission which your goodness hath used toward me in this case."[4] The "interpretation" is dramatized this way in *The Tudors.*

> *Still breathing heavily with excitement, Henry stares*
> *at the jewel, trying to puzzle out its secret meaning.*

HENRY: A ship . . . with a woman on board. What is a ship? What, but a symbol of protection, like the ark which rescued Noah.

> (*beat*)

And the diamond? What does it say in the *Roman de la Rose*? "A heart as hard as diamond, steadfast . . . never changing . . ."

> *He paces around. It hits him.*

HENRY: She is the diamond — and I the ship.

> *His excitement is almost feverish.*

HENRY: She says yes![5]

In the next scene, we see Henry at Hever Castle, engaged in steamy, to-the-brink-of-intercourse sexual play with Anne. They are both overcome with passion, breathing heavily, "eyes bright with desire" and all the other paraphernalia of cinematic lust. "He can take her now if he wants to," the script reads.[6] But he rolls off her, vowing to honor her maidenhead.

Michael Hirst, who created and wrote the series, also provides an ingeniously titillating explanation as to why Henry was corresponding with Anne in the first place. She is at Hever, having left in order to "whet" Henry's appetite for her, and Henry has a dream in which she appears to him (naked at one point) and breathlessly instructs him to "[s]educe me . . . [w]rite letters to me . . . [r]avish me with your words."[7] So he does. We then follow Anne's receipt of each letter, usually read aloud to her brother and father, who are brimming with ambitious fantasies over Henry's deepening desire and offering instruction on how Anne can string him along most effectively. She is reluctant at first, but she soon comes to enjoy the game. And as Henry's passion mounts, so does hers. "How are you?" he asks when she returns to court. "Burning," she answers. "Burning with impatience."

Actually, we don't know when or why the letters were written. They aren't dated, and since Henry presumably destroyed Anne's replies (at any rate, they've never been found), we have to imagine what she wrote on the basis of Henry's references. Historians have struggled for centuries in an attempt to place Henry's letters in coherent chronological context and order, with no definitive conclusion (see sidebar, below). None of the hypotheses correspond to *The Tudors'* clumping of the letters into a single continuous stream. But a dominant tradition does cast Anne in the correspondence as she is cast in *The Tudors* — as an enchantress, with Henry as the besotted recipient of her spells. She knew the fate of those, such as her sister, Mary, who gave in easily, only to be used up and discarded by Henry, and she was determined to avoid that fate. So she keeps him bewitched by carefully and strategically manipulating his emotions. Alison Weir: "[S]he handled him with such calculated cleverness that there is no doubt that the crown of England meant more to her than the man through whom she would wear it . . . [E]verything she did, or omitted to do, in relation to Henry was calculated to increase his ardor. In this respect she never failed."[8]

⸿ Why Was Henry Writing to Anne?

It is notoriously difficult to reconstruct the order in which the seventeen letters were sent and the occasions for their being written. Different scholars have wildly different hypotheses, all of them the product of imaginative reconstruction rather than forensic evidence: Retha Warnicke argues that they began in June 1528, when Anne was sent back to Hever because of an outbreak of the sweating sickness, broke off when she returned to court in July, and then resumed again in September when she was sent back to Hever to keep her out of sight while they awaited the arrival of Cardinal Campeggio, who Henry hoped would quickly resolve his "great matter." James Halliwell-Phillipps claims the occasion was Anne's removal from court in July 1527, "in consequence of reports injurious to her reputation."

(He never says what those were.) Eric Ives breaks them into four groups: one beginning in the fall of 1526, with Henry the beseeching servant trying to make a courtly relationship more serious; the second encompassing the desperate request for an answer, Anne's apparently encouraging gift of the trinket in reply, and his sending her his picture, solidifying the "engagement"; the third during the ten months from December 1527 to October 1528, with Henry reporting, while Anne is at Hever, his progress toward the divorce; and the final group in June 1528, during the outbreak of the sweating sickness. The fact that one scholar (Warnicke) can date as the first the same letter that another scholar (Ives) dates as the last shows how far from transparent these documents are.

I find Eric Ives's ordering and interpretation to be the most convincing—mostly because of the implausibility of the other theories. But really, we just don't know. I spent a weekend cutting out each letter and arranging and rearranging them with small magnets on a large whiteboard. I found plenty of logical and empirical impossibilities in the ordering of each of my three editions of the letters (one of which has a letter full of anxiety over Anne's bout with the sweating sickness coming *before* a letter in which he expresses hope that it will spare her), but I could come up with no fully convincing sequence in which to place the entire set.

What is the basis for Weir's claim that everything Anne did was "calculated" to increase Henry's ardor? Her chief evidence is that Anne "often failed to reply to [his letters]."[9] But we don't know when or whether or in what way Anne replies, for we don't have her letters to Henry. This doesn't stop Weir from describing Anne's replies as though she had them right in front of her. "If she detected a hint of irritation in his letters, she dealt with it by quickly reverting from the unattainable to the affectionate, and sending a loving reply."[10] But the "loving replies" in response to the "hints of irritation" that Weir refers to exist only in her imagination. Henry's letters are unfailingly courteous and deferential; he moans and groans over his lovesick "agony," but he never scolds her. And since we don't have Anne's letters, we can only infer what she said from Henry's. They don't tell us much about what she wrote beyond that he has been left "uncertain" for a length of time and then, at some point, reassured by "demonstrations of your affection."[11] In one letter, Henry ends: "Written with the hand of him which desireth as much to be yours as you do to have him"; in another, he refers to their mutual desire for each other's company.[12] These letters suggest that at a certain point an understanding of shared love had been established between them. But in no way do they imply that some manipulatively "loving reply" had come from Anne in response to irritation from Henry. Weir, however, never gets called out, because our collective "history" has been built up around imaginings such as hers. We don't demand evidence any more than an enthralled child demands evidence that the story of Cinderella is "true." The narrative is so emotionally satisfying that it doesn't require historical confirmation. It's confirmed by its familiarity, its poetic justice, and the ease with which it can be "read."

Add a heavy dose of hot sex to the temptress narrative and you get *The Tudors*. Michael Hirst was well aware that in order to win a contemporary audience for a historical drama, he had to provide plenty of it. He chose his Anne (Natalie Dormer) largely because of the chemistry between the actress and Jonathan Rhys Meyers, and during most of the first season, the relationship between Henry and Anne consists of variations on extended, passionate foreplay. For Hirst, as he shared in an interview with me, the sexed-up version of Henry and Anne's romance was not, however, simply a cynical ploy to get audiences hooked. He admits that he felt the imperative to seduce viewers who expected dry BBC decorum from a series about the Tudors. But he also was making a point. "I do believe that there was a lot of sex at the time. We have this image now that the court was run by middle-aged people, that Henry was prudish, and there was no sex because there was no heating in the palaces, and so forth. But actually, Europe was run by people in their teens and twenties, and they behaved just as you'd expect crazy young people to behave."[13]

I have no idea what happened behind the doors and between the bodies in Tudor England. No one does, as private sexual behavior was, of course, not documented, and unlike some Eastern cultures, there's not even a tradition of erotic art from this period to consult. But, in fact, it's highly unlikely that Anne and Henry were as sexually uninhibited with each other premaritally as portrayed in *The Tudors*. If they had, Henry would have quickly begun to view Anne as just another strumpet who had learned far too many tricks at the French court to be a worthy queen and mother of his future children. Yes, in one letter he mentions her "pretty dukkys" he "trusts shortly to [kiss]."[14] But the exact geography of the desired kiss, and whether it is imagined or remembered, isn't clear; "breasts" covers a lot of territory, much of which, especially in an era when cleavage was in fashion, doesn't imply nudity or nipples. And we really have no way of knowing whether the comment isn't just a bit of slightly risqué but courtly flirtation. Nor do we know just what Anne was thinking about Henry's letters, because we don't have hers. When she sent him that ship, was she agreeing to sex, as *The Tudors* suggests? Was she indicating she would do so if he divorced Katherine? Was it even about sex at all? Several historians suggest, contrary to the dominant "she said no" tradition, that Henry himself may have been the withholding partner, who found sex unthinkable with a potential queen (which, after all, he was seeking at the time) until they were married; the most that could yield was another illegitimate offspring.

Hirst's comparison with our own time also neglects to consider that this was a culture in which sexual consummation does not seem to have been the apotheosis of personal fulfillment that it was to become as physical desire replaced spiritualized, courtly constructions of "longing" in romantic love. Sexual fulfillment, by our time, has been pumped up to the status of a new religion, sold to us (by relationship experts, movies, TV, and advertising) as the "make or break" of relationships, and we expect a lot from it. The bodies are always perfect, the lovers are extraordinarily skilled, the men know just where to put their hands, and the women's breasts never hang or flatten unglamorously. On kitchen tables strewn with plates that get masterfully swept to the floor, on staircases, in bathtubs surrounded by precariously placed candles, material obstacles are no match for the lovers' passion. *The Tudors* imports this worship of matchless, exquisite sex into the sixteenth century. In Henry's time, however, religion was still religion, and sex was . . . well, sex. Henry could have it anytime he wanted — and did. I have always found it hard to believe that Henry's passion could be aroused to such a pitch — and remain there for six years! — just because of a no. He wasn't used to hearing the word, we're told, and that's true; this was a man around whom there clustered no shortage of fresh, flirty damsels to provide pleasure and sexual release, and who took advantage of their adoration — just how freely is debated among historians, but at the very least he did when Katherine (and later, Anne) was pregnant.[15] But his overwhelming drive was for an heir. In April of 1533 — by then, Anne and Henry were married, although he was not yet divorced from Katherine — Chapuys dared to suggest to him that he could not be sure of having children with Anne. Henry flew into a rage. "[Am I] not a man like other men?" he shouted three times.[16] Our own interpretation would probably be that Henry was furious at having his sexual potency called into question. But more likely, it was his reproductive ability; this, at any rate, is how Chapuys interpreted the rage, which he goes on to say led him "to understand that [Henry's] beloved lady was *enceinte*."[17]

Although Henry's pursuit of Anne was unlikely to have been driven by the mere prospect of sex with her, his desire for her to be his queen was probably increased by the enforcement (whether by him or by her) of her virginal status. In the romance of chivalry, on which Henry was raised, the heroine was an unattainable beauty, worshipped by her adoring knights but never to be sexually or emotionally possessed, and therefore always to be incurably desired. Henry's relationship with Anne could not remain in that realm of unrealizable desire — to produce an heir, she had to be brought down to earth, had to become flesh. But so long as there was distance between them, he could imagine himself a fairy-tale warrior and Anne the glittering — but unsullied — prize. His later interest in Jane Seymour "marvelously increased," Chapuys reports, when she sent a letter and gift back to Henry, unopened, with a note saying that she would rather "die a thousand deaths" than sully her honor by accepting anything from him.[18] (By then, Anne was no longer fit, in Henry's eyes, to be an object of worship by any chivalric criteria.)

Cultural Perspectives on Henry's Love Letters

Henry's love letters are extremely difficult to interpret, and not only because of their odd spelling, archaic phrases, and long-winded sentences. For one thing, unlike contemporary bloggers, Tudor correspondents and commentators were constantly mindful of what was respectful, what was pragmatically required, and what (if you weren't king) was downright dangerous. Duplicity was not just acceptable, but recommended, as in Sir William Wentworth's advice to his son, Thomas: "Be very careful to govern your tongue, and never speak in open places all you think . . . Judges, juries, under-sheriffs, and men of influence are to be courted both with flattery and with judicious gifts . . . As for noblemen, be careful not to make them hate you."[19] Those who were closest to the king had to be especially careful, not just because the stakes were so high (and could get hot), but also because Henry was aware of the conventions of flattery and how thinly they could cover plots against him. He was himself a master at contriving affection while planning destruction, lavishing soothing words on Katherine, Wolsey, More, and others moments before they were cut off, not just from their positions but from his company. He didn't like confrontation, and he was notoriously adept at shifting blame. He knew how to use words to create fictions of affection and intention, and naturally was suspicious that others were up to the same thing with him. So his closest advisers had to walk skillfully between suspect flattery and the dangers of honesty, peppering their deference with just the right amount of critical counsel. It was a pretty tricky business, and very few survived intact.

Whether they came from a servant, knight, or king, Tudor words were more like clothing than instruments of (literal) communication; they were used to create an impression, advertise (or defer to) status, armor the naked self with beauty and protective convention. Above all, they were instrumental, chosen with purpose. This cultural context alone makes me skeptical of the claims of David Starkey, who views Tudor documents as the "magical objects . . . hidden in the world's great libraries . . . that can bring a long-gone world vividly to life once more. They are the books, manuscripts, plans and letters that Henry and his contemporaries read, touched, and wrote. Through them, the dead can speak again. It's in these original sources that I hope to find the real Henry."[20] Starkey is a master dramatist, and he makes entering a library look like an episode from an Indiana Jones movie. But the notion that original sources can bring the dead to life again astounds me, as I find most of those documents so opaque that I want to shake them, trying to make the person fall out of the parchment. This is particularly difficult with Henry. "Henry," Thomas More once said to John Fisher, "has a way of making every man feel that he is enjoying his special favors, just as the London wives pray before the image of Our Lady by the Tower, until each of them believes it is smiling on her."[21] This may (or may not) have been a compliment, but it was also a caution: Don't believe everything Henry says or does.

However, that doesn't necessarily mean Henry wasn't "sincere." I put that word in quotes because the original meaning of the word is a particularly revealing example of the difference between the premodern worldview and our own — and unless we appreciate that difference, we can't fully understand Henry. "Sincere" comes from the Latin *sine* (without) and *caries* (decay). Its original meaning was "undecayed," or sometimes "not mixed or adulterated" or "uninjured" or "whole." Just when it came to convey the modern meaning — "without deceit, pretense, or hypocrisy; being the same in actual character as in outward appearance" — isn't clear. But what many scholars believe is that the juxtaposition of "actual character" and "outward appearance" would seem very odd to a man of the sixteenth century.

Here's where philosophers, social theorists, and those who study the evolution of human consciousness can provide insight into a development that "straight" history misses. Philosopher Stephen Toulmin describes it as the emergence of "the inwardness of mental life" — and that's something we take for granted.[22] It feels normal to us to experience ourselves as having a private inner self that is unavailable to others (except through outward giveaway or verbal disclosure). When we lose that sense of self, we feel "depersonalized"; when it is in conflict with what we tell others, we may feel duplicitous; when it harbors nasty urges, we may feel guilty. Whole sciences and disciplines are devoted to its exploration and analysis. Whether we cherish its secrets or spend our lives protecting them, the inner life is a staple of our experience.

Sixteenth-century humans thought and felt, of course. But according to many scholars, they did not experience those thoughts and feelings as *inside* themselves in quite the way we do. "Before the scientific revolution," Owen Barfield writes, "[man] did not feel himself isolated by his skin from the world outside to quite the same extent that we do. He was integrated or mortised into it, each different part of him being united to a different part of it by some invisible thread."[23] The invisible threads that ran throughout the universe knit tightly the relations between people, the various "types" of human beings (phlegmatic, melancholic, choleric, sanguine), human virtues and vices (honor, loyalty, avarice, courage, and so on), and the effect of the planets — and God — on human destiny. And the outer manifestations of those relations spoke for themselves. Lacey Baldwin Smith puts it eloquently: "The tree was known by its fruits: the good pastor could be discerned by his acts of piety, charity and love; and the perfect knight was revealed by his deeds of loyalty, and generosity . . . The possibility that the walls which man presents to the outside world, however transparent they may appear, can obscure and distort the reflection of the true character within, or the concept that bragging can be a sign of insecurity rather than of pride, was totally foreign."[24]

The difference between sixteenth-century and twenty-first-century life, then, went deeper than codpieces and the absence of plumbing. In determining what to do in a particular situation, one didn't "look inside" to consult one's deepest feelings and beliefs; one looked in the book — of the cosmos, of the Bible, of social conventions — and there one found "oneself." As in the original meaning of "sincere," one looked, not for a match between inner experience and outward expression, but for wholeness, for proof that the invisible cords between self and world were unfrayed. It's easy, from a twenty-first-century perspective, to suspect that Henry's invoking the passages in Leviticus when asking Rome for the divorce from Katherine was just a convenient rationalization for his desire to quit the marriage. But for Henry, Leviticus and personal motivation could not be separated in that way.

His restlessness, his roving eye, his growing conviction that Katherine would never give him a son — he found them not so much justified as crystallized, revealed as *whole,* in Leviticus.

All that was to change, gradually, during the Renaissance, the Reformation, and the scientific revolution. The scientific revolution cut the umbilical ties between the human being and the heavens. The Reformation severed salvation from deeds and relocated it in the inner state of faith. Writers from Shakespeare to Montaigne seem at times to be literally *discovering* the difference between what lies inside the self and what is shown to the world. For Henry, however, the ideals of the Renaissance and Reformation were still ideas to be found in books. As an intellectual, he was drawn to them; as a king, he was delighted to find his royal position elevated by them, but they never became habits of being. Self-questioning was never his forte, and like those of his subjects who remained devout Catholics, he never stopped believing that external manifestation of virtue and the state of the soul were one. When he "dissembled" by our standards, he believed he was doing what was required for the greater good, which was his duty and formed his sense of identity. "Lying" suggests a clear understanding of the inner reality behind the outward appearance, but for Henry, the outward appearance of princely honor was the highest "reality." He donned it, when necessary, as he donned his jewel-adorned robes. *We* see those robes as ridiculous in their ostentation and are always aware of the naked body beneath them. But for Henry, robes and body, prince and man, were one and the same. And there was no naked self underneath.

Henry the Courtier

What then of the love letters? Surely, of all his letters and proclamations, they reveal the existence of an "inner" Henry, throbbing with longing for Anne's presence, agony over her absence, and turmoil over his feelings.

My Mistress and friend, my heart and I surrender ourselves into your hands, beseeching you to hold us commended to your favour, and that by absence your affection to us may not be lessened: for it would be a great pity to increase our pain, of which absence produces enough and more than I could ever have thought could be felt . . . at least on my side; I hope the like on yours, assuring you that on my part the pain of absence is already too great for me; and when I think of the increase of that which I am forced to suffer, it would be almost intolerable, but for the firm hope I have of your unchangeable affection for me: and to remind you of this sometimes, and seeing that I cannot be personally present with you, I now send you the nearest thing I can to that, namely, my picture set in bracelets, with the whole of the device, which you already know, wishing myself in their place, if it should please you. This is from the hand of your loyal servant and friend, H.R.[25]

The mere physical act of writing such a letter is by itself an indication of Henry's yearning for Anne. Although intellectually accomplished, he was an impatient and restless personality; in our time, he probably would be diagnosed with ADD. He read voraciously, but only after others had scoured the contents of books for him and presented them in digest form. (To ensure that he knew all sides of an issue, he assigned the same book to different advisers.) He didn't even like to read his letters. And he absolutely hated to respond to them. His secretaries had to cajole him to deal with his correspondence, which he put off as long as possible and wouldn't deal with until he had returned from hunting and had a good dinner.[26] Since he was a terrific athlete whose kinetic energy had been bottled up during adolescence by his protective father and grandmother, his first impulse, on becoming king, was to let loose. Surrounded and cheered on by the like-minded young men he had chosen to be his inner circle, he spent the early days of his reign, as Katherine described it in a letter to her father, "in continual festival."[27] A 1510 description of a day during a typical "progress" — the king and queen, in those days, traveled from court to court and palace to palace, accompanied by a huge retinue — gives us an indication of what the festivities included.

"Shooting [archery], singing, dancing, wrestling, casting of the bar [throwing a wooden or iron baton], playing at the recorders, flute, virginals, setting of songs, making of ballads . . . jousts and tournays. The rest of this progress was spent in hunting, hawking and shooting."[28] In 1517, at a joust in honor of the Spanish ambassadors, Henry wanted to joust against all fourteen competitors. Forbidden to do so by his councilors (an older, more cautious crew than his boy pals), he channeled his desire to show off into "a thousand jumps in the air" before the queens and ladies, exhausting his horse — at which point he continued on one ridden by his pages.[29] At another joust, he forgot to pull his visor down as he advanced toward his competitor and was knocked to the ground, stunned, his eye just barely missed by the lance. Within moments he was back on his horse, ready to go again.

This was the Henry who had been raised on tales of King Arthur's Round Table, virtuous knights, maidens in distress, and chivalrous deeds. When he was knighted — becoming Duke of York at just three and a half years old — he went through all the Arthurian rituals a grown man would have gone through, and after a purifying bath, he was told that his duty, as a knight, was to be strong in the faith of the Holy Church, to love and defend the king, and to protect all widows and oppressed maidens. Undoubtedly, his father or mother must have taken him to Winchester Cathedral, thought to be the site of Arthur's castle and the capital of Camelot, to show him the Round Table that was still there. (When Henry became king, he had his image painted over that of Arthur's.) Nobility, generosity, mercy, justice, and the power of true love were the stuff of his boyish fantasies.

But by 1526, when Henry began to pursue Anne, Arthurian chivalry, a deeply spiritualized ideal, had been transformed into the political "art" of courtly behavior, aimed at creating the right *impression*, even if deceptive, to achieve one's ends. Somehow, I managed to escape college and graduate school without reading *The Book of the Courtier*. So I was surprised to discover that the version of courtly love described by Castiglione was so different from the high-minded ideals and valiant heroes of the legends I grew up with. I was raised on bedtime stories — and later, movies — with strong, pure-of-purpose male leads (which set up some unrealistic expectations of the boys I dated) from Alexander the Great (my father's favorite) to the self-sacrificing Arthur and absurdly handsome Lancelot of Lerner and Loewe's *Camelot*. When I thought of "courtly love," I imagined knights on horseback worshiping ladies from afar and fighting great battles to win their love, their minds full of noble thoughts and dreams of honor. That's how Henry the boy probably imagined chivalry, too, as court minstrels performed and sang of the heroic exploits of Jason, Hector, Charlemagne, Arthur, Lancelot, and Galahad. But by the time Henry was born, the printing press was competing with oral traditions for the hearts and minds of would-be courtiers, and along with print came popular books of "instructions" for courting that, like all guidebooks, replaced romance with formula. This is the genre that Castiglione's *Book of the Courtier* belongs to. It is not so much a celebration of chivalry as it is an advice book on how to "perform" it.

It's full of clever, deceptive strategies for seduction, from ostentatiously "burning sighs" and "abundant tears," to singing outside her house at night, to consulting books teaching men "how women are to be duped in these matters." How could any girl escape such an onslaught of "snares," Castiglione wonders (through one of the characters in his fictional conversations about the virtues and conduct of the ideal courtier). "I could not in a thousand years rehearse all the wiles that men employ to bring women to their wishes, for the wiles are infinite . . ."[30] Castiglione's jaded, ironic tone makes it clear how he regards these practices: as a kind of socially sanctioned harassment (he didn't have the word, but he sure gets close to the concept) in which it was acceptable to dissemble, badger, and lie in order to connive the woman into falling in love with her suitor. Among the more cynical tactics recommended was the fictional suspension of the social positions of lover and beloved. Ignoring actual rank, swearing total allegiance, the lover is advised to address the beloved with deep humility, to be abject before her and totally submissive. But it's all a ploy designed to take advantage of the woman's vanity and gullibility. Or, if she was cleverer or more cynical, to engage her in a pleasurable fiction.

Scholars are in dispute about just how widely practiced "courtly love" was. Some insist that it was just a literary tradition, spread throughout Western Europe in the twelfth and thirteenth centuries largely via the troubadours of southern France, that had little impact on actual courtship practice. This is almost certainly true for most classes in medieval and Renaissance England, but when it came to the better-educated class, the line between "literary" and "actual" is harder to maintain. Poetry, music, and pageants celebrating courtly love were regular entertainments at Henry's court, and both Henry and his best-educated courtiers (those who could read Italian) eagerly sought copies of *The Book of the Courtier* when it was published in 1528. Such published treatments of courtly love were, moreover, based on actual court behavior (in the case of Castiglione, that of the Duke of Urbino; in the case of Andreas Capellanus's *The Art of Courtly Love*, Queen Eleanor's court at Poitiers). It is highly likely that whether or not Henry actually read Castiglione, he was familiar with the practices Castiglione describes.

Earlier treatises, such as *The Art of Courtly Love,* had treated love, in true Platonic fashion, as a god who seizes and obsesses the lover, putting his soul in a state of turmoil. ("When a lover suddenly catches sight of his beloved his heart palpitates"; "Real jealousy always increases the feeling of love"; "He whom the thought of love vexes eats and sleeps very little"; "A true lover is constantly and without intermission possessed by thought of his beloved."[31]) The beloved, on his or her part (depending on whether it's Plato or Capellanus), is more detached, cool, and inclined to play hard to get. Overheated and possessed, the lover must then learn how to manage his passion so it will not self-destruct in rash action, jealousy, or carnality. Castiglione, in contrast, is less concerned with the state of the lover's soul than honing his skill at seducing the beloved. It is she who is to be "managed," not the lover's tumultuous passions. And in the service of that goal, all manner of deception and manipulation is permitted.

There were plenty of critics of this degeneration. Even for Sir Thomas Malory, whose *Le Morte d'Arthur,* published in 1485, was the chief basis for the English version of the Arthurian legend, the "fresh and temperate" love of Lancelot for Guinevere, which lasted for years, was the stuff of fairy tales. ("Today," Malory writes, "men cannot love seven nights but they must have their desires."[32]) But it was a fairy tale that still could inspire. By the time Thomas Wyatt wrote his poem "Of the Courtier's Life" (1539), he has nothing but cynicism for the possibility of living an honorable life at court.

> *I cannot frame my tongue to feign,*
> *To cloak the truth, for praise without desert*
> *Of them that list all vice for to retain.*
> *I cannot honour them that set their part*
> *With Venus, and Bacchus, all their life long;*
> *Nor hold my peace of them, although I smart.*
> *I cannot crouch nor kneel to such a wrong;*
> *To worship them like God on earth alone,*
> *That are like wolves these sely lambs among.*
> *I cannot with my words complain and moan,*
> *And suffer nought; nor smart without complaint:*
> *Nor turn the word that from my mouth is gone.*
> *I cannot speak and look like as a saint;*
> *Use wiles for wit, and make deceit a pleasure;*
> *Call craft counsel, for lucre still to paint.*[33]

Wyatt's poem is not only a protest against pragmatic deception to achieve worldly advancement, it also expresses disgust at those who "set their part with Venus, and Bacchus" — that is, those for whom love has become a game of pleasure rather than the driving force behind honorable actions and spiritual striving. In Europe, Francis's court had the worst reputation for dissolute courtly behavior, but Wyatt, whose most famous poem wrenchingly laments the executions of the men with whom Anne had been accused and condemned, which he watched from a window in the Bell Tower, had lost whatever faith he had in the English court to behave more honorably. "These bloody days have broken my heart," he wrote; a world had been shattered for him.[34]

Where does Henry stand in all this? We find him somewhere between Arthurian honor, which served and protected women as one of its highest goals and for which a king stood nobly and patiently by while his best knight and his wife engaged in a long affair, and a coup d'état that ruthlessly sent a queen and several of the king's best buddies to their deaths without hard evidence of any sort. Raised on the romance of one set of ideals, he was capable of setting aside his dislike of letter writing to pen seventeen love letters to Anne, throbbing with longing for her presence, agony over her absence, and full of declarations of submission and obedience to her wishes, as in this one, in which Henry offers to make Anne his *maîtresse en titre* (official mistress — a form of extramarital monogamy).

On turning over in my mind the contents of your last letters, I have put myself into great agony, not knowing how to interpret them, whether to my disadvantage, as you show in some places, or to my advantage, as I understand them in some others, beseeching you earnestly to let me know expressly your whole mind as to the love between us two. It is absolutely necessary for me to obtain this answer, having been for the whole year stricken with the dart of love, and not yet sure whether I shall fail or find a place in your heart and affection, which last point has prevented me for some time from calling you my mistress; because, if you only love me with an ordinary love, that name is not suitable for you, because it denotes a singular love, which is far from common. But if you please to do the office of a true loyal mistress and friend, and to give up yourself body and heart to me, who will be, and have been, your most loyal servant (if your rigour does not forbid me) I promise you that not only the name shall be given you, but also that I will take you for my only mistress, casting off all others besides you out of my thoughts and affections, and serve you only. I beseech you to give an entire answer to this my rude letter, that I may know on what and how far I may depend. And if it does not please you to answer me in writing, appoint some place where I may have it by word of mouth, and I will go thither with all my heart.
No more, for fear of tiring you,
Written by the hand of him who would willingly remain yours,
H.R.[35]

"I beseech you," "if you please to do," "fear of tiring you," "your most loyal servant," "serve you only." Certainly sounds as if she has him wrapped around her extra little finger. But even at this stage of the relationship, with Henry still besotted with his as-yet-unconquered prize, he was an instrumental thinker — and had been from the beginning of his reign. One of his earliest acts, after he became king, had been to execute two of his father's ministers on fictitious charges of treason, purely in the interests of enhancing his own PR with the people and projecting the image of a new broom sweeping clean. When newly married to Katherine, he had written to her father, King Ferdinand II of Aragon: "Day by day, her inestimable virtues shine forth, flourish and increase, so that even if we were still free, it is she that we would choose."[36] This statement, claims Starkey, proves that Henry was actually in love with Katherine, and not simply — as *Anne of the Thousand Days* puts it — that "England married Spain." But . . . this letter was to King Ferdinand! Katherine's father! Henry's father-in-law! If that isn't enough to raise doubts about the candor of the sentiment, we've got Henry, some years later, using exactly the same rhetorical flourish to prove to Rome that his motives for divorce from Katherine were pious. Were it not for his grievous doubts that the marriage had been against divine law, he assured Campeggio, he would with great joy marry Katherine all over again.

> And as touching the Queen, if it be adjudged the law of God that she is my lawful wife, there was never thing more pleasant nor more acceptable to me in my life, both for the discharge and clearing of my conscience and also for the good qualities and conditions the which I know to be in her. For I assure you all, that beside her noble parentage of which she is descended, she is a woman of the most gentleness, of most humility and buxomness, yea and of all good qualities appertaining to nobility, she is without comparison, as I this twenty years almost have had the true experiments, so that *if I were to marry again, if the marriage might be good I would surely choose her above all other women.*[37] [Emphasis mine.]

This is pretty difficult to buy, as in 1527 he was already writing his beseeching letters to Anne Boleyn, describing being "stricken with the dart of love" for more than a year, begging her to give herself up "body and heart" to him, and sending her charming love tokens such as a freshly slaughtered buck, "hoping that when you eat of it you may think of the hunter."[38] But whether rhetorical or deeply felt, or some combination of both, one thing is clear, which is that at a certain point he was assured that his feelings for Anne were reciprocated, and from that moment on, the two were united in the effort to obtain a divorce.

Reprinted among Henry's love letters to Anne is a "joint production" by the two of them that supports this view. It was sent to Wolsey after Anne had recovered from the sweating sickness and rejoined Henry at court to anxiously await the long-delayed Campeggio. The main letter is by Anne, followed by a postscript from Henry. Popular representations, following Cavendish's reports, have tended to portray Anne's relationship with Wolsey as one of all-out hostility, with Anne harboring a long-standing resentment over Wolsey's ending of her romance with Henry Percy, after which (according to Cavendish) she had vowed to destroy Wolsey at the earliest opportunity. In fact, however, relations between Anne and Wolsey were extremely cordial — about as warm as Tudor relations were capable of being — until the end of 1528, when both she and Henry began to reach the limit of frustration with Wolsey's faltering strategy (not his fault, but that fact was irrelevant to Henry) to achieve the divorce. This letter was written, apparently, during the period of still-amicable relations with Wolsey, but right on the cusp of their breakdown. Anne and Henry had been waiting for months for Campeggio to arrive from Rome and (as they hoped at the time) settle the "great matter"; travel and health difficulties had caused delay after delay, and Henry, as we see from his postscript, was losing patience.

Anne to Wolsey:

My Lord, in my most humblest wise that my heart can think, I desire you to pardon me that I am so bold to trouble you with my simple and rude writing, esteeming it to proceed from her that is much desirous to know that your grace does well, as I perceive by this bearer that you do, the which I pray God long to continue, as I am most bound to pray; for I do know the great pains and troubles that you have taken for me is never likely to be recompensed on my part, but alone in loving you next unto the king's grace, above all creatures living. And I do not doubt but the daily proofs of my deeds shall manifestly declare and affirm my writing to be true, and I do trust you to think the same.

My lord, I do assure you, I do long to hear from you news of the legate; for I do hope, as they come from you, they shall be very good; and I am sure you desire it as much as I, and more, an it were possible; as I know it is not: and thus remaining in a steadfast hope, I make an

end to my letter.
Written with the hand of her that is most bound to be
Your humble servant,
Anne Boleyn.[39]

Postscript by Henry:

The writer of this letter would not cease, till she had caused me like-wise to set my hand, desiring you, though it be short, to take it in good part. I ensure you that there is neither of us but greatly desireth to see you, and are joyous to hear that you have escaped this plague so well, trusting the fury thereof to be passed, especially with them that keepeth good diet, as I trust you do. The not hearing of the legate's arrival in France causeth us somewhat to muse; notwithstanding, we trust, by your diligence and vigilancy (with the assistance of Almighty God), shortly to be eased out of that trouble. No more to you at this time, but that I pray God send you as good health and prosperity as the writer would.

By your loving sovereign and friend,
H.R. [40]

Pray that you never have so "loving" a friend as Henry VIII. For just a little more than a year later, and without a glance backward, Henry had stripped Wolsey of his office of Lord Chancellor and all his accumulated treasures, a culmination of events that many scholars blame on Anne ("Anne and her faction did their work thoroughly," writes Weir [41]), ignoring that it was Henry's pattern, way before he met Anne, to blow hot then ruthlessly cold when things weren't going as he wished. Both Weir and Starkey see Anne as engineering Wolsey's downfall, with Henry the gullible, lust-driven fool skillfully played by her. But there was nothing gullible about Henry; indeed, he was among the most watchful, even paranoid, of rulers. And he was creepily un-flinching in neutralizing perceived enemies, including those who had been lifelong friends and mentors, such as Wolsey and More. Nowa-days, we might diagnose him as a sociopath due to the ease with which he dispatched death to his former buddies and lovers. But then again, kings at that time were trained in royal sociopathy, learning to put their emotions out of reach in the service of "the crown," and Henry, it seemed, became better and better at it with each passing year.

As to Anne, even if she matched Henry's political pragmatism (to put it in the most generous terms), it is unlikely that she had to "wheedle" Henry, as Starkey puts it, into getting rid of Wolsey,[42] just as in this jointly written letter they are of one mind about the need to gently urge him on. It is Henry who supplies the one chilling note, qualifying his expressions of faith in Wolsey with the admission that the delay of Campeggio "causeth us somewhat to muse."[43] (I'm sure Wolsey was quite aware that, Henry's praise for his diet aside, the ominous "musing" was the point here.) Weir describes Anne as having "nagged" Henry to add the postscript, an ungracious choice of words that nonetheless acknowledges that this is no exchange between a besotted courtier and his lady but a domestic snapshot. We can imagine Henry and Anne together, bent over a desk, shoulder to shoulder. Perhaps she's caught at his robe and pulled him over to her as he paced the room, restlessly waiting for her to finish tinkering with her letter so they could go off to hunt or dine or dance, perhaps he's been looking over her shoulder the whole time, poking her in the ribs over this or that turn of phrase. Perhaps she has "nagged," but perhaps she has persuaded him with argument, reminding him that only Henry's seal of approval would get Wolsey to take her seriously. Whatever scene one imagines, this joint letter is one of the very rare moments when we actually get to "hear" Anne and Henry in a kind of conversation with each other, unfiltered by the biases of the various court reporters — and it suggests an intimacy, affection, and shared purpose that doesn't fit at all with Starkey and Weir's "plotting Anne/manipulated Henry" telling of the story.

Of course, everything I've concluded is highly interpretive. That is unavoidable when trying to make sense of what is, in the end, elusive material — and much more complicated than simply an expression of Henry's "softer side" or passionate nature. For not only was the culture in transition, moving from one paradigm of human experience, one set of human ideals, to another, but Henry VIII was himself a barometer of that transition writ large. He was schooled in Arthurian honor, which served and protected women as one of its highest goals. But he could never abide by anything except his own supremacy. He was also an instrumental thinker for whom the ends ultimately justified all means, and he lived in a time when kingly authority — not knighthood — was in flower. Raised on the romance of one set of ideals, he was capable of setting aside his dislike of letter writing to pen seventeen lovestricken letters to Anne. But we are mistaken if we take what he says in those letters too literally. He wanted her, yes. But he was never her servant — not even emotionally — and even in these letters, he never forgot that.

4

A Perfect Storm

Consummation

IN JANUARY OF 1533, after years of negotiating, waiting, strategizing, trial and error, dramatic public confrontations, behind-the-scenes machinations, veiled threats, and outright tantrums from all concerned, Anne and Henry were married secretly—without the pope's blessing. By now, Henry couldn't care less, because with the aid of his new right-hand man, Thomas Cromwell, he was well on his way to supplanting papal authority with his own supremacy as head of the Church of England. Cromwell, like Wolsey (the son of a butcher), was a self-made man who understood that he could not rely on birth but had to use his own ingenuity to further his interests. It's not surprising that Wolsey, in 1523, felt a kinship with Cromwell, and handpicked him from the ranks of young lawyers (by then Cromwell was a member of Parliament) to become his councilor and friend. But unlike Wolsey, who had been educated at Oxford—in those days, virtually a Catholic institution—Cromwell, whose beginnings were far rougher (his father, a Putney blacksmith, was often drunk and violent, and Cromwell left home at the age of fifteen), had a far less conventional "education," roaming Europe, serving as a mercenary in the French army, clerking in Italy, trading in the Netherlands, and finally setting himself up as a lawyer in England at the age of twenty. He had no allegiance to the Catholic Church and relied less on diplomacy — Wolsey's forte, which ultimately failed him — than what we would today call "thinking outside the box." In the case of Henry's "great matter," this translated to ignoring the papacy rather than trying to win its seal of approval for the divorce.

Historians now speculate, calculating from Elizabeth's birth, that Anne had finally slept with Henry in October during an extended trip to meet Francis and his court. The point of the trip was to gain French recognition of Anne as Henry's future queen, and no expense — or humiliation of Katherine — was spared. Anne was given the title of Marquess of Pembroke to elevate her to noble status for the occasion, regal garments were fitted for her, and Henry sent a messenger to Katherine, requesting the return of the queen's official jewels. Katherine, indignant, refused to allow her jewels to adorn the woman whom she called "the scandal of Christendom."[1] The request then quickly became an order. Henry could not, however, order Francis's wife, Eleanor, or his sister, Marguerite, to come to Calais for the occasion; although they knew Anne from her years at the French court, she was still the king's mistress, and — contrary to the common belief that the entire French court was a hotbed of sexual liaisons — they were both very proper when it came to sexual protocol. There is no indication that Anne was angry or hurt.

Once in Calais, Anne and Henry relaxed together for a week, and then, after Henry and Francis had met separately in Boulogne for four days, Henry returned to Calais with Francis for an extravagant reception organized in Francis's honor. It included a dinner of 170 dishes, the firing of 3,000 guns, and a surprise appearance by Anne and six "gorgeously apparelled" masked ladies.[2] Their costumes were "of strange fashion" — more Isadora Duncan than Tudor — loose, gold-laced overdresses of gold cloth with sashes of crimson and silver.[3] But there is no evidence, contrary to *The Tudors*, that they performed a Salome-style seduction dance to the steady beat of drums. At the conclusion of the dance, each of the ladies chose a man to dance with and Anne, as she and Henry had planned, chose Francis. Then the masks were removed, and Francis recognized (perhaps only pretending to be surprised) that he was dancing with the "brunette Venus," Anne.[4] Anne and Francis then spent the better part of an hour in private conversation while the others danced. *The Tudors*, contributing to the mythology that Anne had been promiscuous in France, has Anne refer to "some things, perhaps, which Your Majesty knows about me which I would rather you kept secret and never mention to the king."[5] Francis, ever the gallant Frenchman, promises never to reveal her secrets, which, of course, "every beautiful woman must have."[6] That conversation is invented; we actually don't know what Anne and Francis talked about.

In the days that followed, there was more overconsumption, more dancing, and some manly wrestling. Henry and Francis did not themselves engage in contests of physical one-upmanship, as they had years before at their meeting at the Field of the Cloth of Gold (in that match Henry lost to Francis and didn't take it well), but watched others perform as their surrogates. By the time the French took their leave on October 29, a violent storm and unmanageable tides kept Henry's party in Calais until November 12. There, in sumptuous adjoining suites, Henry and Anne privately celebrated what was already being trumpeted in England — news that was probably prearranged to be released in a timely fashion — as "the triumph at Calais and Boulogne."[7] When it was finally safe to leave, they took their time getting home; although they reached Dover by November 14, they arrived at Eltham only by November 24. Clearly, they were enjoying their quality time alone together. By the time they returned to London, it was very likely that Anne was already pregnant, although too early for her to know it.

By the date of her coronation on June 1, the pregnancy would have been impossible to hide — and probably difficult to endure through the elaborate four-day-long affair that began on May 29 and included a river procession (on the first day), court rituals (on the second), a road procession from the Tower through the City to Westminster (the third day), and the actual coronation and banquet on the fourth day. Then on June 2 there was a more general celebration, with jousts, balls, and "a goodly banquet in the queen's chamber."[8] There are reports that the last months of Anne's pregnancy were hard and possibly tenuous (which, given her later miscarriages, rings true). Yet she was expected, dressed in dazzling but undoubtedly uncomfortable regalia, to shine through it all — despite some notable snubs, such as the absence of Thomas More. Anne may have melted down privately — which would be understandable, considering that she was about six months pregnant. But her stamina was bolstered by the triumph of the occasion, which Henry had made sure would be as pronounced as possible. Naturally, hostile sources, such as Chapuys, reported that the coronation was as "sad and dismal" as a funeral, which seems almost as unlikely as Anne's wearing a dress adorned with tongues pierced with nails. At the very least, the crowds would have been enjoying the free ale and food provided during the processions.

Anne and Henry: In Trouble from the Beginning?

Whether or not the people cheered, as the official report claims, or disrespectfully kept their hats on, as the *Spanish Chronicle* has it, the political, legal, and culture wars were entering the next stage. Anne's enemies continued their vicious character attacks on Anne. Katherine remained stubbornly glued to her "rights." Mary behaved either like an obsessively dutiful daughter or a spoiled brat (depending on your point of view) in refusing to acknowledge Anne as queen. And Henry exacerbated everything by insisting not only on recognition of his authority — which he had received from Parliament, in principle, by its acceptance of the Act of Appeals — but also that everyone pay homage to Anne and relinquish all allegiance to Katherine. As Ives points out, Henry even found time during the coronation "to issue a proclamation warning of the penalties of according royal honors to anyone but Anne."[9]

Henry (through his man Cromwell) fought for his position through official documents and acts. Chapuys and others, at this stage, could only engage in negative gossip, the chief point of which was to keep the opposition's hopes alive. It didn't take long for him to begin predicting that the marriage was in trouble. Even during Anne's pregnancy with Elizabeth, when hopes were presumably high for both Henry and Anne, Chapuys was quick to report any temper tantrums on Anne's part and any indications of Henry's impatience with her.

It's true that it was not uncommon for Henry to graze when his queens were pregnant. No one knows for sure how many of these flirtations were innocent "courtly" play, and how many were actual physical involvements. We do know that he had sexual mistresses when he was married to Katherine, and now that any motive to remain chaste for Anne was gone — he'd won the prize, and it was no longer necessary to play the devoted swain or to avoid possible pregnancies with other women — why should it be any different? On the other hand, he doesn't seem to have been an especially sexually driven man, unlike the rapacious Francis. At the age of forty-one, he told Parliament that he was at an age when "the lust of man is not so quick as in lusty youth."[10] True, he was trying to assure Parliament that his "great matter" was not fueled by lust, but by principle. But still, the statement sounds more like the instrumental sharing of a biological reality that others in Parliament could identify with than an outright lie. And then, too, Anne apparently complained to her sister-in-law Lady Jane Rochford — fatally as it turned out, once treason had been redefined by Cromwell to include speech acts against the king — that the king was neither skilled nor virile.

Whether Henry's affairs were physical or not, what seems hugely unlikely is that he would chastise Anne so harshly when she was so far along in her pregnancy, especially this long-awaited pregnancy, which all the stars and seers had predicted would result in a boy. Even during her final pregnancy, when hopes were not so high, he was careful with Anne. When she purportedly caught the king with Jane Seymour on his knee and "flew into a frenzy," the king, "seeing his wife hysterical and fearing for their child, sent Jane out of the room and hastened to placate Anne. 'Peace be, sweetheart, and all shall go well with thee,' he soothed."[11] Although the reporters of this incident, too, are not very trustworthy (Weir says they came by way of a chain of reports, one passed on to the next, by various ladies at the court), this behavior sounds more like Henry's modus operandi (utter some soothing words, as he did with Wolsey and Katherine, then do what you want) than a king who would risk upsetting a very pregnant wife.

Elizabeth was born on September 7, just a few days after Chapuys wrote Charles about the earlier quarrel, and here, too, Chapuys gives the event his own political spin, claiming that the birth of a daughter was "to the great regret both of him and the lady."[12] This reported reaction has been firmly installed — and embellished — in the popular mythology about Elizabeth's birth, particularly in novels. Paul Rival: "A girl! . . . She heard the whispers of her attendants and Henry's protests and thought to herself: 'If only I could die!'"[13] Norah Lofts: "It was a girl . . . [Anne] knew she had failed, and willed herself away, welcoming the enveloping darkness."[14] Philippa Gregory has an angry Anne pushing the baby away. "A girl. What good is a girl to us?"[15] But historians, too, have played their part, often taking it as highly significant that prepared documents announcing the birth of a prince were hastily altered with an added "s." Antonia Fraser says this "attests to the surprise and displeasure" caused by the birth.[16] Surprise, yes. And undoubtedly disappointment. But was the birth of Elizabeth really the "heavy blow" that David Starkey claims?[17]

Eric Ives, the most careful of scholars, writes that there is "no evidence of the crushing psychological blow that some have supposed."[18] In an age when infant mortality was high, and especially after Katherine's many miscarriages, the mere fact that Anne had given birth to a healthy child was cause for celebration. George Wyatt's account, written during Elizabeth's reign, reports that the king "expressed his joy for that fruit sprung of himself, and his yet more confirmed love towards [Anne]."[19] Wyatt and Chapuys represent opposite ends of the anti-Anne/pro-Anne continuum, and perhaps neither represents it accurately. What makes the most sense, as Ives argues, is that there would have been both delight and disappointment. A healthy child had been born, and she was beautiful and "perfectly formed."[20] But Anne had promised Henry a son, the astrologers and physicians had predicted the child would be a boy, and a huge amount of PR had gone into trumpeting this prediction in justification for the break with Katherine and the marriage to Anne. Henry and Anne may have been personally thrilled with Elizabeth, but her birth represented a crack in the armor of their worldview and public face.

It's interesting that although the notion that Anne was crushed by the birth of a daughter has stuck, it's very rare that she is portrayed — as she is in *The Other Boleyn Girl* — as a cold mother. More commonly, in both fictional and nonfictional accounts, her disappointment is shown as melting in the warmth of the reality of her infant daughter. But post–*Other Boleyn Girl*, which has repopularized the Chapuys-inspired picture of Anne as selfish to the core, some historians have felt the need to remedy the view that Anne was indifferent to Elizabeth. Tracy Borman, from her 2009 *Elizabeth's Women:*

> She lavished affection upon Elizabeth and could hardly bear to be apart from her. When she returned to court after her confinement, she took her daughter with her. Courtiers looked on in astonishment as Anne carefully set the baby down on a velvet cushion next to her throne under the canopy of estate. It was highly unusual for a queen to keep her child with her: surely it ought to be bundled off to the royal nursery, as was customary?[21]

Anne also dressed the infant Elizabeth extravagantly in brightly colored velvet and satin, with satin caps of crimson or white "richly embroidered with gold."[22] No expense was spared, and no efforts. "A purple satin cap required boat journeys from Greenwich to London and back for a fitting and a further trip when the cap needed mending."[23] Although this could be attributed to Anne's own vanity — treating her daughter as an extension of herself or as a new fashion accessory — even Starkey, who generally paints Anne as a self-interested schemer, admits that she "was immensely proud of her daughter and took an unusually close interest in her upbringing and welfare."[24] This is how the relationship is depicted in *Anne of the Thousand Days* and *The Tudors*, and despite *The Other Boleyn Girl*, it seems to have won the debate about Anne's maternal instincts in the popular imagination.

Tracy Borman even claims (as do the Stricklands' 1854 *Lives of the Queens of England* and Alison Weir's 1991 *The Six Wives of Henry VIII*) that Anne wanted to breast-feed Elizabeth, which was unheard of for a noblewoman, let alone a queen. It's impossible to verify this or definitively disprove it because Borman (along with Weir) provides no documentation; presumably, they got it from the Stricklands. But the Stricklands, in turn, got their information from Gregorio Leti, the Italian historian whose 1693 biography of Elizabeth was described by Starkey as a "fictionalised account."[25] On the other hand, Leti did consult English sources for his biography, he is often careful to provide several sides of an argument, and some of what he says about the birth does ring true. He almost certainly fabricated the notion, repeated by the Stricklands, that Henry forbade Anne's breast-feeding Elizabeth because his own "rest would be broken by such an arrangement"[26] rather than for the sake of propriety. But his argument that Anne wanted to breast-feed "*pour se faire mieux valoir*"[27] — to enhance her own value — does not sound like a very romantic "embellishment."

In judging reports of Anne and Henry's "despair" over Elizabeth, we have to consider the original source. In the same letter in which Chapuys tells Charles of Elizabeth's birth, he reports that the new child "is to be called Mary, like the Princess; which title, I hear in many quarters, will be taken from the true Princess and given to her."[28] This (completely false) rumor pleases Chapuys enormously, for "defrauding the said Princess of her title" will "augment" the "indignation of the people, both small and great, which grows every day."[29] This, of course, was an "indignation" that Chapuys tried to inflame every chance he got, for he was well aware (as he tells Charles in the same letter) that it "may grow cool in time, so that it should be used in season."[30] It was also in his interest to convince Charles that, despite appearances, getting rid of Anne was still a real possibility. After Katherine died, his efforts to keep Katherine's cause alive shifted to the restoration of Princess Mary's claim to the throne, and his case against Anne became focused on her "plots" to murder Mary. As we'll shortly see, he was also an active and eager reporter — and possibly a participant — of later matchmaking between the king and Jane Seymour, who Chapuys knew would support Mary's claim.

Many historians, even today, take Chapuys at his word about the decline in Henry and Anne's relationship. It's become fairly standard fare to accept the narrative that after the marriage Anne became shrewish and arrogant and that by the time Anne's fortunes begin to dramatically unravel in March of 1536, "the marriage had been ailing for some time."[31] There seems to have been a collective memory loss, after centuries of repetition, that all the reports of Anne's increasingly "haughty" behavior have come down to us from the Venetian and Spanish records. These descriptions of Anne have to be treated skeptically, given their source. The details of the reports that Henry and Anne were in trouble from the beginning of the marriage invariably turned out to be rumors that, by virtue of their vacillating nature, show how flimsy the evidence is. In December 1533 Chapuys reported that despite the disappointment of Elizabeth's birth, the king is "enthralled" with Anne, that she "has so enchanted and bewitched him that he will not dare say or do anything against her will and commands."[32] (Chapuys, of course, isn't happy about this, which is the most compelling reason for believing him here. He was usually quick to report any loss of the king's favor for Anne.) In September of 1534 the Count of Cifuentes wrote Charles that another ambassador had "heard in France that Ana Boulans had in some way or other incurred the Royal displeasure, and was rather in disgrace with the King, who was paying his court to another lady."[33] By October 3, Cifuentes had corrected himself, writing that the idea that Anne and the King were on bad terms was "a hoax."[34] However, in keeping with the vacillating rumors, a report on October 18 states that "the King no longer loved her as before. The King, moreover, was paying his court to another lady, and several lords in the kingdom were helping him that they might separate him from Anne's company."[35]

Whether or not Henry was involved, relatively early on, with someone else ("Who was this new flame?" Ives asks, skeptically[36]), the quarrels don't appear to amount to anything until Jane Seymour enters the picture. Anne had her outbursts, Henry had his, but they had many more "merry" times, reported throughout the collected papers, and both had to have been well aware that no royal relationship could ride on the twists and turns of passion. If that had been the case, Henry would have sought to divorce Katherine long before he did, instead of waiting until he had become convinced that she was no longer capable of providing an heir. And kings — not even narcissistic Henry — didn't get rid of queens just because they had the occasional jealous outburst. Katherine, too, despite her reputation as the all-accepting, patient Griselda, had had her own vocal quarrels with the king when he first began to seek the sexual company of other women. It was to be expected, for everyone knew that women were weak and ruled by their passions. But ultimately, once the shouting and weeping were over, the queen was required to accept and obey.

This was hard for Anne. Whatever the nature of her romantic or sexual feelings for Henry, Anne was used to being the pursued darling for six years, and now she was expected to behave like a wife. That included accepting Henry's occasional flirtations, innocent and not, something she apparently found difficult to do. She admitted this in her speech at her trial in 1536: "I confess," she said, "I have had jealous fancies and suspicions of him, which I had not discretion enough, and wisdom, to conceal at all times."[37] Whether her jealousy was because she was in love with Henry or because she was fearful of being supplanted as Queen, or if it was simply her pride rebelling, we don't know. But it led to a number of public quarrels, followed by amorous reconciliations ("sunshine and storms" is how Ives describes the years between 1533 and 1536[38]), both of which provided fodder for Anne's enemies to paint a picture of her as shrewish, Henry as either henpecked or philandering depending on the weather, and the relationship as tottering.

It was largely propaganda. If you put all the documentation of the "thousand days" that Henry and Anne were married in chronological order — the letters, the gossip, the various ambassadors' reports — it's a script with a gaping hole if what you think you are reading is a love story in which declining passion and jealousy play the major role. For there is no evidence that either of these was the tipping point that turned Anne's fate around, although they may have contributed to her fall. In fact, there seems to have been no single factor that brought about the disastrous events of April and May 1536, but rather it was a combustion of court atmospherics, political maneuvering, and sheer bad luck. What turned the cherished, hotly pursued consort into the lady in the Tower, awaiting her execution, did not belong primarily to the realm of emotions, but to the gathering of a "perfect storm" of political, personal, and biological events, the absence of any one of which might have resulted in things turning out very differently for Anne.

What Happens When a King Marries a
Woman "Not of Ordinary Clay"

After his years with intelligent but conventional Katherine, Henry had found Anne, whose young womanhood had been shaped by confident women unafraid to speak their minds about virtually any subject, to be an intellectually and erotically stimulating challenge. But the court was still very much a boys' club; Henry had delighted in surprising Katherine by showing up in her bedroom one morning with twelve of his hyperactive companions dressed like Robin Hood and his Merry Men. "The queen," Edward Hall reports, "the ladies and all other there were abashed, as well for the strange sight, as also for their sudden coming."[39] Blushing bride, boisterous husband — it was just the way it was supposed to be. But Anne was not a blusher. Spontaneous and intense in an era when women were supposed to silently provide a pleasing backdrop for men's adventures, Anne had never "stayed in her place" — which was exciting in a mistress, but a PR problem in a wife. Even if Henry's own fascination with Anne had remained unwavering (which it probably did not; after such a long unrealized pursuit, even the most enchanting woman would have to seem a little too "real"), her involvement (read: interference) in the political and religious struggles of the day was a continual annoyance to her enemies, who saw her as the mastermind behind every evil that properly should have been laid at Henry's feet, from the destruction of Wolsey and More to the harsh treatment of Katherine and Mary.

We know from her actions that Anne was not content to flirt with power through womanly wiles and pillow talk. She was a player. Although a few historians are still insistent that Anne's contribution to "The King's Reformation" (as G. W. Bernard titles his book) was exaggerated by later Protestant "rehabilitators" of Anne's image, by now most historians agree that Anne was not just the face that launched the Reformation, but an active participant. She was an avid reader of the radical religious works of the day (many of them banned from England and smuggled in for her), both in French and English. Her surviving library of books includes a large selection of early French evangelical works, including Marguerite de Navarre's first published poem,

"Miroir de l'âme pécheresse" (1531), which was later to be translated into English as "Mirror of the Sinful Soul" in 1544 by Anne's eleven-year-old daughter, Elizabeth.[40] Anne's library also included Jacques Lefèvre d'Étaples' French translation of the Bible, published by the same man (Martin Lempereur) responsible for publishing Tyndale's New Testament and numerous other French evangelical tracts. She had Tyndale's English-language New Testament (which was to become the basis for the King James Bible) read to her ladies at court. She also introduced Henry to Tyndale's antipapal *The Obedience of a Christian Man* and probably also to Simon Fish's *Supplication for the Beggars*. James Carley, the curator of the books of Henry and his wives, also sees it as highly significant that *all* the antipapal literature Henry collected that supported his break with Rome dates from after he began to pursue Anne.[41] Although she may not have supplied the actual readings herself, the couple was almost certainly discussing the issues and theological arguments involved, as both were avid readers of the Bible.

This was a time of religious anarchy, and although clear-cut divisions between various sects were not yet established — in fact, the Protestant/Catholic divide was just forming — Anne clearly stood on the "evangelical" side of issues. In those days, that chiefly meant a belief that the word of God was to be found in the Bible, unmediated by the interpretations of popes and priests. But direct, "personal" access to the Bible required, for all but the classically trained elite, that it be available to people in their own language. This was a cause Anne passionately supported. She secured the appointment of several evangelical bishops and deans when Henry created the newly independent Church of England. She attempted to intervene on behalf of reformists imprisoned for their religious beliefs. Multiple corroborating sources from her own time remember her as "a patron of rising evangelicals, a protector of those who were harassed," both "a model and champion" of reformers, "in England and abroad."[42]

The promotion and protection of the cause of reform was an especially dangerous business for Anne to engage in, because it was such a divisive issue (to put it mildly), and men's careers (and sometimes heads) could flourish or fall depending on which side was winning. Anne took a risk in showing Tyndale and Fish to Henry, but it was one that initially paid off, as he immediately saw that they were on the side of kings rather than Rome when it came to earthly authority. (Henry's reported reaction to discovering Tyndale — "This is a book for me and all kings to read" — is one of those quotes, enshrined even in *The Tudors*, that has become a pop signature of his recognition that he didn't have to argue with the pope, just ignore him.) But even if Henry had no objection to Anne's tutelage, others did, and their objections were a potent mix of misogyny and anti-Protestant fervor. Much of the gossip that circulated around court and through Europe came from the tongues (and pens) of those for whom being antipapal was to be prodevil. "Lutheran" women (an incorrect appellation for Anne, who did not subscribe to Lutheran doctrine) enraged Catholic dogmatists, who were quick to accuse them of witchcraft — an old charge against "talkative," impertinent women that was particularly handy when the women were "heretics." From "heretic" to "witch" was a short step, and from "witch" to "insatiable carnal lust" and "consorting with the devil" took barely a breath.[43] The same year that Anne was executed, an effigy of evangelical Marguerite de Navarre, on a horse drawn by devils wearing placards bearing Luther's name, appeared during a masquerade in Notre Dame.[44]

Protestants, of course, could be no less zealous than papists in their diatribes against women who presumed to interfere in men's business — particularly when women who threatened to bring Catholicism back to the throne were on the horizon. Actually, the Protestants could be even more vehement, as they had a religious doctrine within which the Father, whether God, king, or husband, was the model of all authority. Which side you stood on — Catholic or Protestant — determined which presumptuous women were most offensive to you. When Mary Tudor became queen of England in 1553, her Catholicism added fuel to the fire that was already burning in Protestant reformer John Knox, who argued, in his famously titled *The First Blast of the Trumpet Against the Monstrous Regiment of Women*, "that any woman who presumed 'to sit in the seat of God, that is, to teach, to judge, or to reign above a man'" was "a monster in nature."[45] And then the old familiar charges came pouring out again. "Nature . . . doth paint them forth to be weak, frail, impatient, feeble, and foolish, and experience hath declared them to be unconstant, variable, cruel, and lacking the spirit of counsel and regiment."[46] No wonder Elizabeth felt it important that people see her as having "the heart and stomach of a King"![47]

Anne Boleyn's problem, though, as far as public relations went, was the pro-Katherine, papist faction. It was they who called her a "whore," a would-be poisoner, and a vicious corrupter of otherwise sweet-tempered King Hal. It was they who later spread rumors that she bore physical marks of the devil on her body. It was they who were most terrified of her insidious influence on the king's politics. Her actual contribution to the scourge of Lutheranism, far from being minimized as it later was in the writings of early-twentieth-century historians, was inflated to unbelievable proportions. In one letter to Charles, Chapuys goes so far as to blame "the heretical doctrines and practices of the concubine" as "the principal cause of the spread of Lutheranism in this country."[48]

It was preposterous, and Henry certainly didn't believe it. But it created a political/religious "wing" of anti-Anne sentiment that was exploited by Cromwell when he turned against Anne, and it was a powerful obstacle in the way of Anne's acceptance by the (still largely Catholic) English people. In gaining that acceptance — and with it some protection from the winds of shifting politics — Anne already had several strikes against her. She had supplanted a beloved queen. She was rumored to be "haughty" and suspiciously "French" — and even worse than that, a vocal, intellectual, "interfering" woman. Jane Seymour, when she entered the picture in 1536, was no less the "other woman" than Anne was (and probably more deserving of the charge of using her virginity as bait than Anne was), but when she became queen, her apparent docility miraculously spared her from the antipathy that Anne inspired. True, Jane was a believer in the "old ways" and a supporter of Mary's rights, which would have endeared her to Chapuys no matter what her personality. But although later historians would question just how docile Jane actually was, in her own time she was constantly commended for her gentleness, compassion, and submissiveness, which she advertised in her own motto: "Bound to obey and serve." With few exceptions, that stereotype has not lost its grip on popular culture.

With Anne it was quite the opposite. Even those who shared her religious views, such as Cromwell, had no scruples about spreading nasty rumors when it suited their purposes. For Anne's reputation as a woman who simply would not behave as she should had created an atmosphere that did not incline men to be her protectors, but rather freed them to take the gloves off when fighting with her. And while her unwillingness to occupy her "proper place" was not in itself the cause of Cromwell's turn against her, it certainly contributed to their standoff, unleashed his ruthlessness, and ensured his success in planning her downfall. "Had she been gracious and modest," writes nineteenth-century commentator James Froude, "she might have partially overcome the prejudice against her."[49] "Gracious and modest" seem like laudable qualities. But what they meant in the context of the times and why Anne could never play the part is laid bare by David Loades: "Anne . . . could not pretend to be a fool or a nonentity, and the self-effacement customary in a royal consort did not suit her style at all . . . In many ways her sharpness of perception and readiness of wit made her more suitable for the council chamber than for the boudoir."[50] But women did not belong in the council chamber.

Anne recognized that she had overstepped the boundaries of appropriate wifely behavior. At her trial, insisting that she was "clear of all the offences which you have laid to my charge," she went on to acknowledge not only her "jealous fancies" but also her failure to show the king "that humility which his goodness to me, and the honours to which he raised me, merited."[51] Anne's recognition that she had not shown the king enough humility, in this context, shows remarkable insight into the gender politics that undoubtedly played a role in her downfall. She stood accused of adultery and treason. Yet she did not simply refute those charges; she admitted to a different "crime": not remaining in her proper "place." In juxtaposing these two transgressions, Anne seems to be suggesting that not only did she recognize that she had overstepped the norms of wifely behavior, but that this transgression also was somehow related to the grim situation she now found herself in.

The idea that Anne was aware that she had fatally defied the rules governing wifely (and queenly) behavior may seem, at first, like the

wishful, anachronistic thinking of a twenty-first-century woman looking for would-be feminists in the shadows of every historical era. But
actually, educated women of her time were very much aware of the
various debates concerning the "*querelle des femmes*," which was first
introduced by Christine de Pizan in the late fourteenth and early fifteenth centuries, and which had a particular resonance in Britain,
where the issue of whether or not women were suitable to rule became
more than just theoretical during Henry VIII's reign. Pizan is most
famous for her *The Book of the City of Ladies* (1404–5), which gathers
heroines from history and Pizan's own time to refute ancient views of
female inferiority, and which was published in England in 1521 around
the same time that Anne was about to return from France. Historians
of women have made a strong argument that Pizan's book became part
of an ongoing debate about "the woman question" in England, beginning with Juan Luis Vives's *The Education of a Christian Woman* (1523),
written expressly for Mary, that insisted, against Pizan's arguments, on
the necessarily subordinate role of women. The debate continues in
1540 and 1542 with Sir Thomas Elyot's refutation of Vives, *Defence of
Good Women*, and Heinrich Cornelius Agrippa von Nettesheim's *Of the
Nobilitie and Excellencye of Womankynde*, which historian Constance
Jordan describes as "the most explicitly feminist text to be published
in England in the first half of the century."[52] In its original Latin form,
published in 1509, it was dedicated to Margaret of Austria, who was to
be Anne's first model of queenly behavior. Anticipating later Enlightenment thinkers, Agrippa argues that the differences between men
and women were only bodily and that "the woman hathe that some
mynd that a man hath, the same reason and speche, she gothe to the
same ende of blysfulnes [spirituality], where shall be no exception of
kynde." Why then are they everywhere subordinate to men? Because
they are not permitted to make the laws or write history, and therefore
they, as Jordan paraphrases Agrippa, "cannot contribute to or criticize
the intellectual bases on which they are categorized as inferior."[53]

To describe Anne Boleyn as a feminist would be an anachronism
— and not nearly as appropriate an anachronism as in the case of
Marguerite de Navarre and others who openly championed female
equality. Marguerite did not have the word, but she was conscious of a

women's "cause." There's no evidence that Anne felt similarly. But she had learned to value her body and her ideas, and she ultimately recognized that there was something unsettling about this for Henry and understood that this played a role in her downfall. "I do not say I have always shown him that humility," she said at her trial, insistent even then on speaking what she believed.[54] Anne wasn't a feminist. But she did step over the ever-moving line that marked the boundary of the comfort zone for men of her era, and for all the unease and backlash she inspired, she may as well have been one.

Anne as a Piece on the Chessboard of Politics

By 1536 Henry was well aware that public opinion, especially after the executions of Bishop Fisher and Thomas More (for refusing to take the oath declaring Henry Supreme Head of the Church of England), was not exactly riding in his favor.

Besides anger over Fisher and More, who were generally admired, there was growing public resentment over the mistreatment of Katherine and Princess Mary, whom Henry kept separated from each other, treating them as if they were discarded limbs. The abuse of Mary was especially acute, as she was forced to wait on her younger sister, Elizabeth, and was allowed no audience with the king, who had formerly been an affectionate father, so long as she refused to acknowledge Anne as queen. This she would not do, not even after Anne had personally offered her friendship and a home at court on that one condition. Despite a huge amount of evidence that Henry was in a rage over his daughter's "obstinacy" and hardly required any goading to punish and humiliate her, Chapuys blamed her mistreatment entirely on Anne, whom he believed turned the king against Mary, and he did all that he could to ensure that every other person who would listen to him saw it that way.

Even those who knew better, such as Thomas Cromwell, realized that blaming the king for Mary's mistreatment could create a huge public relations disaster and encouraged Chapuys in his Anne-blaming. As early as October of 1534, Chapuys met with Cromwell, who reassured Chapuys of Henry's "paternal affection" for Mary and claimed that "he loved her 100 times more than his last born" and that he and Chapuys should do all that they could to "soften and mend all matters relating to her," for "in time everything would be set to rights."[55] Although I am often skeptical of Chapuys' second- and thirdhand "intelligence," the manipulative, self-serving speech he attributes to Cromwell has, to my ears, the ring of truth.

> True it was [Cromwell said] that the King, his master, had occasionally complained of the suit which Your Majesty had instituted against him at Rome, but he [Cromwell] had fully shown that Your Majesty could not help stirring in favour of Queen Katherine, bound as she was to you by the bonds of consanguinity and royal rank; and that, consider- ing the King, his master, if in your Majesty's place, might have acted as you did there was no fear of his now taking in bad part your interfer- ence in the affairs of so close a relative. He himself had so strongly and so often inculcated that reasoning upon the King, that, in his opinion, no cause now remained for disagreement between Your Majesty and his master, save perhaps the affair of these two good ladies [Katherine and Mary]; to remedy which, as he had signified to me, it was needful that we both should agree upon a satisfactory settlement of all com- plaints, and the knitting of that lasting friendship which might other- wise be endangered. Cromwell ended by saying in passing that it was perfectly true that great union and friendship existed now between France and England, but that I could guess the cause of it. He did not say more on this subject. Your Majesty, by your great wisdom, will be able to judge what Cromwell's last words meant.[56]

Of course, the "cause" that was implied here was Anne — who Crom- well "hinted" was standing between the repair of relations between England and Spain in a double way: first, because she was known to be a Francophile, and second and more important, because she was the obstacle standing in the way of reaching a "satisfactory settlement of all complaints" by Katherine and Mary.[57] Chapuys also took Cromwell as hinting "that there was some appearance of the King changing his love."[58] He wasn't sure whether to take this seriously — for Cromwell was quite capable of dissembling when it suited his purposes — but what seems crystal clear is that Cromwell was buttering up Chapuys in the interests of Henry's PR and future good relations with Charles, and that Anne was already being used by him to take the heat off Henry.

Why would Cromwell, who shared Anne's religious proclivities, want to stir up the anti-Anne pot with Chapuys and Charles? After all, he had been the chief engineer of the break with Rome and, as a reformist himself, had been Anne's strongest ally at the start of her relationship with Henry. At one point, it was generally believed that Cromwell, as Chapuys later put it, was "Anne's right hand."[59] What had happened? At this point, nothing of grave significance. But Cromwell was a man who was ever alert to the slightest changes in the weather of power politics, and Anne had just had a miscarriage in July of 1535. It was not publicly reported, but this can be inferred from comments made about her "goodly belly" in April and Henry's postponement of a trip to France that summer "on account of her condition."[60] Then in July—silence. There now had been two unsuccessful pregnancies as far as the issue of a male heir was concerned. Moreover, although Elizabeth was born healthy and beautiful, this child had not even gone to term—a far more ominous sign for superstitious Henry. Was he already wondering whether God disapproved of this marriage? And did he share his misgivings with his "most beloved" Cromwell?

Cromwell and Anne, although they inveighed against Rome and fought for the divorce together, had a serious break brewing. Even though they may have shared the same "theory" of reform (although we don't know for sure, as what became English Protestantism was only just evolving), they disagreed sharply on what should be done with the spoils of disbanded churches and monasteries. From the beginning of his ascent to power—and among the reasons why he was able to keep the favor of the nobility even after Wolsey was deposed —Cromwell "actively assisted the King in diverting revenues from the suppressed monasteries, originally granted to Wolsey's two colleges, to the purses of Henry's cronies at court."[61] Anne, in contrast, favored using the funds to set up educational and charitable institutions, and was shocked to learn that the money was being diverted for private use. This difference between them would not explode until April of 1536, but it seems that in sidling up to Chapuys, Cromwell was already preparing for the possibility that there might be a showdown that would result in his own fall from favor, and he was seeking an alliance with Chapuys to prepare for a possible strike against Anne.

Cromwell was aware that developing a friendship with Chapuys was risky, but assessing the situation at the time, he wasn't overly concerned. In June of 1535 he told Chapuys that if Anne knew how close he and Chapuys were, she would see Cromwell's head off his shoulders. At the time, Cromwell shrugged it off, telling Chapuys that "I trust so much on my master, that I fancy she cannot do me any harm."[62] But the differences between Anne and Cromwell were escalating — not just over the use of confiscated money but also over international alliances (Anne favored France, while Cromwell was beginning to lean toward some kind of accommodation with Charles) — and the mere fact that Cromwell was already assessing his security relative to Anne's displeasure with him suggests that he was aware she could, under the right circumstances, be a danger to him and that he was making preparations.

Cromwell also undoubtedly became aware, in the fall of that year, that a new family was rising in the king's favor: the Seymours. Edward Seymour, who had hosted a visit from Henry to Wolf Hall in September, was becoming a special favorite. Henry had always enjoyed the company of vital, masculine, young men ("thrusting, acquisitive and ambitious" is how Derek Wilson describes them[63]) and as his own athleticism and sense of masculine potency declined, hobbled by leg ulcers and increasing obesity, he may have begun to live vicariously through them, "unconsciously sucking new life from their physical and mental vigor."[64] By 1535, Seymour's circle — John Dudley, Thomas Wriothesley, Ralph Sadler — had come to serve this function for Henry. They were also courting Cromwell, whom they rightly saw as having the king's ear and who was seemingly, at this point, the architect of England's future. They hated the Boleyns. And Edward Seymour had a sister.

The Other Women: Katherine and Jane

On January 7, 1536, Katherine of Aragon died, most likely of cancer of the heart (a real illness, but an apt bodily metaphor as well). It was an enormous relief to both Anne and Henry. For Anne, it meant that at last she was the only queen of England. And both of them hoped that Katherine's death, removing the chief reason for the emperor's breach with Henry, would repair relations with Charles and tip the balance in England's favor vis-à-vis Francis (who now would have to court Henry in order to be sure that England did not ally against him with Charles). "The next day," Ives reports, "the king and queen appeared in joyful yellow from top to toe, and Elizabeth was triumphantly paraded to church. After dinner Henry went down to the Great Hall, where the ladies of the court were dancing, with his . . . daughter in his arms, showing her off to one and another."[65] Whether or not their yellow clothing was a mark of their joy, as Ives says, or a sign of respect for the dead has been much debated. But whatever the meaning of the color of their clothing, neither had a political reason at this point to mourn Katherine's death — and Henry, over the years of battle with Katherine, seems to have lost any trace of affection for her.

Chapuys was horrified by their reaction; grief stricken at having lost his longtime friend, whom he had comforted and championed over the years, he quickly began spreading rumors that Katherine had been poisoned by Anne. But good news was to come a bit later that month when Chapuys reported, thirdhand as usual, that one of the king's "principal courtiers" said that the king had confessed to another lady and her husband "that he had been seduced and forced into this second marriage by means of sortileges and charms, and that, owing to that, he held it as null. God (he said) had well shown his displeasure at it by denying him male children. He, therefore, considered that he could take a third wife, which he said he wished much to do."[66] Even Chapuys, ever alert to promising signs that Anne would be supplanted, finds this report "incredible." Anne was in her final month of what was to be her last pregnancy; how could the king be sure that God would not bless the marriage with a male heir this time around? Was someone whispering in Henry's ear, planting suggestions about Anne?

It seems that this is exactly what was happening. By April 1 Chapuys was writing to the emperor, informing him that the king was "paying court" to Edward Seymour's sister, Jane, and that he had "heard" (from the Marchioness of Exeter) that Jane had been "well tutored and warned by those among this King's courtiers who hate the concubine, telling her not in any wise to give in to the King's fancy unless he makes her his Queen, upon which the damsel is quite resolved. She has likewise been advised to tell the King frankly, and without reserve, how much his subjects abominate the marriage contracted with the concubine, and that not one considers it legitimate."[67] The marchioness also requested, at this time, that Chapuys aid in whatever way he can the "meritorious work" of removing Anne and thus not only protecting Princess Mary from Anne's evil plotting and ridding the country of the "heretical doctrines and practices" of "Lutheranism," but also "clearing the King from the taint of a most abominable and adulterous marriage."[68]

In the four months between Katherine's death and Henry's open courting of Jane, two momentous events had occurred. On January 24, Henry had a bad jousting accident, which left him unconscious for two hours, and this undoubtedly stirred up his anxiety about his own diminishing physical competence and reminded him of his mortality — something he had been trying to avoid all his life through a hypochondria bordering on obsession. Then, on January 29, Anne miscarried. Although it was probably too early in the pregnancy for attendants to determine the sex of the child, which was later described by Nicholas Sander as a "shapeless mass of flesh," it was reported by both Chapuys and Wriothesley to have been a male. This was a "huge psychological blow" to Henry.[69] We have only Chapuys to rely on for details — "I see that God will not give me male children," he reports Henry as saying and then ominously telling Anne that he would "speak to her" when she was up — but whether the quote is accurate or not, it makes sense that the loss of a potential heir, especially after at least one other miscarriage and his own recent brush with death, would have affected Henry deeply.[70] Anne, on her part, was distraught. She appealed to Henry, telling him that the miscarriage was the result of the shock over his accident, which is not improbable, although Chapuys dismisses it. In a letter of February 17, he wrote to Charles that Anne's inability to bear male children was due to her "defective constitution," that "the real cause" of this particular miscarriage may have been the king's "behavior toward a damsel of the Court, named Miss Seymour, to whom he has latterly made very valuable presents."[71]

Jane was a startling contrast to Anne: "fair, not dark; younger by seven or eight years; gentle rather than abrasive; of no great wit, against a mistress of repartee; a model of female self-effacement against a self-made woman."[72] Plus, whether through coaching or inspiration of her own, she refused the king's gifts, saying that her greatest treasure was her honor and that she would accept sovereigns from him in "such a time as God would be pleased to send her some advantageous marriage."[73] She may have not been of "great wit," but she (or her brother) knew that this would increase Henry's ardor. The refusal of sovereigns happened after Anne's miscarriage, an event that undoubtedly emboldened Jane and her supporters. For if Anne had produced a living son, all the rumblings about Anne, both at court and among the people, and all the conniving of the Seymours, would have crashed against a brick wall. But it was Anne's disastrous luck that not only did she miscarry, she miscarried soon after Katherine died. Initially, this had been a cause for celebration. What Anne did not take into account (or perhaps did, but had no reason to consider probable at this point) was that with Katherine's death, Henry could have his marriage to Anne annulled, or invalidated in some other way, without having to deal with Katherine's claims to the throne. Disastrously and without precedent, it was the "some other way" that prevailed.

The Storm Breaks

There are a number of theories as to what allowed the unthinkable — the state-ordered execution of a queen — to happen. One theory, first advanced by Retha Warnicke and then adopted by a number of novels and media depictions, is that the miscarried fetus was grossly deformed, which led to suspicions of witchcraft. If Henry truly believed that Anne was guilty of witchcraft — which, of course, was a possibility in those times — he would have virtually no choice but to destroy her, as he would have to do with anyone in league with Satan. But although Henry complained at one point that he had been bewitched by Anne, that was a notion that, as in our own time, was freely bandied about in a very loose, metaphorical manner. It could mean simply "overcome beyond rationality by her charms" — as Chapuys means when he complains that the "accursed Lady has so enchanted and bewitched him that he will not dare to do anything against her will."[74] Moreover, none of the charges later leveled against Anne involved witchcraft, and there is no evidence that the fetus was deformed.

Another theory, which Alison Weir puts forward in *The Six Wives of Henry VIII* but revises in *The Lady in the Tower*, is that Henry, fed up with Anne, newly enamored of Jane, and eager "to rid himself" of his second wife but not knowing how, eagerly embraced Cromwell's suggestion in April that he had information that Anne had engaged in adultery, and then asked Cromwell to find evidence to support the charges.[75] But even if we accept the idea that Henry would cynically encourage a plot designed to lead to Anne's execution, and despite his flirtation with Jane and disappointment over the miscarriage, Henry did not behave like someone looking to end his marriage until Cromwell put the allegations before him. Whatever he was feeling about Anne, recognition of his supremacy was still entwined with her, and even after the miscarriage, he was still working for imperial recognition of his marriage to "his beloved wife" Anne. With Katherine gone, that seemed a real possibility. And, in fact, in March the emperor offered, in return for the legitimation of Mary, imperial support for "'the continuance of this last matrimony or otherwise,' as Henry wished."[76] The deal didn't work out due to Henry's refusal to acknowledge that anything about his first marriage — including Mary — was legitimate. He was utterly committed to maintaining his own absolute right to the organization of his domestic affairs, and that meant both recognition of Anne as lawful wife and Mary as bastard.

Most scholars nowadays (with a couple of exceptions I'll discuss later) believe, following Eric Ives, that the plot against Anne was orchestrated by Thomas Cromwell without Henry's instigation or encouragement. Things had been brewing dangerously between him and Anne for some time, and by April she probably knew that he had become friends with the Seymours and had also been sidling up to Chapuys. On April 2 Anne had dared to make a public declaration of her opposition to his policies by approving a potently coded sermon written by her almoner, John Skip, in which he (implicitly) compared Cromwell to Haman, the evil Old Testament councilor (which would make Anne Esther to Henry's Xerxes). The specific spur for the sermon was proposed legislation to confiscate the wealth of smaller monasteries, which was awaiting Henry's consent and against which Anne was trying to generate public sentiment. But by then, the enmity between Anne and Cromwell had become more global than one piece of legislation. Still, as he told Chapuys, Cromwell felt more or less secure in Henry's favor until a crucial meeting between the ambassador and the king on April 18, in which Henry, who had seemed to be in favor of the reconciliation with Rome that Cromwell had been negotiating with Chapuys, now revealed his true hand and refused any negotiation that included recognition of his first marriage and Mary's inclusion in the line of succession. Cromwell was aghast at Henry's stubbornness, as he had been working hard toward the rapprochement with the emperor, burning his bridges with France and (because of his relationship with Chapuys) with Anne and her faction as well. Earlier in the day, it had seemed that some kind of warming between Chapuys and Anne was being orchestrated. Chapuys had been invited to visit Anne and kiss her hand — which he declined to do — then he was obliged to bow to her when she was thrust in his path during church services. Later, at dinner, Anne loudly made remarks critical of France, which were carried back to Chapuys. But when Henry took Chapuys to a window enclosure in his own room for a private discussion after dinner, he made it clear that he wouldn't give.

"Far from the issue of April 1536 being 'When will Anne go and how?'" Ives writes, "Henry was exploiting his second marriage to force Europe to accept that he had been right all along."[77] Cromwell was furious, humiliated, and fearful that he had unexpectedly found himself on the wrong side of Henry's plans. In a letter to Charles, Chapuys wrote about the April 18 meeting, and what he wrote suggests that what was already on high heat between Cromwell and Anne was about to boil over. Chapuys reports that one reason why he would not "kiss or speak to the Concubine" and "refused to visit her until I had spoken to the King" was because he had been told by Cromwell that the "she devil" (Chapuys' appellation, not Cromwell's) "was not in favor with the King" and that "I should do well to wait till I had spoken to the King."[78]

With the king still pushing for her recognition, Anne must have felt deceptively safe. On April 25 Henry wrote a letter to Richard Pate, his ambassador in Rome, and to Stephen Gardiner and John Wallop, his envoys in France, referring to "the likelihood and appearance that God will send us heirs male [by] our most dear and most entirely beloved wife, the Queen."[79] But something had already begun to seem wrong to Anne, who sought out her chaplain, Matthew Parker, on April 26 and asked him to take care of Elizabeth, should anything happen to her. And in the days that follow, Chapuys was clearly (and gleefully) aware that plots were being hatched against Anne. He wrote to Charles that there was much covert discussion at court "as to whether or not the King could or could not abandon the said concubine," and that Nicholas Carew was "daily conspiring" against Anne, "trying to convince Miss Seymour and her friends to accomplish her ruin. Indeed, only four days ago the said Carew and certain gentlemen of the King's chamber sent word to the Princess to take courage, for very shortly her rival would be dismissed."[80] When the bishop of London, John Stokesley, expressed skepticism, "knowing well the King's fickleness" and fearful that should Anne be restored to favor, he would be in danger, Chapuys reassured Stokesley that the king "could certainly desert his concubine."[81]

In fact, after the April 18 meeting, Cromwell, claiming illness, had gone underground to begin an intense "investigation" into Anne's conduct. On April 23 he emerged and had an audience with Henry. We have no record of what was said. But many scholars believe that the illness was a ruse — that during his retreat he carefully plotted Anne's downfall, and that what he told the king on April 23 were the deadly rumors about Anne that eventually led to her arrest and trial. The king, however — perhaps dissembling for public consumption or perhaps unconvinced by what Cromwell had told him — was still planning to take Anne with him to Calais on May 4 after the May Day jousts and was still pressing Charles to acknowledge the validity of his marriage to Anne. Then on April 30, Cromwell and his colleagues laid all the charges before Henry, and court musician Mark Smeaton was arrested.

Anne had no idea that Cromwell and Henry were meeting to discuss the "evidence" that she had engaged in multiple adulteries and acts of treason. The evening of April 30, while Smeaton was being interrogated (and probably tortured), there was even a ball at court at which "the King treated [Anne] as normal."[82] He may have been awaiting Smeaton's confession, which didn't come for twenty-four hours, to feel fully justified in abandoning the show of dutiful husband. Although we don't know for sure what message was given to Henry during the May Day tournaments, it was probably word of Smeaton's confession, for the king immediately got up and left. Anne, who had been sitting at his side, would never see him again; the very next day, as her dinner was being served to her, she was arrested and conducted to the Tower.

5

The Tower and the Scaffold

Rushing to Judgment

WHEN CHAPUYS HEARD of Anne's arrest on May 2, he could barely suppress his glee. He marveled at "the sudden change from yesterday to this day" and declared that "the affair" had "come to a head much sooner and more satisfactorily than one could have thought, to the greater ignominy and shame of the lady herself."[1] Anne and Smeaton, he reported, were charged with adultery, and Henry Norris and George Boleyn were sent to the Tower for not having revealed what they knew of the "adulterous connexion" between the spinet player and the queen.[2] Until the actual charges were formally made — and sometimes long after — reports of who was arrested and why were often inaccurate. The bishop of Faenza told Protonotario Ambrogio that the queen was arrested along with "her father, mother, brother, and an organist with whom she had been too intimate"[3]; Philipp Melancthon wrote to Justus Jonas that those arrested for adultery were "her father, brother, two bishops, and others."[4] John Hannaert wrote Charles that "the so-called Queen was found in bed with her organist, and taken to prison. It is proved that she had criminal intercourse with her brother and others, and that the daughter supposed to be hers was taken from a poor man."[5] False gossip circulated throughout Europe concerning the arrests, with Chapuys, for once, getting it mostly right. His intelligence was muddled with respect to the charges—for Norris was already under suspicion of adultery (although it's possible that wasn't yet revealed)—but accurate with respect to those arrested. For Francis Weston and William Brereton were not arrested until May 4.

Anne may have unwittingly contributed to those later arrests. "M. Kyngston," she asked when brought to the Tower, "do you know wher for I am here?"[6] In a state of shock and disbelief, she searched her mind for the reasons for her arrest and shared her anxious musings with Kingston (who reported everything to Cromwell) and also with the ladies-in-waiting whom Cromwell had chosen to spy on her. In particular, Anne fretted about a possibly incriminating conversation she had with Norris, a longtime supporter of the Boleyns and the Groom of the Stool in the King's Privy Chamber. Norris, who was honored to oversee Henry's intimate bodily functions—Groom of the Stool, unbelievable as it may seem today, was a privileged spot in the king's service—was closer to Henry than anyone else except for Charles Brandon. On May Day, when he left the jousts, Henry had asked Norris to go with him, and they had ridden together, discussing some serious matter. That evening, Norris was arrested.

The serious matter may have had to do with an exchange Norris had with Anne late in April, which had made its way to Cromwell, undoubtedly in garbled form. The actual details only came out when Anne, wondering why she had been arrested, speculated about it out loud with Kingston. Anne had been verbally jousting with Norris about his constant presence in her apartments and had chided him for "looking for dead men's shoes, for if aught should come to the King but good, you would look to have me."[7] This particular statement must have alarmed Norris, who replied that "if he should have any such thought, he would his head were off."[8] There was good reason for his alarm. In 1534, Cromwell had engineered an extension of the legal definition of treason, which was passed by Parliament and made it high treason to "maliciously wish, will or desire by words or writing" bodily harm to the king.[9] Under this new definition, Anne's remark could be construed as referring to Norris's desire for the king's death. Anne apparently eventually "got it," too, for after Norris made the comment about his head, she then told Norris that "she could undo him if she would."[10] What had (probably) begun as casual teasing ended with both of them ostentatiously declaring their horror at the thought that either one of them entertained fantasies of Henry's death.

But Anne worried that this wasn't enough. Later, realizing that their remarks may have been overheard, she asked Norris to go to John Skip and "swear for the queen that she was a good woman."[11] Unfortunately, this attempt at damage control only worked to make Skip suspicious. He confided his suspicions to Sir Edward Bayntun, who then went to Cromwell, who surely felt that gold from heaven had fallen into his lap. All this happened in late April. So clearly, at the point of Anne's arrest on May 2, Norris was suspected of more than simply withholding information about her purported affair with Smeaton. However, the full details of the conversation may only have been revealed by Anne in her rambling self-examination with Kingston.

Anne also told Kingston about how she had teased Francis Weston, then reprimanded him for telling her that he, too, frequented her apartments out of love for her. Under other circumstances, it would undoubtedly have been regarded as innocent courtly banter. But Cromwell was on the hunt, attempting to assemble a case that would be overwhelming, if not in the evidence, then in the sheer magnitude and scope of the charges. Both G. W. Bernard and Suzannah Lipscomb suggest, too, that Anne's banter with Weston had "crossed the acceptable boundaries of courtly interchanges."[12] But I suspect that what was considered "courtly" and what was suspected to be something more had changed since Anne had learned the rules and that Cromwell was able to take advantage of the different climate with regard to heterosexual behavior.

Anne was trained in traditions of courtly love within which flirtatiousness, far from being suspect, was a requirement of the court lady. But it must never go too far; the trick was to go just to the edge and then back off (without, of course, hurting the gentleman's feelings). Purity was required, but provocative banter was not just accepted, it was expected. Especially in the French court, a relaxed atmosphere was the norm in conversations between men and women. As the Middle Ages segued into the Renaissance and then into the Reformation, however, conversations that would have been seen as entirely innocent may have begun to be viewed differently. In an earlier chapter, I looked at the change from Capellanus's version of courtly love, still rooted in Plato, that cautions young men to turn their backs on carnal pleasure and aim for spiritual transcendence of mere bodily love, to Castiglione, with his cynical advice for the most effective ways to overcome the resistance of their female prey. If actual behavior followed ideology, then by the time Cromwell mounted his conspiracy against Anne, people may have been disposed to believe things, based on the exchanges with the men she was charged with, that would have been dismissed as ridiculous forty years earlier.

In addition to his spies in the prison, Cromwell may have had some malicious female accomplices helping him out. One of those could have been Jane Parker (George Boleyn's wife), who many historians believe provided the incriminating "evidence" against her husband — that she had seen the siblings kissing on the mouth and that Anne had told George first about her last pregnancy. Both of these were completely appropriate behavior for a brother and sister, but by the time they reached the point of formal indictments, tongues and other body parts had been added to raise the suspicion that the pregnancy was the result of George's having "carnally" known Anne "at Westminster [and] also did on divers days before and after at the same place, sometimes by his own procurement and sometimes by the Queen's."[13] Jane is also said to have told Cromwell that the two had mocked the king for being unskilled and having "neither potency nor vigor" in bed.[14]

Jane's role has not been definitely confirmed, however. Her involvement is hinted at by Chapuys (not the most reliable source, admittedly); stated outright by George Wyatt, who calls George's "wicked wife" the "accuser of her husband"; and accepted by later historians Gilbert Burnett, Peter Heylin, and others who attribute her turn against her husband and sister-in-law to Jane's jealousy of Anne's close relationship with George.[15] Alison Weir, more plausibly, I think, points to a possible self-protective switch of political allegiance from the Boleyns to the Seymours. Jane saw which way the wind was blowing and followed its course. Howard Brenton, in his play *Anne Boleyn*, portrays

Jane as actually a close ally of Anne's. She was, however, a weak person in Brenton's telling, and she capitulated to Cromwell's pressure on her. The latter two explanations — self-protection and pressure from Cromwell — rather than animosity toward Anne and George seem most convincing to me.

Another accomplice appears to have been Elizabeth Browne Somerset, Countess of Worcester, the sister of a member of the Privy Council, Sir Anthony Browne, who accused Anne of relations with both Smeaton and George. This accusation, as related in a poem by Lancelot de Carles written after Anne's death, was made by Lady Worcester after one of her brothers (which one is not made clear) had criticized his sister for her own "dishonorable love," to which she replied that "it was little in her case in comparison with that of the Queen."[16] To my ears, this sounds very much like a desperate attempt to deflect attention from her own guilt, as a child will do when accused. But this was the sort of stuff on which Cromwell's case was built. The tactic seems to have been to create as much smoke as possible and to count on people believing there must therefore be a fire.

And then, of course, there was the intimidation factor. Thomas Cranmer, the archbishop of Canterbury, who shared Anne's religious inclinations and had been a champion of hers since before the marriage, was in emotional turmoil on hearing of Anne's arrest. On May 3 he wrote to Henry, his soul clearly in struggle, wanting to defend Anne but fearing for his own safety. "I am clean amazed, for I had never better opinion of woman; but I think your Highness would not have gone so far if she had not been culpable. I am most bound to her of all creatures living, and therefore beg that I may, with your Grace's favor, wish and pray that she may declare herself innocent."[17] Still, he cautiously hedged his bets. "Yet if she be found guilty, I repute him not a faithful subject who would not wish her punished without mercy."[18] The "if" evaporated in the middle of his letter writing after Cranmer was called to the Star Chamber by Cromwell and his cronies. When he returned to his desk, having "chatted" with Cromwell, Cranmer concludes his letter: "I am sorry such faults can be proved against the Queen as they report."[19]

It is astonishing how quickly events proceeded from then on, both in the criminal investigation and trial, and in the disintegration of whatever remained of Henry's relationship with Anne. On May 4 Francis Weston and William Brereton, a Groom of the Privy Chamber who was married to Elizabeth Savage, a second cousin of Henry's, were arrested. The charges for both: high treason and adultery. On May 5 Thomas Wyatt and Sir Richard Page were arrested. It was rumored that Wyatt (who is credited with introducing the sonnet into English) and Anne were romantically involved before Anne's marriage to Henry, and several of his love poems, although ambiguous, seem to refer to his feelings for her, which had to be abandoned because she "was Caesar's."[20] However, whatever Wyatt felt, there is no evidence that Anne reciprocated. Wyatt was brought in for questioning at the Tower of London, but he was later released. Richard Page had been appointed a Gentleman of the Privy Chamber for his support for the king's "great matter," and had been helpful in bringing Wolsey down. Like Wyatt, Page was later released from the Tower. Unlike the other nobility who had been arrested, neither was a member of "the Boleyn faction" at court.

On May 12 Smeaton, Brereton, Weston, and Norris were tried. Three of the men — Norris, Brereton, and Weston — pleaded "not guilty." Smeaton, who had earlier confessed under torture, "pleaded guilty of violation and carnal knowledge of the Queen, and put himself in the King's mercy."[21] They faced a handpicked jury that was well aware of the verdict Henry wanted, and there was no effort to keep them from gossip. In fact, questions were put to potential jury members about their knowledge of the case, and the more they "knew," the more fit they were considered for service. The trial itself would have been very speedy — any crime, from petty theft to grand larceny to murder, took only thirty minutes to try at the most. And, of course, when a king or queen had a vested interest in a case, they would be favored. As Wolsey once remarked, "If the Crown were prosecutor and asserted it, justice would be found to being in a verdict that Abel was the murderer of Cain."[22] The verdict of guilty was no surprise, and the convicted men were sentenced to be hanged and drawn and quartered.

Anne must have felt great anguish on hearing of the verdict. She could not know yet if Henry would spare her own life, but she knew how drastically the verdict would affect the families of these men, who would not only lose their husbands, fathers, sons, and brothers, but their livelihoods as well. And with the crown's judgment against the men, she knew she automatically stood judged as an adulteress. The only question that remained was what punishment would be handed down to her.[23]

The sentences were a gross injustice; an overwhelming number of the purported sexual encounters would have been impossible by virtue of the queen's absence from court or highly improbable due to her being pregnant or recently postpartum on the dates specified. But two "smaller" yet horrible cruelties were visited on the condemned men. On May 16 Henry signed all the death warrants. But although the men were due to die the next day, they were left in suspense as to the method of their execution, which normally was commuted for royals and nobles from hanging (to be followed by drawing and quartering) to beheading. As late as after dinner on that same day, Kingston was begging Cromwell to let him know how they were to die, but word didn't come until much later, possibly the following morning. George and the other nobles thus spent many unnecessarily agonizing hours anticipating the more excruciating, humiliating death. In the end, all of them — even Smeaton, who was a lowly musician — met death by beheading.

Henry was apparently too occupied with other activities to worry about such an inconsequential decision as choosing the method of the men's deaths. On the day of the arrests, "to cover the affection which he has for [Jane Seymour]," Henry had "lodged her seven miles hence in the house of the grand esquire, [Sir Nicholas Carew]."[24] Oddly, while Jane was sequestered at Beddington, the king was often seen at "banquets" with diverse ladies, "sometimes remaining after midnight, and returning by the river . . . accompanied by various musical instruments" and "singers of his chambers."[25] Was this some sort of final fling, a smoke screen for his intentions with Jane, a show of macho bravado? It isn't clear. Chapuys remarked that he never saw a man "wear his horns more patiently and lightly," which to him was an indication of how little he cared about Anne's future.[26] Suzannah Lipscomb's explanation is more penetrating. If we accept the premise that Henry believed Anne guilty of at least some of the charges, then it would have gravely wounded Henry's sense of masculine honor, already made less sturdy by his physical decline and inability to perform the athletic feats that brought men glory.

> Honor was chiefly a measure of one's ability to conform to the ideals demanded of one's gender. For a man, it meant exerting masculin- ity, imposing patriarchy, controlling the women in one's household, maintaining a good reputation and demonstrating physical and sex- ual prowess . . . Anne's very behavior, if assumed to be true, testified to the king's lack of manliness, and, as if this weren't enough, Anne and Rochford's ridicule of the king on this very matter drove the point home.[27]

It was out of a desperate need to feel himself a man that Henry both escalated the relationship with Jane and "felt the need to cavort himself with the ladies . . . [He] did it to restore the patriarchal order and to prove his manhood."[28]

On May 13 preparations were made for the trials of Anne and her brother. The grand juries were commanded to furnish the indictments, and Constable Kingston received a precept from Thomas Howard, the duke of Norfolk (Anne's uncle), ordering him to bring the prisoners to trial on Monday, May 15. Norfolk also sent a precept to Ralph Felm- ingham, sergeant-at-arms, to summon at least twenty-seven "peers of the Queen and Lord Rochford, by whom the truth can be better made to appear."[29] While these official legal steps were being taken, physical preparations were also begun to make the King's Hall in the Tower amenable to two thousand spectators, with benches lining the walls and a high platform for the interrogator and the condemned, so that all could see. "The King was determined," Alison Weir writes, "that justice would be seen to be done" and was sure of the judicial strength of the evidence.[30] Weir argues, as Lipscomb does, that he was honestly convinced that the charges were true and that "he had nourished a viper in his bosom" who had "betrayed and humiliated him, both as a husband and a king."[31] Other scholars are not so sure. But whatever his actual beliefs about Anne's guilt or innocence, for Henry the outcome was such a foregone conclusion that on the same day that preparations

were being made for the trial, he ordered Anne's household dissolved
and her servants discharged. On May 14 Jane was brought to Chelsea
to be within quick reach when the sentence was pronounced on Anne.
Henry, as always, was an excellent recycler of resources; Jane was installed in Thomas More's former home, which Henry had taken over
and lavishly redecorated after More was executed.

In the Tower

While Jane waited patiently in the various lodgings to which she had
been moved, already being treated (and apparently regarding herself)
as a queen, Anne was in the Tower of London. Her moods, according
to Kingston, vacillated wildly from resignation to hope to anxiety. She
had always had a wicked sense of humor, and no irony was ever lost
on her. When taken to the Tower, she had asked, "Master Kingston,
shall I die without justice?"[32] He replied, "The poorest subject the king
hath, had justice."[33] Hearing this, despite her fear, Anne laughed. She
was too sophisticated and savvy about the dispensing of royal power
to swallow the official PR. But she also seized on any glimmer of hope,
and she had reason to believe that in the end she might be spared.
She was the queen, after all, and no one in England had ever executed
a queen. Isabella of Angoulême and Isabella of France, both married
to English kings, had been adulterous, but only their lovers were executed. Even those who had been involved in acts of treason — the
most famous of all being Eleanor of Aquitaine, who almost succeeded
in toppling Henry II from his throne — were put under house arrest at
most. It was almost unthinkable to Anne that Henry would have her
put to death. But so, too, was her imprisonment, which had come so
suddenly and seemingly without reason.

Until very near the end, she still harbored the belief that Henry
might pardon her. It was not an unreasonable expectation. The last-
minute rescue of the condemned queen was a centerpiece of the romance of chivalry, which was still being avidly consumed at court
via Malory's *Le Morte d'Arthur*. In the Arthurian legend, Guinevere is
condemned to death twice for treason (the second time for adultery
with Lancelot) and both times is saved from the stake by Lancelot —

with King Arthur's blessings. Arthur had, in fact, suspected the queen's infidelity for years, but because of his love for her and for Lancelot, had kept his suspicions a secret. When Modred and Agravain, plotting their own coup d'état, told the king about it, he had no choice but to condemn his queen, while privately hoping she would be rescued. It was a romantic fantasy — but one that Henry and Anne had grown up with and that had no doubt shaped their ideas about love. Henry had been an adroit and seductively tender courtier who had pledged himself Anne's "servant" and swore his constancy. The pledges may (or may not) have been made manipulatively, but his infatuation was real and the gestures were convincing. Why wouldn't Anne, whom Henry had, in fact, honored for six years as if she were Guinevere, cherish the hope that she, too, would be rescued from death?

From the time she was taken to the Tower, then, a razor-thin edge separated hope and doom for Anne. She had been treated very gently and with great respect by Constable Kingston, and no doubt the fact that she was housed not in a dungeon but in the lodgings she had slept in before her coronation lent an ambiance of (mistaken) comfort to her stay in the Tower. After a visit from Cranmer on May 16, she appears to have been offered hints — or even proposed — some sort of "deal," in which her admission of the illegitimacy of her marriage and Elizabeth might win her life in a nunnery instead of death. Cromwell had been working to find a way to annul the marriage and bastardize Elizabeth. Two likely "impediments" to the lawfulness of the marriage were a possible precontract with her young love Percy and the "consanguinity" of the king's affair with Mary Boleyn. Percy denied the precontract, so Cranmer was sent to get Anne to admit that she knew of the relationship with Mary when she married Henry. Weir speculates — accurately, I believe — that Cranmer may have suggested to Anne that if she admitted to the impediment, the king might spare her life. After Cranmer left, Kingston reports that Anne was in a "cheerful" mood and talked about her hopes of being spared death. Instead, the only "mercy" Henry had planned was her death by a skilled French swordsman, who was on his way even before Anne's trial.

Anne's emotional vacillations — from terror to prayerful resignation to black humor (speculating the night before her execution that her enemies would remember her as "la Royne Anne sans Tête") suggest that the strangeness of what was happening to her was at times impossible for her to assimilate. Just a few short months before, she had been pregnant. Just a few weeks before, Henry had been insisting that Charles V acknowledge the legitimacy of their marriage. Now she was in the Tower, condemned to death. Her fortunes had turned around so swiftly and extremely that it must have been difficult to keep a steady grip on reality. Yet she managed, at her trial on May 15, after nearly two weeks in the Tower and the certain recognition, after the verdicts of the men accused with her, that she would be found guilty, to summon her renowned pride and dazzling confidence for the grim occasion. Dressed in black velvet over a scarlet petticoat, her cap "sporting a black-and-white feather," she "presented herself with the true dignity of a queen, and curtseyed to her judges, looking round upon them all, without any sign of fear . . . impatience, grief, or cowardice,"[34] according to Crispin de Milherve, whom Alison Weir cites as an eyewitness at the trial, but who may have been Lancelot de Carles. When it was time for her to speak, after hearing the full charges for the first time — including trivial, noncriminal but "atmospherically" damaging accusations that she had made fun of the king's poetry and taste in clothing — she made such "wise and discreet answers to all things laid against her" that "had the peers given in their verdict according to the expectations of the assembly, she had been acquitted."[35] But, of course, the verdict was not dependent on the impression Anne made or how convincing her defense was. When she protested against Smeaton's confession "that one witness was not enough to convict a person of high treason," she was simply informed "that in her case it was sufficient." Also "sufficient" were numerous bits of gossip that nowadays would be regarded as worse than hearsay, since they came from obviously prejudiced sources. George Wyatt, writing about the trial later, says that he heard nothing that could be considered evidence. Instead, as author Jane Dunn described the case, it was "a ragbag of gossip, innuendo, and misinterpreted courtliness."[36]

Anne almost certainly expected the guilty verdict that followed, which makes her calm, clear, and highly intelligent (according to numerous observers) responses to the charges all the more remarkable. It is less likely that she expected the sentence that followed: "that thou shalt be burnt here within the Tower of London on the Green, else to have thy head smitten off, as the King's pleasure shall be further known of the same." On hearing the verdict, several onlookers shrieked, took ill, and had to leave the hall. But Anne, as Chapuys observed, "preserved her composure, saying that she held herself '*pour toute saluee de la mort*' [always ready to greet death], and that what she regretted most was that the above persons, who were innocent and loyal to the King, were to die for her."[37] And then, as summarized by several onlookers but reported in the greatest detail by the witness identified by Weir (controversially) as Crispin de Milherve, she delivered the extraordinary speech that I quoted from briefly in the previous chapter.

My lords, I will not say your sentence is unjust, nor presume that my reasons can prevail against your convictions. I am willing to believe that you have sufficient reasons for what you have done; but then they must be other than those which have been produced in court, for I am clear of all the offences which you then laid to my charge. I have ever been a faithful wife to the King, though I do not say I have always shown him that humility which his goodness to me, and the honours to which he raised me, merited. I confess I have had jealous fancies and suspicions of him, which I had not discretion enough, and wisdom, to conceal at all times. But God knows, and is my witness, that I have not sinned against him in any other way. Think not I say this in the hope to prolong my life, for He who saveth from death hath taught me how to die, and He will strengthen my faith. Think not, however, that I am so bewildered in my mind as not to lay the honour of my chastity to heart now in mine extremity, when I have maintained it all my life long, much as ever queen did. I know these, my last words, will avail me nothing but for the justification of my chastity and honour. As for my brother and those others who are unjustly condemned, I would willingly suffer many deaths to deliver them, but since I see it so pleases the King, I shall willingly accompany them in death, with this assurance, that I shall lead an endless life with them in peace and joy, where I will pray to God for the King and for you, my lords.[38]

The clarity and confidence of Anne's declaration here, her insight into her lack of humility, and her reference to "bewilderment" of mind are all, I believe, support for the theory, which many scholars have challenged, that a purported "last letter" to Henry written by Anne on May 6 is indeed authentic. The letter was found among Cromwell's possessions after his death, apparently undelivered to the king. The handwriting doesn't correspond exactly (although it is not radically dissimilar) to Anne's other letters, but it could easily have been transcribed by someone else or written in Anne's own hand, which could have been altered by the distress of her situation. On May 5 Anne *did* ask Kingston to "bear a letter from me to Master Secretary."[39] Kingston then said to her, "Madam, tell it me by word of mouth and I will do it."[40] She thanked him, and after that, we hear no more of it in Kingston's reports, so we don't know if the letter was ever written or dictated. But the one found among Cromwell's papers, dated May 6, begins with a statement that is so startlingly precise in its depiction of Anne's state of mind at the time that it's hard to imagine anyone else, in the decades following her death, writing it.

Your Grace's displeasure and my imprisonment are things so strange to me, that what to write, or what to excuse, I am altogether ignorant. Whereas you send to me (willing me to confess a truth and so obtain your favour), by such a one, whom you know to be mine ancient professed enemy [Cromwell]; I no sooner received this message by him, than I rightly conceived your meaning; and if as you say, confessing a truth indeed may procure my safety, I shall, with willingness and duty, perform your command.

But let not your grace ever imagine your poor wife will ever be brought to acknowledge a fault, where not so much as a thought ever proceeded. And to speak a truth, never a prince had a wife more loyal in all duty, and in all true affection, than you have ever found in Anne Bulen — with which name and place I could willingly have contented myself if God and your grace's pleasure had so been pleased. Neither did I at any time so far forget myself in my exaltation, or received queenship, but I always looked for such alteration as I now find; for the ground of my preferment being on no surer foundation than your grace's fancy, the least alteration was fit and sufficient (I knew) to draw that fancy to some other subject.

You have chosen me from a low estate to be your queen and companion, far beyond my just desert or desire; if then you found me worthy of such honour, good your grace, let not any light fancy or bad counsel of my enemies withdraw your princely favour from me, neither let that stain — that unworthy stain — of a disloyal heart toward your good grace ever cast so foul a blot on me and on the infant princess, your daughter [Elizabeth].

Try me, good king, but let me have a lawful trial, and let not my sworn enemies sit as my accusers and as my judges; yea, let me receive an open trial, for my truth shall fear no open shames; then shall you see either mine innocency cleared, your suspicions and conscience satisfied, the ignominy and slander of the world stopped, or my guilt openly declared. So that whatever God and you may determine of, your grace may be at liberty, both before God and man, not only to execute worthy punishment on me, as an unfaithful wife, but to follow your affection already settled on that party [Anne knew of Henry's affection for Jane Seymour], for whose sake I am now as I am; whose name I could some good while since, have pointed unto: Your Grace being not ignorant of my suspicions therein.

But if you have already determined of me, and that not only my death, but an infamous slander, must bring you to the enjoying of your desired happiness, then I desire of God that He will pardon your great sin herein, and, likewise, my enemies, the instruments thereof, and that he will not call you to a strait account for your unprincely and cruel usage of me at his general judgment-seat, where both you and myself must shortly appear; and in whose just judgment, I doubt not (whatsoever the world think of me) mine innocency shall be openly known and sufficiently cleared.

My last and only request shall be, that myself may only bear the burden of your grace's displeasure, and that it may not touch the innocent souls of those poor gentlemen, whom, as I understand, are likewise in strait imprisonment for my sake.

If ever I have found favour in your sight — if ever the name of Anne Bulen have been pleasing in your ears — then let me obtain this request; and so I will leave to trouble your grace no further: with mine earnest prayers to the Trinity to have your grace in his good keeping, and to direct you in all your actions.

From my doleful prison in the Tower, the 6th of May.

Ann Bulen[41]

Most of Anne's modern biographers believe this letter to be a forgery, in part because it is so daringly accusatory of Henry and in part because the "style" is not like Anne's. "Its 'elegance,'" writes Ives, "has always inspired suspicion."[42] Well, not always. Henry Ellis and other nineteenth-century commentators believed it was authentic. And the "style" argument is an odd one, because we have so few existing letters of Anne's and they are such businesslike affairs that it's hard to see how anyone could determine a "style" from them. If Henry had saved her responses to his love letters, we might have a better idea of what Anne was like as a writer, but they were destroyed. As it stands, though, we do have the account of her speech at her trial, and it exhibits many of the same qualities as this letter. In both, Anne stands her ground bravely and articulately, but more striking, goes beyond the conventions of the time to venture into deeper "psychological" and political territory: the insight into her lack of humility, the inference that this might have had something to do with her fall from grace, her reference to the "bewilderment" and "strangeness" of finding herself accused of adultery and treason.

As to the letter's bold attitude toward Henry, this was characteristic of Anne, and (as she acknowledged in her trial speech) she was aware that it overstepped the borders of what was acceptable. Her refusal to contain herself safely within those borders was what had drawn Henry to her; she could not simply turn the switch off when it began to get her in trouble. To do that would have been to relinquish the only thing left to her at this point: her selfhood. Ives says that it would "appear to be wholly improbable" for a Tudor prisoner to warn the king "that he is in imminent danger from the judgment of God."[43] But Anne was no ordinary prisoner; she had shared Henry's bed, advised and conspired with him in the divorce strategies, debated theology with him, given birth to his daughter, protested against his infidelities, and dared to challenge Cromwell's use of confiscated monastery money. Arguably,

it was her failure to be "appropriate" that contributed to her downfall. Now, condemned to death by her own husband, to stop "being
Anne" would have been to shatter the one constancy left in the terrible
"strangeness" of her situation.

I don't know for certain, of course, that this letter is authentic. But I
have to wonder whether skeptics have been influenced by Anne's reputation as a woman known for her "feminine" vivacity, emotionality, and
sexuality. Henry Ellis called this letter "one of the finest compositions
in the English Language."[44] Ellis lived at a time when women writers
had begun to come into their own. But perhaps not every historian has
been as ready to acknowledge that Anne could possibly have written
"one of the finest compositions in the English language."

Approaching the Scaffold

Expecting to die on May 18, Anne took the Sacrament at two AM, having prepared her soul for many hours. She had insisted that Kingston
be present when she took confession so her assertion of innocence
of the charges would be public record. Even her old enemy Chapuys
was impressed by the fact that Anne, before and after receiving the
Sacrament, affirmed to those who had charge of her "on peril of her
soul's damnation, that she had not misconducted herself so far as her
husband the King was concerned."[45] In the sixteenth century, to speak
anything other than the truth at such a time would be to invite the utter condemnation of God. Anne had nothing to gain and her salvation
to lose by lying. By now all who were in close contact with her must
have been convinced of her innocence, whatever their politics.

She was prepared to die. Yet, cruelly, the execution was delayed
twice, once in order to clear the Tower of possible sympathetic observers, the second time because the executioner had been delayed. The
first delay dismayed Anne, who thought that at the newly appointed
hour she would already "be dead and past my pain."[46] Kingston, who
seems to have been an absurdly literal man, took her to be referring to
the physical pain of the execution itself and reassured her that "there
should be no pain, it was so subtle."[47] Anne replied with her most famous line: "I heard say the executioner is very good, and I have a little

neck."[48] And then, according to Kingston, "she put her hand about [her neck] laughing heartily."[49] Kingston flat-footedly interpreted this to mean that Anne had "much joy and pleasure in death."[50] He apparently did not "get" Anne's irony or that she was probably becoming a bit unhinged at this point. At the news of the second delay, she was distraught. But "It was not that she desired death," as she told Kingston (or perhaps she told one of the ladies, who then told him), "but she had thought herself prepared to die, and feared that the delay would weaken her resolve."[51] So much for Kingston's theory that Anne felt "joy and pleasure" at the prospect of death.

What she may have felt was something closer to what psychologist James Hillman describes as the state of mind that often precedes an attempt at suicide: a desperate desire to shed an old self whose suffering has become unbearable and thus must be "reborn" in the act of dying. This imagined rebirth, for Hillman, has nothing to do with belief in reincarnation or even in heaven, but with the perception, ironically, that the soul cannot survive under existing conditions. What Anne had been through was certainly enough to shatter any hold her previous life may have exerted on her. She had been discarded by the man who had pursued her for six years, fathered her daughter, and seemingly adored her for much of their time together. The person she was closest to in the world—her brother—had been executed on the most hideous and shameful of charges. The rest of her family, as far as we can tell, had either abandoned her or—as Anne believed of her mother—was awash with despair and grief over what was happening. Still recovering from a miscarriage, her body and mind undoubtedly assaulted by hormonal changes and unstable moods, she had been sent to prison on absurd, concocted charges and "cared for" there by women who were hostile spies. She knew she would never see her daughter again, and—unlike the fictional Anne of *Anne of the Thousand Days*, who predicts that "Elizabeth will be queen!"—she had no hope, after Cranmer's visit, that her child would ever be anything more than what she had seen Mary reduced to: a bastardized ex-princess forced to bow down to any children the new wife might produce for Henry. She had been given reason to hope that she would be allowed to live, only to have those hopes crushed at her sentencing. In a sense, she had already been through dozens of dyings. Nothing was left but the withered skin of her old life, which she was ready to shed.

As she mounted the scaffold, wearing a robe of dark damask (black in some reports, gray in others) trimmed with white fur, with a red kirtle (petticoat) underneath — red being the liturgical color of Catholic martyrdom — political and national affiliations continued, as they had through her reign and would for centuries to come, to shape the descriptions of her appearance and behavior. To an author of the *Spanish Chronicle*, she exhibited "a devilish spirit."[52] A French witness who had sneaked in despite the ban on strangers wrote that "never had she looked so beautiful."[53] An anonymous observer described her as "feeble and half-stupefied"[54] (which would be understandable, and not incompatible with her looking beautiful as well). Thomas Wriothesley says she showed "a goodly smiling countenance."[55] Frenchman de Carles commented on the beauty of her complexion, pure and clear as though cleansed by all the suffering. For all, the spectacle of a queen, wearing the white ermine of royalty and mounting the stairs to the scaffold, was unnerving.

Unlike her trial speech and her "last letter," Anne's remarks on the scaffold made the more conventional bows to the goodness and mercy of the king — in this highly public context, it was virtually required, if only to prevent any retribution against surviving relatives — and asked the people to pray for her. She did not admit to guilt for the offenses with which she was charged or accuse the judges of malice, but she did make reference to the "cruel law of the land by which I die."[56] By now, the four young ladies who had accompanied her to the scaffold (clearly not the hostile spies who had lived with her in the Tower, but others, more intimate with her, whom she had been allowed to have with her in these last moments) were weeping. Anne, having helped them take off her robe — an act that in itself must have demanded great composure and courage — "appeared dazed" as she kneeled down, modestly covering her feet with her dress, and asked the executioner to remove her coif lest it interfere with his stroke. The executioner realized that she was afraid of the pain of an impeded blow; she kept looking around her, her hand on her coif, anticipating the moment. Clearly "distressed" at the task he was to perform, he told her that he would wait until she gave the signal. "With a fervent spirit" she began to pray, and the Portuguese contingent, unable to bear it, huddled together and knelt down against the scaffold, wailing loudly.[57]

Anne gave the signal. But either the executioner or someone else in charge had devised a scheme to distract Anne at the last moment, so the fatal blow would come when she wasn't expecting it; the executioner turned toward the scaffold steps and called for the sword, and when Anne blindly turned her head in that direction, he brought the sword down from the other side and swiftly "divided her neck at a blow."[58] As these things went — others had died only after multiple clumsy hackings — it was an easy death. If the naturalist Lewis Thomas has it right, it was far easier than her weeks of suffering in the Tower. "Pain," he writes, "is useful for avoidance, for getting away when there's time to get away, but when it is end game, and no way back, pain is likely to be turned off, and the mechanisms for this are wonderfully precise and quick. If I had to design an ecosystem in which creatures had to live off each other and in which dying was an indispensable part of living, I could not think of a better way to manage."[59] He quotes Montaigne, who nearly died in a riding accident and later described the "letting go" that he experienced at what could have easily been the very end.

> It was an idea that was only floating on the surface of my soul, as delicate and feeble as all the rest, but in truth not only free from distress but mingled with that sweet feeling that people have who have let themselves slide into sleep. I believe this is the same state in which people find themselves whom we see fainting in the agony of death, and maintain that we pity them without cause . . . If you know not how to die, never trouble yourself; Nature will in a moment fully and sufficiently instruct you; she will exactly do that business for you; take you no care with it.[60]

Dostoevsky, too, had experienced a close brush with death — by the czar's firing squad, a sentence from which he was reprieved at the last moment — and fictionalizes his experience through a character in *The Idiot.* His account, though very different from Montaigne's or mine, nonetheless describes a radically altered state of consciousness, not characterized by pain but by a sense of the infinity of time, stretching his final moments into an extended reflection culminating in the "melting" of oneself with nature.

About twenty paces from the scaffold, where he had stood to hear the sentence, were three posts, fixed in the ground, to which to fasten the criminals (of whom there were several). The first three criminals were taken to the posts, dressed in long white tunics, with white caps drawn over their faces, so that they could not see the rifles pointed at them. Then a group of soldiers took their stand opposite to each post. My friend was the eighth on the list, and therefore he would have been among the third lot to go up. A priest went about among them with a cross; and there was about five minutes of time left for him to live.

He said that those five minutes seemed to him to be a most interminable period, an enormous wealth of time; he seemed to be living, in these minutes, so many lives that there was no need as yet to think of that last moment, so that he made several arrangements, dividing up the time into portions—one for saying farewell to his companions, two minutes for that; then a couple more for thinking over his own life and career and all about himself; and another minute for a last look around. He remembered having divided his time like this quite well. While saying good-bye to his friends he recollected asking one of them some very usual everyday question, and being much interested in the answer. Then having bade farewell, he embarked upon those two minutes which he had allotted to looking into himself; he knew beforehand what he was going to think about. He wished to put it to himself as quickly and clearly as possible, that here was he, a living, thinking man, and that in three minutes he would be nobody; or if somebody or something, then what and where? He thought he would decide this question once and for all in these last three minutes. A little way off there stood a church, and its gilded spire glittered in the sun. He remembered staring stubbornly at this spire, and at the rays of light sparkling from it. He could not tear his eyes from these rays of light; he got the idea that these rays were his new nature, and that in three minutes he would become one of them, amalgamated somehow with them.[61]

Anne's preparations for dying, facing the inevitability of her execution, may also have been filled with internal good-byes, existential confrontations with the mystery of "being" and "nothingness," and imaginings of becoming one with nature. I like to think of her final hours as immensely rich, in a way that I cannot comprehend but that were sustaining to her even beyond her more conventional — but extremely deep, for Anne — religious faith. And then, at the end, I hope that nature or God (it makes no difference) gave her no more to figure out, no more to regret, no more to say good-bye to, no more work to do, and took care of her dying.

The Executioner's Sword and the Red Bus

While I was in London conducting interviews for this book and visiting sites of importance, I had an experience that reminded me of Lewis Thomas's essay. Returning to my hotel from a daylong visit to the Tower, I was obediently following the crowd across a busy intersection when I heard a voice call out, "Watch out!" and, struck on my lower back, I was knocked to the ground. The impact was forceful and disorienting; I had no idea what had happened. Then, out of the corner of my eye, I saw the red of a London bus. *I'm about to be run over by a bus!* I thought, disbelieving but sure; it seemed impossible, on my innocent little research trip, that I should die in this arbitrary, unexpected way, but that was clearly what was about to happen. I tried to lift myself up and realized that although I was hurt, I wasn't about to be crushed, for I'd been hit not by the bus I'd seen out of the corner of my eye, but by an impatient bicyclist; the bus had slowed to a stop by the time I was on the ground.

I was bleeding from a bad scrape on my arm, and sharp darts of pain in my back and side accompanied every breath in a way that I recognized from a hairline rib fracture I'd once received in an auto accident. I suppose I ought to have gone to the hospital just to be sure everything was okay, but I didn't. And eventually, everything did heal. The only injury that remained was existential: the memory of that moment when I was sure that I was about to be extinguished, just like that, without warning. I had felt terror, yes, but then, when the fatal blow seemed inevitable, an eerie calm overcame me. It seemed useless to struggle—a feeling that I had never before experienced in a life devoted to making things happen, protecting myself and those I love, and constantly moving forward. For a moment, when I thought I was about to be struck by that bus, I relaxed into the unfamiliar sense of "letting go." It was only for an instant, and then, when I realized that the bus had stopped and escape from the traffic was still possible, the self-protective fear returned, and I scrambled to my feet and hobbled across the street to the sidewalk where my husband was standing, looking alarmed.

Sometimes we know when our death is coming—when we are desperately ill, say. But we all "know"—although we rarely allow the knowledge to seep in—that even if we are in perfect health, even if we occupy the most privileged position in the world, even if we believe ourselves to be protected through prayer, good works, or youth, that, without warning, with a blind eye and an unhearing ear, the back of the universe can turn, the earth can tilt, and death can take you. This was how it happened to Anne—and it is why the image of the red bus, out of the corner of my eye, wouldn't leave me for weeks after the incident. My accident had not been fatal; it was not even serious. But my turning head had channeled the moment when Anne's life, anxiously turned toward an imagined death, was struck down by the executioner's sword coming at her—kindly, cruelly, unexpectedly, and irrevocably—to command the reality of her death.

6

Henry: How Could He Do It?

THE NIGHT OF Anne's execution, Henry returned to Hampton Court, the magnificent palace that Henry had refurbished for Anne after appropriating it from his longtime mentor and (at the time Henry took possession, soon to be former) Lord Chancellor, Thomas Wolsey. Jane Seymour followed Henry at six the next morning. They were betrothed at nine o'clock. The palace had been divested of all the emblems and other evidence of Anne's queenship (save the ones missed by the furiously scrambling revisionist carpenters and stonemasons). Soon it would be renovated, once again, to accommodate Prince Edward, the long-prayed-for male heir.

The execution of a queen was unprecedented, extreme, and shocking, even to Anne's enemies. Henry had invested six years of time, energy, intellect, money, and blood in making the marriage happen. They were married less than three years. There is no evidence of an unbridgeable emotional estrangement between them. His earlier love letters to her, admittedly written in the bloom of fresh passion, portray a solicitous, tender suitor whom it is impossible to imagine coldly ordering a wife's death. There are plenty of explanations for Henry's desire for a new marriage — Anne's failure to provide a male heir; Jane Seymour, waiting in the wings, fresh and fertile; Henry's recognition that Anne was creating problems with his image; and perhaps the need to reaffirm his declining masculinity with a new, more pliant bride. There are also plenty of theories, as we've seen, as to whether or not he believed Anne guilty of adultery and treason. Retha Warnicke argues that Anne's miscarriage of a deformed fetus convinced Henry that Anne was indeed a witch. G. W. Bernard (going on nothing more than a "hunch") believes that Anne was, in fact, guilty of at least some of the charges laid against her. Alison Weir, while herself maintaining Anne's innocence, considers that the charges were "more than enough to arouse fury in any husband, let alone an egotistical monarch" and that from the moment the Privy Council reported the charges to him, Henry was "convinced that he had nourished a viper in his bosom, and that Anne had betrayed and humiliated him, both as a husband and a king."[1] In the end, whichever account you find most convincing, it still takes a leap of comprehension to find any of them sufficient to explain Henry's willingness — seeming eagerness, in fact — to sign the order for Anne's *execution*. We are still left asking ourselves: How could he do it?

The answer to that question requires going deeper into Henry's character, both as a man and as a king, in search of precisely that piece of his being that made the order to execute Anne possible for him. And here, too, there are plenty of theories. David Starkey sees him as a once "virtuous prince," full of high ideals and generosity of spirit, who became a ruthless tyrant as his equanimity was assaulted by years of battle with the Church, declining health, and a disastrous domestic life. Others argue that from the first he was cold-bloodedly "devoted to his own interests and inclinations" and "inherently cruel."[2] Some historians, as well as the fictional *Wolf Hall*, have viewed Henry as impressionable and dependent, intimidated by Anne, and easily manipulated by those, such as Wolsey and then Cromwell, with a clearer plan of action. On this view, Henry didn't "act" with full agency when he signed the order for the execution, but instead passively surrendered himself to the more dominant Cromwell. Suzannah Lipscomb sees Henry, in the year Anne was executed, as having undergone a crisis of masculine honor, brought on by a bad fall from his horse that left him with a permanently disabled leg, unable to joust, and vulnerable to any rumors — such as those that Cromwell whispered in his ear about Anne — that questioned his manhood. She points to the "exaggerated, tragicomic manner" in which Henry complained of Anne's having bewitched him, then betrayed him with more than one hundred men.[3] Henry's motivation: to convince others — and himself — that he had not been cuckolded due to his own lack of sexual competence, but because Anne was the embodiment of feminine voraciousness and evil. As such, he was not killing an ordinary woman, but destroying a succubus who was eating away at his ability to perform as a king and as a man.

At the other end of the spectrum from Lipscomb is the hypothesis that Henry had a rare genetic disorder that was responsible both for Katherine's and Anne's frequent miscarriages *and* Henry's own physical and mental problems after middle age. Announced by headlines such as KING HENRY VIII'S MADNESS EXPLAINED, the theory is wonderfully embracing of virtually everything that went bad in Henry's life.

> Henry VIII . . . was basically the Brad Pitt of his day when he was younger . . . Yet he is most remembered for being gluttonous, impaired and executing wives.
>
> What happened?
>
> Research conducted by bioarchaeologist Catrina Banks Whitley . . . and anthropologist Kyra Kramer, leads them to speculate that the numerous miscarriages suffered by Henry's wives could be explained if the king's blood carried the Kell antigen . . . If Henry also suffered from McLeod syndrome, a genetic disorder specific to the Kell blood group, it would finally provide an explanation for his shift in both physical form and personality from a strong, athletic, generous individual in his first 40 years to the monstrous paranoiac he would become, virtually immobilized by massive weight gain and leg ailments.
>
> "It is our assertion that we have identified the causal medical condition underlying Henry's reproductive problems and psychological deterioration," write Whitley and Kramer.[4]

Pretty confident conclusion. Of course, it could be argued that Katherine's and Anne's miscarriages do not really require explanation. The sixteenth century's version of good nutrition during pregnancy (or during any stage of life) was very different from ours, and would be frowned on by modern medicine. Prenatal care for queens involved isolation in a chamber hung with tapestries covering the walls, doors, and ceilings. (Fresh air was considered unnecessary, even dangerous.) Advice for prenatal bleeding was to avoid "fire, lightning, thunder, with monstrous and hideous aspects and fights of men and beasts, by immoderate joy, sorrow and lamentation."[5] As to Henry's various ailments, it's possible that Henry could have suffered from McLeod syndrome, whose symptoms include heart disease, muscular and nerve impairment, and paranoia and mental decline after forty. But, as Retha Warnicke points out, "Could is the big word. It's an interesting theory and it's possibly true, but it can't be proven without some clinical evidence, and there is none."[6] The gap between "could" and "true" widens to the point of absurdity when Whitley and Kramer speculate that their genetic hypothesis "could explain why Henry shifted from supporting Anne to having her beheaded."[7] This is to collapse the three-year trajectory of a politically troubled, emotionally intense marriage into a diagnosis from *House*. Except on the television show, House's assistants would go scurrying off to perform the blood tests to confirm or disprove the theory, whereas "bioarchaeology," like evolutionary psychology, is heavy on theory and light on proof.

Ideas about Henry fall into one of two categories. There are the "turning point" theories that see the young Henry and the older Henry as two very different men, with some crisis or set of crises responsible for the change. Lipscomb's and Starkey's theories fall into this category, and so does Michael Hirst's. Hirst, creator of *The Tudors*, described in an interview with me what he views as a shattering of Henry's psyche brought on by the recognition that he had spent years of his life, shed the blood of friends, and broken with the Church of his childhood, only to be proved mistaken in the supposition that this was what God wanted of him. In this interpretation, Anne's failure to produce an heir was not just a blow to the security of the Tudor line but also a sign that the hope he had built his entire life around was based on an illusion.

He had attacked the Church on the basis of a love affair, largely. But he felt sure of what he was doing at the time, and Anne had mistakenly promised him a son. After she'd given him a daughter and had the miscarriages, it began to seem to him as though he'd gone horribly wrong. He was plunged back into reality, which is messy and not perfect. And I think that as he confronted the huge seriousness of it, he began to think in weird ways, that she was a witch and so forth. This, of course, shows how juvenile he still was. And he did have an absolutely ruthless streak that his father, too, had possessed. But beyond that, he did suffer a severe psychological crisis, knowing he had been so deluded. He came out of that crisis a much worse person, a complete tyrant and monster, who killed off the best part of himself in the attempt to reconcile his psychological issues.[8]

Hirst dramatized this transformation with a chilling last scene in the final episode of the second season of *The Tudors*. This was the episode in which Anne is executed, and scenes of her suffering in the Tower were punctuated with the image of Henry, gazing contemplatively at two beautiful swans — creatures known to mate for life — nuzzling in the pond outside the palace. His mood and thoughts are left deliberately ambiguous; perhaps, the viewer imagines, he is thinking back over his love for Anne and the life they shared together, once imagined to be as enduring as that of the swans, perhaps he is having regrets, feeling sorrow for the beauty that is about to be lost? No. After the execution scene, we are immediately taken to the king at his table, looking forward to his breakfast, which is being brought to him in a large gilt tureen on a silver platter. The lid is lifted, and the servants and nobles surrounding Henry gasp and applaud in delight. There on the platter is one of the swans, roasted and decorated with its own beautiful wings, posed as gracefully as if it were still swimming in a lake. Hirst, referencing Charles Laughton's famous eating scene but giving Henry's voraciousness a menace missing from Laughton's comic depiction, has Henry tear off a wing, plunge his hand into the body of the swan, and begin eating, oblivious to the greasy drool spilling from his mouth.

The theory of a great transformation depends, in part, on believing the enthusiastic PR that surrounded Henry when he first came to the throne, at eighteen years of age, and was hailed as ushering in the dawn of a bright new age. Thomas More, on the occasion of Henry's coronation, wrote a prose poem welcoming him to the throne.

> This day marks the limit of our slavery, the beginning of our freedom, the end of sadness, the source of joy . . . Now the people, freed, run before their king with bright faces. Their joy is almost beyond their own comprehension. They rejoice, they exult, they leap for joy and celebrate their having such a king. "The King" is all that any mouth can say.[9]

More, Greg Walker writes, was implicitly contrasting the erudite, exuberant, generous new king with his father, Henry VII, whom More and many others saw as a calculating, money-hoarding tyrant with little respect for the law and less for his people. Certainly, Henry did everything that he could to dramatize the contrast, forgiving those who had incurred enormous debts under his father and surrounding himself with humanists such as More and Erasmus, who had very strong ideas about what constituted a good prince. In *The Education of a Christian Prince* (1516), which Erasmus had sent to the young Henry, he argues that "whoever wants to bestow on himself the title of prince and wants to escape the hated name of tyrant must win it for himself by benevolent actions and not through fear and threats . . . The tyrant brings it about that everyone is under his thumb, either in law or through informers; the king delights in the freedom of his people."[10] Yet by the end of his reign and in descriptions after his death, "tyrant" was exactly what many were calling Henry, including Sir Walter Raleigh.

> If all the pictures and patterns of a merciless prince were lost in the world, they might again be printed to the life out of the story of this king. For how many servants did he advance in haste (but for what virtue no man could suspect) and with the change of his fancy ruined again; no man knowing for what offense? To how many others of more desert gave he abundant flowers from whence to gather honey, and in the end of harvest burnt them in the hive? How many wives did he cut off, as his fancy and affection changed? How many princes

of the blood (whereof some of them for age could hardly crawl toward the block) with a world of others of all degrees (of whom our common chronicles have kept the account) did he execute?[11]

But the contrast between More's young prince and the tyrant that Raleigh describes does not depend on disbelieving More or postulating a radical change of character in Henry. Walker argues that for his first eighteen years as king, it was easy for Henry to "deliver on the early promise" that More extols. "Avoiding tyranny," he writes, "was mainly a matter of not oppressing his people with unnecessary financial demands, of being pious, affable, and successful on the battlefield" and welcoming counsel and encouraging their candid advice without fear of retribution.[12] So long as Henry and his advisers were on the same page, this was easy to do. But when he launched his "great matter" and found many—perhaps the majority—of his advisers and most of the people in opposition, "the results were wide-ranging and catastrophic."[13] Henry's apparent equanimity, beneficence, and open-mindedness had depended on there being no challenge to what he wanted. Opposition unleashed the ruthless bully who had, in a sense, been lying in wait behind the carefully crafted posture of the virtuous prince.

There are many indications that, although Henry's resilience, emotional balance, and temper may have degenerated as he got older, his personality and character were essentially the same from the beginning of his reign to the end. Chief among the characteristics that pop up throughout both early and later descriptions are his unpredictability and capriciousness. Francis I, in 1536, described him as "the hardest friend in the world to bear: sometimes so unstable . . . other times so obstinate and fiercely proud that it is almost impossible to bear with him."[14] That was said during 1536, the year Tudor scholars regard as Henry's "annus horribilis." But Thomas More had told a young courtier—in 1520, before any "crisis" had occurred in Henry's reign—that having fun with the king was like "having fun with tamed lions—often it is harmless, but just as often there is the fear of harm. Often he roars in rage for no known reason, and suddenly the roar becomes fatal. The pleasure you get is not safe enough to relieve you of anxiety.

For you it is a great pleasure. As for me, let my pleasure be less great — and safe."[15] George Boker, in his 1850 play, compared Henry to "the shifting sand that tumbles in the tide, taking new form from every wanton surge . . . careening now to passion's fiery gust, now to the other side prostrated flat by self-styled reason's icy hurricane."[16]

Lacey Baldwin Smith argues that Henry was *always* a man of many faces, a "baffling composite of shifting silhouettes" who could be good-natured, generous, and charming one moment and dangerously cold as stone the next, highly emotional yet rigidly stubborn, a genuine searcher of his conscience for "God's will" yet able to subordinate all moral scruples and guilt to solidifying his own authority or satisfying his own desires.[17] The combination of informal warmth and lethal self-interest meant that even the closest relationships with him were never on solid ground. Thomas More, of all of Henry's contemporaries, was the most perceptive about the inherent danger of making too much of the king's outward gestures of affection. He told John Fisher that "[t]he king has a way of making every man feel that he is enjoying his special favor."[18] It may have been a compliment, but it was also a warning. More realized, as he told his son-in-law William Roper, that even though he was favored by the king "more singularly" than any subject in the realm, "I have no cause to be proud thereof, for if my head could win him a castle in France, it should not fail to go."[19] In the end, Henry was just that cavalier with More's life, although not over a castle in France. Henry had promised, years before, that he would always allow More to avoid any declarations or actions that went against his conscience. But when Henry's own supremacy was at issue, More's conscience — and his head — proved to be easily dispensed with. On the day of More's execution, Henry went hunting in Reading. This was the way Henry dealt with all his executions of old friends and lovers: Go hunting, have a party, be merry. Move on. It may have been a survival mechanism to defend himself against normal human feelings of regret or grief.

The problem with theories that postulate a crisis that turned Henry from a virtuous prince into the sort of man who could order the execution of a wife is that Henry was *always* capable of decisively and irrevocably turning off the switch of affection, love, tender feeling, and shared memories; striking a fatal blow; and refusing to look back. In fact, those whom he loved the most — Wolsey, More, Anne, Cromwell — were most at risk. Because he loved them, they had the most power to disappoint him — and for Henry, disappointment could never be "slight." All wounds to his authority, his manhood, and his trust were bloody gashes that he could repair only by annihilating the one who inflicted the wound. This, perhaps, is what distinguishes Henry's pattern from "ordinary" royal imperiousness. Kings execute people. Kings have grandiose ambitions. Kings are threatened by challenges to their authority. Kings can become drunk on power, and often do. But Henry may be unique among famous authoritarian kings in that his close relationships had only two switches: on and off. As Howard Brenton put it in an interview with me, "With Henry, you were either totally in or you were dead. He would have someone close to him, he'd elevate them, and they'd be terrific and virtually run everything on his behalf, and then when something went wrong, or a wind came his way, he would turn 180 degrees against them and they would be out. It happened to Wolsey, it happened to More, it happened to Anne, it happened to Cromwell."[20] Although it didn't result in their deaths, it happened to Katherine and Mary as well. Mary, in particular, so enraged Henry when she refused, even after Anne was dead, to take the oath recognizing her father as Supreme Head of the Church of England, that Cranmer had to talk him out of ordering her execution.

In 2012, this kind of personality would probably be diagnosed as borderline or narcissistic. Of course, those designations were unknown in the sixteenth century, and some would argue that the inclination to categorize and medicalize people into "types" is an invention of a later era. But we don't have to go that far to see that phenomenologically — that is, without attempting to put a medical label on Henry, but simply looking at his patterns of behavior — some of the descriptions of what we call "borderline" personality are apt — for example, the phenomenon that therapists call "splitting."

The world of a borderline, like that of a child, is split into heroes and villains. A child emotionally, the borderline cannot tolerate human inconsistencies and ambiguities; he cannot reconcile another's good and bad qualities into a constant coherent understanding of that person. At any particular moment, one is either "good" or "evil"; there is no in-between, no gray area. Nuances and shadows are grasped with great difficulty, if at all. Lovers and mates, mothers and father, siblings . . . and friends may be idolized one day, totally devalued and dismissed the next.[21]

In a certain sense, of course, the medieval worldview was itself a "split" universe, in which God and Satan, the saved and the fallen, were at starkly opposite poles, and "history was an extended moral homily upon the actions of men behaving rightly or wrongly."[22] It wasn't until the psychological turn of the nineteenth century that human beings began to be seen as mixtures of good and evil, ego and id, light and dark. But a dualistic ideology and a personality for whom others are either "for you" or "against you" are two very different things. In philosophical or religious dualism, it is God (or the universe) who assigns the categories of good and bad, which are relatively stable; for Henry, his own shifting needs were the measure of all things. "He is a prince of a royal disposition, and hath a princely heart," Wolsey told Kingston in 1529, long before Kingston became Anne's warder in the Tower, but "rather than he will either miss or want any part of his will or appetite, he will put the loss of one half of his realm in danger."[23] But Henry's "will" was not always easy to discern. In the screenplay of *A Man for All Seasons*, Robert Bolt brilliantly captures, in one brief action, not only the trembling uncertainty this produced in those around him but also Henry's delight in it. Henry's boat has just arrived at Chelsea, More's home, and the king (Robert Shaw), robust and athletic, has jumped off the deck and, unexpectedly, into a pool of mud. He glares menacingly at the oarsmen, who quake appropriately. Henry then bursts into a hearty, howling laugh, and the tense atmosphere among the men is transformed into playtime as they take their turns jumping into the mud.

There's no evidence that Henry took such childish pleasure in manipulating the emotions of his subjects — although there are plenty of occasions when he used his ability to make people cower in order to show his magnanimity (e.g., staging last-minute pardons) or assert his authority. Those tactics were pretty standard for kings, whose image was essential to maintaining power. But Henry's turnabouts do not seem to have been always under his control. The letters of ambassadors, even from the early years of his reign, describe sudden, explosive angers, "tears and tantrums."[24] In 1535, the king's fool almost lost his life over a joke about Anne Boleyn; a year later, Henry was weeping uncontrollably while hugging his illegitimate son by Bessie Blount, relieved that he was now safe from "that accursed whore" who had slept with more than a hundred men. A hundred? That would have meant a new man every ten days of her queenship. Yet it's possible that Henry believed something near to this, for his emotional switch, for whatever reasons, had turned against her, and she was now as wholly evil in his eyes as she once was wholly virtuous.

If we want to go beyond the phenomenology of Henry's "splitting" to causal explanation, we could find it in his childhood, which was itself split between the "cosy feminine world" of his mother and sisters and the cold indifference, then hostile domination, of his father. "As the only boy in the royal nursery," writes Robert Hutchinson, Henry "was thoroughly spoilt and tenderly protected from the hard knocks and bruises of childhood misfortune. The toddler prince was cosseted, his grumpiness and tears sweetly cooed away, and his every whim swiftly fulfilled by the doting matronly ladies who cared for him."[25] It's not clear, however, that naturally energetic Henry was entirely happy with all this "doting," which, after Arthur's death, kept him "as locked away as a woman" out of fear that the precious spare heir would also be lost.[26] But the masculine attentions of his father came with a high price too. Until Arthur's death, his father had virtually ignored Henry, leaving him to the care of the women; after Arthur died, however, he became obsessively focused on preparing Henry for the throne, and in the process, Henry became subject to his father's famous rages when he didn't do exactly as was required of him. Henry VII was so strict with the child that he gave the impression to Reginald Pole, Henry's contemporary, that he had "no affection or fancy unto him."[27] You don't need to venture into contemporary developmental theory to imagine Henry growing up with the belief that relationships were an either/or business, defined by gender: You could be extravagantly loved but smothered by women (perhaps part of the reason why he was initially drawn to both Katherine and Anne, and later to Katherine Parr, all of whom were strong-minded women whose strengths he came to resent). Or you could excel in the competitive world of men, where you might exercise power and command fear but never achieve the unconditional adoration you crave. Perhaps this intense desire for male love, in addition to the freedom from the restrictions of his childhood, helps to explain both his attraction to a father figure such as Wolsey, and also why Henry was at his happiest, most generous, and most exuberant among the young men he hunted and cavorted with. But in the end, everyone — with the exception of Charles Brandon and Katherine Parr, the two "survivors" of life with Henry — was bound to fail him. And they, too, walked a precarious tightrope in keeping Henry's favor. Brandon was exiled from court for a time when he married Henry's sister without the king's permission. And Katherine came very near to arrest for her Protestant sympathies, managing to talk Henry out of it at the last moment by humbling herself before him and begging his tolerance for her "womanly weaknesses and natural imperfections."[28]

Whatever the origins of Henry's personality, his problems were vastly exacerbated by the fact that he was, after all, king. As such, he was continually flattered and pampered, his every whim indulged, his grandiosity rarely challenged, his illusions carefully maintained. All of this encouraged his sense of omnipotence. "When you believe in yourself as morally superior, and at the same time do not scrutinize yourself," writes Francis Hackett in his perceptive biography, "when you dispense with this scrutiny because you are Defender of the Faith, A Knight of the Garter, Knight of the Golden Fleece, and a vast number of other distinguished things make you an automatic gentleman, you do not descend from the height of your scruples, even though they are spavined, to the level of mother earth. You are knighted for all time."[29] The closest comparison from our own time might be to the cult of the sports superhero, who not only gets away with abuse — and sometimes, like O. J. Simpson, murder — but remains immune to any sense of guilt or regret. Neither Simpson nor the high-school athletes who raped a mentally handicapped girl in the basement of one of their homes, then had the whole town rally round them in support, were born without a conscience; their senses of absolute entitlement were conferred on them through years of adulation and "getting away" with bad behavior.

Henry's inability to see himself as in the wrong made it all the riskier for those around him to show anything less than absolute allegiance. And proving allegiance, even obedience, put one at risk, ironically. For Henry wasn't a fool; he knew those around him were afraid, and so never fully trusted anyone. When he was young, he sought out people such as More and encouraged them to be honest with him, seeking some solid ground on which to base a relationship. But it was a zero-sum game; when More ran up against Henry's need to be the center of the universe, More's once-cherished independence of mind became worse than "nothing" in Henry's "all or nothing" demands on relationships.

It's hard to know exactly what threw the switch with Anne. Her final miscarriage may have convinced him that God was not on the side of their relationship. He may have believed in the charges of adultery — although his exaggerated estimates of her infidelities make me less rather than more likely to believe that; if he truly believed she had slept with five men, including her own brother, surely that would have been enough to "justify" his outrage without dragging half the men in court into her bed. Or the humiliation of hearing that Anne gossiped about his lack of sexual prowess may have been all that was needed. We will never know, and it really doesn't matter. It was sufficient, whatever it was, to shut off any currents of empathy, memory, and attachment that Henry felt for Anne. This is where *Anne of the Thousand Days* has it so wrong. The play and movie both open with Henry tormented by the decision whether or not to order Anne's execution. In Maxwell Anderson's play, which is written in verse, Henry muses:

> *This is hard to do*
> *when you come to put pen to paper.*
> *You say to yourself:*
> *She must die. And she must —*
> *If things are to go as planned.*
> *Yes, if they are to go at all.*

If I am to rule
And keep my sanity and hold my England off the rocks . . .
Go back to it, Henry, go back to it.
Keep your mind
On this parchment you must sign.
Dip the pen in the ink; write your name . . .
It's only that a woman you've held in your arms
And longed for when she was away,
And suffered with her — no, but she promised you an heir.
Write it down —
Write Henry Rex, and it's done.
And then the headsman
Will cry out suddenly, "Look, look there!"
And point to the first flash of sunrise,
And she'll look,
Not knowing what he means, and his sword will flash
In the flick of sun, through the little bones of her neck
As she looks away,
And it will be done.
It will be done.[30]

It's romantic and moving, and beautifully written. But it is not, I believe, the poetry of Henry's reality. In that reality, they handed him the parchment. He dipped the pen in the ink. He signed his name: Henry Rex. And it was done.

PART II

Recipes for "Anne Boleyn"

7

Basic Historical Ingredients

CHAPUYS EXULTED OVER Anne's fall: "I cannot well describe," he wrote Charles, "the great joy the inhabitants of this city have lately experienced and manifested, not only at the fall and ruin of the concubine, but in the hope that the Princess will be soon reinstated in her rights."[1] Yet even in letters written in the hours immediately after her execution, qualifications creep into his reports: "[A] few" people, he admits, "find fault and grumble at the manner in which the proceedings against her have been conducted, and the condemnation of her and the rest, which is generally thought strange enough."[2] Moreover, people have begun to question the king's role in all this, a "slander" that Chapuys fears "will not cease when they hear of what passed and is passing between him and his new mistress, Jane Seymour."[3] They have heard that Henry has been out making merry on his barge at night, showing "joy and pleasure" at what Chapuys compares to the anticipation of "getting rid of a thin, old, and vicious hack in the hope of soon getting a fine horse to ride."[4] Despite the snide remarks and reassurance of the people's "joy," it seems from this letter that even Chapuys is beginning to have his doubts about Anne's guilt. "No one ever shewed more courage," Chapuys admits, than the used-up, scraggly mare in the face of her execution.[5] And then, too, there is the disquieting fact—relayed to Chapuys by "the lady" attending Anne in prison who had been secretly reporting her every word to him —that both before and after receiving the Sacrament, Anne "affirmed, on peril of her soul's damnation, that she had not misconducted herself so far as her husband the King was concerned."[6]

Chapuys knew, as we've seen, about Cromwell's duplicity regarding Anne, as he himself had been encouraged to do everything he could to turn the king against her, and had done so with relish. (When he heard that Anne blamed him for her ruin, he told his friend Antoine Perrenot de Granvelle that he was "flattered."[7]) Yet it seems that he did not expect it to happen by means of invented charges. Cromwell, on the other hand, bragged to Chapuys, in June, that because of the "displeasure and anger" he had incurred with the king after his diplomatic efforts had failed, he had "set himself to arrange the plot (*a fantasier et conspirer led. affaire*)" against Anne.[8] It had "taken a great deal of trouble" but now that Anne was dead, he assured Chapuys, "matters would be more easily arranged than before."[9] Chief among those "matters" was the reinstating of Princess Mary. Chapuys was doubtful, still fearing "the obstinacy of the King towards the Princess."[10] And indeed, Chapuys' instincts were better than Cromwell's on this score (or, more likely, Cromwell was spinning things in the best light for Charles's consumption). For even with Anne dead, Henry continued to demand that Mary accept the invalidity of his marriage to her mother and warned Jane Seymour, when she expressed sympathy with the Catholic rebels who, among other things, were Mary's champions, that her predecessor had died "in consequence of meddling too much with state affairs," implying that she should take care that the same thing not happen to her.[11] Insisting that others bow to his will, clearly, had become more important to Henry than personal history, blood relations, emotional bonds, or even international alliances. Perhaps it had always been that way for him. Or perhaps—I believe this to be more likely—he was feeling greater and greater need to bolster his authority, which was no longer ensured by the free love of his subjects, but had to be bolted down through absolute submission. He was no longer the dashing and generous young king, bringing learning, light, and intellectual freedom into the realm, but a destroyer of two wives, a callous father, and a plunderer of monasteries who could not endure any dissent from his wishes and decrees. The less love he felt from his subjects, the more he needed the oaths and genuflections to his authority; the more acts of tyranny that followed, the less he was loved — a vicious circle.

In private, people had begun to doubt the justice of what had been done to Anne, George, Norris, Brereton, Weston, and Smeaton. Alexander Ales, a Scottish Protestant theologian and friend of Cranmer's, who resided in court at the time but who could not bear to go to the executions himself,[12] had dinner with his landlord and some of the spectators the night of Anne's beheading. The charges, evidence, and outcome were being discussed; it had become the hot topic of the day, as the verdict of the O. J. Simpson trial was among twentieth-century observers. Charge by charge, the dinner guests took apart the evidence and found it lacking, concluding that "no probable suspicion of adultery could be collected; and that therefore there must have been some other reason which moved the king" — the desire for a male heir, Anne's interference in negotiations with Spain and Germany,[13] his fear that the Catholic princes of Europe would band together against him, and so on. None of them knew yet about Jane Seymour.[14] In the middle of the conversation, a servant of Cromwell's arrived, and when asked for news, he replied cynically that just as the queen had betrayed the king by "enjoying herself with others" so now "while the Queen was being beheaded, [the king] was enjoying himself with another woman."[15] The other dinner guests were shocked and disbelieving — but, of course, they soon found out that it was true, for even as they dined, the king was already betrothed to his third wife.

Ales, who was sympathetic to Anne because of her reformist activities, recounted this story in a 1558 letter to Anne's daughter, Queen Elizabeth, and was one of the first to speak openly (and, due to Elizabeth's accession, quite safely) of his high regard for Anne. By then, Ales was convinced that Anne had been the victim of a conspiracy of papists (Chapuys as well as various bishops) who were responsible for all "the hatred, the treachery, and the false accusations laid to the charge of that most holy Queen, your most pious mother."[16] Ales was not exactly right about this. Although the hostility (and in Chapuys' case, machinations) of papists certainly contributed to Anne's fall, it is now generally agreed that it was Cromwell who engineered the coup, with or without the instigation of the king. Cromwell was a reformist, and he and Anne had once been collaborators of a sort in bringing reformist ideas to court. But Cromwell was a pragmatist, raised in the school of very hard knocks, and he looked after himself above all else.

Whomever one thought responsible for the plot, once the facts were assembled, it required a defiance of reason to believe in Anne's guilt. Reason, however, has never played a very large part in attitudes toward Anne. Henry's first successor (Edward VI, his son by Jane Seymour), no doubt influenced by his father's version of things, bitterly described Anne as "more inclined to couple with a number of courtiers rather than reverencing her husband."[17] Edward may have sincerely believed this, but he and his chief minister, John Dudley, also had political motives. Because they were intent on skipping over Mary and Elizabeth in the line of succession,[18] it suited their purposes that Elizabeth's mother remain the Great Whore in people's eyes.

When Edward's appointed successor (and very Protestant) Lady Jane Grey was executed, in a coup d'état even more staggeringly swift and brutal than Cromwell's against Anne, and with the aggressively Catholic (and still resentful) Mary Tudor on the throne, there was little chance that Anne's reputation would be rehabilitated. Mary had been badly treated by Anne — while awaiting her death, Anne confessed that this was the one thing that she repented of and wished to apologize for — and had seen her mother and her mother's religion moved from an unassailable position in her father's life to an obstacle in the way of his authority and his love life. Virtually abandoned by her father, forbidden to see her mother, she had formed close bonds with Eustace Chapuys, who brought her his own version of events, which cast Anne as Mary's would-be poisoner. According to Jane Dormer (a lady-in-waiting to Mary when she was queen), Mary never stopped believing that this had been the case, and she also was convinced — or at least, made a great public show of insisting — that Elizabeth was the daughter of Anne and Mark Smeaton. Mary's eventual husband, Philip II of Spain, came from a country that was not only devoutly Catholic but fiercely anti-Anne. Fed by Chapuys' portrait of the satanic schemer who spent half her time thinking of ways to get rid of Katherine and

Mary, and the other half of her time plotting to spread the Lutheran heresy throughout the world, the Spanish saw Anne as a militant offender against church and state, with Mary as the great avenger of her mother and defender of the faith. It was likely that Mary hated Anne to her dying breath, and it was thus prudent for those who had a different view to remain silent during her reign.

Elizabeth's ascension to the throne brought Anne's Protestant defenders out of the closet, determined not just to exonerate her of the charges that brought her down, but also to create a new martyr to their cause. Alexander Ales, who wrote to Elizabeth about the dinner-table discussion and who in the same letter tells a memorable story about Anne and Henry quarreling near the end, with Elizabeth in her "sainted mother's arms" as Anne beseeched the immovable Henry for sympathy, declared that "True religion in England had its commencement and its end with your mother," and vowed to write the true history of her death "to afford consolation to the godly."[19] John Foxe went several hundred steps further in the monumental *The Acts and Monuments of the Church* (better known as the *Book of Martyrs*), the 1563 edition of which (one of the four that Foxe revised and enlarged over his lifetime) was dedicated to Elizabeth. An earlier tribute to Anne, printed in 1559, had praised her beauty as well as her "many great gifts of a well instructed spirit: gentleness, modesty and piety toward all (particularly toward those who were in dire poverty) and most especially, a zeal for sincere religion."[20] In the 1563 version, Foxe credits Anne with much more, asserting that papal power in England "began utterly to be abolished, by the reason and occasion of the most virtuous and noble lady, Anne Bullen . . . by whose godly means and most virtuous council, the king's mind was daily inclined better and better," and detailing Anne's charitable activities and support of reformist authors, including her introducing Henry to Simon Fish's *Supplication for the Beggars.*[21]

Ironically, the Protestants and Catholics were in agreement with regard to the significance of Anne's influence in what Protestants called "the English Reformation" and Catholics called "the Anglican Schism." But after the emphasis on her important role all agreement ends. The difference between "reforming" and fomenting a "schism" pretty much tells it all. Where Foxe (and William Latymer, Anne's chaplain, whose own work in praise of Anne provided much of Foxe's information) saw Anne's efforts as a heroic accomplishment for which she paid with her life, Catholic polemicists such as Nicholas Sander saw her as a harlot and seductress who led Henry into heresy, filled the court with fellow heretics, and gave birth, both literally and metaphorically, to the most monstrous heresy of all: Elizabeth. Sander's book, *Schismatis Anglicani (The Rise and Growth of the Anglican Schism)*, which was written expressly to provide a counterhistory to Foxe's account of Henry's and Mary's reigns, is especially important to the creation and international spread of some of the most enduring myths about Anne. Although originally published in Latin (1585), it had a lively, colloquial style bursting with salacious tales about the Tudor royalty and colorful analogies to well-known Bible stories; and it was quickly translated into French, German, Italian, Portuguese, Polish, and Spanish. Described as "the basis of every [subsequent] Roman Catholic history," it was even turned into a school play (called *Henricus Octavus!*), which was performed in Louvain (the home of Sander and many other self-imposed exiles from Elizabeth's England) in 1624.[22]

Unlike Chapuys, whose letters to Charles had shied away from explicit references to Anne's sexuality and physical appearance, Sander, as we've seen, wallowed in descriptions of Anne's body as the deformed but alluring gateway that ensnared Henry and led him through the doors of heresy. Of course, "monster Anne" was a fantasy. It would have been unthinkable for Henry to have taken as his queen a woman whose beauty was so "corrupted" by deformity — or as promiscuous as Sander, who confuses Anne with her sister, makes her out to be. Whether Mary's reputation was deserved or not (and Alison Weir has claimed, recently, that it was not), it was Mary Boleyn, not Anne (as Sander has it), who was nicknamed the "English mare" — according to the gossip — for having been mounted so often while at the French court. But for Sander, the entire tribe of Boleyn women was a spreading miasma of shameless sexuality. Anne, he claims, was actually the offspring of her mother and Henry VIII! ("A claim," comments one contemporary critic, "that must have startled even the most cynical Catholic reader."[23])

Sander's influence on ideas about Anne has been deep and wide, providing a blueprint for dozens of later representations, even in portrayals that are more sympathetic to Anne, in no small part because they strike an archetypal chord. The idea that she had black hair, which has its origins in Sander, has persisted, in cartoons and contemporary art, and in other imaginative depictions. (In *The Tudors* shooting script, Anne is described as "a very beautiful woman with jet-black hair."[24]) And the sixth finger has been pretty firmly established in popular lists of historical trivia. In Spain, Sander's influence has been especially enduring. For hundreds of years the annual Corpus Christi festival in Toledo featured a float with a *tarasca* (or monster) represented by a small female figure known as "Ana Bolena." Spanish playwright Pedro Calderón de la Barca's 1627 drama, *The Schism in England*, which takes all its main ideas about Anne from Sander, portrays Henry, at the end, railing against Anne: "That woman, that fierce animal, that blind enchantment, false sphinx, that basilisk, that poisonous serpent, that enraged tigress, Anne Boleyn, arrest her!"[25] In Spain, Katherine remains the legitimate wife and protector of the true religion; Anne the heretical usurper.

The first prominent Protestant response to Sander came from George Wyatt, grandson of the poet, who begins his defense of Anne with an all-out attack on the "see of Rome" in the "full tide of all wickedness," "outrageous corruptions and foaming filth" — and goes on to celebrate "the bright beams of [Anne's] clearness," in trying to further "the blessed splendor of the Gospel."[26] The point of his book, he tells the reader, is to dispel the "black mists of malice . . . instructed to cover and overshadow her glory with their most black and venomous untruths."[27] As we've seen, he challenges Sander's physical descriptions of Anne point by point, admitting when there was a small basis in fact — such as Anne's vestigial nail — and, like Foxe, he praises Anne for her numerous virtues, including her support for reformist writing and activity,[28] and exonerates her from all charges of adultery and treason, declaring them "incredible" and "by the circumstances impossible" (which was true).[29] Unfortunately, the circulation of Wyatt's counter-Sander manuscript, unlike Sander's book, was highly limited until the beginning of the nineteenth century, when it was printed along with the first published edition of Cavendish's *The Life of Cardinal Wolsey.* The latter had been written in 1641 but was widely circulated before that, during Mary's reign, in manuscript form, contributing in its own way to the anti-Boleyn mythology. Cavendish was more intent on praising his former master's life than he was on smearing Anne, but smear Anne he did, blaming Anne for Wolsey's downfall and portraying her as the "instrument" of Venus, a beautiful temptress who was relatively innocent in the beginning, but grew hungry for jewels and power once she realized "the great love that [the king] bare her in the bottom of his stomach."[30]

It's from Cavendish and Wyatt that we get the stories of Anne's early romances with Henry Percy and Thomas Wyatt that would so captivate later fiction writers and moviemakers, from Madame d'Aulnoy's 1680 *The Novels of Elizabeth, Queen of England,* which re-creates a "secret history" written by Elizabeth that features Anne and Percy longing for each other throughout Anne's reign, to Philippa Gregory's *The Other Boleyn Girl,* in which Anne actually has sex with Percy before she is banished to France in disgrace (eventually to return and steal the king from her kindhearted sister). None of this is in Wyatt or Cavendish, but the theme of love thwarted by royal interests is. The affair with Percy, as Cavendish recounts it, was the more serious, reciprocal one, with the couple already precontracted for marriage when Henry instructed Wolsey to break it up. "Wherewith Mistress Anne Boleyn was greatly offended, saying, that if it ever lay in her power, she would work the cardinal as much displeasure"—which Cavendish believes she did, goading Henry to see Wolsey as responsible for the sluggish pace of the divorce and spiriting Henry away on an early morning picnic so that Wolsey, who was expecting to talk to the king that morning, would have no chance to defend himself.[31]

Wyatt, on the other hand, as his grandson emphasizes, was never a real contender for Anne's affection because he was already married. That didn't stop Henry, but Wyatt was a more honorable courtier, and so contented himself with writing poetry and charming Anne with flattery and entertaining conversations. Courtly and "innocent" though they were, Wyatt's attentions (his grandson tells us) were noticed by Henry, who "was whetted the more to discover to her his affection" and "in the end fell to win her by treaty of marriage."[32] In between the whetting of the king's interest and his serious pursuit of Anne, the king and Wyatt "sport" at bowls together, and a playful dispute arises about a particular winning throw. "Wiat, I tell thee it is mine," Henry pronounces with a smile and points to the bowl, ostentatiously displaying on his finger a ring that Anne had given him.[33] Wyatt, perceiving that the issue in question is not really who has won the throw but who had won Anne's heart, offers to measure the throw, with the "hope it will be mine."[34] The measuring device, which he takes from around his neck, is a string of lace on which hangs a small jewel that he had mischievously stolen from Anne. Henry recognizes that it is Anne's, and the game is over. "It may be so, but then I am deceived," Henry mutters, and stomps off, "showing some discontentment in his countenance."[35] But Anne clears things up, assuring Henry that Wyatt had pilfered the jewel, and "satisfied the king so effectually" that within days Henry is announcing his intentions to Anne's father, "to whom we may be sure the news was not a little joyful."[36]

From Chapuys until the middle of the nineteenth century, the Protestant/Catholic divide was the major determinant in how Anne was portrayed. Put starkly, the Protestants loved Anne; the Catholics despised her — and each side could be equally fanciful in dramatizing their allegiance. Sander demonized Anne. But John Banks's *Vertue Betray'd: or, Anna Bullen* (1682) sanctified her. Banks's play, which was hugely popular in its day, presents Anne as the hapless victim of "royal tyranny allied with Catholic conspiracy."[37] Banks's Henry is a megalomaniac, intent on establishing his own supremacy; Wolsey is the Platonic form of the decadent, corrupt priest. The former is heartless and cruel to Anne; the latter plots with Henry's ex-mistress, Elizabeth Blount, to bring Anne down. And Henry Percy is there as a reminder of what might have been. Banks's play was among the most popular of the emotion-rousing public entertainments emerging at that time, which many see as forerunners to the development of the romantic novel. But those entertainments, often dismissed nowadays as sentimental tearjerkers, could also be quite "political" — and *Vertue Betray'd* was an undisguised grenade in the Protestant/Catholic culture wars. At the end of the play, long-suffering Anne goes to her death in magnificent fashion, proclaiming to all the saints, cherubim, and other martyrs in heaven that she is coming to them, and ending many long and lofty speeches with an even loftier prediction of her daughter's future (and, through her, the glorious future of Protestantism).

> Thou, little Child [Elizabeth], Shalt live to see thy Mother's Wrongs o're paid In many Blessings on thy Womans State. From this dark Calumny, in which I set, As in a Cloud; thou, like a Star, shalt rise, And awe the Southern World: That holy Tyrant, Who binds all *Europe* with the Yoak of Conscience, Holding his Feet upon the Necks of Kings; Thou shalt destroy, and quite unloose his Bonds, and lay the Monster trembling at thy Feet. When this shall come to pass, the World shall see Thy Mothers Innocence reviv'd in thee.[38]

The "holy tyrant" and "monster," of course, is the pope. Elsewhere in the play, little Elizabeth slings her own anti-Catholic imagery around, referring to Wolsey as "that red thing there . . . that devil."[39] When Henry protests, "He is no devil, he's a cardinal," Elizabeth argues, "Why does he wear that huge, long coat then? Unless it be to hide his cloven feet."[40]

The play makes a hash of history, of course (Elizabeth was two and a half when Anne was executed, and Wolsey died in 1530 before Anne had even become queen), but then, too, so did Shakespeare's plays about historical figures. His *The Famous History of the Life of King Henry the Eighth* — subtitled *All Is True* (1623) — is full of creative alterations of history. But in the seventeenth century, marking the distinction between "fiction" and "history" wasn't yet an issue; in fact, "history" as a distinct genre of writing was just appearing. Also, fidelity to fact wasn't yet seen as equivalent to "truth." That was to come with the scientific revolution, which had only just begun; at this stage, "truth" wasn't a matter of correct dates or exact measurements, but a metaphysical ideal. Neither Shakespeare nor Banks was interested in an "objective" view of Henry's reign; they probably wouldn't have understood exactly what that meant or why anyone would be interested in achieving it. Presenting the moral/religious/political "truth" in a dramatic, emotionally stirring form that would be accessible and engaging to audiences was the goal. This is why Shakespeare could meaningfully subtitle his play *All Is True*, even though it was clearly not all factual. Literary critics have debated about just what "truth" Shakespeare was going for in this play (it's notoriously disjointed, and perhaps written in collaboration with John Fletcher), but in Banks's play, it's very clear that the truth of history was found in the subordination of individual fortunes to the birth of the Golden Age of Elizabeth.

8

Anne's Afterlives, from She-Tragedy to Historical Romance

Gender Wars

THERE ARE SOME other "truths" in Banks's play as well — and they have to do with what we would call "gender issues." It's a mistake, as I argued earlier, to see consciousness of such issues as a modern development. "Gender" as a concept is of extremely recent vintage, but an awareness of male/female inequality is not, and debates surrounding female fitness to rule, sexual differences between men and women, and so on are as old as Plato and Aristotle. What had begun to change in those debates, beginning (as we've seen) with some medieval writers and picking up speed in the seventeenth century, is the participation of women themselves in those debates. And around the time that Banks was writing, interesting things were happening in France, where the salon had long been an arena for women poets, storytellers, and visionaries to express their "politics," sometimes in deceptively amusing forms.

An important but relatively unknown figure in this development was Marie-Catherine Le Jumel de Barneville — or as she was known in her anonymous works, Madame d'Aulnoy. D'Aulnoy wrote memoirs and travel literature, both of which became popular in England at the beginning of the eighteenth century. However, her most famous writings were her many fantastical fairy tales. Some literary scholars, in fact, credit d'Aulnoy with originating the genre, which in her day was designed to entertain adults in the French salon rather than children at bedtime. D'Aulnoy's most popular tales often featured enterprising, clever girls whose lives were tyrannized by wicked kings and fathers — very different from the stories of the better-known Charles Perrault, whose heroines are marked by their modesty, obedience, and reliance on the ingenuity of a prince to save them from the spell of a wicked stepmother or witch. But d'Aulnoy's less conventional heroines found another home in the "secret histories" she (and others) published dealing with historical figures from other times and places but, under that disguise, critiquing the court and culture of Louis XIV. Among these works was d'Aulnoy's *The Novels of Elizabeth, Queen of England, Containing the History of Queen Ann of Bullen.* Despite its title (which was a diversionary tactic), it's really about Anne, not Elizabeth, and as d'Aulnoy tells it, the book is virtually a "real life" dystopian version of the fairy-tale form she favored — clever, generous, and beautiful girl, wicked king, but no happy ending.

D'Aulnoy's "secret histories" of English royalty were quickly translated and circulated in England in the 1680s, where they clearly wound up in Banks's hands, who imported key plot elements of d'Aulnoy's version of the Anne Boleyn story into his own play. One of those elements is a tortured, unending relationship with Percy (meant to represent what male-female relationships could be like if allowed to develop freely and equally); another is the scheming of the king's former mistress, Elizabeth Blount, who, abandoned by Henry, collaborates with Wolsey in plotting against Anne. But it's not plot devices but the gender of the protagonist that was the most radical innovation Banks took from Aulnoy. In Shakespeare's play, Anne Boleyn hardly figures at all except as a sexual motive for Henry and the incubator of Elizabeth. In *Vertue Betray'd,* as in d'Aulnoy's "secret history," Anne's trials and tribulations are the heart and spine of the work. This was something new. In fact, having any kind of tragic female hero(ine) was new. Katherine suffers nobly and dramatically in Shakespeare's play, but she can't be said to be the "heroine" of a play that ends in the celebration of the birth of Elizabeth. In *Vertue Betray'd*, it is Anne's life and death that generate Elizabeth and are vindicated by Elizabeth. She is the tragic hero of the play. As such, she is not simply a martyr to a cause, as she appears in Foxe and Wyatt, but someone whom we are encouraged to suffer along with as we imagine Henry's betrayals, the terror of imprisonment, and the grief over the loss of her daughter.

Although the experience of sympathetic identification with the emotions and fate of an entrapped or abused heroine is commonplace to those of us raised on romantic fiction, it was so novel at the end of the seventeenth century that it was hailed (or derided, depending on your point of view) as a new genre, known as the "she-tragedy." Anne, of course, was a perfect subject for this genre, which introduced some metaphors — such as the "prison" of subordination — that later would become staples of Enlightenment feminist writing. Anne was actually imprisoned, of course, but Banks has her metaphorically imprisoned as well, long before the arrest. In her first appearance in the play, just after her coronation, she is distraught over the loss of autonomy she has suffered through marriage to the king: "Has then a Throne cost me so dear a Price," she muses, "as forfeit my Liberty of Thinking? Do Princes barter for their Crowns their Freedoms? Good Heav'n! Not think! Nor pray if I have need — If I am Queen, why am I not obey'd?"[1] Here, the demand to think her own thoughts (most particularly with respect to religion) — and, as queen, to have them respected — which Anne's contemporaries had found so outrageous in her behavior, is presented as a legitimate "right." Banks's Henry is also the first portrayal — though definitely not the last — to equate Henry as political tyrant with Henry as sexual predator, who controls the state with the same ruthless, invasive force with which he dominates his wife. Describing sex with a resistant Anne, he recalls, not without pleasure, how "[s]he struggles like the Quarry in the Toil: And yields herself unto my loath'd Embraces."[2]

❦ Jonathan Swift's Marginalia on Henry VIII, Found Handwritten in One of His Books

"I wish he had been flayed, his skin stuffed and hanged upon a gibbet. His bulky guts and flesh left to be devoured by birds and beasts for a warning to his successors forever. Amen."[3]

This was radical sexual politics for England at the time. But male chroniclers of the period did not see the politics; they only saw the focus on "domestic" relations, which was viewed as of "special" interest to female viewers, but of little relevance to the important issues of the day. When "history" began to carve itself out as a genre, it carried the distinction along with it in the contrast between "particular history" and "general history" — a distinction that at least one influential historian, David Starkey, maintains to this day, with his complaints against "feminised history," which has turned "proper history" into a profitable "soap opera."[4] "Unhappy marriages are big box office," he says.[5] But neither d'Aulnoy nor Banks was interested in creating romance simply for the sake of soaking audiences' handkerchiefs; d'Aulnoy used the Henry/Anne story to raise questions about the court culture of her own time, and *Vertue Betray'd,* as Tracey Miller-Tomlinson argues, uses its virtuous heroine and tyrannical villains to engage political controversies of the time, including the threat of counterreformation conspiracies to control the English throne and thwart a Protestant succession. Even in terms of "gender politics," Anne and Henry's union was no ordinary marriage. Anne's suffering, although it may have moved female audiences of *Vertue Betray'd,* was not merely that of a wife tyrannized and betrayed by a husband, but a female monarch struggling for religious autonomy and her own authority in the face of the implacable absolutism of a male-dominated state and church. That issue was hardly "domestic"; it had shaped the course of English history since Henry decided that only a male heir would do.

ꝰ Jane Austen on Anne and Henry (from Her Playful *The History of England,* Composed in 1791, When Austen Was Sixteen)

"It is . . . but Justice, & my Duty to declare that this amiable Woman was entirely innocent of the Crimes with which she was accused, of which her Beauty, her Elegance, & her Sprightliness were sufficient proofs, not to mention her solemn protestations of Innocence, the weakness of the Charges against her, & the King's Character . . . The Crimes & Cruelties of this Prince, were too numerous to be mentioned, (as this history I trust has fully shown) & nothing can be said in his vindication, but that his abolishing Religious Houses & leaving them to the ruinous depredations of time has been of infinite use to the landscape of England in general, which probably was a principal motive for his doing it, since otherwise why should a Man who was of no Religion himself be at so much trouble to abolish one which had for ages been established in the Kingdom."[6]

Although Anne may have served larger political and religious causes in *Vertue Betray'd,* the play also made her — for the first time in the English-speaking world — a subject with a story in her own right, and not just Henry's Helen of Troy, or martyr for the cause of reform, or second in a series of wedded and dead/discarded wives. But Elizabeth Benger's 1821 *Memoirs of the Life of Anne Boleyn, Queen of King Henry VIII* was an even more significant contribution. At first glance, Benger's novel, the first full-length book devoted entirely to Anne, doesn't seem that different, in its politics, from Foxe, Wyatt, or Banks. Benger believed the Protestant Reformation to be a glorious achievement, and she credited Anne with significant influence in bringing it about. She also emphatically disputes the notion that Anne was sexually manipulative and power hungry: "She had employed no artifice to obtain pre-eminence in the King's regard . . . and rejected his passion with disdain, till it assumed the character of honorable love. Even after Henry approached her with a legitimate object, she is said to have expressed repugnance to the idea of supplanting her Queen."[7] This kind of refutation of Anne's bad reputation was pretty standard stuff for pro-Protestant texts, which were still wrangling with Sander's slander. Where Benger breaks new ground, however, is not only in the historical detail that she draws on, but also in her explicit — and surprisingly sophisticated — analysis of the role played by gender expectations in the breakdown of Anne and Henry's relationship.

Benger begins by challenging any expectation that Henry, the proud and domineering monarch, was someone who could "scarcely tolerate any superiority in a woman."[8] This assumption would be a mistake, for when he met Anne, "he had not entirely lost the sensibilities of his youth, [which] had been favorable to the female character."[9] The examples of the women who brought him up, as well as other "distinguished women of that age" such as Margaret of Austria and Marguerite de Navarre, had taught him to admire "individuals who might sanction the pretensions of their sex to intellectual equality."[10] Benger was clearly not an "essentializer" of men, and was capable of appreciating the qualities in Henry that drew him to Anne's intellect and ambition. She also credits Henry as admiring Anne's boldness, as well as her "gaiety" and "softness" — an appealing mix of masculine energies and feminine charms that made her a perfect match for Henry, then in the prime of his life and no longer stimulated by Katherine's more conventionally queenly strengths.[11] Katherine was a powerful woman — much more forceful than she is made out to be in most depictions of her — but she did not engage in courtly fun and games, and generally kept her views to herself and her close advisers. Anne's upbringing, being both courtly and French, had taught her that being flirtatious and intellectually challenging was not outside the rules of appropriate behavior. Henry was refreshed by her, desired her, respected her, and fought for her.

However, Henry was also accustomed to the "unbounded indulgence of [his] imperious will" and little able to "brook the necessity of submitting to privation or restraint."[12] And Anne, as Benger argues, changed as she developed as a women and a queen.

Her mind expanded, her character developed; instead of being merely the private gentlewoman, whose highest ambition was to attract or please, she was become the partner of the throne, the generous queen, who aspired to be a true and affectionate mother of the people.

The enthusiasm she delighted to inspire was far from pleasing to Henry, now that the fervor of passion had subsided, and that he no longer required talents or courage, but unwearied adulation and unconditional obedience. To a jealous egotist her best qualities had, perhaps, the effect of diminishing her attractions; by the zeal with which she carried into effect her plans of reformation, she must have offended one accustomed to consider himself as the sole and exclusive object of attention. It was, perhaps, fatal to her safety, that, in the first transports of affection, Henry had admitted her to full participation of all the honor and sovereignty formerly conceded to Katherine, and that he not only caused her to be proclaimed Queen Consort of England, but Lady of Ireland. When love declined, it might be suggested that he had sacrificed dignity, and even hazarded security, by this prodigal dispensation.[13]

And then came Jane Seymour. Here, Benger stresses that Jane had none of Anne's graces or sensibilities, and appealed to Henry for that very reason. For, having "lost his youthful susceptibility of imagination, and perhaps original delicacy of taste . . . it is probable that the inferiority of Jane's mental attainments . . . contributed to turn the balance in her favor."[14]

Whether or not you accept this analysis of Anne's fall from favor with Henry, the interpersonal dynamics that Benger focuses on are strikingly "gendered." Without accusing Henry of being born a possessive, macho tyrant, Benger does argue that Anne's strength and independence did eventually become a psychological (and possibly political) threat to him. At that point, the king becomes vulnerable to the charms of a younger, less formidable female. Starkey might dismiss this analysis as "soap opera," but some version of it has become a staple of twentieth-century histories of Henry VIII, including Starkey's. Here he considers why Henry might have fallen for Jane, a woman of "no family, no beauty, no talent."

But maybe Jane's very ordinariness was the point. Anne had been exciting as a mistress . . . But [now] Henry wanted domestic peace and the quiet life. He also, more disturbingly, wanted submission. For increasing age and the Supremacy's relentless elevation of the monarchy had made him ever more impatient of contradiction and disagreement. Only obedience, prompt, absolute and unconditional, would do. And he could have none of this with Anne. Jane, on the other hand, was everything that Anne was not. She was calm, quiet, softspoken (when she spoke at all) and profoundly submissive at least to Henry. In short, after Anne's flagrant defiance of convention, Jane was the sixteenth-century's ideal woman (or at least the sixteenth-century *male*'s ideal woman).[15]

It's often been the case in the history of "history" that when women do something, it's considered tangential and trivial, while when men do it, it's labeled a breakthrough of decisive historical importance. Male historians disdained Benger, along with Agnes and Elizabeth Strickland and other biographers of famous women who began to produce their "memoirs" and "lives" during the Victorian era. They were derided as "sentimental," "gossipy," "minute," "trifling," "twaddling," "amusing," and "tiddle-tattle," and charged with a chief interest in frivolous matters such as dress, diet, education, and manners — in other words, the stuff of what we nowadays call "social and material history." Some prominent male historians, including Thomas Babington Macaulay (*The History of England*, 1848), were enthusiastically praised for tackling "domestic and everyday life" and "the revolutions which have taken place in dress, furniture, repasts, and public amusements."[16] But Macaulay's social history was viewed as "general" interest and an expansion of the proper domain of the historian, whereas attending to a woman's "sphere" — even that of royalty — was seen as a specialized, miniaturizing focus.[17] In the twentieth century, philosopher Simone de Beauvoir gave us a concept — the woman as "other" — that aptly describes this dualism: What men do is "essential," representative of the interests of "human beings," and what women do is seen as particular to their sex. As such, all women writers, from the extremely sophisticated Benger, whose details of the everyday worlds of the French and English courts are always of social significance, to a trifle such as the Countess of Blessington's 1848 *Book of Beauty, or Regal Gallery,* which is more a prescription for decorous female conduct than a biography of Anne, were lumped together as the work of "literary ladies." Often, the books themselves were materially linked to women's sphere: Francis Palgrave, in an 1843 review of Mrs. Forbes Bush's *Memoirs of the Queens of France,* wishes the writer would have remained content with "marking pinafores and labeling pots of jam."[18] Margaret Oliphant, a fellow author, derides the Stricklands' *Lives of the Queens of England* as "a shower of pretty books in red and blue, gilded and illustrated, light and dainty and personal, that fall upon us from [their] hands."[19]

The Stricklands can make one squirm, but it's not because they deal with the details of clothing and court manners. Those passages, in fact, are among the most interesting (and often plundered by male historians looking for colorful detail to enliven their own work). And the books are far from "light and dainty" in their heavy moralizing, done in the typically prudish language of instruction in proper feminine comportment. Anne "lacked the feminine delicacy which would make a young and beautiful woman tremble at the impropriety of becoming an object of contention between two married men."[20] Not only had she "overstepped the restraints of moral rectitude" simply by flirting with the king but at the very "hour that Anne Boleyn did this, she took her first step towards a scaffold, and prepared for herself a doom which fully exemplified that warning, '*Those who sow the whirlwind, must expect to reap the storm*' [emphasis mine]."[21] In the service of (their own or the reader's) "delicacy," they also eliminated some historically irrefutable facts, such as Anne's sleeping with Henry before their marriage. After all, as Jane Hunter describes in *How Young Ladies Became Girls,* "measured reading of improving texts [that is, texts aimed at instilling virtue in the reader] was part of the regimen of many Victorian girls."[22] And "the reading of history was especially praiseworthy."[23] It was important that reading not degenerate into a salacious vice, corrupting young women with tales of extramarital sex between kings and their female subjects.

But prudishness with regard to Anne and Henry's sex life was not limited to female writers; virtually no Victorian historian, male or female, mentioned it. (Elizabeth, it was either stated or implied, was very premature.) And idealized "feminine" descriptions, mostly of Katherine but sometimes of Anne, too, blossomed in all their sticky sweet fragrance on the pages of male writers as well. Tom Taylor's popular 1875 play, *Anne Boleyn*, gives us an Anne who is haunted by the plight of "that poor Queen whose place I took"[24] and whose love for the king is so virtuous that when she sees what a mess their romance is causing, she reminds him that "It's not yet too late for pausing. Think, my lord, if you repent, there's no harm done — 'tis but to chase me from you, to look back on a four years' golden dream."[25] The king refuses; it's his lust, not Anne's connivance, that moves events forward. Even more striking — and probably more influential — in creating a popular image of Anne as the romantic victim of Henry's tyranny were two paintings: *Anne Boleyn in the Tower* (Edouard Cibot, 1835) and an 1838 depiction of Anne saying a final farewell to Elizabeth by Gustave Wappers. If the Victorians "feminized" history, it had more to do with a gender ideology that men and women shared rather than which sex held the pen (or the brush).

What Victorian Kids Were Taught About Anne Boleyn

From Oliver Goldsmith's *The History of England* (1771):

"It happened that among the maids of honour, then attending the queen, there was one Anna Bullen, the daughter of Sir Thomas Bullen, a gentleman of distinction, and related to most of the nobility. The beauty of Anna surpassed whatever had hitherto appeared at this voluptuous court; and her education, which had been at Paris, tended to set off her personal charms. Her features were regular, mild, and attractive, her stature elegant, though below the middling size, while her wit and vivacity exceeded even her other allurements. Henry, who had never learned the art of restraining any passion that he desired to gratify, saw and loved her; but after several efforts to induce her to comply with his criminal desires, he found that without marriage, he could have no chance of succeeding. This obstacle, therefore, he hardily undertook to remove; and as his own queen was now become hateful to him, in order to procure a divorce, he alleged that his conscience rebuked him for having so long lived in incest with the wife of his brother . . .

". . . Anna Bullen, his queen, had always been a favourer of the reformation, and consequently had many enemies on that account, who only waited some fit occasion to destroy her credit with the king; and that occasion presented itself but too soon. The king's passion was by this time quite palled with satiety; he was now fallen in love with another, and languished for the possession of Jane Seymour, who had for some time been maid of honour to the queen . . .

". . . The queen and her brother were tried by a jury of peers . . . Part of the charge against her was, that she had declared to her attendants that the king never had her heart; which was considered a slander upon the throne, and strained into a breach of a law-statute, by which it was declared criminal to throw any slander upon the king, queen, or their issue. The unhappy queen, although unassisted by counsel, defended herself with great judgement and presence of mind . . . but the king's authority was not to be controlled; she was declared guilty . . .

". . . She was beheaded by the executioner of Calais, who was brought over, as much more expert than any in England. The very next day after her execution, Henry married the lady Jane Seymour, his cruel heart being no way softened by the wretched fate of one that had been so lately the object of his warmest affections."[26]

From Charles Dickens's *A Child's History of England* (1854):

"We now come to King Henry the Eighth whom it has been too much the fashion to call 'Bluff King Hal' or 'Burly King Henry' and other fine names but whom I shall take the liberty to call, plainly, one of the most detestable villains that ever drew breath . . . He was a big, burly, noisy, smelly, small-eyed, large-faced, double-chinned, swinish looking fellow in later life (as we know from the likenesses of him, painted by the famous Hans Holbein), and it is not easy to believe that so bad a character can ever have been veiled under a prepossessing appearance . . . He was a most intolerable ruffian, a disgrace to human nature, and a blot of blood and grease upon the History of England.

". . . All this time [while Henry was trying to divorce Katherine], the king and Anne Boleyn were writing letters to each other almost daily, full of impatience to have the case settled; and Anne Boleyn was showing herself (as I think) very worthy of the fate which afterward befell her."[27]

From Lady Maria Callcott's *Little Arthur's England* (first published in 1835 and widely used in home schooling):

"I told you Anne Boleyn was very young and beautiful. She was also clever and pleasant and I believe really good. But the king and some of his wicked friends pretended that she had done several bad things; and, as Henry had become very cruel as well as changeable, he ordered poor Anne's head to be cut off. On the day she was to suffer death she sent to beg the king to be kind to her little daughter Elizabeth. She said to the last moment that she was innocent; she prayed God to bless the king and the people, and then she knelt down, and her head was cut off."[28]

From Samuel Gardiner's *English History for Students* (1881):

"After Henry had been married for some time he grew tired of his wife, Queen Catharine, and wanted to marry a sparkling beauty named Anne Boleyn. He suddenly discovered that he had done wrong in marrying his brother's widow . . . Anne brought him a daughter Elizabeth, who was to be more famous than any son could be . . . Her mother was suddenly accused of the vilest misconduct to the king her husband. Whether she was guilty or innocent cannot now be known."[29]

From Lydia Hoyt Farmer's *The Girl's Book of Famous Queens* (1887):

"On the day of Catharine's burial, King Henry wore mourning, but Anne Boleyn clothed herself and all her ladies in yellow, exclaiming 'Now am I queen!' . . . Neither King Henry's arrogant power nor Anne Boleyn's pernicious influence could prevent the widespread and lasting effect of the Christian death-bed of Catharine . . . And now Anne herself was to suffer the penalty of her wicked ambition."[30]

The old Protestant/Catholic divide was still in operation too. And despite the growing tendency to distinguish between "commercial" biographies, appealing to the sensibilities of female readers, and "real" history, which had "accuracy and importance" as its guiding lights, no works of the period, by men or women, were free of undisguised, and often strident, moral agendas and biases. Henry William Herbert, in *Memoirs of Henry the Eighth of England: With the Fortunes, Fates, and Characters of His Six Wives* (1856), refers condescendingly in his preface to "the lighter and more gossiping sketches of the lady-biographers of the queens" and accuses both Benger and the Stricklands of being motivated by "false sympathy for their sex."[31] This is the way, he says, "in which ladies write history concerning ladies."[32] But Herbert's view of Anne and Katherine is not much different from the old Catholic propaganda: Anne was a "vain," "wily," and "cruel persecutress," while Katherine was a living saint: "I know of no woman, recorded in veritable history, or portrayed in romance, who approaches so nearly to perfection . . . there was no speck to mar the loveliness, no shadow to dim the perfection, of her faultless, Christian womanhood."[33] He criticizes John Knox for his "fierce, intolerant, fanatic" hostility toward Queen Mary, but although Knox was a blatant misogynist, it is only Benger and the Stricklands who are charged with "buckler[ing] the cause of their sex, rather than that of truth."[34] He is especially furious with Benger for having not even "the smallest regard to consistency or truth"[35]; but his own work is peppered with both the old mythology, taken unquestioningly from Chapuys and Sander, and some new embellishments, as novelistic as anything found in the "ladies' histories."

> I see, in her every move, a deep determination to win the game, at all
> hazards; I see it in her coyness at one time, in her consent in another;
> and above all, I see it in the implacable, unrelenting hatred with which
> she pursued all those who opposed her marriage to the king, — Wol-
> sey to ruin; More and Fisher to the block . . . I read base rivalry [with
> Katherine] and cruel triumph; I mark her ungentle persecution of the
> fallen queen's orphan child, bastardized for her aggrandizement; I see
> the triumphal dress of yellow[36], worn on that fallen rival's funeral day;
> I hear the exulting speech — "At length I am the queen of England" —
> it needs not the imagination of a Shakespeare to conceive, if it might
> tax his powers to create, the phantom of the abused, departed royalty,
> floating in vengeful majesty athwart the path of the exulting beauty,
> and replying to the wicked vaunt, "Not long! not long!"[37]

Actually, although Herbert presents himself as a professional historian, his "histories" were not much more than a hobby. A sportswriter by profession, Herbert was better known as the author of *Frank Forester's Fish and Fishing of the United States and British Provinces of North America*. But recognized historians, too, still openly took sides in the "Anne versus Katherine" construct, without apparently thinking that they were being anything but "objective." At this point (from about 1850 onward) most of the *Letters and Papers, Foreign and Domestic, of the Reign of Henry VIII*, as well as foreign state calendars and correspondence, were available, resulting in much more detailed and documented work, including recognition of Chapuys' role in the creation of "bad Anne" and "good Katherine."[38] But it's going too far to write, as Alison Weir does, that this "new tradition in historical study" was increasingly "free of religious bias" and "more rational" in its assessment of Henry's queens.[39] The two exemplars she refers to — James Anthony Froude and Paul Friedmann — may debunk the romantic view of Anne as the tragically wronged heroine of the Protestant Reformation. But in its place, as we saw in chapter 1, they substitute a refurbished version of Chapuys' scheming adventuress. Froude is an enthusiast for the Protestant cause, but Anne was an "unworthy," "foolish and bad woman" who had "stained the purity" of Henry's cause and made herself universally "detested for her insolence and dreaded for her intrigues."[40] After conceding that "imperfect credit" must be given to Chapuys' stories, he goes on to claim that "the existence of such stories shows the reputation which Anne had earned for herself, and which in part she deserves."[41] He concludes, "Anne, it is likely, was really dangerous."[42] Friedmann (*Anne Boleyn: A Chapter of English History*, 1884) agrees. Although he admits that there "was no trustworthy evidence to sustain the specific charges," he is "by no means convinced that Anne did not commit offenses quite as grave as most of those of which she was accused."[43] And Albert Frederick Pollard (*Henry VIII*) goes still further than Friedmann concerning Anne's guilt: "[I]t is not credible that the juries should have found her accomplices guilty, that twenty-six peers, including her uncle, should have condemned Anne herself, without some colourable justification."[44] His assessment of Anne's character: "Her place in English history is due solely to the circumstance that she appealed to the less refined part of Henry's nature; she was pre-eminent neither in beauty nor in intellect, and her virtue was not of a character to command or deserve the respect of her own or subsequent ages."[45]

In no way am I claiming that Froude, Friedmann, and Pollard were nothing more than anti-Anne polemicists. Their detailed, informative histories represent an enormous advance in our knowledge of the king's "great matter" and the events that followed. But whether religious, gender, or national antipathies are the cause, or frustration with the idealized Anne of the Elizabethans and Romantics, or some combination of all of these, Froude, Friedmann, and Pollard return us to the scheming adventuress of Chapuys' letters. They don't achieve balance; they simply tip the scales in the opposite direction.

Anne Makes Her Debut in the Novel

As she sat there alone in the room, her chin in her hand, her dark eyes heavy with anxieties, the thought that had slipped some time ago, shamefaced and sly, into the back of her mind edged more and more into the open . . . What if she played her last card — her precious card — herself! . . .

. . . 'I dare not,' she whispered to herself, and then in a strangled voice, 'I dare!'

She grew aware at last that her clasped hands were clutching each other so tightly that the rings were cutting into the flesh. She drew off the ring from the sharpest cut. It was one of Henry's earliest gifts to her, a plain gold band with 'Thy virtue is thy honor,' graved within it . . . Her virtue — God alone knew how she had hugged that comfort to her smarting pride against the secret sneers she divined about her. Yet now . . . [t]he ring slipped from her fingers and rolled out across the floor. A bit of rush blocked it and it toppled and dropped through an open knot hole. The augury seemed to her complete. She laughed — and then something, like a hand upon her throat, seemed to strangle the laughter at its source and she quivered back among the cushions, her hands hiding her face like some poor shamed thing.

That year the Christmas revels were gayer than ever and King Henry was scarce an instant to be parted from his marchioness.[46]

This is as close as Mary Hastings Bradley, in *The Favor of Kings* (1912), the first full-length novel about Anne, comes to describing the moment when Anne decided to let Henry have — gasp — sex with her. It was a huge advance in sexual candor, however, over the Victorians, who had mangled Elizabeth's stage of development at birth and/ or Anne and Henry's marriage date in order to avoid acknowledging that Anne and Henry had bedded together before marriage. Bradley, an English major and graduate of Smith College who went on to lead quite an adventurous life, was committed to staying as true to "actual situations . . . real incident, and dialogue" as possible and did extensive research among the collected foreign and domestic letters and papers of Henry's reign; the then-prominent histories of Friedmann, the Stricklands, David Hume, and others; and at historical sites.[47] In her foreword, she acknowledges her use of these sources and also indicates where she has "taken liberties" with history (an admission that was quite common among novelists in the first half of the century and that has, unfortunately, gone completely out of fashion today). But she stresses that her aim is not to "enter an historical controversy" but "to suggest the truth of the colors of the picture I have tried to paint, and to offer the Anne Boleyn of this story, a very human girl."[48]

I want to pause for a moment over those two words: "human" and "girl." Bradley doesn't say exactly what she meant, but I speculate that "human" is to be counterposed to "Historical Figure" and "girl" is to be contrasted with "queen" as well as "woman." Bradley wanted Anne to be someone whom readers could identify with, not observe from afar as a player in a grand historical pageant, "The Tudor Saga" or "The Reformation Crisis." She wasn't interested in either redeeming or vilifying Anne. She wanted readers to understand her. And a large part of what would make this understanding possible is the imaginative conjuring of Anne's feelings and thoughts before she had been subjected to and transformed by "the favor of kings" — a title Bradley means sardonically — but was still a creature of fantasies and dreams, "gay and fearless and rashly proud, as the likeness of that Anne who dared and lost so long ago and whose blood was the first of any woman's to stain an English scaffold."[49] And so, for the first time, an author ventures into the "inner life" of Anne, the young girl.

> [Wolsey's] cold arrogance that treated her mercilessly as a wooden pawn to be moved hither and yon quickened her to the fiercest resentment her fiery little heart had ever thrilled with . . . It was just such a night as [this] one that she had last met Percy, and under all the fierce surge of her anger came stealing the pain of the nevermore. Nevermore would they meet there — it might be they would never meet again. The poignancy of such denial was strange to her, but she divined that it was but the beginning of sorrow. Memories that had suddenly become an agony enwrapped her, and an aching presentiment of grief to come.[50]

In making Anne "human," Bradley's narrative introduces some elements that are absent from previous ideas about Anne but that have since become stock features of later fictional portrayals. One is the manipulation of Anne by her father and uncle, whose ambitions for the family are behind their desire for the match between her and the king. With all that we now know about social history, the history of the family, and the position of women in the sixteenth century, it seems incredible that Anne would have been the all-powerful, autonomous prime mover that Chapuys and the histories that take his word for it make her out to be during the six years that the king pursued her. But ideology and hostility were much stronger forces than common sense in those accounts, and sociological thinking, completely unknown to the early polemicists and still a very young discipline even at the end of the nineteenth century, did not play much of a role in the first histories and biographies of Anne and Henry. Neither did the idea that Anne, as a young woman, might have been a less formidable personality than she would become as queen. Only the Stricklands and Benger seem to recognize that Anne, in fact, was once a young girl. Perhaps the fact that they, too, were once girls makes it harder for them to see Anne, as Froude, Friedmann, and Pollard do, as having sprung fully formed from the French court — a mature, ambitious agent of her own destiny.

But then, too, so little is actually known about Anne's life as a girl that historians, although they indulge in creative license in their imaginings of Anne the woman, may have felt that Anne's early life was off-limits. Novelists, who freely admitted to filling in the blanks, felt no such limitations. Sometimes the early twentieth-century portraits were little more than anachronistic transplants of the Gibson girl into the sixteenth century, as in Reginald Drew's 1912 *Anne Boleyn*.

> [Young Anne] was a vision of loveliness. She was radiant and dimpled, and her beautiful face, pink-hued and lily white, rippled with laughter and bubbled with vivacity. She had sparkling eyes, wavy, golden-brown hair which framed her face like a picture, and which her coif could not either confine or conceal. She rode her palfrey perfectly, flicking her whip with her daintily gloved hand; her whole being personified emotion, her carriage was that of a queen, and her musical laughter sounded like rippling water to the thirsting.[51]

Drew wasn't the last to turn Anne into a creature of his own fantasies while ignoring the historical evidence (slim as that evidence is, we do know a few things, and among them is that she did not have "golden-brown hair"). It's been a continuing tendency of Anne's imaginers, whether they are painters, novelists, or casting directors, to project the beauty standards and feminine ideals of their own day onto Anne. The Victorians were fond of depicting Anne, in scenes with Henry, as a mature, curvaceous (but, of course, corseted) fair-haired beauty, properly clinging to her husband; interestingly enough, she looks most like the "real" Anne — dark-haired and slender — in the paintings that mourn her fall. In the first decades of the twentieth century, Anne starts to look — and act — like the audacious "new girls" of the twenties and thirties, full of spunk and fun, "speeding joyously along on her bicycle [substitute "horse"] . . . women's rights perched on the handlebars and cramping modes and manners strewn on her track."[52] She's slender and clever, flirtatious and emotionally spontaneous; she doesn't know when to hold her tongue.

Bradley's Anne is of this model, which actually suits what we know of the historical Anne much better than the Victorian versions. It's a very sympathetic picture, while not an idealizing one. Although Anne's girlish high spirits, in the novel, are ultimately disfigured by ambition, it is the machinations of her father and uncle that are responsible for her loss of innocence. Yet, the "seeds" of her destruction are also "in" her — not in her vanity or defiance of sexual morality, as the Stricklands have it, but in her proud, independent nature. In the passage that follows, Bradley presents the young Anne to us through the (retrospective) perspective of poet Thomas Wyatt, who never gives up his thwarted love for Anne and who represents the one who sees "the truth" in the novel.

He looked at her now [after Anne becomes queen], jeweled and gauded till her slender body was like the glittering image of some idol . . . [B]ehind her chair in smiling converse, were her father and uncle, suave images of insincerity, assiduously grimacing upon her, and at the sight Wyatt's heart filled with yet heavier dejection. Those elegants were like vultures feeding on her youth, he thought, in bitter clarity of vision . . . He had never thought before of Anne as over-young and helpless, but now . . . for all her heavy robes of state, her jewels, her air of command, he saw the girl in her as he had never seen it when she was yet younger; the flushed face that smiled so proudly under the drift of dark hair was a child's face, its woman soul unawakened, its eyes smiling in a dream, unopened to the abyss ahead.[53]

The paradigm of Anne as a vivacious, high-spirited young girl whose life was profoundly—and tragically—altered by becoming Henry's queen has remained the narrative spine of the twentieth-century novels that are sympathetic to her. But sympathy is not the same as idealization, and the Anne of the early twentieth century has very "human" faults. Some of those faults—such as pride and ambition—are not so different from the charges laid against her by Friedmann, Froude, and Pollard. But in the early novels, they no longer mark her as a "type": a *bad* woman. This is due partly to the more flexible imagination of the creative writer. And it's due partly to changes in the ideology of femininity: Sexuality was no longer consistently seen as the line that divided good girls from bad girls, and female "ambition" was more likely to be viewed with uneasy ambivalence rather than pure horror. But Freudian and developmental psychology, as well as the perspectives of sociologists and anthropologists, had also created new frameworks for imagining the interaction of external environment and personality; and the power of the change in Anne's circumstances, once the king had singled her out—and then even more dramatically when she became queen—began to be seen as more significant to her story.

The Anne of most twentieth-century fiction is not a bred-in-the-bone she-devil. Rather, she is a strong-willed young woman with personal qualities that are quite attractive but, when unleashed by her elevation, proved dangerous to her. Even as a young girl, she was "audacious," "confident," and above all, "proud," as Bradley, through Wyatt, describes her. "By the law of her nature," she writes elsewhere in the novel, "she might command, coax, dominate, divert, bewitch, enthrall; but implore—never!"[54] It's Anne's proud nature, in Bradley, that distinguishes her from her pliant sister and that motivates her sexual resistance to the king.[55] Her Anne does not withhold her favors out of manipulative ambition, as later narratives would have it, but because she was "too high of pride, too maiden of spirit, to surrender to such ignoble fate"— and because she was still in love with Percy.[56] For the first third of the novel, Anne hopes that her persistent refusal would "weary Henry" and that "he would find some newer face, some fresher fancy."[57] The turning point comes only when she realizes that Henry means to make her queen.

Anne is surprised and confused by this prospect rather than (as in other depictions) having schemed to bring it about: "The glade seemed to whirl about her. She felt the rushing of vast wings, the elation of airy heights. To be queen — to be Queen of England!"[58] But the thrill is not only due to the sudden, unexpected fantasy of being queen. Anne's pride, wounded by Wolsey's ability to rearrange her fate — and in this novel, Katherine's unwillingness to intercede — is also vindicated, and the "recklessness" of her nature is challenged. "A fierce, cruel wave of joy swept over. To be queen on Katherine's throne — Oh, what an exquisite, what an infinitely ironic retaliation! Dared she trust herself to the mad project? Dared she undertake the humbling of one queen, the crowning of another? Aye, she dared! Her blood rushed on in faster time: with feverish recklessness it sang songs of triumph and power in her veins. There was little that wild blood would not dare!"[59]

This Anne is no maiden whose virtue was plundered by a rapacious monarch. But neither is she the temptress/witch incarnate. She's a young woman whose temperament, for all her flirtatiousness, was more unnervingly "masculine" than was usual for her time: confident, excited by her own potential to effect action in the world, capable of fierce resentments, daring ambitions, bold action — and unwilling to be anyone's plaything or political tool. As Francis Hackett sums it up: She was the mother of Elizabeth, not "an understudy of Queen Victoria."[60] And she has a sexual life, too, although her erotic temperament and tastes vary wildly from novel to novel, and — especially as historical fiction became a thriving commercial specialty — could be quite extravagant. Elizabeth Louisa Moresby, writing under the pen name of E. Barrington (*Anne Boleyn*, 1932), while insisting that her story "is as true to history as the consultation of many authorities can make it," apparently consulted some very odd authorities because her Anne, while sexually frigid with everyone else and thoroughly repulsed by Henry, is smitten with Dionysian Smeaton.

She could fancy him dancing alone in the wild woodlands at Hever — yes, in that haunted spot where the oaks fell back and left an open space for moonlight. There, looking up at the searing moon with wild hair flying back from his forehead, he would caper like a goat and beckon, and the woodland creatures would crowd in a furry ring . . . He smelt of woods and fresh turned earth dewy in the night . . . A faun come to Court who had never changed his ways for Henry or another! All this he seemed to her, perhaps wholly mistakenly, for the man lived his life like others, so they told her. But she dangerously liked his love-making — wild, careless love with drifts of bird-music and no more responsibility than a cuckoo's.[61]

Despite appearances, Barrington was not hinting that the charges of adultery with Smeaton might have been true; later in the novel, it's very clear that her Anne is innocent of adultery. Barrington, a devotee of Buddhism who also wrote fantasy novels, seems to have been motivated more by an aversion to the institution of marriage, which took the spontaneity, freedom, and "natural" flow out of relationships, than she was in painting Anne as a sexual libertine. Elsewhere in the novel, she has Anne reflecting on "the weariness of married companionship with nothing new to say or do together" and "the tedium of a wife who loves calmly, securely."[62] Smeaton is used, I believe, as a symbol of the freedom Anne gives up when she marries Henry. "We are both creatures of fairy blood," he tells Anne. "We know at bottom that neither Pope, Church, nor King matter a jot, but only the wild hearts of men that carry them into strange places. When you have flung his son into his arms come away with me and let him find another to nurse his leg . . . and bear his humour — some milk-blood bit of curd he cannot break, that will dissolve in whey if he looks at it! Come away, Anne, and we will wander the world singing for our bread and lying in meadows by a running river to eat it."[63]

In striking contrast to Barrington, Paul Rival's 1936 novel, *The Six Wives of Henry VIII*, has Anne discovering her true womanhood in Henry's arms. Originally written in French and quickly translated into English by Una Vincenzo, Lady Troubridge, Rival's novel was reprinted in paperback form in 1970 with the front cover reading: NOW A MA-

JOR NETWORK TV SERIES, TAKING ITS PLACE BESIDE *THE FOR-SYTE SAGA*. The series was the BBC six-part *The Six Wives of Henry VIII*, with Keith Michell as Henry and Dorothy Tutin as Anne. But the novel bears little resemblance, in style or content, to that subdued, very proper British series. Rival's language is dizzyingly intense and dramatic, and his interpretation of Anne and Henry's attraction for each other seems a combination of early French existentialism (which Gabriel Marcel had introduced in the twenties) and Freudian theory (very much in vogue in the thirties). For Rival's Henry, the thought of a child with Anne is more than a desire to secure the Tudor line, it is a way of making the "ethereal" creature into an earthly — Simone de Beauvoir would say "immanent" — body.

> Henry was invaded by a powerful and perverse fascination that dwelt in the thought that this small, dancing creature would be enslaved, would endure long months of a bewildered weakness until she became a mother. The more elusive [Anne] seemed, the more he burned to possess her. She stirred and re-awoke in him bygone mystical dreams, which took upon themselves new significance: "I shall take her in my arms and compel her to materialize, to become mere flesh of this earth. I shall fashion a woman out of this flame; I shall mingle my being with that of this sinuous snake, this Melusine. An essential particle of my body will inhabit her unreality, will slowly come to life, to birth and to the light of day, and the child will be myself and this small elusive Anne."[64]

Henry's desire for Anne is thus premised on what Sartre would later describe as the desire to capture the elusive freedom of another person by "incarnating" it as flesh. But Anne, on her part, is a more Freudian kind of girl, who realizes her own sexuality only when she gives up everything that is "masculine" about her — the "huntress," with her own plans and ambitions — and submits totally to Henry, as she finally does at Calais.

> That night, in the conventional room which had been assigned to her in the castle of Calais, she opened her arms to Henry. She humbled herself and allowed him to possess her. The gentle wash of the waves

was audible through the windows, the tapestries waved in the night breeze, and a dying log fire flowed upon the hearth.

They remained more than a week at Calais. Francis had gone and the chill air of November emphasized the silence. They had lived so long in a dream that reality surprised and alarmed them. Anne was at length a woman; Henry had delivered her from her own unbalanced fancies and revealed her to herself, finding her interior rhythm, giving her serene happiness, the pleasure of ceasing to think, of allowing her mind and her nerves to be lulled to sleep, of being no more than a physical vessel, utterly fulfilled and submissive. For her there were now order, peace and repose. The sky was tranquil and colourless, the sea more grey than the sky with faint ripples and reflections and a few drifting sails. The nights unfolded themselves, long and blissful.[65]

In Francis Hackett's *Queen Anne Boleyn* (1939), it's Wyatt who holds the key to Anne's libido, possibly because his bold, poetic nature makes for more ecstatic romance than the somewhat weak-kneed Percy of earlier novels.

Anne shuddered as the force of her feeling for Thomas took impetus from the hours they had had together, hours borrowed from another plane of existence, borrowed from eternity. In those hours she had come into something of her own buried self—almost as if she had learned to walk or learned to talk. The proud woman in her, as well as the calculating, gave way to a creature of blinding tenderness, and this sweeping tenderness rolled through her, ran ramparts that advanced as they mounted, one surging on the other, until they broke with the dazzling submission of a wave. It was a succession of rapture she had not been prepared for. She was stunned by it, yet ached to return to him through it.[66]

Steamy sex aside, Hackett's novel is extremely well researched, its portrait of Anne complex and subtle, and its skepticism about the received wisdom of the historians who recycled Chapuys (and each other) is refreshing and astute.[67] The first Anne novel to become a *New York Times* best seller, *Queen Anne Boleyn* was also the first to benefit from the creation, in 1939, of the paperback book format, announced in

the *New York Times* as "the most important literary coming-out party
in the memory of New York's oldest book lover. Today your 25 cent
piece leaps to a par with dollar bills. Now for less than the few cents
you spend each week for your morning newspaper, you can own one
of the great books for which thousands of people have paid from $2 to
$4."[68] When the paperback of *Queen Anne Boleyn* came out that same
year, the first page quoted from its many excellent reviews from pres-
tigious papers, but the back cover was clearly designed to sell copies to
a broader audience than those who read the *Christian Science Monitor*,
the *New Statesman*, or the *Saturday Review*. SHE CONQUERED THE
HEART OF A KING — AND LOST HER LIFE FOR HER LOVE, reads the
bold headline, and below it ran the following text:

> In all of history there are few stories as enthralling as the astonishing
> rise and tragic fall of Anne Boleyn. Born the daughter of a commoner,
> her proud beauty won the heart of mighty Henry the Eighth — but
> to sanctify their love, they faced a battle that shook the foundations
> of the Western World. Against the might of the Church, the opposi-
> tion of the nobility, and the rage of an Emperor, she rose to become
> Queen of England — and to die on the block at the hands of the man
> she loved.

Anne was now a full-fledged heroine of the historical romance, and
a major commercial item.

9

Postwar: Domestic Trouble
in the House of Tudor

WORLD WAR II interrupted Anne's fictional career — possibly because people didn't want to read about the love life of a long-gone tyrant when they were dealing with one who was very much alive, and far more evil. But as soon as the war ended, Anne was back full force and with more "pluck" and independence than before. Passive, dependent heroines were no longer appreciated by middle-class female readers, who during the war had not only their own independence tested, but who also had been treated, at the movies and in women's magazines, to feisty, spirited female characters. At the same time, there was considerable anxiety about what would happen when the men returned. Most young women longed to reunite with their husbands and boyfriends and start a family, and the machinery of culture — films, magazines, advertisements, how-to books — encouraged them. But was it possible to have it all? While decades later the answer would be (a completely unrealistic) "Hell, yes!," in the years immediately after the war, culture vacillated back and forth between celebrating and condemning the woman who tried to live as an equal with men.

Consider the contrast between two films, released a mere seven months apart. *Adam's Rib* (1949) is one of the last gasps of admiration (for the time being) for the "urban," egalitarian marriage, in which husband and wife (Spencer Tracy and Katharine Hepburn) work, play, flirt, and spar together, equally matched in intelligence, humor, and passion (and capable of aiming the occasional whack at each other).[1] *Father of the Bride* (1950) and its 1951 sequel, *Father's Little Dividend*, are advertisements for the freshly romanticized, newly commercialized "old-fashioned" gendered division of labor, with a kittenish, thoroughly domesticated bride (Elizabeth Taylor) unable to tie her shoelaces without the help of her sturdy provider groom (Don Taylor). In this suburban world, teenage girls could be (mildly) rebellious, and learning to wrap men around their pretty little fingers was part of the fun of "being a girl." But once married, they were expected to settle down and content themselves with the thrill of new appliances and decorating the baby's room.

Margaret Campbell Barnes's *Brief Gaudy Hour*, published the year before *Father of the Bride* was released, follows this blueprint. But in Barnes's novel, unlike the film, it all goes bad. Barnes's Anne is a flirtatious, ambitious, but very likeable teenager. But over the course of the novel, because she doesn't know her "place," she becomes the housewife from hell.

In the first chapter, we find Anne studying her own nude body in the mirror at Hever, contemplating her coming time at the French court. "'Thank God,'" she thinks to herself, "'it is exquisite enough for the most exacting lover.'" She was glad that her parents, through some freakish caution or ambition, had omitted to arrange a betrothal for her in infancy. Unlike her sister and her girlfriends, she was still free. Free to choose her own lover . . . [t]he kind of man who wouldn't stop to write a sonnet to one's eyes, but who would sweep one into compelling arms and stop all protests with a kiss."[2] She breezes about her bedroom, trying on flirtatious looks and playfully shocking her (invented) stepmother with her boldness. There's a generation gap between Anne and her elders — a new theme for fictional Annes very much in keeping with the time during which "teen" culture was born. Previous novels had dealt with Anne's early years. But Barnes's young Anne is the first to "read" as a teenager. In fact, there are many times that the novel sounds exactly like a story from one of the upbeat teen magazines that began to be published in the midforties. Anne is depicted learning how to dress, how to attract a man, and how to manage her own sexual impulses. And, as the magazines promise, when she meets "the one" — Henry Percy — she knows it immediately.

At that point, romance novel and teen magazine part ways. Where *Seventeen* would have them "dating" (or *Father of the Bride* would have her planning a wedding), *Brief Gaudy Hour* plunges Anne into a passionate, doomed — and fully sexually realized — affair. Anne is the one to urge it ("Take me now while there is yet time"[3]); Percy the one to caution her to hold back ("But Nan, my dear, my very dear, the shame"[4]), and it's Anne whose boldness trumps his scruples. But it is a "brief, rich transport": "Throwing aside security and favour, she made the reckless surrender which could have kept her sweet."[5] It's very *True Confessions*. Barnes's Anne is feisty, independent, high-spirited, and smart — and Henry adores this about her. ("You have been brought up to think — to have a mind of your own," he tells her, "so that a man may be richer for your company."[6]) But, ruined by memories of her night with Percy, she never develops any love in return for the king. Still, she coldly and skillfully plays Henry, lying to him about her virginity (which has already been lost to Percy) and doling out her kisses and caresses as if they were precious gems. It is she who introduces the idea of marriage to him, then seals the deal with a sinuous dance that turns Henry into a big, sloppy lapdog, ready to roll over at her whim.

Brief Gaudy Hour is a very enjoyable novel; in fact, it's often still listed by fans of historical fiction as one of their favorites. But without disputing its pleasures, I did find its portrait of Anne very odd — and, in hindsight, a harbinger of things to come. Anne the teenager is charming and "real." But Anne the queen becomes virtually demonic. Here, for example, Barnes traces the beginnings of Henry's turning against Anne[7] to her response to Katherine's death. Henry has just returned from Westminster to find Anne celebrating with her maids and courtiers in wild, Dionysian revelry, complete with pagan horns.

And now it was time for her to don her antlers, for the Queen, leaving her bevy of saffron-gowned maidens, was beginning to lure the men dancers within the magic circle Smeaton had chalked upon the floor, turning them, by her lascivious dancing, into beasts. Through the noise they made, the stamping and laughter, they did not hear the commotion of the King's unexpected arrival . . . From velvet cap to rolled, slashed shoe, he was clad in black velvet, with only a plain silver dagger hanging from his belt . . . Anne noticed that his eyes were puffed and red . . .

"I saw the lights of your orgy," he said, his blue eyes no longer blinking, but flicking like a whip over everybody present and taking in every frivolous detail . . . "Take off that unseemly dress," he ordered sharply, "and go pray for some sense of fitness!"[8]

"Saffron" (as in "saffron-gowned") here refers to the color yellow, which Chapuys says *Henry* wore after Katherine's death. Scholars have reached no firm conclusion as to what it meant. Some claim it was the Spanish color of mourning; others say it was a blatant gesture of celebration. In Barnes's scene it clearly signifies celebration, and it is Anne and her fellow revelers, not Henry, who are wearing it. As to grief-stricken Henry, his eyes puffed and red, it's a brand-new fiction. In reality there's no evidence that he was any less relieved than Anne over Katherine's death, or that any tender feelings for Katherine remained. Katherine, after all, had fought him tooth and nail for six years, stubbornly refusing all attempts to provide her with a dignified exit, seemingly unconcerned that she was tearing England apart with her resistance. Henry was furious with her, and the equally obstinate Mary, for defying his authority and bringing England to the brink of war with Spain. On the Sunday following Katherine's death, he appeared in extremely high spirits with Elizabeth in his arms in the middle of a dance at the palace. But Barnes's Henry is incapable of such callousness, and becomes meaner as the novel goes on only because Anne, "through years of trickery and sex enslavement," had "schooled him to shut up his compassion."[9]

Norah Lofts' *The Concubine* (1963) is another postwar novel that takes a dark view of the relationship between Henry and Anne. Lofts's

This sixteenth-century portrait (artist unknown), often referred to as "the NPG portrait" because it hangs in the National Portrait Gallery in London, is thought to be one of the few surviving copies of an original painting. Although it's not discernible in this black-and-white photograph of the portrait, Anne has chestnut—not black—hair.

© Heritage Images/Corbis

This anonymous portrait, hanging at Hever Castle, Anne's childhood home, captures a childlike innocence not usually seen in depictions of Anne.

Hever Castle & Gardens

Anne in an Elizabethan collar. Depictions of Anne have often followed the fashions of the artist's era, not Anne's.

Alfredo Dagli Orti/The Art Archive at Art Resource, NY

In the nineteenth century, the early days of Henry's relationship with Anne became a subject of romantic imagery, with Henry a tender suitor and Anne his adored (and blonde) darling.

Copyright and courtesy of Rotherham Heritage Services

A less idealizing nineteenth-century view of Henry that imagines a cold, unwavering Henry with a voluptuous, fainting Anne behaving according to Victorian stereotypes.

© Bettman/Corbis

Anne as tragic heroine. Early nineteenth-century French painters often drew on unjustly condemned historical figures, such as Anne and Lady Jane Grey, to comment on the politics of their own time.

Erich Lessing/Art Resource, NY

Lubitsch's 1920 *Anna Boleyn*, with Emil Jannings as a predatory Henry and Henny Porten as a sweet, suffering Anne.

© *Paramount Pictures/Photofest*

a novel by Francis Hackett

QUEEN ANNE BOLEYN

The magnificent epic of a love affair that changed the course of history "As rowdy and vital as the times it treats of." —*The New Yorker*

QUEEN ANNE BOLEYN

Francis Hackett

SHE CONQUERED THE HEART OF A KING —AND LOST HER LIFE FOR HER LOVE

In all of history there are few stories as enthralling as the astonishing rise and tragic fall of Anne Boleyn. Born the daughter of a commoner, her proud beauty won the heart of mighty Henry the Eighth—but to sanctify their love, they faced a battle that shook the foundations of the Western World. Against the might of the Church, the opposition of the nobility, and the rage of an Emperor, she rose to become Queen of England—and to die on the block at the hands of the man she loved.

FIRST TIME IN PAPERBACK

POPULAR LIBRARY

Although it wasn't the first historical novel to feature Anne, Francis Hackett's 1939 novel, the first to be issued in paperback, made her a best-selling fictional heroine for the first time.

Queen Anne Boleyn, *Popular Library*

This scene—a publicity still—never appears in Alexander Korda's 1933 *The Private Life of Henry VIII*, which dispenses with Anne (the gorgeous Merle Oberon) very early in the film to focus on the exploits of Charles Laughton's gluttonous, lecherous Henry. The wives, from left to right: Elsa Lanchester (as Anne of Cleves), Binnie Barnes (as Katherine Howard), Everley Gregg (as Katherine Parr), and Oberon as Anne.

© United Artists/Photofest

To this day, Geneviève Bujold's fiery, proud Anne remains the quintessential portrayal for many viewers.

© Universal Pictures/Photofest

Dorothy Tutin brought gravity and maturity to her portrayal of Anne in the Masterpiece Theatre television series *The Six Wives of Henry VIII.*

Photofest

Natalie Dormer, who fought to make Anne more than just a seductress in the second season of *The Tudors,* is shown here in one of Joan Bergin's anachronistic (but award-winning) costumes, fixing her sights on Jonathan Rhys Meyers's Henry.

© *Showtime/Photofest*

Anne as Mean Girl: Natalie Portman in *The Other Boleyn Girl*.

© *Columbia Pictures/Photofest*

Howard Brenton's 2010 play *Anne Boleyn* (with Anthony Howell as Henry and Miranda Raison as a blonde Anne) is the first popular depiction to emphasize Anne's reformist activities as well as her flirtatious side.

Manuel Harlan/Shakespeare's Globe Press Office

✄ cut here

Sarah Mensinga is among the contemporary artists who have used irony and wit to present what is arguably a feminist perspective on Anne's execution.

Sarah Mensinga

LE TEMPS VIENDRA ♀

Anne continues to fascinate. Emily Pooley's stunning waxwork creates a sense of intimacy with a young Anne, whom it is easy for girls and young women of today to identify with. If you look carefully, you can also see Anne's controversial sixth finger, which Pooley included to point ominously ahead to the false rumors that were spread by her enemies after her death.

Emily Pooley

Anne, unlike Barnes's, has no time of childish innocence; the novel begins with Wolsey's breaking up of the relationship with Percy, so in our first introduction to Anne, she has already become cynical and guarded, and so proud that she doesn't shed a tear over Percy, even though she is, in fact, heartbroken. She has contempt for her sister and never develops lasting affection for Henry. When he offers marriage, she immediately begins bargaining — "How long would it take?"[10] — and when it all drags on, calculates that a pregnancy will speed things along, so she sleeps with him. But after their first night together, he is disappointed and depressed. "All that promise, that hint of some peculiar and precious joy in store, was mere illusion," a "trick"; "[b]etween the sheets, in the dark, she was no different from Katherine, Bessie Blount, Mary Boleyn."[11] Anne, on her part, feels as cold and alone as "in her grave."[12] But she was not disappointed, for she had "expected nothing"; she'd known "ever since her forced parting from Henry Percy, that from this part of life enchantment had gone forever."[13] Thinking of Percy, she stifles an impulse to cry, then decides that dwelling on that is a "waste of time."[14] She had done what she had planned — "every word, every gesture, every smile almost, directed to the one end" — and consoles herself with the thought: *My child will be King of England.*[15]

Something surprising happens in *The Concubine.* For only one of two times in her career as a heroine of romantic fiction, Anne actually does commit adultery — three separate acts, with three different men — in order to secretly get pregnant again after she's lost the child she'd been carrying by the king. What's bizarre — and not very credible, even in a work of romantic fiction — is that none of her partners "could say truthfully that he had sinned with the Queen," for each coupling had happened during a masked ball, and Anne, in costume and with her voice disguised, "had made absolutely sure that no man could look at her next day and think . . ."[16] The reader is left in the same position with respect to whom she had sex with, for we're never told. This was the last time fictional Anne would actually be guilty of any of the charges laid against her until 2001, when the first truly despicable Anne since Chapuys' letters became the reigning queen of historical fiction.

Barnes's and Lofts's Henry and Anne are never soul mates or even lovers in anything but the most mechanical sense; they are bad romances from the start. In contrast, Maxwell Anderson's *Anne of the Thousand Days,* which premiered December 8, 1948, the year before Barnes's novel was published, is the story of a true love affair gone sour. Drama critic Brooks Atkinson called the play "the story of two violent, willful people who act on each other without mercy."[17] That may be going a bit too far. The violence amounts to a slap across the face, but "willful" is on target — and so is the passion that Anne and Henry's battle of wills brings about. It's truly a match between equals, in every respect except the fatal inequality of Henry's power over Anne's life and death. And in a season that also brought *South Pacific* and *Death of a Salesman* to Broadway, it was a surprisingly popular success, despite the fact that it is written in a combination of prose and verse, and often wanders into long, somewhat pretentious poetic monologues. The key to its popularity: Although the play is peppered with fragmentary (and often confusing) references to "large" historical issues and events, the central drama is domestic — a battle of the sexes between Henry and Anne, within which they behave more like a man and a woman than a bluebeard and a vixen in a Grand Historical Drama.

Most audiences of the play would have been familiar with the Henry played by Charles Laughton, who in Alexander Korda's *The Private Life of Henry VIII* (1933) bequeathed to us the enduring image of Henry devouring a chicken, tearing off a chunk, taking one bite, then chucking each piece over his shoulder as he dives for the next while burpingly lamenting the death of civility. "There's no delicacy nowadays. No consideration for others [belch]. Refinement's a thing of the past! . . . Manners are *dead!* [Belch.]"[18] Some might have remembered Emil Jannings's gluttonous, volatile lecher from Ernst Lubitsch's melodramatic silent movie, *Anna Boleyn* (1920). From prevailing representations they would have expected a buffoon; a leering bloated tyrant; or "Bluff King Hal." In *Anne of the Thousand Days* they got manly, handsome Rex Harrison (who won a Tony for the role), charming and suave, but also calculating, arrogant, and utterly unused to being refused anything, even by God. ("I pray," he says, "and God answers."[19])

As for Anne, her previous appearances on stage and in film exhibited little in the way of "character." Shakespeare's play is not and never was among his most popular, and the real show-stealing speeches are given to Katherine. In Gaetano Donizetti's 1830 opera, *Anna Bolena,* Anne is pure victim, tormented by the loss of her first love, Percy (a theme undoubtedly picked up from *Vertue Betray'd*), manipulated and treated coldly by Henry, and ultimately driven mad by everything that has happened to her (the high point of the opera finds Anne in the Tower careening between hallucinations from a happier past and hysterical confrontation with her present agony). In Lubitsch's version, Anne is also a victim, a virtuous — and blonde — sacrificial lamb very much in the tradition of the wide-eyed, demure heroines that Mary Pickford made famous. Barely post-Victorian, she goes to her death unadorned, in a plain white smock.[20] Merle Oberon (Korda's Anne) was the first of many elegant, hypnotic beauties who helped create the more glamorous version of femininity that reigned in the thirties — and that seems to be her main function in the film. She has only a few scenes to play, and each one seems designed to highlight the actress's regal (and, in those days, "exotic"[21]) beauty. As she prepares for her execution, she gazes into the mirror, fusses with her hair, ponders which headdress to wear. She preens, she suffers a bit, she looks beautiful, and then she's gone. Relieved of Anne, the Korda film can then go on to play future episodes in Henry's "private life" mostly as comedy — although with dark undertones. Before Anne is executed, for example, we are given a scene of Anne's ladies-in-waiting fluttering about, preparing the king's bed and gossiping with each other over Anne's impending execution and Jane Seymour's takeover.

1ST LADY: So that's the king's bed.

NURSE: Yes, my dear. And he has not long left it — feel!

1ST LADY: I wonder what he looks like — in bed.

2ND LADY (*a rival beauty*): *You'll* never know!

1ST LADY (*annoyed*): Well, there's no need to be spiteful, is there, Mistress Nurse?

NURSE (*consolingly*): No, my dear; and you've as good a chance as another when the king's in one of his merry moods.

   The girls laugh.

1ST LADY: Oh! I never meant . . . I never thought . . .

2ND LADY: *Didn't* you, darling?

NURSE: Now, ladies! You're not here to quarrel, but to get busy with your needles. Look — all these A's must come out, and J's go in. Hurry, ladies, hurry!

Anderson's Anne (played by petite but feisty Joyce Redman) was clearly not influenced by these earlier stage and film depictions. Perhaps Bette Davis's Elizabeth I in *The Private Lives of Elizabeth and Essex* (1939), which was based on a stage play that was also written by Anderson, helped shape his image of Anne. Perhaps — as Francis Hackett claimed — Anderson was influenced by Hackett's 1939 novel. There, as with his portrait of Henry in his 1929 biography *Henry VIII: The Personal History of a Dynast and His Wives,* Hackett was determined to go beyond the clichés and stereotypes to show readers that "it is creatures of flesh and blood . . . who make great history."[22] With Henry, this required going beyond the caricatures of Bluff King Hal, the jovial serial collector of wives, a cartoon figure described by Hackett as "one of the most vulgar and fatuous and horrible of illusions."[23] With Anne, he wanted readers to understand how this woman — and only this woman, with the exceptions, perhaps, of his grandmother and Katherine Parr — could have, for so long, matched Henry eye to eye, power for power, in the relationship. His Anne has a personality that refuses to be vanquished; this is what draws Henry to her, while infuriating everyone else.

If ever a slip of a girl owed it to the established order to satisfy her lover by a union outside the bonds of matrimony, this was a clear instance; and Cardinals and ambassadors and blood-relations and the pope were soon beside themselves with eagerness to learn that this chit would remain simply Henry's mistress. Her father grew weary of her obstinacy. Her uncle Norfolk resented her ambition. Her sister could not understand Anne's rigorousness. But she was not a coquette nor a wanton. She was a high-spirited, high-minded girl who made this marriage a term of her being and who, in spite of this, delivered herself to ruin.[24]

It's a pretty accurate description of Anderson's Anne too.[25] Fiercely independent and apparently without a drop of fear, "the slip of a girl" refuses Henry's advances and calls him out: "You are spoiled and vengeful and malicious and bloody. The poetry they praise so much is sour, and the music you write's worse. You dance like a hobbledehoy; you make love as you eat — with a good deal of noise and no subtlety."[26] Although in "real life" this attitude would probably have resulted in her head going missing much earlier in the story, in the play it inflames Henry's desire for her, and he vows that "[i]f it breaks the world in two like an apple and flings the halves into the void, I shall make you queen."[27] Anderson's Anne also has a sexual past — she confides to Percy, her first love, that she slept with men while she was in France and even before that. Sander and others had claimed that too. But what is striking here is how irrelevant it is to the play's assessment of Anne's moral character. She's not a virgin — big deal. The king knows it and doesn't care. Neither does Percy. She tells him about it matter-of-factly, without a hint of coyness; she's more the modern "liberated" woman than either the trembling virgin or the temptress who endows sexuality with subversive power.

When Henry and Anne finally sleep together, it is a wildly transporting experience for both of them: "I'm deep in love," Anne declares (so deep she no longer cares about the divorce), and Henry proclaims it "a new age. Gold or some choicer metal — or no metal at all, but exaltation, darling. Wildfire in the air, wildfire in the blood!"[28]

The irony (and existential essence and dramatic spine of the play) is that falling in love with Henry after years of hating him is the beginning of Anne's downfall, for it finally releases him from his erotic bondage to her. "After that night," she muses later in her room in the Tower, "I was lost."[29] What follows is the speech that gave the play its title.

> From the day he first made me his, to the last day I made him mine, yes, let me set it down in numbers. I who can count and reckon, and have the time. Of all the days I was his and did not love him — this; and this; and this many. Of all the days I was his — and he had ceased to love me — this many; and this. In days — it comes to a thousand

days—out of the years. Strangely, just a thousand. And of that thousand—one—when we were both in love. Only one, when our loves met and overlapped and were both mine and his. When I no longer hated him, he began to hate me. Except for that one day. One day, out of all the years.[30]

I've always loved that speech for its psychological acuity about the kind of love that is fueled by challenge and pursuit, as Henry's desire for Anne was. Whatever her motives, Anne was not easily conquered. This may have inflamed Henry's passion, but it also meant there was a danger to Anne in finally giving in. For what he found in his arms was a real woman rather than a fantasized ideal—and as a real woman, Anne, having been elevated in Henry's imagination by years of longing, was bound to disappoint.[31] This is a new theme in Anne's fictional afterlives, one which Norah Lofts develops in chilling detail after his and Anne's first sex together. (It affects even Henry's sense of smell.) "For years and years, whenever he had been near her he had been conscious of the scent of her hair, not oversweet, not musky, in no way obtrusive, a dry, clean fragrance, all her own; but now, nearer to her than he had ever been, he was only aware of his own freshly soaped odor and the scented oil which he had rubbed into his hair and beard . . . He could have cried when he thought of how he had soaked and scrubbed himself, put on his finest clothes and his jewels."[32] All that for "just another woman in a bed!"[33]

Anne and Henry's sexual attraction for each other does not degenerate so starkly or decisively in *Anne of the Thousand Days*. Even after Henry has begun to court Jane, he still can be aroused by Anne; when her fury is ignited, so is his desire for her. And furious she often is —over his betrayal, over the prospect of Elizabeth's being made a bastard, and over Henry's underestimating of her integrity. No fictional Anne before had ever been so proudly defiant, so insistent on her own autonomy, so utterly unintimidated by Henry. For drama critic Joseph Wood Krutch, this is what made Anderson's Anne so "intriguing." "In her own way she is as ruthless as Henry, no dove snatched up by an eagle, but an eagle herself. What she has is a prideful integrity incapable of a sin against herself, though quite capable of most of the other sins in the calendar."[34] This inability to "sin against herself" ultimately sends her to her death, but it's also what gives her enormous power. She will risk anything, endure anything, in order to retain her self-respect. Even at the end, condemned to death, she continues to challenge Henry, tormenting him with a lie that is also a final show of her unwillingness to "do all this gently," as Henry would like.

> Before you go, perhaps you should hear one thing—I lied to you. I loved you, but I lied to you! I was untrue! Untrue with many![35]

She thus leaves Henry with an uncertainty that he will "take to the grave" (as she puts it).[36] Did she? Didn't she? Unknowable and elusive once again, she goes to her death knowing that her own power in the relationship has been restored.

As successful as it was, *Anne of the Thousand Days* was not made into a movie until twenty years later. It was deemed untouchable by movie studios in 1949, as it dealt with subjects — adultery, incest, illegitimacy, even the word "virgin" — that the Motion Picture Production Code would not permit. It wasn't until the sixties that the code began to be killed off, bit by bit, by the "foreign invasion" of sexually franker European films and the need for American movies to offer something that television could not. In 1966, Mike Nichols's screen adaptation of Edward Albee's *Who's Afraid of Virginia Woolf?* — a less fatal but more foul-mouthed "bad romance" than *Anne of the Thousand Days* — did the code in. And Anderson's Anne was ready to be revived — and, as I will argue, reimagined — for a new generation.

PART III

An Anne for All Seasons

10

It's the Anne That Makes the Movie: *Anne of the Thousand Days*

I N THE EARLY 1960s, Hal Wallis, producer of such distinctively American hits as *True Grit, Casablanca, Barefoot in the Park,* and all of Elvis Presley's movies, and known as one of the "Jews who invented Hollywood," was about to realize a deeply held longing. The child of immigrants from Russia and Poland, Wallis had grown up in a Chicago tenement, in an Eastern European Jewish enclave of garment workers and small shopkeepers. And from an early age, he adored all things British. As soon as he had made enough money, from early hits such as *Little Caesar* and *Yankee Doodle Dandy,* he built himself a huge manor in the San Fernando Valley, with fireplaces, woodwork, and furniture imported from Britain. And he began to dream of making films that would introduce British history — which he had studied, on his own, since childhood — to movie-going audiences. He so succeeded in this goal that Queen Elizabeth II, at a 1972 Royal Command Performance of *Anne of the Thousand Days,* shook his hand and whispered, "Thank you, Mr. Wallis. We're learning about English history from your films."[1] A year later, Wallis was honored with the title of Commander of the British Empire by order of Elizabeth.

Discounting *The Adventures of Robin Hood* (1938), Wallis's first foray into British history had been *The Private Lives of Elizabeth and Essex* (1939), with Bette Davis and Errol Flynn. He most enjoyed turning distinguished plays into popular movies, and when he saw Jean Anouilh's *Becket* in 1960, he knew he had to make the movie version. *Becket* turned out to be a huge success, starring Peter O'Toole as Henry II and Richard Burton as his wenching buddy Thomas Becket, who become tormented adversaries in a battle between allegiance to king and the demands of conscience. But when Wallis first suggested it to Paramount execs, they balked. "A picture about an archbishop and a king would have no commercial value in today's market," they told Wallis.[2] And Charles Bluhdorn, who owned Paramount, could not see how mass audiences would accept a "plot predicated on what was essentially an intellectual argument."[3] It was only after Wallis reassured him that he would dress up the intellectual content with beautiful locations and gorgeous costumes that Bluhdorn agreed. The movie went on to receive ten Oscar nominations and encouraged Wallis's ambition to make a series of historical dramas.

Wallis had seen and admired *Anne of the Thousand Days* when it was playing on Broadway in 1949, but apparently he didn't think of making it into a movie until Richard Burton suggested it, begging to play the part of Henry VIII. At least, that's the story that Wallis tells in his autobiography, *Starmaker*. Richard Burton, in an interview with Michael Munn for his book, *Richard Burton: Prince of Players* (these titles don't shy away from hyperbole), insists he had no interest in making the film. "I thought it was a poor attempt to try to make a 'classic,'" he told Munn, and after he finally agreed — under threat of a lawsuit — he remained apathetic: "I had rarely begun any film so disinterested."[4] There's no way of knowing for sure whose version is accurate, but however it came about, in 1964, when Wallis first acquired the rights to the play, the *New York Times* announced that he was negotiating with Elizabeth Taylor and Richard Burton to play the roles of Anne and Henry. According to Wallis, however, he never actually considered Taylor for the role — perhaps he was just leading a reluctant Burton on. In any case, Wallis recalls a lunch with Liz in 1967, in which "Elizabeth hung on my every word. I was surprised by her attention, as there was no part in the picture for her. Over an elaborate dessert she took a deep breath and said, 'Hal, I've been thinking about it for weeks. I have to play Anne Boleyn!' My fork stopped halfway to my mouth. *Anne Boleyn?* Elizabeth was plump and middle-aged; Anne was a slip of a girl. The fate of the picture hung in the balance. I could scarcely bring myself to look at Richard."[5] Burton, however, "handled it beautifully. He put his hand on hers, looked her directly in the eye, and said, 'Sorry, luv. You're too long in the tooth.'"[6] Any hard feelings were handled by a huge fee for Burton ($1,250,000 plus) and cameos for Liz (as a masked dancer at a ball) as well as for Burton's daughter Kate and Taylor's daughter Liza.

The young woman Wallis settled on for Anne, after the usual "exhaustive search," was a virtually unknown French-Canadian actress named Geneviève Bujold, whom Wallis spotted in an independent Canadian film called *Isabel* (directed by Bujold's then-husband, Paul Almond). Finding her, Wallis recalls, was a "miracle."[7] "The minute [Geneviève] appeared on the screen, I was riveted. I saw a tiny, seemingly fragile woman made of steel — willful, passionate, intense. She was exactly the actress I wanted to play Anne Boleyn. Even her French accent was perfect: Anne had been educated in France. I hired the girl without meeting her or testing her. [When] we met, everything about her confirmed my prediction that she was a very special personality: unique, perfect for Anne."[8] Wallis hired a special coach to help Geneviève get the accent just right — British tinged with French rather than the other way around — and gave her books to read on Boleyn.[9] In a personal interview with me, Bujold recalls him as a wonderful "guide" to interpreting Anne — something that I admit surprised me.[10] Before I talked to Geneviève, I associated Wallis with big blockbuster "American" movies. But Geneviève set me straight. "He had an insatiable curiosity that took him outside American films in his search for Anne, and he had a hunger for discovery" that responded when he saw Bujold.[11] So much for my stereotypes about Hollywood producers.

Bujold's performance, and a few key changes in the play, were to make quite a dramatic transformation in the Maxwell Anderson original. Anderson's play, despite its fireball Anne, was really Henry's story and, like Hackett's biography, was intent on exorcising the ghost of

Bluff King Hal, described in Hackett's biography (published well before *The Private Life of Henry VIII* made it to the screen) as "the sort of man who eats a baron of beef and says Arise, Sir Loin; the sort of man who cuts off his wife's head, ha-ha, out of a big, jovial, exuberant good humor. Off with her head! Off with the next one's head! The more, the merrier."[12] Charles Laughton played precisely this kind of Henry with such gusto and ingenuity that many viewers (and reviewers) believed that they were seeing the "real" Henry. John Gamme, in *Film Weekly*, described Laughton as "drawing a full-blooded portrait of the gross, sensual monarch in whom lust and the satisfaction of vanity are the ruling passions."[13]

Hackett and Anderson, however, considered this kind of portrait to be a caricature. Their respective Henrys are not piggy old souls, but tortured monarchs. Hackett's was a "man of open manner and gracious fellowship ... and the magnet of a facile imagination"[14] who, due to an inability to imagine himself and his personal needs as anything other than orchestrated by God, had "managed to plunge himself and his country in the thick of an inextricable jungle." Anderson's Henry is an even more tragic figure than Hackett's. He truly loves Anne, but gets caught in the net of his own obsession with an heir, masculine pride, and self-indulgence. Ultimately, he comes to see that he has paid an enormous price, but that "nothing can ever be put back the way it was."[15] In the final speech of the play, Henry muses on the magnitude of what has changed for his country ("the limb that was cut from Rome won't graft to that trunk again"[16]) and, with Anne's ghost hovering in the background, he begins to realize that "all other women will be shadows" and that he will seek Anne "forever down the long corridors of air, finding them empty, hearing only echoes."[17] "It would have been easier," he now recognizes, "to forget you living than to forget you dead."[18]

In Anderson's play, it's Henry who has the final word, who makes the final pronouncements about history, whose torments we are left to imagine. The film, however, ends very differently. The screenplay, adapted from the play by Bridget Boland, John Hale, and Richard Sokolove, has Henry, in our last glimpse of him, listening for the signal sounding Anne's death, then galloping off to see Jane Seymour with nary a second thought. In place of his sober, sad reflections at the end of the play, we see little Elizabeth, a sprig of flowers in her hand, toddling down the path toward greatness (actually in the gardens of Penshurst Castle) while her mother's voice in the background predicts her daughter's glorious future. The voice-over is a repeat of part of an earlier speech, one that has viewers cheering for Anne to this day. As in the play, Henry visits Anne in the Tower, and she lies to him about her fidelity to him. In the movie, however, she embellishes her lie with more detail — "I was untrue to half your court. With soldiers of your guard, with grooms, with stable hands. Look for the rest of your life at every man that ever knew me and wonder if I didn't find him a better man than you!" — and Henry, rattled and enraged, shouts, "You whore!" Anne, who knows she has hit the mark of his manhood but has even sharper arrows in her quiver, goes on.

> Yes. But Elizabeth is yours. Watch her as she grows; she's yours. She's a Tudor! Get yourself a son off of that sweet, pale girl if you can — and hope that he will live! But Elizabeth shall reign after you! Yes, Elizabeth — child of Anne the Whore and Henry the Blood-Stained Lecher — shall be Queen! And remember this: Elizabeth shall be a greater queen than any king of yours! She shall rule a greater England than you could ever have built! Yes — MY Elizabeth SHALL BE QUEEN! And my blood will have been well spent!

Yes, it's overblown. And it's utterly without historical foundation. Henry never visited Anne in her room in the Tower, and Anne never delivered a speech like this; indeed, at this point, Anne knew the chances of Elizabeth ever becoming queen were extremely slim. Two days before her execution, her marriage to Henry was declared null and void by Henry's lawyers, and Elizabeth was bastardized. In the movie, she is given a choice that the real Anne never had: To live, if she will willingly end the marriage, freeing Henry to marry Jane Seymour and making Elizabeth illegitimate in the bargain. Or to die, with Elizabeth still a rightful heir. She turns Henry down flat.

It was all invention, but of a particularly potent and timely sort for 1969. This was a period of convention smashing in film: *Bonnie and Clyde, The Graduate, In the Heat of the Night, Midnight Cowboy, The*

Wild Bunch, Butch Cassidy and the Sundance Kid, and *Easy Rider.* But with the exception of Bonnie Parker and Mrs. Robinson (but strikingly *not* her daughter, Elaine), the female characters in the New American Cinema played by the rules. It was the men who challenged the status quo, and the men who paid heroically for it.[19] Hale and Boland's Anne, long before *Thelma & Louise,* is the first female heroine to ride off the cliff, in full consciousness of what she is doing, to preserve her own integrity (and, in this case, the future of her daughter and England).

It struck a chord, even with me. In 1969 I was a pretty cynical moviegoer. The antisentimentalist Pauline Kael, who did movie reviews for the *New Yorker,* was my idol, and I hated anything that smacked of pretention or high-mindedness. I was not a feminist in anything but the most inchoate sense of the word. While friends of mine were joining consciousness-raising groups and attending demonstrations, I scorned and was made anxious by what I thought of as "groupthink." My own personal rebellion was to drop out of school, have a lot of mindless sex, marry someone I didn't love, and then suffer a nervous breakdown that made me unable to leave him. But I did manage to make it to the movies — and *Anne of the Thousand Days* was one of them. It was my first introduction, since the boring, sexless Tudor history I'd read in high school, to the story of Henry and Anne. I had no idea what was invented and what was historically documented, but it made no difference. I loved fiery, rebellious Anne. I loved the way she bossed Richard Burton's Henry around like a surly twentieth-century teenager. I loved the fact that Geneviève Bujold's hair was messy as she delivered that speech to Henry, loved her intensity, loved her less than perfectly symmetrical beauty, loved the fact that someone that small could pack such a wallop.

Anne's speech in the Tower might have seemed melodramatic if it had been played by a young Bette Davis — or, heaven forfend, Elizabeth Taylor! But Bujold's fire, issuing from her petite frame and elfin face, her hair disheveled, her dark eyes glittering with pride, desperation, hurt, and vengeance, transformed the potentially hokey into an indelible, iconic moment. Even at a recent festival of Burton's films, held by the British Film Institute, the audience was stirred, crying out, "Go, Anne, go, you tell him!"[20] "After watching this," writes one contemporary Tudorphile, "you come away with the feeling that if that ain't the way it really happened then it should've. I love the pride she displays even after Henry slaps her. She's right, he's wrong, and they both know it. As she goes on talking down to him, you can see him shriveling little by little and he nevermore was the man he'd once been. Seems she got the last laugh in more ways than one."[21]

Bujold also did something with Anne's famous — and famously ambiguous — behavior in the Tower that contributed to the believability of that final speech. Anne's actions and comments, as she awaited her sentencing and then her death, provide some of the most intriguing clues to her personality. Unfortunately, they were recorded by Constable Kingston, a man who seems to have been tone-deaf to her sense of irony. In one iconic moment, for example, Anne had said to Kingston, upon arrival at the Tower and being told that she would be housed in the apartment she stayed in before her coronation, that it is "too good for her."[22] Kingston reports that she then "kneeled down weeping, and in the same sorrow fell into a great laughing."[23] One can interpret the weeping as relief and the laughter as hysterical, but Anne also laughed — in the same conversation with Kingston — when he told her that "even the King's poorest subject hath justice."[24] It's hard to read that laughter as anything other than mocking Kingston's naivete about the King's "justice." Similarly, Anne's laughter over being housed in her coronation room can be read as a reaction to the bizarre, bitter irony of her situation. For a queen, of course, the apartment would hardly be "too good." By saying so, Anne may have been pointing out to the clueless, uncomfortable Kingston that she was still, after all, the queen of England.

These are matters of interpretation that can make a huge difference in an actress's portrayal of Anne. When Anne delivered her best-known line — "I heard say the executioner was very good, and I have a little neck" — then put her hands around her neck and "laughed heartily" (as Kingston described it), he took her to be showing "much joy and pleasure in death."[25] The actresses who have played Anne have been too smart to accept that interpretation, but then they have been left with the task of figuring out just what *was* going on. Merle Oberon and Dorothy Tutin eliminate the laughter entirely and have Anne say the line wistfully, as if in resigned acceptance (and in the case of Oberon, with a touch of narcissism) of the reality of the coming confrontation between steel and flesh. Natalie Dormer plays the "little neck" speech as a moment when the unimaginable stress that Anne is enduring breaks through her composure, and both the absurdity and the terror of her situation erupt in a crazy joke and then, hysterical laughter — an interpretation that fits well with the evidence that Anne's behavior in the tower was frequently unhinged. But Bujold chooses to emphasize Anne's intelligence and pride rather than her emotional instability, and plays the line as a sardonic response to Kingston's lame reassurances that the blow would be so "subtle" there would be no pain. Her Anne recognizes cowardly, self-serving bull when it's thrown at her, and will have none of it. She was, and probably always will be, the proudest of Annes.

The enthusiastic critical reception to Bujold's performance was an exception to the lukewarm — and frequently hostile — reviews that the movie received when it opened. Vincent Canby complained that it was "unbearably classy" and "conventionally reverential."[26] But he also said (somewhat condescendingly, I think) that Bujold was "a constantly delightful surprise" whose intelligence was "an unexpected dividend" to her beauty.[27] John Simon, in a piece for the *New York Times* called "Oscars: They Shun the Best, Don't They?", described the movie, which had garnered ten nominations, including Best Picture, as "a sluggish dullard of a film [that] conforms to Hollywood's and, for all I know, Dubuque's idea of a grand, historic document in which regal, larger-than-life-size dummies bestride the screen with pachydermous portentousness, their mouths full of spine-chilling platitudes."[28] *Time* magazine began its review by saying that "it appears to have been made for one person: the Queen of England."[29] After describing *The Private Life of Henry VIII* as "a superior treatment of the same subject," the magazine singled out Bujold as nearly, but not quite, saving the movie. "It would have been easy to play the spider ensnared by her own web, but Bujold knows better . . . The performance establishes the star, but not her setting. A great king may be enough to restore a country; a noble queen is insufficient to save a base film."[30] The *New York Times* attributed the film's ten Oscar nominations to the beef stroganoff and champagne served at the thirty-five special screenings for Academy members.[31] But many critics complained when Bujold, nominated for Best Actress, lost to Maggie Smith in *The Prime of Miss Jean Brodie* and celebrated when Geneviève won the Golden Globe.

The critics' harsh reaction to the film was in part due, I believe, to the tenor of the times. The year before *Anne of the Thousand Days* was released, American soldiers massacred 347 civilians at My Lai. President Lyndon Baines Johnson, the target of antiwar rage, said he would not seek reelection. Martin Luther King, Jr. had been assassinated on the balcony of a Memphis motel, and the inner cities exploded. Just days later, SDS students at Columbia barricaded themselves in the president's office while black students occupied a separate building. In May, Parisian students went on strike, tearing up the cobblestones of Paris. A few weeks later, moments after victory in the California primary, Bobby Kennedy was murdered in the kitchen of a Los Angeles hotel. A few days before, a marginal member of Andy Warhol's circle, Valerie Solanas, also the founder of SCUM, the Society for Cutting Up Men, shot him in the stomach. Prior to the shooting, she had written a manifesto calling for "systematically fucking up the system, selectively destroying property, and murder."[32] It was not a time for reverence, not a time to romanticize the privileged, and not a time for "stuffiness" of any sort. In 1969, the once-daring *Anne of the Thousand Days* seemed tame and "conservative."

Wallis also had a crush on history that was not very fashionable during this period in America. He was obsessed with making sure the costuming and settings — and even much of the music — were period appropriate. (Outside scenes were filmed at Hever Castle, Anne's actual childhood home, and Penshurst Castle, a fourteenth-century manor house a few miles from Hever.) And unlike *A Man for All Seasons* (1966) — which was actually much more reverential toward its subject — *Anne of the Thousand Day's* language remained "lofty" and without the touch of the casual, slangy ambiance that kept Robert Bolt's screenplay (from his play) down to earth and seductively intimate, despite its idolatry of Thomas More. Sixties audiences could identify with the witty, antiestablishment dropout (played by Paul Scofield), who remained so cool throughout *A Man for All Seasons* — something the real Thomas More, a ferocious heretic hunter, certainly was not. In contrast, Richard Burton was physically stiff and unfashionably leering. He hated wearing the costumes and was uncomfortable "hiding" behind the beard he had grown for the film. He didn't like the dancing sequences (and it shows). If it weren't for his wonderful voice, his Henry would have had no presence at all, especially when compared to the robust performance of Robert Shaw (Henry in *A Man for All Seasons*). That role was much smaller, but whenever Shaw came on screen, his playful but dangerous Henry dominated.[33]

Geneviève, unlike Richard, had an immediate sense of identification with Anne. Wallis "recognized something that was already a part of me," she told me.[34] Still, to be picked to play Anne was a complete surprise. She had already been in several well-received films, but, as she told me, "was still something of an unwritten page. At the time I was married to Paul Almond, living in the East End of Montreal, and enjoying my life. But I definitely had ambition. When that call came, I was shocked. Pleasantly so, of course."[35] There were aspects that made her nervous. She was panicked about the prospect of reading love scenes with Richard Burton. ("I can laugh about it now, but it was agonizing.") And "the English lines were unfamiliar. I'd been schooled in French-Canadian theatre and suddenly I had one hundred and ten pages of English as Anne Boleyn would have spoken it."[36] But the character of Anne "felt extremely natural to me."

Her own history had prepared her well to play a young woman breaking through the confinements of convention. She had grown up in a devout French-Canadian Catholic household and spent her first twelve school years in a convent; in an online biography, she is quoted as saying that at the time she felt "as if I were in a long, dark tunnel, trying to convince myself that if I could ever get out, there was light ahead."[37] But something about her religious training made its way into her attitude toward acting. When asked in 2007 how she prepared for her roles, Bujold answered, "You pray for grace. If you've done your homework and, most of all, are open to receive, you go forward . . . Preparation for me is sacred."[38] But going forward with her own life required rebellion as well as grace; she finally "got out" of the tunnel by being caught reading a forbidden book. Liberated to pursue her own designs for her life, she enrolled in Montreal's free Conservatoire de Musique et d'Art Dramatique due Québec. While on tour in Paris with the company, she was discovered by director Alain Resnais, who cast her with Yves Montand in the acclaimed *La Guerre Est Finie.*

Resnais taught her an acting lesson that "still is in me, will always be with me. 'Always go to the end of your movement,' he told me — don't short-circuit the emotion, the bodily expression, the commitments of the personality you are playing, allow them to fully unfold."[39] That's something that Geneviève saw in Anne as well. "You can't put something into a character," she said, "that you haven't got within you. Every little thing in life is fed into the character . . . a word, a thought. I had read something on Anne Boleyn that Hal gave me and I could look at her with joy and energy; Anne brought a smile to my face."[40] I asked her what elicited that smile. "Independence. A healthy sense of justice. And she knew herself and was well with herself. She obviously had such profound integrity in that respect. She was willing to lose her head to go to the end of her movement."[41] That's what we see, too, in Bujold's portrayal of Anne, especially in that final speech, and it's why "My Elizabeth shall be queen!" still has audiences cheering for her, unconcerned with the historical liberties.

Most movies of the late 1960s have not worn exceptionally well, particularly with today's generation of viewers, for whom many of the lifestyle protests of the time seem dated and silly. My students snoozed through *Easy Rider.* With *Anne of the Thousand Days,* the passing years and changing culture have had the opposite effect; my students adored it, especially loving an Anne who seems to become "truer" as the generations have become less patient with passive heroines and perhaps a bit tired of the cutesy, man-focused femininity of many current female stars. "Everything I imagine Anne really was"[42]; "How I always picture Anne — as a strong woman not a sniveling girl"[43]; "The gold standard of Annes"[44]; "When I imagine Anne, it is her that I see"[45]; "The definitive Anne Boleyn for me"[46]; "Pitch-perfect"[47]; "So powerful that she turned a big, tough guy like me into a whimpering fool"[48]; "A remarkable actress. I will never forget the scene where she and Henry go riding from Hever . . . Purely from her body language, she radiates suppressed hatred toward Henry — just by sitting on a horse! And who can forget her in the blue gown, with jewels in her hair, looking devastatingly beautiful and in total command of herself and the situation."[49]

Before I said good-bye to Geneviève in our interview, I asked her whom she would pick to play Anne today. She admitted that she hadn't seen either Natalie Portman or Natalie Dormer; she lives a fairly reclusive life in Malibu and rarely sees movies or watches television. "But is there anyone who you think would do the part justice?" She was silent for a while, then asked me if she could be honest. Of course, I said. "Maybe it's selfish, but . . . the way I feel . . ." Geneviève had been so warm and generous throughout the interview, praising all her mentors and influences in her life, but she was clearly a bit uncomfortable with what she wanted to say. So I pressed a bit more, and she responded with an intensity that recalled her performance and made me smile with delight.

"No one," she replied. "Anne is mine."[50]

11

The Tudors

WHY HAVE THOUSANDS of young girls, in the first decade of the twenty-first century, become obsessed with Anne Boleyn? In no small part, the answer is Showtime's *The Tudors*—and Natalie Dormer's smoldering, brainy Anne. In the years between Bujold and Dormer, other actresses have played Anne —Dorothy Tutin, Charlotte Rampling, Helena Bonham Carter, Jodhi May—but none have inspired the passionate devotion of Bujold's and Dormer's fans. Of these four, only Dorothy Tutin is memorable. Charlotte Rampling was a credible vixen in a truly horrible 1972 condensation of the six-part BBC miniseries, which, as in the original, stars Keith Michell; Michell does an excellent job, but the events of Henry's reign are so compressed that we don't even get to see Anne's execution (one review said the made-for-TV movie should have been titled "Henry VIII and, By the Way, His Six Wives"[1]). Helena Bonham Carter, playing Anne to Ray Winstone's Henry in the 2003 *Henry VIII* (a pretty decent TV movie that no one remembers anymore), was fine but indistinguishable from Helena Bonham Carter in any other role. The 2003 BBC version of *The Other Boleyn Girl* was almost entirely improvised, allowing the actors to interpret their roles as the mood struck them; Jodhi May, who was selected for the part of Anne on the basis of the fact that she was sensual but not conventionally pretty, was most notable for the excited deep heaving of her bosom, which never let up no matter what was happening in the plot. Excited: heave, heave. Anxious: heave, heave. Plotting: heave, heave. Awaiting her beheading: heave, heave, heave.

None of these actresses brought anything to their roles that suggested the strength of character that Bujold brought to her Anne, perhaps due to the lack of directorial vision and guidance. The 1970 BBC miniseries was different. From the start, the creators were committed to the then-innovative conception of a Henry modeled on history rather than either the boorish caricatures of Emil Jannings and Charles Laughton or the tormented egotist of *Anne of the Thousand Days*. Long before Jonathan Rhys Meyers appeared on the scene, the BBC series broke new ground by showing the young Henry "as an excellent scholar who spoke four languages other than his native tongue . . . a student of mathematics and astronomy, a gifted musician, and a superb athlete . . . most likely England's first civilised king."[2] The first episode, "Katherine," was a revelation for many viewers. In the story people were used to, Katherine is the rejected and ultimately discarded wife. In this episode, we see her young and eager, chasing through the castle and tumbling under the sheets with an equally young, ardent Henry. When things begin to go wrong, she is less a piously downtrodden wife than a stubborn defender of her (and her daughter's) rights. This was also the first and last Katherine whose fair skin and golden hair were faithful to historical description rather than Spanish stereotypes. Annette Crosbie won a BAFTA award for her performance, and deservedly. In her Katherine, we saw a consistent personality develop over time, from a bubbly but regal young woman to a steely monarch who, unlike more clichéd, contemporary portraits, never descends into long-suffering pathos.

Crosbie was helped by the fact that her character appeared in only one episode, written by just one screenwriter, Rosemary Sisson, who had a clear and steady vision of her heroine. Anne's role, in contrast, was spread out over two episodes that were written by two authors with very different views of her. She appears at the end of Sisson's episode as a coldhearted, gossipy, and cackling harbinger of what is to come for Katherine. Then in Nick McCarty's episode, devoted almost entirely (except for a brief montage of happier days) to Anne's fall, she suddenly becomes dignified, principled, and much more sympathetic. Between the harpy of the "Katherine" episode and the stoical queen of the "Anne" episode, there is a vacuum, which viewers filled as they pleased. But although the role was not coherent, and some said she was too old (perhaps true for the first episode but not for the second), Dorothy Tutin brought a solidity to her Anne that those who followed her lacked. All of them emphasized cunning and sexual flirtatiousness —traits that, while they may have been true to aspects of Anne's personality, made her seem too much of a lightweight to fuel the six-year obsession of the king, especially when played by such young actresses. Tutin projected more; she understood that it was not just Katherine who had dignity.

I saw the BBC series when it first aired on television, and I found it anything but stuffy. For viewers of that era, *Masterpiece Theatre* and its ilk, while usually dealing with "classics" heavily encrusted with "Britishness" (Alistair Cooke introduced each show sitting in an imaginary English country house), were our first experience of what has become *the* most popular form of American television addiction: the prime-time miniseries. It didn't feel "classic-y," it felt intimate and involving. Until then, only comedy, action, and variety shows had given us ongoing interaction with familiar actors and characters; drama (with the exception of the daytime soaps) began and ended in the space of an hour. Now I became frantic if I had to miss one of the twenty-six episodes of *The Forsyte Saga* (this was pre-TiVo and DVR, even pre-VCR for ordinary people), was riveted by *I, Claudius* and *Elizabeth R,* remained devoted to Sunday night PBS through *Brideshead Revisited* and even some series that have disappeared from collective memory almost entirely: *Danger UXB* followed the lives and loves of the young men who detonated unexploded bombs in the streets of London during World War II. Arguably, these shows were the forerunners and inspiration for American prime-time series such as *Roots, Lonesome Dove,* and *The Winds of War.* Ultimately, with *Dallas* and *Dynasty,* the nighttime series fare became far schlockier. In the early seventies, our tastes were not classier; they were just less jaded, less numbed. We didn't need sex and scheming to become engaged; a good story that lasted for a while was juicy enough.

By the time Robert Greenblatt, the award-winning producer of HBO's *Six Feet Under*, then president of Showtime and known as "the man who out-HBO'd HBO"[3] with such innovative series as *Dexter*, *The L Word*, and *Weeds*, got the idea to do a series on the Tudors, those once-delicious PBS shows had come to seem (as various writers and actors associated with *The Tudors* put it) "old-fashioned," "wooden," "stiff," "starchy," "rigid," and — as Greenblatt described it — "safe in a, you know, 'BBC' way."[4] (Jonathan Rhys Meyers, more crudely, referred to previous approaches as "period puke."[5]) Greenblatt's goal for the series he had in mind was to "breathe new life" into the Henry VIII story by offering a "younger and sexier version," with plenty of beheadings and "more sensual reality."[6] Greenblatt had a certain amount of experience with "young and sexy" when he was executive vice president of prime-time programming for the Fox Broadcasting Company, where he had helped to develop such hits as the original *Beverly Hills, 90210*; *Melrose Place*; *The X-Files*; *Party of Five*; *Ally McBeal*; and *King of the Hill* (as well as the pilots for *The Sopranos* and *Dawson's Creek*).

Michael Hirst, who studied English literature at Oxford and wrote the screenplay for *Elizabeth* (and later, the sequel), was commissioned to do the pilot and was expressly asked to do it by Reveille Productions founder Ben Silverman as a "kind of American soap opera" about politics, power, and sexuality, like *The West Wing* and *The Sopranos*. "I hadn't worked in TV before," Hirst told me in a 2011 phone interview. "And although I had seen *The Sopranos*, I didn't really know what he was talking about. Was he asking me to dumb down the story?"[7] This was not what Hirst was interested in doing. In fact, one of his pet passions, in imagining a series on the Tudors, was to open up a fresh understanding of the Reformation, so often simply glorified as leading to the "golden age" of Elizabeth and Shakespeare. But in Hirst's view, it left deep "psychic wounds" in England. He was skeptical about the possibilities of doing this without becoming "didactic," but after reviewing episodes of *The West Wing*, which he hadn't seen before, Hirst became convinced that it was possible to "be entertaining and commercial but about serious things. You could develop ideas, and I could actually talk about important things like the Reformation, but without lecturing."[8] So he decided to "have a go" and wound up in love with the project.

Among the ideas Hirst was most interested in developing was a revision of the "cartoon vision of Henry VIII as this fat, bearded monster. People seem not to understand that historical figures, behind the iconography, were human beings. That's the way I approached Elizabeth, and I did it with Henry."[9] At the center of this revision was the actor chosen to play the most post-Holbein, post-Laughton — and, one might say, postmodern — Henry yet. He was not just young, but *very* young, brown-haired, as physically taut as a J.Crew model, and pulsing with dangerous sensuality. The actor chosen was Jonathan Rhys Meyers, the pillow-lipped Irish actor who had won a Golden Globe for his performance in the CBS miniseries *Elvis*. Hirst felt that Rhys Meyers would actually bring the Tudor king more in line with historical reality. "Jonny, by instinct, has many of the same qualities as Henry," he said in an early interview. "He has a short attention span. He never thinks there's anything he can't do."[10] Brian Kirk, one of the show's directors, pointed out that Jonny's knowledge of the Hollywood star system would give him a "parallel experience to draw on" as the "rock star" of the court.[11] Meyers, who admits to having done very little research for the role, continues the comparison: "Henry's court at that time was the fastest court in the world. If you weren't in Henry's court, you were nobody . . . It was the Mecca of entertainment."[12] Um, historians of Francis's court might have something to say about that.

On the darker end of the comparisons, Rhys Meyers has also been reported to be a heavy partier and womanizer, with poor impulse control. "Jonny has always been on the brink of going really off the rails," says a friend, after Rhys Meyers became aggressive with the airport staffer who woke him up after he fell asleep, drunk, on the floor of the airport.[13] "He is a clever boy and likes to play mind games," says another.[14] Henry's behavior — whether aggressive or sexual — was, of course, usually well contained by his sense of the necessary kingly image, but he was prone to sudden outbursts of rage, particularly in later life, and his "mind games" were well-known.

The younger Henry was also known for his athleticism and was often described as extremely handsome. Of course, there was a certain amount of required flattery going on in these descriptions. But the fact that Henry was over six feet tall, well-built (in his youth), and vividly complected in an era in which life was "nasty, brutish, and short" counted for a lot. Compact, wiry Jonathan Rhys Meyers, seen in terms of Tudor standards, was a very odd choice; a taller, more robust Henry — think, for example, of a slimmed-down Russell Crowe — would have preserved some aesthetic continuity with the real Henry. Joan Bergin, in her costuming, tried to do just this by creatively combining authentic Tudor styling with fashion from other eras — Degas paintings, Balenciaga couture — in order to achieve a "more modern sensibility." She called this process "deconstructed Tudor."[15] But Jonathan Rhys Meyers wasn't even a "deconstructed" Henry; he was a radically resculpted one.

Meyers, apparently, called quite a few of the shots here. He refused, for example, to gain weight — or to wear prosthetics — as the series went on. Both Hirst and Meyers have tried to justify this. Hirst has given a few different explanations. In a 2008 interview, he said that he didn't want people to say, "Oh, look. That is Henry VIII. We wanted to get closer to the spirit of the thing, to a kind of reality. And the reality was that Henry was young, virile, very charismatic, very dangerous."[16] In his 2011 interview with me, he began by saying that a "big body suit" would have looked ridiculous on Rhys Meyers's "small head," and he "never wanted to go down the line of a slightly comical Henry."[17] Eventually, however, Hirst admitted to me that "we simply couldn't have gotten Jonny to do it. He would not have been able to tolerate looking grotesque."[18] Rhys Meyers has tried to justify his refusal in commercial terms. "Listen," he told the *Sunday Times* when the show aired in the U.S. in 2007, "you're trying to sell a historical period drama to a country like America — you do not want a big, fat, 250-pound, red-haired guy with a beard. It doesn't let people embrace the fantastic monarch he was, because they're not attracted to the package. Heroes do not look like Henry VIII. That is just the world we live in."[19] Of course — setting aside the insult to redheads and Americans — Henry didn't become fat overnight, and by the time that he did, he was hardly a "hero." In another interview, Rhys Meyers admits that "I just didn't want to be Fat Henry."[20] That seems to have been the bottom line.

Natalie Dormer, the twenty-six-year-old actress who was chosen to play the role of Anne Boleyn, approached her assignment very differently. A longtime British history buff who had, in fact, hoped to study history at Cambridge (she misunderstood a question on her A-level exams and failed to get the necessary grade for acceptance), Natalie has strong opinions about the real Anne, and when she got the role, she was excited over the prospect of embodying her as accurately as possible. "I didn't want to play her as this femme fatale — she was a genuine evangelical with a real religious belief in the Reformation."[21] Dormer also came to the role well aware of the stereotypes and gender biases that had dogged Anne, both in her lifetime and in later representations.

"Anne really influenced the world behind closed doors," she told me in our 2010 interview. "But she's given no explicit credit because she wasn't protected. Let's not forget, too, that history was written by men. And even now, in our postfeminist era, we still have women struggling in public positions of power. When you read a history book, both the commentary and the firsthand primary evidence, all the natural gender prejudices during the period will certainly be there.

"Anne was that rare phenomenon, a self-made woman. But then, this became her demise. The machinations of court were an absolute minefield for women. And she was a challenging personality, who wouldn't be quiet and shut up when she had something to say. This was a woman who wasn't raised in the English court, but in the Hapsburg and French courts. And she was quite a fiery woman and incredibly intelligent. So she stood out — fire and intelligence and boldness — in comparison to the English roses that were flopping around court. And Henry noticed that. So all the reasons that attracted [Henry] to her, and made her queen and a mother, were all the things that then undermined her position. What she had that was so unique for a woman at that time was also her undoing."[22]

I was extremely lucky to meet Natalie after her contract with Showtime was over and she felt free to cease acting as a spokesperson for the show and to speak her mind. We arranged to meet in a small boutique hotel in Richmond upon Thames, where she lived at the time. When she arrived (I had been there for a half hour, the only woman in the room without a hat, nervously checking my recording equipment), the staff immediately sprang into action to make things comfortable for us in the bar; she clearly is the town celebrity. But, except for her dramatic expressiveness and striking beauty, which singled her out from everyone else at the bar, there was no aura of celebrity about her. Despite her success and the legions of fan clubs devoted to her, she regards herself as very much at the start of her career and seemed genuinely excited to talk to someone else who was waist-deep in the world of Anne Boleyn, a place that she had occupied with intensity and dedication over the last several years. We were in sync from our first exchange, and for over an hour and a half, nestled like longtime girlfriends in the corner of the bar. Accompanied by her younger sister, Samantha, we shared our love of Anne and her story, lamented how it had been misrepresented both in Anne's time and our own, discussed Tudor history, and reflected on the struggle of Anne, women actors, and young women today to escape the limitations and expectations placed on them. It was in this interview that Natalie revealed, for the first time, just how hard she had struggled to "not betray" Anne, as she put it, in the series.[23]

The first challenge came almost immediately. Natalie had auditioned in her natural hair color, which is blonde, fully expecting that if she got the role she would play Anne as a brunette. She knew her history, and it never occurred to her that the executives at Showtime would have anything else in mind. She was concerned, in fact, that her strong physical differences from Anne — including her blue eyes — would disqualify her for the part. She reassured herself about the eyes — "They aren't the right color, but just like Anne, I've been told they are my most becoming feature." (Actually, there's not a feature on Natalie's face that isn't dazzling.) But she knew the hair would have to be changed. So after she received the phone call telling her she'd won the part — largely on the basis, Hirst told me, of the "physical chemistry" between her and Rhys Meyers (Natalie describes it as "a lot of heaving bosom stuff") — she became "hysterical with joy" and then immediately dyed her hair.[24]

When she arrived on set, Dee Corcoran, chief of the hair department, who won an Emmy for her work on the show and was "almost like an Irish mother" to Natalie, took her aside. "Okay, we've got a really serious problem — you dyed your hair. They are really unhappy. Really unhappy."[25] "They" were the Showtime execs.

"So they sent me back to the hairdresser and they tried to dye blonde back in. But any hairdresser will tell you that it doesn't work to put peroxide blonde on jet black. I looked like a badger! I was terrified that I'd lose the role. I mean, what did they have planned, now that I was multicolored — to put me in a blonde wig?" Dormer wasn't sure she could accept that. "Anne's hair color is such an important detail! For one thing, it was the basis of a lot of nasty labels — Wolsey calling her the 'night crow' and so on. And also, in being a confident brunette she was defying the ideal of what it meant for a female to be attractive at that time.[26]

"So we're all barely cast, and I went to Bob Greenblatt with my heart in my mouth and told him how important it was that Anne be dark. 'Bob, I have to play her dark. It's so important. You have to let me play her dark!' Some might say I was being melodramatic and self-important. But I thought it would just be a direct betrayal of Anne. Of her refusal to step into the imprint of the acceptable norm at the time.[27]

"Greenblatt, who is a very shrewd man, just said, 'I'll think about it.' I assumed I'd lost the job. I felt completely and utterly depressed. But then I got a phone call a few days later, telling me that Bob had decided I could be dark."[28]

Natalie didn't try to hide her pride and pleasure from me. "It was a major coup at the time! A major coup!"[29] It was clear that by "coup" Natalie didn't mean that she had bested the executives with a power play, for she was well aware that they called the shots and that her casting had hung precariously in the balance. It was, rather, a victory for the values that she hoped would be brought to the series — authenticity, a recognition of what was unusual about Anne, and a willingness, on the part of those in charge, to listen and learn.

But there were more challenges ahead. Michael Hirst freely admitted to me that when he wrote the first season of *The Tudors*, he wasn't all that interested in Anne Boleyn. "I didn't even know if we'd be picked up for a second season at that point, and Anne was one of many people swimming in the ether. Wolsey and More — and, of course, Henry — were the more dominant figures."[30] His ultimate goal was to introduce television viewers to the tumultuous events behind the English Reformation. But he knew that history-as-entertainment was "a giant leap" for most viewers, and he wasn't afraid to make use of — some would say, invent — the sexier side of the story. He had wanted Natalie Dormer for the role of Anne largely because of the sparks between her and Jonathan Rhys Meyers, and felt that to win audiences over to a historical drama they "had to push the boundary" when it came to sexuality. But, he insists, "It wasn't entirely cynical."

> I did want to show, unlike high school history, that there was a lot of sex at the time. All the courts of Europe were run by people in their teens and twenties . . . that's why they were so crazy. We have this image now that the court is always middle-aged, but it wasn't true. You know, Henry was eighteen when he became king, and I thought it was ridiculous that people were telling me he was really rather prudish and there was no sex because there was no heating in the palaces. But it's quite true that it was also a way of gaining an audience for something that wouldn't otherwise have been watched. Once I had my audience, I could develop more complicated issues.[31]

Some members of the cast, however, did not apparently care much about those "complicated issues." Sam Neill, who played Cardinal Wolsey, described the series as "above all, about sex. Sex drives everything, including Wolsey, who had a mistress. The vow of celibacy didn't mean a lot to the good cardinal. Yes, sex drives everything. That's what makes [the series] such fun."[32] Amazingly enough, this view of the period did not hamper Neill from doing a pretty fair job as Wolsey.

Today, Hirst admits that he may have gone too far. "We probably had a little too much sex in the beginning," he conceded.[33] I certainly thought so, not for reasons of prudishness but because the sexual overkill was ludicrous, historically inaccurate, and turned all the women, save hair-shirted Katherine, into mindless tarts. The debut of the series coincided with the beginning of my own research for this book, and I had the passion of a new convert to the cause of "the real" Anne and Henry. Their sex lives are not so easy to uncover, of course, but partly that's because they were so much more discreet than the out-in-the-open antics of *The Tudors*. "They were much more sexually gregarious in the sixteenth century than they are today," Rhys Meyers claims; how he knows that is a mystery, but even if it were true, Henry would not have paraded his adventures in view of the court.[34] That much we can say with certainty. Beyond that, there is speculation. Henry, many scholars believe, may not have been the most expert of lovers; some think he was plagued by intermittent impotence. There's no proof of either of those claims; it all depends on whether you believe that Anne was speaking truthfully (and not merely spitefully) when she told Jane Rochford that the king had neither skill nor vigor in bed. But one thing upon which most historians agree is that Henry was not especially promiscuous and took relatively few mistresses — when compared, say, to Francis. For Francis, affairs were a sport; for Henry, they were mostly confined to the periods when his wives were pregnant — or when he had truly soured on his current mate (as happened with both Katherine and Anne). If there were indeed as many beddings as shown in *The Tudors*, we don't know about them precisely because he was so careful to keep them private.

This was a man, too, we should remember, who apparently kept himself chaste for six years while he waited for Anne to become available, a restraint that some scholars believe was Henry's idea, not Anne's. It does make sense that having settled on Anne as queen, Henry would not have wanted to jeopardize the scenario he hoped for — marriage and then an indisputably legitimate male heir — with an illegitimate child by her or any other woman. Hirst retains the notion that Henry waited for Anne (showing Henry masturbating in a little pot held by a manservant to get some release). But a Henry who would have been capable of such restraint doesn't square very well with the rambunctiously horny Henry of previous episodes, who merely has to wink at one of his boys and nod in the direction of a pretty wench in order to have her delivered to his rooms that night. In the very first episode, he spends all of four minutes discussing the pros and cons of war with France before he declares that "it's time to play" and goes off to have cinematic sex with his mistress, Elizabeth Blount. Blount *was* his mistress, and the mother of Henry's illegitimate son, Henry Fitzroy, so there's some justification for introducing her early on. But later on in the same episode — it seems to be the next day — he invites another maid — a "Lady Jane," unknown to the historical record — to his bedchamber. And on it goes, until Henry is struck with the dart of love for Anne. In these pre-Anne romps, Henry is such an expert undresser, buttocks-slapper, muff nibbler, and nipple stroker that it's hard to believe the man was raised in a Catholic household, let alone suffered from any confidence problems.

None of this stopped me from becoming addicted to the series. And none of it truly offended me until, in the third episode, Francis's sister Marguerite de Navarre, the intellectual light of Francis's court, a critic of male sexual aggression, and a deep believer in platonic love between men and women, appears as a visitor to the English court, bosom spilling out of her dress, casting hot glances across the dining hall at Henry as both of them bite into their roasted thighs and wings, Tom Jones fashion. The liaison gets arranged effortlessly, and later that night, we see two guards stoically keeping watch while Henry and Marguerite grunt and moan behind his bedroom door. Most viewers would not have realized that a distinguished historical figure — Marguerite is often called "the mother of the Renaissance" — was being turned into a trollop for the sake of ratings, but for those of us who know something about the period, it seemed not merely gratuitous (as "Lady Jane" had been) but nasty. Having talked to Michael Hirst at length, I know he is neither nasty nor disrespectful of women. But doing *The Tudors*, as he admits, was a learning curve for him when it came to the intellectual and religious role of the female players in the larger historical drama. And at this point along the curve, someone such as Marguerite would have been even farther out "in the ether" than Anne. I suspect he just assumed that Francis's sister would have had the same proclivities as her brother.

Hirst, in his zeal to make the series deliciously digestible to primetime viewers, did not initially do justice to Anne either. Although, in his interview with me, he described her as "one of the heroines of English culture . . . who did a great deal to support and foster the advancement of the Protestant faith," but whose "name has been blackened because she was the Other Woman who came between Henry and his rightful queen," the Anne of the first season of *The Tudors* (and partway into the second) did not do much to disrupt that "blackened" image.[35] Throughout that first season, Anne entices, provokes, and sexually manipulates her way into the queenship, allowing Henry to get to every base except home, driving him mad with pent-up lust. "Seduce me!" she orders Henry, and a moment later we see her stark naked[36]; a few episodes later, she taunts him to find a piece of ribbon that she has apparently hidden inside her vagina. In the last episode of the season, they ride into an appropriately moist and verdant forest, tear at each other's clothing, and just about do it before Anne pulls herself away from the embrace, leaving him to howl in frustration — and reminding me, unpleasantly, of high school. (We're told, early in the second season, that Anne had become acquainted, while a teenage resident at the French court, with the hand job. Why didn't she make use of it? It would have spared Henry and viewers alike some agony.) At the beginning of season two, it is also suggested that while at the French court, Anne slept with half the courtiers and possibly the French king. When Henry presents her, newly anointed as the Marquess of Pembroke, to Francis and his court, she performs a Salome-style dance that makes one wonder just which historical series one is watching. At home, her bold flirting, confiding, and cuddling with Mark Smeaton makes the later charges of adultery with him quite plausible — and completely out of character with Anne, who was obsessed with being accepted as queen and would never have condescended to treat a court musician in such an openly familiar fashion.

The show premiered in the United States in April 2007. The first reviews were neither outraged nor particularly enthusiastic. Alessandra Stanley, in the *New York Times*, called it "enjoyable but not exhilarating, engaging but not hypnotic."[37] Ted Cox, in the *Daily Herald*, asked: "What do bare breasts and rampant sex scenes add to the life of Henry VIII?" and concluded that while "history certainly goes down easier when it's being mixed with bodice-ripping romps in bed," the show "never really ignites dramatically."[38] Ginia Bellafante, in a later review, referred to the first season as "somnolent."[39] A lot of viewers, apparently, didn't agree; the preview episode gave Showtime its highest viewing figures for a series debut in three years.

It was when the show premiered on BBC six months later that the steam hit the fan, as the British reacted to the marathon sexuality and what in virtually every review was described as the gross, pandering "Americanization" of English history. "Perfectly preposterous. There are so many pouting babes and dashing blades in Henry's court, *The Tudors* looks like a *CSI: Miami* pool party with ruffles"[40]; "a Wikipedia entry with boobs"[41]; "sexed up" and "dumbed down" for American audiences[42]; "a porno-style historical semi-drama quite obviously not aimed at the serious television watcher"[43]; "*Entourage* goes historical"[44]; "if Jackie Collins wrote a dramatic version of Simon Schama's *History of Britain*, it might come across like this."[45]

When the historians got in on the action, criticisms of the historical inaccuracies were added to the complaints about the sex. Retha Warnicke, a historian who has advanced her own somewhat eccentric view of Anne's fall, later incorporated in both *The Tudors* and *The Other Boleyn Girl* (a deformed fetus taken as a sign of witchcraft), "shuddered" at the conflation of Henry's sisters, Mary and Margaret, into one person. "Truly dreadful," she said of the merging of the two, which was done, according to Hirst, so that staff on location would not be confused when "Mary" was called to the set.[46] Leanda de Lisle, who has written several well-regarded Tudor biographies, stated: "With inaccuracies in almost every sentence, the BBC is dumbing down the Tudor period."[47] Alison Weir compared the series to a Hollywood "fairytale." "For a program to be made with integrity, it has to take account of the facts."[48] David Starkey (a self-confessed "all-purpose media tart," who has created controversy in virtually every interview he has done) called the series "gratuitously awful" and "a Midwest view of the Tudors . . . made with the original intention of dumbing it down so that even an audience in Omaha could understand it."[49]

There were some exceptions. There were historians who pointed out that simply by igniting interest in the period the series had done a service to Tudor history. Tracy Borman, who writes about Anne in

Elizabeth's Women, while acknowledging that the show was often historically inaccurate, admitted to having become "strangely addicted" and praised it for "re-creating the drama and atmosphere of Henry VIII's court, with its intrigues, scandals, and betrayals."[50] John Guy, who has written more than a dozen scholarly books about Tudor England, agreed. "*The Tudors* conveys brilliantly the claustrophobic atmosphere of Henry's court; it's a place where back-watching is second-nature, plotting endemic . . . If you value true and accurate history, this isn't for you. But then, it isn't meant to be. It's a rumbustious romp through the life and times of 'Horrible Henry and the Terrible Tudors,' a fiction loosely based on fact, and when the facts get in the way, they're ditched. If you can accept that, then watch and enjoy, for that's what the real-life characters would have done. Thomas More, who always loved a comic turn, will be spinning in his grave if he's watching this new series. But at least he'll be smiling."[51]

Hirst had never claimed the series was 100 percent historically accurate, and to be fair to *The Tudors,* there's not a film or television series — or play or novel, for that matter (and few biographies) — that can lay claim to that. "What?" a reader wrote in response to a critical *Guardian* story, "It's NOT historically accurate?? Thanks goodness I know that Robin Hood *is* an American with a number 1 soundtrack, King Arthur is an old Scotsman, and the Americans single-handedly won the Second World War!"[52] He makes a strong point. *Anne of the Thousand Days,* in addition to numerous other alterations of history, has that invented — yet somehow perfect — scene in the Tower between Anne and Henry. *The Private Life of Henry VIII* turns Anne of Cleves into a wisecracking cardsharp who is physically disgusted by Henry rather than (as history tells it) the other way around. *A Man for All Seasons* neglects to mention that Thomas More, besides being a witty intellectual, also burned quite a few heretics and was apparently not quite the devoted husband he appeared to be. The BBC production of *The Six Wives of Henry VIII* barely notes that there was a conflict of authority between Henry and the Church, beyond the issue of the divorce; it's actually much more the wife-centered, "feminized" history that Starkey berates than *The Tudors,* which spends a lot of time on the more "masculine" (and for Starkey, historically central) end of things: diplomatic skirmishes, wars, and court politics. Hirst, in his interview with me, pointed out with some justice that while *The Tudors* got slammed for its gaps and inventions, Hilary Mantel's *Wolf Hall* gets nothing but praise for its liberties with history. *Wolf Hall*, he says, is "complete fiction. But nobody says that. They all say: 'What a wonderful book, what insights it brings to the Tudors.' Isn't that bizarre?"[53]

Mantel's quirky, magisterial portrait of Thomas Cromwell *is* a wonderful book, an imaginative tour de force that makes the precarious yet oddly cozy world of the Tudor court seem both completely familiar and utterly strange. Yet Hirst is right, it doesn't shy away from tweaking the facts. Ignoring the fact that Cromwell and Anne had many of the same religious commitments for most of Anne's reign, Mantel paints Anne through Cromwell's eyes as a predatory calculator, brittle, anxious, and cold — a view that Cromwell is unlikely to have held during the period that *Wolf Hall* takes place. Mantel's 2013 sequel, *Bring Up the Bodies*, which deals with the chilling, sudden turnabout of Anne's fortunes "as it might have looked from Thomas Cromwell's point of view,"[54] goes even further, presenting a "theory" about Anne's fall that is quite different from what most historians now believe — namely, that Cromwell played the leading hand in cooking up the ruthless plot that cost Anne her life. Mantel's Cromwell, less the master strategist of a political coup than the nimble, pragmatic servant of Henry's fickle love life, has some fortunately timed gossip fall in his lap and simply follows the wind, never quite sure of the truth himself — and leaving the historically uninformed reader unsure as well. "What is the nature of the border between truth and lies?" Mantel has Cromwell musing as the bits and pieces of rumor pile up. "It is permeable and blurred because it is planted thick with rumour, confabulation, misunderstanding and twisted tales."[55] In *Bring Up the Bodies*, Mantel brilliantly re-creates that permeable and blurred experience (even Anne's guilt or innocence remains undecided at the end of the novel), which is what makes her fiction remarkable. Yet it is as blurred with regard to the truth as the false rumors that swirled around Anne's sexual behavior.

It's worth reflecting on our shifting standards with regard to the historical accuracy of fictional representations. Although historians complain about the distortions of history in *The Tudors*, the show actually sticks much more closely and in greater detail to the historical record than any other production. Ironically, that has made it more vulnerable to criticism. With the leisure of four seasons, the series is able to deal with much more of what actually happened; therefore, it has much more "data" to not get quite right or alter deliberately for dramatic purposes. And despite the condescending remarks of the British press, the show is actually intellectually far more demanding than *The Six Wives of Henry VIII*. Perhaps its chief offense is being "pop" rather than "literary." I adored *Wolf Hall* (despite its nasty portrait of Anne), but I know a great deal about the period and have to wonder how many of those who praised it actually were able to follow it. It's an extremely dense, demanding work of art, particularly for those who aren't familiar with all the cultural references; even keeping all the Thomases straight is a challenge. Perhaps critics were afraid to question its fidelity to history because, like students in a high-theory college course, they were afraid of displaying their own ignorance.

Among historians, what is seen as "dreadful" and what slides by is often a matter of whom and what you care about. As an Anne scholar and a feminist, I bristle most when she is dragged through the sexist muck. Some depictions get away with nonsense because they were created long enough ago that they are viewed as dusty, cultural artifacts, and as such are not held to standards of factual accuracy. Television and movies, because they carry with them the illusion of verisimilitude — real bodies, real action, and often in highly realistic settings and costumes — are more likely to be criticized for historical inaccuracy no matter how often their creators, as Hirst does, insist that they are not meant to be entirely factual. If they comport themselves with enough dignity, however — like the BBC productions or *A Man for All Seasons* — they are off the hook. And then there is the post–Oliver Stone, "postmodern" problem: We no longer have much assurance that viewers or readers will be able to distinguish between fact and fiction, so special anxiety about the transgressions of *The Tudors* or *The Other Boleyn Girl* is "justified" by virtue of a cultural milieu in which the created image (whether computer-generated visuals or concocted narratives) is consumed, without scrutiny, as "reality."

The Tudors' chief offense, I believe, is not that it is "dumb" or especially riddled with inaccuracies, but that it exploits audience's tastes for eye candy, cinematic sex, and soap-opera drama. If the series had aimed at more refined tastes, I believe, fewer historians would have found the Mary/Margaret conflation so outrageous. They would have been respectfully curious as to the reason for it, but they would not have so readily cried "shame!" — as though the Virgin Mary had been slandered. My most serious problem with the show's pandering to soap-opera tastes is that it inevitably led to recycling the image of Anne Boleyn as the seductive, scheming Other Woman. That's the classic soapy element of the story, after all: Sexpot steals husband from mousy, menopausal first wife. Hirst says he never intended this and attributes it less to the script than to "deep cultural projections." He had initially seen Anne, he told me, as a victim of her father's ambitions, and believed he was writing the script to emphasize that. He was surprised when "critics started to trot this line out: 'Here she is, just a manipulative bitch.' Well, actually I hadn't written it like that. But they couldn't get out of the stereotypes that had been handed down to them and that's what they thought they were seeing on the screen. It didn't matter what they were actually seeing. They had already decided that Anne Boleyn was this Other Woman, this manipulative bitch."[56]

I agree with Hirst about the power of the history of cultural images; but it's odd that he would be so naïve about the way that the show's own imagery reinforced them. Dormer believes it was indeed unconscious on Hirst's part, that in capitalizing on the sexual chemistry between Henry and Anne, and while portraying Katherine as virtuous and long-suffering, he slipped into a very common male mind-set. "Men still have trouble recognizing," she told me, "that a woman can be complex, can have ambition, good looks, sexuality, erudition, and common sense. A woman can have all those facets, and yet men, in literature and in drama, seem to need to simplify women, to polarize us as either the whore or the angel. That sensibility is prevalent, even to this day. I have a lot of respect for Michael, as a writer and a human being, but I think that he has that tendency. I don't think he does it consciously. I think it's something innate that just happens and he doesn't realize it."[57]

Natalie was in a bind. "I had to reconcile the real person and the character of Anne Boleyn as created in the text. For the actor, the text is your bible. You can try to put a spin on the nuances, but in the end our job is to be the vehicle of the text." Yet she often felt "compromised" by the way Anne's character was written for the first season and got tired of "flying the flag of Showtime" in interviews, justifying the show's hypersexuality and inaccuracies "when in the pit of my stomach, I agreed wholly with what the interviewer was saying to me. I lost many hours of sleep and actually shed tears during my portrayal of her, trying to inject historical truth into the script, trying to do right by this woman whom I had read so much about. It was a constant struggle, because the original script had that tendency to polarize women into saint and whore. It wasn't deliberate, but it was there."[58]

At the point at which I spoke to Michael Hirst, after the last season of the show was completed, he had become much more aware of the long legacy of negative stereotypes of Anne, the tendency of fiction writers and some historians to simply recycle them, and his own complicity. But at the time of the first reviews, he was surprised when some critics "dismissed Anne as your typically manipulative, scheming bitch" and was distressed that "some of this criticism hurt Natalie very much."[59] But Natalie wasn't about to let it rest with that. During a dinner with Hirst, while he was still writing the second season, she shared her frustration and begged him "to do it right in the second half. We were good friends. He listened to me because he knew I knew my history. And you know, he's a brilliant man. So he listened. And I remember saying to him: 'Throw everything you've got at me. Promise me you'll do that. I can do it. The politics, the religion, the personal stuff, throw everything you've got at me. I can take it.'"[60]

She told Hirst of her wish that audiences, when the series got to Anne's fall, would empathize with her. Talking to me in Richmond upon Thames, Natalie was especially passionate about that subject.

"It happened very shortly after she miscarried, remember. To miscarry is traumatic for any woman, even in this day and age. And to be in that physical and mental state, having just miscarried, and be incarcerated in the Tower! If only she'd had that child! It's horrific to confront how much transpired because of terrible timing, and how different it could have been. It's one of the most dramatic 'ifs' of history. And it's why it's such a compelling, sympathetic story. But I knew by the time we'd finished the first season that we hadn't achieved it. That audiences would have no sympathy for her because the way she'd been written, she would be regarded as the other woman, the third wheel, that femme fatale, that bitch. Who had it coming to her."[61]

Hirst listened to her and took her seriously, and the result was a major change in the Anne Boleyn of the second season. Still sexy, but brainy, politically engaged and astute, a loving mother, and a committed reformist. Scenes were added, showing Anne talking to Henry about Tyndale, instructing her ladies-in-waiting about the English Bible, quarrelling with Cromwell over the misuse of monastery money. No longer was Anne simply a character "in the ether." Rehabilitating her image became part of Hirst's motivation in writing the script: "I wanted to show that she was a human being, a young woman placed in a really difficult and awful situation, manipulated by her father, the king, and circumstances, but that she was also feisty and interesting and had a point of view and tried to use her powers to advance what she believed in. And I wanted people to live with her, to live through her. To see her."[62]

The execution scene was especially important to Natalie: "By the end of the season, when I'm standing on that scaffold," she told Michael, "I hope you write it the way it should be. And I want the effect of that scene to remain with viewers for the length of the series. I want the audience to be standing with her on that scaffold. I want those who have judged her harshly to change their allegiance so they actually love her and empathize with her."[63] However the scene was to be scripted, this would require a lot of Natalie, especially since the show was not filmed in chronological sequence and the execution scene was shot before the episodes that led up to it. At dawn, standing in the courtyard of Dublin's Kilmainham Jail, the site of many actual executions, she had "a good cry" with Jonathan Rhys Meyers. "It was incredibly haunting and harrowing — I felt the weight of history on my shoulders." But because she had "lived and breathed Anne for months on end" and had "tremendous sympathy for the historical figure," it did not require a radical shift of mood to prepare herself for the scene. "I was a real crucible of emotions for those few days. By the time I walked onto the scaffold, I hope I did have that phenomenal air of dignity that Anne had." Anne's resigned, contained anguish did not have to be forced, because by then Natalie was in mourning for the character. "As I was saying the lines, I got the feeling I was saying good-bye to a character. And when it was over, I grieved for her."[64]

Hirst, too, recalls the heightened emotions of shooting that scene. "That was an amazing day. Extraordinary day. After, I went in to congratulate her. She was weeping and saying, 'She's with me, Michael. She's with me.'"[65]

The episode averaged 852,000 viewers, according to Nielsen, an 83 percent increase over the first season finale and an 11 percent increase over the season premiere, and for many viewers — particularly younger women — the execution scene became as iconic as Geneviève Bujold's "Elizabeth shall be queen" speech.[66] When I showed the episode to a classroom of historically sophisticated honors students, none of whom had watched the series, there were many teary eyes; among devoted *Tudors* fans, for whom it was the culmination of a building attachment to the character, the effect of the scene — whose last moments were both graphic and poetic, lingering on Anne postexecution, her now-lifeless face still bearing her final, sad, unbelieving expression, caught midair, suspended in space — was emotionally wrenching.

> I have watched many actresses walk to the scaffold as Anne Boleyn and I read every book I can get my hands on fiction or nonfiction about her and I have never seen anyone do it with the grace I believe that Anne had except Natalie. The scene where she is walking through the crowd and they are actually touching her, you can see in her eyes and her mouth and the way she breathes that she is trying to hold it together and stay calm. Episode 9 and 10 of season two are stunning due to Natalie.[67]

Many viewers, in fact, watched the show listlessly after Dormer as Anne left; the rest of the story seemed anticlimactic to them. "Natalie

Dormer basically ruled *The Tudors*!," wrote one viewer. "Her performance was absolutely passionate, genuine, and convincing and that's why I was devastated when her character died and she left the show."[68] The feelings of this commentator were shared by many. The following season's finale had the show's second smallest audience (366,000 viewers), and among those who stuck with it and continued to enjoy it (as I did) there remained a void where Natalie's Anne Boleyn had been. The ads for the remaining two seasons were successively more sensationalizing—the third season depicting Henry sitting on a throne of naked, writhing bodies, the last season described (on the DVD) as a "delicious, daring . . . eight hours of decadence."[69] But "those of us who were glued to this sudsy mix of sex and sixteenth-century politics know the spark went out of the series when Dormer's Anne Boleyn was sent to the scaffold,"[70] wrote Gerard Gilbert in the *Independent*.

Today, hundreds of fan sites are devoted to Natalie Dormer, who managed, despite being cast on the basis of "sexual chemistry," to create an Anne Boleyn who is seen by thousands of young women as genuinely multidimensional. Natalie still gets letters from them every day and finds them gratifying, but also a bit depressing. "The fact that it was so unusual for them to have an inspiring portrait of a spirited, strong young woman—that's devastating to me. But young women picked up on my efforts, and that is a massive compliment—and says a lot about the intelligence of that audience. Young girls struggling to find their identity, their place, in this supposedly postfeminist era understood what I was doing."[71]

12

Chapuys' Revenge

Fiction Becomes Fact Once Again

IN 2002 ROBIN MAXWELL, who had written a highly praised novel about Anne, *The Secret Diary of Anne Boleyn,* was given a new manuscript to read. Arcade editor Trish Todd wanted to know, would Robin give it a blurb?

The manuscript took Maxwell by surprise. Most novels about Anne that were written in the 1980s and '90s had been quite sympathetic toward her. Maxwell's own book (1997) is constructed around the delightful fiction that Elizabeth discovers Anne's diary and learns how much her mother loved her and how "cruel and outrageously unjust" her father had been; the knowledge redeems Anne in her daughter's eyes and sets Elizabeth up for a lifetime of caution about giving the men in her life too much power.[1] In Jean Plaidy's beautifully wrought *The Lady in the Tower* (1986), we find Anne imprisoned, thinking back on her life, wondering "how had I come to pass from such adulation to bitter rejection in three short years"; her reflections are those of a mature, regretful, clear-sighted woman, capable of recognizing her own faults, but very much aware of how her own missteps had been cruelly exploited by others.[2] This new book, however, seemed to Maxwell to be a modern re-creation of the old Catholic view of Anne as a scheming viper.

"I was appalled," Robin recalled in a phone interview with me. "It was a great read, a page-turner. But she had taken every rumor, every nasty thing that anyone had ever said about Anne Boleyn, and turned it into the truth in her book. You can argue that she had every right because she's a historical fiction author, but I refused the blurb on principle because of its vicious, unsupportable view of Anne."[3]

The book was Philippa Gregory's *The Other Boleyn Girl*. In it, the character of Anne is indeed more selfish, spiteful, and vindictive than she had appeared in any previous novel, a nasty, screechy shrew who poaches Henry from her generous, tenderhearted (and very blonde) sister and proceeds to tyrannize her (and everyone around her), barking out orders, plotting deaths, appropriating her sister's child, and — when she miscarries her final pregnancy with Henry — coercing her brother to have sex with her. Neither *Sleeping Beauty* nor *Cinderella* strikes a more clear-cut division between the good and the wicked woman, with Anne playing the role of the wicked witch and Mary the long-suffering, virtuous heroine. As in any other fairy tale, however, the good are ultimately rewarded and the evil are punished. Anne, having gone to "the gates of hell" with her brother in order to get pregnant, miscarries a deformed child (an idea that Gregory picked up from Retha Warnicke's 1989 biography), is accused of witchcraft, and goes to the scaffold (in far less dignified fashion than history records) while Mary, with Elizabeth in her arms, retires to a bucolic life with her husband and children.[4]

Gregory describes herself as a "feminist historian, and a radical historian" and Mary Boleyn as a feminist heroine — apparently because she has sex and yet isn't portrayed as "bad."[5] (I thought we went past that — and then some — with *Bridget Jones's Diary*, *Ally McBeal*, and *Sex and the City*.) "It is no coincidence," Gregory says, "that our prejudiced opinions of women of the Tudor court are drawn from the devoted Victorian historians who were the first translators and publishers of the original Tudor documents, but were deeply committed to their own view of women as either saints or whores."[6] Her novel, in contrast, allows Mary to be both sexual and saintlike, and despite having been "used" sexually by Henry, she is rewarded with the best ending of anyone in the book (which just happens to be a life of domestic happiness). "Mary's story is one of absolute independence and victory," Gregory says, and a "triumph of common sense over the ambition of her sister Anne."[7] Huh? Sex is allowed, but ambition isn't? What kind of feminism is this? The answer to that appears to be: an opportunistic, infinitely malleable one. Gregory, in a more recent interview, complains about how "one-eyed some historians have been" in their depictions of women of power: "They are always portrayed as power hungry, pretty ambitious, manipulative, cold or proud."[8] This sounds like a pretty fair description of her portrayal of Anne Boleyn.

The book was well reviewed and has been fabulously successful with general readers. It stormed the U.S. market, selling more than a million copies in the U.S. alone, and it has by now been published in twenty-six countries. It won the Parker Pen Novel of the Year award, the *Romantic Times* fictional biography award, was adapted for the BBC as a television drama, and was made into a film starring Scarlett Johansson as Mary Boleyn, Natalie Portman as Anne Boleyn, and Eric Bana as Henry VIII. It has legions of devoted fans, who write gushing tributes on Gregory's website. But other novelists and historians, both professional and amateur, range from the politely critical to the seething when *The Other Boleyn Girl* is mentioned. Most are offended less by the "viciousness" of its view of Anne than by its many historical inaccuracies. Hilary Mantel notes that the notion that Anne gave birth to a deformed child is an "eccentric interpretation" that has "gained traction" because of its sensational elements.[9] Robin Maxwell criticizes Gregory for "knowing the truth" as a scholar but then going with what is "most dramatic" for her readers, even when there is "zero evidence."[10] Michael Hirst, who knows what it's like to be charged with distorting history, describes Philippa Gregory as "having no historical sensibility at all. Her characters are all middle-class people wandering into a historical situation and behaving in a very modern middle-class way . . . Her Anne is like someone in the dorm of your university."[11] One Facebook group, which calls itself the History Police, will not even call Philippa Gregory by name, instead referring to her sarcastically as "our favorite historical novelist" and engaging in fantasy conversations involving sending snipers to her public talks.

There's no doubt that Gregory plays fast and loose with history in *The Other Boleyn Girl* (see the sidebar "*The Other Boleyn Girl* Fact-Checker," on page 224, for specifics) and even more so when the book was made into a movie. The screenplay, written by Philippa Gregory and Peter Morgan (*The Queen, The Last King of Scotland, Frost/Nixon*), contributed fresh inventions to the story. Michael Grandage, who directed the Donmar Warehouse production of *Frost/Nixon,* credits Morgan with the ability to weave a fictional storyline "so deeply" into a factual situation "that audiences don't know where the boundaries of truth lie."[12] In the case of *The Other Boleyn Girl,* the "interwoven" fantasies/fictions included a gratuitous (and utterly out-of-character) rape of Anne by Henry, Mary begging Henry for a last-minute pardon for Anne, and a heroic capture of Elizabeth by Mary, who strides into court after Anne's execution, grabs her niece, and — with the whole court watching and not lifting a finger — leaves the palace with the future queen in her arms. Oh, and another trifle — the movie "manages to virtually edit out a rather large historical fact: the Reformation."[13] As Gina Carbone puts it in her review, "Let's just say you shouldn't watch this and base any *Jeopardy!* answers around it."[14]

The actors, apparently, did little research beyond reading the novel (Gregory commends Scarlett Johansson for having "her copy of my book in her hand practically all the time she was on set"[15]), learning how deeply to curtsy from an etiquette coach ("It was those kinds of things," says Johansson, "that added to the freshness and authenticity of the period"[16]), and mastering the English accent. Natalie Portman admits to not "relating" to the character of Anne Boleyn, but appears to be so postmodern in her approach to history (perhaps due to her Harvard degree) that it didn't matter much: "You have to accept that all history is fiction . . . there are all these different versions."[17] Eric Bana didn't even bother with checking out the history books. "Look," he told director Justin Chadwick when he was offered the part, "I never envisaged myself playing a king, or Henry VIII, or anybody" but "Henry, the guy, the man in this script, I said, I think I can get to the core of him and I wanna play him just as a man. That's all I know. So I just used that. I didn't get too bogged down in history or any of that stuff, because I felt like at the core of it, it was kind of irrelevant."[18]

Not getting "bogged down" in history matters to some and not to others. "No matter what criticisms *The Tudors* may have received for its inaccuracies," one blogger wrote, "the Showtime series seems like a History Channel documentary compared to this movie."[19] Respected historical novelist Margaret George, in an e-mail exchange with me about the actors' comments, was less circumspect.

> I think they are all a bunch of ignoramuses. Lazy. Un-intellectually curious. As for hiding behind such a dumb and dismissive statement as "all you got from historians was competing views, anyway," I wonder if they carry that philosophy over into their medical treatments? ("What the heck, they can't decide how many cigarettes it takes to cause lung cancer, so I'll just ignore it all!") Frankly, they all gave dismal performances in TOBG because they were all miscast, except for Scarlett, who acted somnolent through the whole thing even though from a distance she kind of looked like Mary Boleyn. And sorry, Natalie is just not convincing as someone who could topple a throne. Maybe if they'd studied their history a little, they could have done a better job.

But others didn't care whether or not, for example, Anne actually propositioned her brother. "It makes for a juicy and shocking footnote," shrugged Rex Reed, tellingly conflating the apparatus of scholarship with an "event" that has been pretty thoroughly shown by scholars to be Cromwell's invention.[20] And now that it has become culturally referenced by the film, a whole new generation, with little background in history but with an extensive media education, has become vulnerable, once again, to the argument. WELL DONE AND BEAUTIFULLY PRODUCED, proclaims the headline of one review, SATISFACTORILY EXPLAINS THE INCEST CHARGE AGAINST ANNE BOLEYN.[21] Another online reviewer admits that "near the finale, the dim recollection of my studies and the few facts that I've gleaned from other films combined their meager forces as one of Henry's daughters is named, and my inner monologue actually mixed Hollywood and history and noted 'I think that baby girl grows up to be Cate Blanchett.'"[22] This is what theatre critic Mark Lawson has called the "Oliver Stone phenomenon," referring to the sizeable number of Americans who believe Oliver Stone's film *JFK* to be an accurate portrayal of an actual conspiracy to kill Kennedy.

The Other Boleyn Girl Fact-Checker

Concocted Fictions:

Anne deliberately "steals" Henry from Mary (Henry's affair with Mary was over before he began to pursue Anne).

Anne forces Mary to give up her son to be raised at court.

Anne says she wants Wolsey dead.

Anne behaves viciously to her sister on many occasions.

Anne induces a miscarriage (third pregnancy) when she thinks the fetus is dead.

Anne has sex with her brother in order to conceive a child.

No Evidence or Contrary Evidence:

Intense rivalry between Anne and Mary (no evidence).

Mary Boleyn has two children by Henry, one of whom is a son. (Elizabeth Blount, Henry's former mistress, had Henry's son. Whether or not Mary had any children by Henry is not known.)

Anne has sex with Henry Percy (no evidence).

George Boleyn has an affair with Francis Weston. (This comes from Retha Warnicke's theory of a "homosexual ring" at Henry's court. It's possible, of course, but there's no evidence.)

Mary was a virgin before her first marriage. (There are many reports of sexual activity in Francis's court.)

Anne's mother hides evidence of Anne's miscarriage (second pregnancy) by burning the miscarried fetus. (It's possible that Anne hid a miscarriage, but it's speculation. There's no evidence at all that her mother burned a fetus.)

Anne gives birth to a "horridly malformed" baby. (This is Retha Warnicke's theory, but there is no evidence for it. In contemporary accounts, the fetus is referred to only as "a shapeless mass.")

Added in the Hollywood movie (screenplay by Peter Morgan):

Henry was attracted to Anne first, but got turned off when she humiliated him horseback riding. (In fact, Henry had an affair with
Mary before he became interested in Anne.)

In disgrace, Anne was exiled to France after marrying Henry Percy.
(Anne did not marry Percy, and she was sent to the Hapsburg
Court and then France when she was twelve, to be educated and
"finished.")

After Mary has just given birth to Henry's son, Anne (worried that this
will foil her own designs on Henry) orders Henry never to talk to
Mary again if he wants to have Anne. Henry agrees and walks out
of the room, indifferent to his infant son.

Henry becomes hostile and indifferent to Anne sexually even before
the marriage. (Henry pursued Anne for six years before they married—a prolonged courtship missing from the movie—and there
is no evidence that he became hostile to her until very late in the
marriage.)

Henry VIII rapes Anne Boleyn.

Mary intercedes on Anne's behalf and tries to get Henry to pardon
her sister.

Mary Boleyn walks into court after Anne's execution and takes Elizabeth with her.

Of course, if my book has demonstrated anything at all, it's that neither *The Tudors* nor *The Other Boleyn Girl* has a monopoly on the creative uses of a history that, after all, has some very large holes in the record. Nell Gavin, whose ingenious and moving *Threads* follows Anne
through several reincarnations, is based on a metaphysical premise
that many readers find dubious; *Anne of the Thousand Days* cooks up

a fictional exchange between Henry and Anne that not only did not happen but is also almost unimaginable; Norah Lofts's *The Concubine* has Anne engaging not just in one but multiple anonymous acts of adultery, Robert Bolt's *A Man for All Seasons* conveniently omits Thomas More's heretic burnings from among his other hobbies; and Hilary Mantel's *Wolf Hall* has Cromwell suspicious of Anne from the very beginning of their relationship, whereas, in fact, they were far from enemies for much of her reign. These depictions are not just accepted without protest, they are prizewinning, beloved, and admired. So why the special outrage over Gregory?

Perhaps what is most offensive to critics are not Gregory's distortions of fact, but her insistence on the historical rigor of her work. "Because I am a trained historian," she wrote in 2008,

> I described the story of the Boleyn girls in the full context of the dramatic political, religious and social changes of the time. Without realizing it, in so doing I invented a new way of writing the historical novel in which the "history" part of the equation is just as important as the "novel" part. The fact plays as great a part in the story as the fiction, and when there is a choice of fact or fiction, I always choose the factual version.[23]

She describes herself as applying "very strict rules of accuracy" to her novels."[24] What does she supply as a novelist? Only "the bits that we don't know" and "feelings . . . because we don't know how people felt."[25]

Fine, for a novelist, and there's certainly plenty of "bits we don't know" when it comes to the story of Anne Boleyn. But Gregory doesn't like to view herself as imaginatively inventive. She wants to defend her narrative choices as history too. In one interview, Gregory described the "made up bits" as speculation about what was "fairly likely." In a Q-and-A appendix to *The Other Boleyn Girl*, however, she went further, claiming that all her choices "can be defended as historical probability" and then she goes still further, with bold statements such as Anne Boleyn "was clearly guilty of one murder"[26] (and probably another, she implies) and — in another interview — "Anne's incest is powerfully suggested by the historical record."[27] ("The historical record" here seems to be that she was found guilty by Henry's rigged court.) In the production notes for the television version of *The Other Boleyn Girl*, she backs off a bit, admitting that having Anne proposition her brother is "speculative history."[28] But then, perhaps feeling the need to justify her "choice" further, she goes on: "You could argue that would have been quite a sensible thing to do if she could get away with it."[29] As for the alleged "murder" — the attempted poisoning of John Fisher — it is simply defended as "fact," although there's no evidence that Anne had anything to do with it.

It's Gregory's insistence on her meticulous adherence to history that most aggravates the scholars.[30] Both Margaret George and Hilary Mantel, in contrast to Gregory, make the fictional status of their novels clear. George includes a guide to what is factual and what is invented in her books. "Readers seem to really want that — they need to know whether this or that scene really happened, or where certain information came from. I think more and more writers are asking that it be included."[31] Mantel, in an e-mail exchange with me, described *Wolf Hall* not as "history" but as "part of a chain of literary representation."[32] In an author's note to *Bring Up the Bodies,* her sequel to *Wolf Hall,* Mantel describes that book as "making the reader a proposal, an offer" of "how a few crucial weeks might have looked from Thomas Cromwell's point of view."[33] She warns the reader against taking her as "claiming authority." Gregory's website, in contrast, intones the mantra that the hallmarks of her writing are "her love for history and commitment to historical accuracy."[34] "I'm passionate about getting things right," she says in a 2008 interview.[35]

My reason for highlighting all this is the fact that many of her readers take her at her word and consider *The Other Boleyn Girl* to be a historically accurate re-creation of events that actually happened. I've gotten plenty of direct evidence of this from audiences at my talks when I ask the opening question: "What do you know about Anne Boleyn?" "Six fingers" comes first (one myth Gregory isn't responsible for). Then: "She slept with her brother." "She gave birth to a deformed child." Sometimes people will argue with me over the "facts" that they've learned from the book. As a Tudor blogger wrote, "The novel's portrayal of Anne as promiscuous, immoral and thoroughly nasty, I think, is what most people came away from TOBG assuming must have been more or less true . . . [P]eople find it impossible or improbable that a novelist would claim historical credibility but would then make up SO much about one of the most famous women in British history."[36] Even members of my Facebook page — unusually well educated in things Tudor — frequently admit that before they began to delve deeper into the history, Philippa Gregory was their authority.

> I completely took TOBG as fact when first reading it in tenth grade!
> I had no real background knowledge on Anne before reading it, so I
> took what the book said as fact, especially after reading the author's
> note. Ms. Gregory is a very good and CONVINCING author, and it
> took me reading some other books afterwards to "detox" Gregory's
> Anne from my mind![37]

This reader eventually got "detoxed" and learned "not to take historical fiction at face value." And to be fair to Gregory, she often does "bring history to life" for many readers, sparking interest in the periods she writes about and inspiring further research. Parents praise Gregory for luring their teenaged daughters out of the mall and into an appreciation for history, and teachers credit her novels with humanizing historical figures for their students.

> One learns to put themselves in their shoes and start asking hard
> questions about the people, the times, and about themselves. Ulti-
> mately, historical fiction creates an interest in the actual events, and a
> need to learn more. I have done more research, just out of curiosity,
> after reading a novel than I would have ever thought. Reading histori-
> cal fiction has caused me to become a more informed person, and a
> great success at trivia games. As a teacher, I love them as a way to
> spark enthusiasm in my students. They make the facts come alive.[38]

The problem with "the facts coming alive" in Gregory's books, however, is that her most ardent fans do not distinguish between well-researched trivia of the sort that can give you an advantage in board games and the lively — and perhaps "humanizing" but inaccurate — "facts" about what the characters said and did. Neither, it appears, does Gregory, who seems to believe that knowledge about manners, dress, food, or the bad breath of the pretoothpaste Tudors is enough to keep her novels grounded in historical fact. Sometimes Gregory's training in literature sneaks up on her, and she suddenly becomes more seemingly aware of the dangers of verisimilitude. I was surprised when I read a recent scholarly piece by Gregory to find her decrying "putting a convincing lie on the record."[39] "A convincing lie," she writes, "is a wicked thing because it replaces the truth. If a lie is told with conviction and accepted as the sound coin of fact then no one will question it. It becomes something we all think that we know. It becomes something we rely on. It becomes the self-evident fact."[40] It's a thoughtful comment — but it's very puzzling that Gregory does not see that her own work is guilty of that.

The seductions of the "convincing lie" have become even more acute in our media-dominated, digitally enhanced era in which people are being culturally trained to have difficulty distinguishing between created "realities" and the real thing. If the created reality is vivid and convincing enough (whether it is a flawless computer-generated complexion or a "spin" on events), it carries authority — and that's the way advertisers and politicians want it. The movies, which are often extremely attentive to historical details, creating a highly realistic texture for the scaffolding surrounding the actions of the characters, make it even harder for audiences to draw the line. Directors, who are, after all, focused on entertaining rather than educating, may not *want* audiences to draw that line. Critic Thomas Sutcliffe describes Peter Morgan as "brilliant at sidestepping the usual shrieking reflex of anxiety about mixing fantasy and truth."[41]

The novelists I interviewed would agree that too much "anxiety" about the fact/fiction divide would make the work of historical fiction impossible. Margaret George laughingly told me about overhearing someone say, about her *The Autobiography of Henry VIII*, "This is just a lie! Henry VIII never wrote an autobiography!"[42] But George also expressed concern that in an age when most people get their history from TV and movies, we are losing our collective sense of "what really happened." As I write this, a controversy about this loss has been freshly stirred up by Roland Emmerich's movie *Anonymous*, which suggests that Edward de Vere, the seventeenth earl of Oxford, was the real author of Shakespeare's plays. Although among most Shakespeare scholars "the idea has roughly the same currency as the faked moon landing does among astronauts," former English literature professor Stephen Marche worries that thanks to the movie, "undergraduates will be confidently asserting that Shakespeare wasn't Shakespeare for the next 10 years at least, and profs will have to waste countless hours explaining the obvious."[43]

For thoughtful creators of fiction (whether written or cinematic), "shrieking anxiety" and "anything goes" are not the only alternatives. There's the responsible middle ground of recognizing that there is an unavoidable tension between the demands of history and the requirements of fiction. As Hilary Mantel puts it:

> You have to think what you owe to history. But you also have to think what you owe to the novel form. Your readers expect a story. And they don't want it to be two-dimensional, barely dramatized. So (and this is queasy ground) you have to create interiority for your characters. Your chances of guessing their thoughts are slim or none; and yet there is no reality left, against which to measure your failure.
>
> Fiction is commonly more persuasive than history texts. After *Wolf Hall* was published, I was constantly being asked, "Was Thomas More really like that? We thought he was a really nice man!" I could only answer, "I am trying to describe how he might have appeared if you were standing in the shoes of Thomas Cromwell, who, incidentally, did not dislike him." But of course what I was really up against was *A Man for All Seasons*: the older fiction having accreted authority, just by being around for two generations. When I say to people, "Do you really think More was a 1960s liberal?" they laugh. "Of course not." But (again, for the sake of honesty) you constantly have to weaken your own case, by pointing out to people that all historical fiction is really contemporary fiction; you write out of your own time.[44]

The Return of Chapuys' Anne

"All historical fiction is really contemporary fiction."[45] Mantel's remark is also a premise of this book. But historians and biographers write "out of their own time" too. And although it may be more subtly done, some of the most popular historians of our own time are not all that far from Gregory's perspective on Anne as a ruthless human predator. I earlier quoted David Starkey, whose bloodthirsty Anne hunts down all enemies and rejoices at their deaths. More recently, perhaps influenced by the more balanced assessments of Eric Ives, Suzannah Lipscomb, David Loades, and others, Starkey has been making Anne-friendly comments in his public lectures. But even as late as the 2009 documentary *Henry VIII: The Mind of a Tyrant,* Starkey goes as far as to credit Anne with having turned Henry from a gentle, poetry-loving Renaissance prince into "something colder, harder, and more brutal." (This incredible theory, which Starkey also puts forward in his *Six Wives* [2003], makes Anne, in a sense, responsible for her own death, since she was the one who turned Henry into the tyrant who ordained it.) In the documentary, a pair of dark, scheming eyes flashes on the screen — no face, just eyes — when Starkey discusses Anne while Katherine is represented by an open, sweet, smiling face.

Alison Weir, too, is not above using dramatic but unfounded stereotype and rumor to spice up her portrait of Anne. In her 1991 *The Six Wives of Henry VIII,* she describes Anne as "an ambitious adventuress with a penchant for vengeance"[46] who "handled [Henry] with such calculated cleverness that there is no doubt that the crown of England meant more to her than the man through whom she would wear it."[47] No doubt? Really? We don't have Anne's letters or, indeed, much of anything said or written by her that has not been filtered through the colored perspectives of her contemporaries. I would say that under such circumstances there isn't much about which there is "no doubt" except for the recorded events of the birth of Elizabeth and Anne's execution. *The Lady in the Tower* — by far Weir's most compelling book — is focused less on assessing Anne's character than in detailing the plot against her, but even so, there are moments when the "ambitious adventuress with a penchant for violence"[48] makes an appearance: "She had hounded Wolsey nigh unto death; she had repeatedly urged Henry to send Katherine of Aragon and Mary, his own daughter, to the scaffold; she had been ruthless against her enemies. Five years earlier, rumor had placed her faction behind an attempt to poison John Fisher ... and only a couple of months ago, it had been bruited that Katherine of Aragon had been poisoned, and that Anne was the culprit."[49]

Weir, like Starkey, has become more Anne-friendly in the last few years. In a 2008 interview, she says that had Anne lived, "she would have gained a reputation as the matriarch of the English Reformation."[50] She credits the reputation Anne has as "the Other Woman in an eternal triangle" as the result of Boleyn's history being "what it was."[51] By that I assume she means that Anne deserved her reputation. However, it's not "history" but those who have reported it who have made Anne the disreputable "Other Woman" rather than the mother of the English Reformation, and Weir is hardly blameless. Her own 1991 book — unlike, for example, Eric Ives's *The Life and Death of Anne Boleyn* (2004) — does not devote more than a few passing references to Anne's reformist activities and religious sympathies. Then, in her more recent book, *Mary Boleyn* (2011), she revives the old Chapuys-originated rumor that Anne had been sexually "corrupted" at the French court, with no more evidence than Chapuys himself presents — namely, an uncorroborated private conversation he reports having had with Henry *after* Henry had already turned against her. It's an old story, first retold in Paul Friedmann's 1884 biography of Anne and having about as much credibility as Henry's claim (again, reported by Chapuys) that Anne had "criminal connexion" with "upwards of 100 gentlemen" after she had become queen.[52] As Weir acknowledges, there isn't any "solid evidence" of the corruption (whatever it entailed, which isn't specified). But she then goes on to provide a handy explanation. "Anne was discreet and clever enough to ensure that barely a soul knew of these early falls from grace."[53]

Do we know the truth of Anne's sexual activity — or lack of it — while in France? No. She may have been scrupulously careful to never stray from the game of "courtly" flirtation. Or she may have had some discreet sexual affairs, rumors of which never saw the light of day—hard as that is to believe in Henry's gossipy court—until she was accused of adultery. We just don't know and probably never will. What we do know is that despite the paucity of dependable evidence, scheming, sexually provocative Anne still clings tightly to popular narratives.[54] When it comes to the male players in the drama, old images are continually being energetically deconstructed. *The Tudors* has replaced Charles Laughton's blustering, chicken-chomping buffoon with Jonathan Rhys Meyers's lean, athletic bad boy. *Wolf Hall* exposes Thomas More as coldly, viciously pious and turns the ruthless, calculating Cromwell we know from depictions of his role in Anne Boleyn's death into the true "man for all seasons": warm, loyal, and opportunistic only because his survival requires it. These revisions—particularly the arresting portraits of *Wolf Hall*—have made us question how much received wisdom about the Tudors, most of which we learned in the school of popular culture, is sedimented mythology turned into "history" by decades of repetition.

In this skeptical, revisionist moment, it's striking how Anne the temptress just keeps bubbling up—for example, in G. W. Bernard's *Anne Boleyn: Fatal Attractions* (2010), a sensationalistic, poorly argued extension of an equally flimsy scholarly article from 1991, in which Bernard claims that "Anne indeed committed adultery with Norris, probably with Smeaton, and possibly with Weston" largely on the basis of what he himself calls "a hunch."[55] The reasoning behind this "hunch": a poem by Lancelot de Carles—well-known for years by scholars, but rightly regarded as not much more than a description of a chain of gossip and accusation—and Anne's flirtatious behavior, "hinting at what might be called a liberated, certainly an un-puritan, attitude toward sexuality."[56]

Serious scholars of the Tudor period will recall that Eric Ives and Greg Walker had already challenged Bernard's views on Anne's fall in a series of scholarly responses in 2002. But that was before the success of *The Other Boleyn Girl* and *The Tudors,* and since Bernard's article was hidden in the pages of a scholarly journal, why not trot it out again for a mass audience? It's difficult to imagine that this book was motivated by much beyond a craving to cash in on the wave of Tudormania. But although many academics privately shook their heads over the shabby logic and wild imaginings of the book, Bernard was too eminent a personage to get taken much to task in public. David Starkey, who never misses an opportunity to shower uncensored scorn on feminist historians, was gravely respectful. "There will undoubtedly be something in what Professor Bernard has got to say. He's a very serious scholar with a profound knowledge of the period."[57] Peter Marshall, in a piece in *Literary Review,* is similarly deferential. Although he (like Starkey) doesn't buy Bernard's conclusion, he strains to end his review with praise. "(Bernard) . . . at the very least can be said to have shown it to be not entirely impossible that the charges had some substance."[58] Bolstered by these kinds of endorsements, the mass media jumped on it: ANNE BOLEYN DID HAVE AN AFFAIR WITH HER BROTHER; THE POEM THAT "PROVES" THE ADULTERY OF HENRY VIII'S QUEEN, reads the headline of a *Daily Mail* piece on the book, accompanied by a photo of Anne from *The Tudors* with the legend: "Promiscuous."[59]

In the even more freewheeling world of historical fiction, Gregory's Anne has continued her career, most sordidly in Carolly Erickson's *The Favored Queen* (2011), a recycling of the winning good girl/bad girl premise of *The Other Boleyn Girl* with Jane Seymour now playing the role of the abused innocent and Katherine in the supporting cast as such a self-sacrificing Christian soul that she even tends Anne when Anne gets the sweating sickness. Erickson's Anne, in contrast to these angels of mercy, dwarfs Gregory's Anne in her malevolence, and she's even more unhinged from history. I could cite chapter and verse detailing the various poisonings, tormentings of servants, and illicit affairs that Erickson's Anne commits but the summary on the flyleaf will spare me that task.

> Born into an ambitious noble family, young Jane Seymour is sent to court as a maid of honor to Katherine of Aragon, Henry VIII's aging queen. She is devoted to her mistress and watches with empathy as the calculating Anne Boleyn contrives to supplant Katherine as queen. Anne's single-minded intrigues threaten all who stand in her way; she does not hesitate to arrange the murder of a woman who knows a secret so dark that, if revealed, would make it impossible for

the king to marry Anne. Once Anne becomes queen, no one at court is safe, and Jane herself becomes a victim of Anne's venomous rage.[60]

Although I hesitate to mention it in the same breath as Erickson, even Hilary Mantel's *Wolf Hall,* which won the Man Booker Prize in 2010, follows the old stereotype in her portrayal of Anne as a scheming predator. Mantel's Anne is a nervously "calculating being" with "small teeth, white and sharp"[61] and "a cold slick brain at work behind her hungry black eyes."[62]

> Her eyes passed over him [Cromwell] on her way to someone who interested her more. They are black eyes, slightly protuberant, shiny like the beads of an abacus; they are shiny and always in motion, as she makes calculations of her own advantage. Uncle Norfolk must have said to her "There goes the man who knows the cardinal's secrets," because now when he comes into her sight her long neck darts; those shining black beads go click, click, as she looks him up and down and decides what use can be got out of him . . ."[63]
>
> . . . At the feast Anne sits beside Henry on the dais, and when she turns to speak to him her black lashes brush her cheeks. She is almost there now, almost there, her body taut like a bowstring, her skin dusted with gold, with tints of apricot and honey; when she smiles, which she does often, she shows small teeth, white and sharp.[64]

Mantel, of course, cannot be compared as a writer with Erickson (or with Gregory, for that matter), and her artistry brings touches that distinguish her Anne from the cartoon schemers of historical romance. Her Anne is brittle, anxious, tightly wound, and skinny; she exudes the nervous energy of a modern-day anorexic, her true self and laser focus carefully hidden away, constantly calculating how to keep up appearances lest her secrets be exposed. And, of course, she's only a bit player in the novel, which is the world according to Cromwell. Yet it seems clear, especially with the publication of *Bring Up the Bodies,* that Mantel's Anne is not just an "offering" of how Cromwell might have seen her, but Mantel's own rejoinder to the more sympathetic portraits of other writers and filmmakers.

In both novels, for example, Mantel excludes some key historical material that, coincidentally, might cause readers to question (her) Cromwell's view of Anne as a cold "strategist," with whom he feels some identification but little affection,[65] "a woman without remorse" who would "commit any sin or crime."[66] Among the most famous material that she rejects are Anne's eloquent speeches at her trial and on the scaffold, left out, Mantel says in her author's note, because they "should be read with skepticism."[67] The explanation via skepticism over the authenticity of this material is odd, not only because there are multiple corroborating reports of both speeches, but because she has just told readers that she claims no *historical* "authority" for her version of things. Certainly, she doesn't let history get in the way of other narrative choices. For example, it's a matter of historical record that Anne's longtime ally Cranmer, shocked by Anne's arrest, sat down to write a letter to Henry expressing his amazement at the charges and his belief in Anne's virtue. His writing was interrupted (as Cranmer relates when he resumes) by a visit from Cromwell and his cronies. They apparently helped him "change his mind" about Anne's guilt, for the letter ends very differently than it begins, with poor Cranmer, clearly quaking in his boots, acknowledging that she must be guilty.[68] Mantel chooses not to tell us about Cromwell's interruption, although, of course, it's part of his story. But this detail would have made Cromwell seem like more of a thug than Mantel wants to present him.

Mantel is creating a fiction, of course, and can do what she wants. But if she gives herself such free rein with Cranmer's letter (and other incidents), it seems disingenuous to justify the absence of Anne's speeches (and her final letter) on the basis of skepticism about their factual nature. Is this history or a novel? Mantel would be the first to acknowledge that it's a novel. But her choices of what to include and what to eliminate from the historical record suggest that she (and not merely her Cromwell) is intent on building a case against Anne — not necessarily for the commission of the crimes with which she was accused (she leaves that ambiguous) but certainly as a cold, self-seeking manipulator.

I love Mantel's writing; no other novelist has given us such a textured, unsettlingly "real" re-creation of Henry's court and the tight-rope nature of survival within it. But I can't help wondering why, in an imaginative work of great depth and subtlety, we find the old, one-sided, extremist view of Anne as a wily schemer. Perhaps this is our "default" Anne, who insinuates herself in the imagination whenever we aren't specifically focused on rehabilitating her. In *The Tudors,* it took the concerted efforts of Natalie Dormer to knock her off the page and replace her with someone more complex. And when Howard Brenton's play *Anne Boleyn* opened in 2010 — the first popular depiction of Anne since her early Protestant defenders to present her as a heroine of the Reformation — it was hailed as "fresh and sympathetic,"[69] a "radically revisionist work" that "challenges received wisdom,"[70] "an alternative history,"[71] "eye opening,"[72] "a re-materialization of . . . an Anne we have, until now, never seen,"[73] which will "have the historians scratching their heads."[74] The praise for the vibrant, witty play was deserved, but few responsible historians would scratch their heads over Anne the reformist (Brenton himself credits his interpretation to historian Eric Ives). That Brenton's sexy but spiritual Anne was "eye-opening" says more about the intransigence of temptress stereotypes than Brenton's "radical" revision of history. And even in those appreciative reviews, the "received wisdom" kept popping up in the descriptions of Anne. She "used her sexual stranglehold over Henry VIII to pursue the idea of religious reform,"[75] "advances herself in court — and Henry's heart — by dedicating herself to the spirituality of William Tyndale's low church, while simultaneously allowing a drooling, still-Catholic Henry to inch ever further up her leg over seven long years"[76]; "Her irresistible wickedness is a fiery companion to Anthony Howell's fiercely lusty Henry as she tempts, resists and subsists to his advances over seven years."[77]

I spoke with Brenton when the play first opened and can say with confidence that he had no interest in portraying Henry as "drooling" and Anne as having a "sexual stranglehold" over him. In fact, we talked at some length about those stereotypes and their indebtedness to the puritanical strain of Protestantism that had not yet developed in Anne's own time.

I do think that even in England, the mind/body split, or the soul/body split, the fallen body, all that, which came out of Calvin, really, was only beginning to make its way into the reformist faction at this time. Come the turn of the century, it had taken hold, and it was warfare between the different sections of Puritans, really. But I thought, well, maybe it hadn't really got hold by the time of this play. And that's reflected in Anne's version of Protestantism.[78]

In other words: Yes, Anne was sexual (and Brenton's play definitely portrays her as such), but our reading of this as "wicked" (even if deliciously so) is a puritanical leap that would have baffled Anne. I'm not sure that I agree with Brenton's chronology or genealogy regarding the mind/body split. What was clear from talking to him, though, was that he was much less interested in Anne's hold over Henry than her advocacy of Tyndale's Bible. That, and her courage: "What was extraordinary to me about her was her recklessness. The Tudor court was unbelievably dangerous and yet she got to the very center of it, and the only way out was either bear a male child or death. There was no other way out. There was no retreat, and that I thought was an extraordinary existential place to end up, and I thought the recklessness of it, the courage that took, was amazing."[79]

Who Let the Bitch Out?

What is it about Anne the temptress/predator? Why do we keep returning to her, even though serious scholars have challenged the stereotype? The "femme fatale" is a long-standing archetype in many cultures, of course, and Anne is only one of many: Eve, Delilah, Salome, Jezebel, the sirens, Medea, Cleopatra, Morgan le Fay, Vampira, the Dragon Lady, and all their various incarnations and evil sisters in mythology, novels, fin-de-siècle painting, film noir, and television soaps. There are many explanations — cultural, psychological, feminist, and misogynist — for her appeal. Camille Paglia, in *Sexual Personae*, follows Freud and Nietzsche and argues that the femme fatale is "one of the most mesmerizing of sexual personae," who will always have a cultural presence because "Woman," beginning first of all with the mother, represents the seductions, betrayals, and "uncontrollable nearness of nature," "a malevolent moon that keeps breaking through our fog of hopeful sentiment."[80] Bram Dijkstra sees her less as a permanent fixture grounded in the facts of women's biological role and more as a periodically erupting, misogynist icon, whose popularity waxes and wanes historically. He illustrates this in *Idols of Perversity* through the culture of fin-de-siècle Europe, arguing that a wave of literary, artistic, and scientific "fantasies of feminine evil" flooded that period, externalizing its misogyny and developing evolutionary racism. One of my Facebook page readers offered a more "Jungian" view: that Gregory's Anne, like Scarlett O'Hara, acts out parts of the self that most of us are afraid to put into public scrutiny.

> In the great autobiography that is my inner monologue, I am the heroine of my story sometimes, and an anti-heroine other times. We aren't supposed to like Scarlett O'Hara, but we admire her and talk about her almost a century since she debuted in the public consciousness . . . She fascinates those who like her, who hate her, or those who admire but do not necessarily like her. I would argue that Anne Boleyn — the real one — and just like me and Scarlett O'Hara and you, was a complex human with good intentions mingled with bad. Philippa Gregory's Anne has the disadvantage of being fictional, of having her thoughts and intentions broadcast by their author, whereas real people are able to conceal their intentions behind words and perspectives.[81]

Putting this comment into Jungian terms, wicked Anne belongs to the repressed "shadow" that is part of the storehouse of our collective unconscious. We all secretly identify with the behavior of those who dare to act out our more libidinous (sexual and aggressive) fantasies and impulses. And perhaps when they are punished, it psychologically wipes clean our own slates, exorcises our demons, makes us feel purified.

My own view is that while the femme fatale can't be simply dismissed as a creation of Western sexism, the fact that she has flourished in certain specific cultural contexts rather than in others is striking.

She may be part of some collective unconscious, but there are (historical) moments when she is fairly quiet, and others when the "bitch is loose." The end of the twentieth and turn into the twenty-first century seems to be one of those — and since this is more and more a global culture, the dominion of the bitch is too. Postwar popular culture had its share of scheming vixens on *Dallas*, *Dynasty*, and the rest. But they played a supporting role to Mary Tyler Moore, Claire Huxtable, Murphy Brown, *Designing Women*, and other independent but likeable prime-time women — and they clearly were marked as "villainesses." Nowadays, really, really mean girls, backstabbing "frenemies," and defiantly materialistic sluts are not just dots on the landscape, but truly in the ascendancy. And unlike Alexis Carrington, they don't even scheme in secret. They're proud of their materialism and their aggression, which Bravo highlights in the self-defining snippets that open each of their *Real Housewives* shows. ("If it doesn't make me money, I'm not interested in it."[82] "There may be younger housewives, but no one is hotter than me."[83] "I don't try to keep up with the Joneses; I *am* the Joneses."[84]) Women crave power, hell yes! And they lust over designer shoes and handbags. And yes, they will beat one another up, verbally and physically — call one another whores, pull one another's wigs off, overturn tables — given half the chance. Deal with it! The only difference between these characters' behavior and the "selfish, boorish ways that once got men called 'chauvinist pigs,'" Hampton Stevens writes in the *Washington Times*, is that "critics describe them with glowing words such as 'assertive,' 'edgy,' and, heaven help us, 'sassy.' However, what these women actually are, generally speaking, are utterly awful human beings: vain, selfish, shallow and controlling — a generation of 'Mean Girls' grown, not surprisingly, into mean women."[85] And consumed with relish — and often admiration — by viewers.

Compare this cultural moment to the late 1980s, when Glenn Close's character in *Fatal Attraction* aroused a storm of indignation and controversy over a depiction of an unstrung, bunny-boiling adulteress. When *Fatal Attraction* was released, we were still pre–Dinesh D'Souza, Camille Paglia, and Christina Hoff Sommers; Allan Bloom's *The Closing of the American Mind* had only just been published. "Politically correct" had not yet become a handy ubiquitous put-down of feminists and other critics of sexism, racism, and ethnocentrism. And while preview audiences demanded to see the bunny boiler killed off by the betrayed wife (an original ending, which had Alex commit suicide to the strains of *Madame Butterfly*, didn't wash and was replaced), the new ending (along with the portrayal of Alex as a murderous sociopath) was seen by many reviewers as an indictment and vicious punishment of the single career woman. Today, jaded by the slew of copycat female sociopaths that followed the success of the film (*Single White Female; The Hand That Rocks the Cradle*, etc.) and knowing that the culture is not very welcoming of "old-fashioned" feminism, movie and television reviewers are unlikely to beef about sexist imagery or ideology. It isn't cool.

Who let the bitch out? Clearly, she is being warmly welcomed by an unhinged consumer culture that gratifies all tastes, no matter how sleazy or degrading, so long as the product sells. But just what tastes are being gratified, and what is being sold? Susan Herbst, in *Rude Democracy*, says, in speaking about the escalation of vicious attacks among politicians and from news commentators, that "conflict sells and excites in a way that calm political dialogue never will."[86] In the case of the outrageous behavior of reality-show contestants, this might be even more simply summed up as "It's hard to turn your eyes away from a train wreck." But arguably, reality-show contestants also hold a fun-house mirror up to viewers, acting out tendencies that our culture encourages in all of us — competitiveness, materialism, self-indulgence — but in an over-the-top way so we can feel superior. When Scott Dunlop created *The Real Housewives of Orange County* (the first in the Bravo series, which was meant to be a one-season feature), his intention was for it to be "a satirical look at life in affluent gated communities."[87] (*Desperate Housewives*, too, was originally marketed as a satire; it didn't sell until rebilled as a prime-time soap opera.) But Bravo discovered that viewers didn't see satire. They saw actual people leading enviably successful lives, whose behavior they could dissect and dis around the water cooler at work or talk about in blogs online.

Chillingly, the behavior of the housewives may not even seem all that awful to many viewers. In an increasingly mean culture, it may read as all the more "real." Our polarized political discourse, by the time *The Real Housewives of Orange County* aired in 2006, had already degenerated into name-calling. And the Internet had teased the bitch out in the rest of us, enabling "users to làsh out at individuals without forethought."[88] Laura Stepp, in the *Huffington Post,* makes an apt comparison. "Tweets, blog posts and comments on Facebook are like the wicked notes girls used to pass in high school."[89] It's no accident that the housewives all have their own blogs, in which they stoke one another's fires between episodes. These sorts of blogs, David Denby points out in *Snark,* encourage nastiness to "metastasize as a pop writing form: A snarky insult, embedded in a story or post, quickly gets traffic; it gets linked to other blogs; and soon it has spread like a sneezy cold through the vast kindergarten of the Web."[90]

Let's not forget, though, that *Housewives* and *Bachelor* viewers are overwhelmingly women. And unlike *Dallas* and *Dynasty,* whose prime-time villainesses were made up, these shows reinforce the worst stereotypes about real women. So why do women, apparently, adore these shows? Have we been brainwashed to take delight in the demeaning and demonizing of our hard-won power? Susan Douglas, in "Where Have You Gone, Roseanne Barr?" (the *Shriver Report*), says:

> The chief culprit is the use of an arch irony — the deployment of the knowing wink that it's all a joke, that we're not to take this too seriously. Because women have made plenty of progress because of feminism, and now that full equality is allegedly complete, it's OK, even amusing, to resurrect sexist stereotypes of girls and women. After all, TV shows such as "Are You Hot?" or magazines like *Maxim* can't possibly undermine women's equality at this late date, right?[91]

I would go further than this. It's not just that sexist stereotypes are seen as "okay" but that they aren't even seen as sexist anymore but rather as proof of women's triumph over sexism in a culture that is viewed as "beyond feminism." In this culture, our sexuality is seen as a potent form of power. Bitchery shows that we aren't simpering, whining weaklings, that we've "come a long way" from our subservient ancestors. The "just do it" mentality has released all brakes on competitiveness; the harder we fight, the more we demonstrate that we have the right stuff. Unlike their mothers, the bubby-flaunting femmes of reality television aren't afraid to "go for it." They won't allow anyone to make them feel ashamed of their ambitions or their aggressions. And they refuse to be stifled. "I've finally found my voice!" says one housewife, in the snippets that introduce the show. "I'm my own person," says another. They announce themselves with feminist tropes. But they don't need feminism. They already have power; just look at the size of those boobs and bank accounts. Both are usually the result of their husbands' (or ex-husbands') high-paying jobs, but puh-lease, don't give me that tiresome libber crap. Get a life, Gloria Steinman (or whatever her name is).

The "heroines" of reality television are, in a sense, the inevitable flowering, in popular culture form, of the protest against "victim feminism" that Naomi Wolf, Camille Paglia, and Katie Roiphe inaugurated in the early 1990s. "Victim feminism," as Wolf described it in her book *Fire with Fire*, "casts women as sexually pure and mystically nurturing, and stresses the evil done to these 'good' women as a way to petition for their rights."[92] It has turned "suffering into a virtue, anonymity into a status symbol, and marginalization into a mark of the highest faith."[93] It is also "obsolete" because "the psychology and the conditions of women's lives have both been transformed enough so that it is no longer possible to pretend that the impulses to dominate, aggress, or sexually exploit others are 'male' urges alone."[94] Katie Roiphe *(The Morning After)* translated this into a critique of feminist ideas about date rape, arguing that in many cases, charges of rape were a "victim-feminist" excuse for a woman's own bad behavior "the night before."[95] Camille Paglia went even further, charging all second-wave feminism with "paranoia" about male oppression and declaring that women, in fact, are "the dominant sex."[96]

It may seem like a huge leap to go from rejecting "victim feminism" to behaving like a housewife from hell. But ideas that are ripe for development move fast from conception to materialization in a consumer culture, and as they find their audience, they gather steam. A door is opened, taboos are lifted, something sounds a resonant note with buyers, and within short order, much more is permitted — even celebrated — than would have been dreamed of five years before. Popular culture, with its expert nose for profitable icons and images, skipped quickly from "power feminism" and its proponents to *Sex and the City* and *Ally McBeal,* which tested — and demonstrated — that old-fashioned feminism, with its horror of sexual "objectification," was dead. Get out your short skirts, and show off those legs (shaved, of course)! Then came the *Mean Girls* books, a whole slew of them, dedicated to demonstrating that girls were just as aggressive as boys, only more underhanded. *Desperate Housewives* discovered that women plotting against other women would not sell as satire; we wanted our schemers straight up — and, ultimately, with the opportunities provided by reality television, "real." And then, inevitably, came the self-help books celebrating the "inner bitch," such as Sherry Argov's *Why Men Love Bitches,* which argues that "releasing your inner bitch" can help you land the right male.[97]

The headlines of the movie reviews of *The Other Boleyn Girl* almost all exploited this cultural moment: RIVAL SISTERS DUKE IT OUT FOR THE PASSION OF A KING (the *New York Times*),[98] CATFIGHT IN THE HOUSE OF TUDOR (the *Chicago Sun-Times*),[99] SISTERS FACE OFF IN "OTHER BOLEYN GIRL" (the *San Francisco Chronicle*).[100] The *Boston Globe* describes the movie as having "the DNA of a 'Gossip Girl' episode."[101] Putting the novel in the context of a "power-feminist" celebration of female competitiveness and aggression may also explain why it seems, to Gregory and many of her most devoted readers, that her Anne is not a villainess, but rather — in contrast to earlier novels such as Plaidy's and Maxwell's — a bold, assertive, "nonvictim" (or, to put it in currently fashionable academic terms, an "agent") who, in the final analysis, made her own bed. Explaining part of the success of her books, Gregory says that it's appealing to readers "to see women empowering themselves with no help at all; they find it immensely inspirational."[102] The fact that this perspective doesn't square at all with Gregory's other comments about the triumph of Mary's goodness over Anne's ambition doesn't seem to bother her, as she is equally capable of turning right around and celebrating Anne's bid for power.

> Despite the gains made by feminism — and I am a feminist and great supporter of equal rights — you look at Anne Boleyn who gets from nowhere to be queen of England, and has the King of England danc-

ing for six years — during which time he turns the history of England upside down in order that he might get into bed with her, and she won't allow it! You know, that's a woman who, well, I mean these aren't wiles, this is campaign-level strategy.[103]

"Just say no" as campaign-level strategy! You have to hand it to Philippa Gregory.

13

Anne Gets the Last Word (for Now)

Viral Anne

DESPITE THE FACT that the splashiest Annes of recent years have tended to reproduce some of the oldest, most negative iconography—the bitch, the schemer, the sexual temptress—they haven't had the last word. The following is a smattering of comments from some of the members of *The Creation of Anne Boleyn* Facebook page, a site I created with historian Natalie Sweet in the spring of 2011, chiefly in order to survey young women's impressions of Anne Boleyn for this book. Through e-mail interviews with girls and women ranging from twelve to twenty-six and on-site postings of questions to which women (and some men) of all ages, nationalities, and "political" persuasions responded, I discovered that Anne is an inspiration for many of this generation.

> Anne was beautiful, a spark of life, a feminist in a time when it was not accepted, a powerful woman. Why am I "obsessed" with her? Because that's what I want to be. She makes me feel like I could be that, like I have power too.

> She had dreams and visions for her future and she went after what she wanted. And even in the end, knowing she'd pay the ultimate price,

she was strong and brave and died boldly. I think that's admirable in a woman, especially a woman living in such dark, chauvinistic times when men usually determined women's fates. It's great to have such a strong woman to look up to.

She was a nobleman's daughter, trained to "catch" a husband & to be the chattel of her father & husband. Yet she rose above that training and became a strong, independent woman with opinions of her own . . . Anne is fascinating for her intelligence and determination, and then finally the immense courage and grace with which she met her death.[1]

To me Anne is unique because she had such a strong personality and voice at a time when women were essentially bargaining tools. She didn't fit the societal norm and I think that's what attracted Henry in the first place but also what made him stray in the end. People see her as either a victim or a vixen, but she was so much more complex than that. She wrote her own story and was uniquely in control of her life which makes her end all the more tragic. I see Anne as an inspiration . . . Her confidence and ambition have really driven me because if she, as a woman, in 1530 could be as much of a force and presence as she was, I can be one in 2011.[2]

I am still amazed that she kept Henry VIII waiting for SEVEN YEARS, and refused to be a mistress to him. It's quite an accomplishment for a woman to do that to a man in the fifteenth century, let alone for a woman to do that to a KING. I also admire her courage and bravery when facing her tragic end. The dignity she displayed in the face of her detractors is quite inspiring to me. She was essentially a powerful, strong, and independent woman in a world where all of those qualities were seen as deplorable for a female to possess. She did not change who she was, even for the king of England! I think Anne was a 21st century spirit born in a 15th century body![3]

I was a relative latecomer to the online community of Tudorphiles, which emerged out of the tentative seedings of longtime Tudor fans and, after *The Tudors* caught hold, sprouted limbs and shoots all across the Internet. Lara Eakins, whose *Tudorhistory.org* was among the first, began in 1994 with "a little GIF of Elizabeth I" and a "very simple page about the Tudors."[4] Lara's initial impulse, as she describes it, was just to share: "Here's something that interests me."[5] She was surprised when numerous e-mails began arriving, some asking for help with school assignments, but many from people for whom the Tudors had been a secret passion. "I thought I was the only one interested in Tudor history!" wrote some; "My friends and family are tired of me talking about it."[6] Now they would have a place to indulge freely without driving others away. Lara began to suspect that her site had tapped into a community of Tudor fans, each one thinking he or she was the "only one." Then, the publication of *The Other Boleyn Girl* turned Anne Boleyn into "one of the biggest topics of interest" among the followers of her Q-and-A page, and "once *The Tudors* started, the questions started flooding in."[7] Many were interested in sorting out fact from fiction in Gregory's novel and the television show, and that delighted Lara. "It was nice to know that there is at least some fraction who will dig deeper and try to learn more about the actual history."[8]

As part of the prepublicity for *The Tudors*, Showtime created a number of websites in 2007, one of which was a wiki — like Wikipedia, a compendium of knowledge built by viewers themselves. In addition to informational postings about the show and Tudor history, the moderators posted questions soliciting readers' opinions. Discussions ranged from the historical controversies that had engaged longtime Tudor scholars — was Anne born in 1501 or 1507? Did she sleep with her first love, Henry Percy? Was her last stillbirth deformed? — to playful questionnaires such as "If Henry's wives were alive today, what jobs would they have?" and "What magazines would they read?" Participants, at one point, were asked to submit the question they would most want to ask Anne if she was contacted in a séance. Their questions reveal their personal engagement, even sympathetic identification, with Anne. "Was Henry good in bed?" "Did you really have extra toes and fingers?" "If you had to do your life again would you marry the king if you knew all we know today?" "Do you think you had an impact in your daughter's life?" "How did you find the strength to endure the trial and imprisonment without any support from your family?" "Did the beheading hurt?"[9]

Not everyone was a fan of Anne's, however. Claire Ridgway, who started *The Anne Boleyn Files* in 2009, encountered a good deal of hatred of Anne and, by extension, her site. "Being someone who runs an Anne Boleyn site has left me open to abuse, offensive e-mails, and even death threats because I dare to defend a woman who for some really is the 'scandal of Christendom.'"[10] Either encouraged or angered by *The Tudors'* tendency to sanctify Katherine and Jane Seymour, "Team Boleyn" members and "Team Aragon/Team Seymour" members became mean, squabbling girls themselves. Sue Booth, one of the first moderators of the *Tudors Wiki*, was struck by the "fierce loyalties" that arose among the members of the Katherine of Aragon and Anne Boleyn "camps."[11] "It never ceased to amaze me," she recalls, "how strongly these women felt about something that happened more than four hundred years ago."[12] Natalie Sweet, who joined the wiki in 2008 while she was studying for a master's degree in history, remembers these battles as proving the truth of the comment made by sportswriter Clay Travis that "the dark corners of the Internet message board made talk radio seem like a midday stroll in a well-kept garden." Viewers, encouraged by the anonymity of Internet conversations, didn't hold back on slinging mud at one another, and for moderators of the site, it became a "challenge maintaining the line between constructive criticism and negative character bashing."[13] Barb Alexander, who runs *The Tudor Tutor*, is puzzled by all this. "I can never figure out why there is such a 'fangirl' or 'bully' attitude toward any of these people — they have been dead for about five hundred years! I like to see an educated passion for a historical figure, and if that figure is not your cup of tea, a respectful disagreement is fine. But they lived centuries ago, in a different climate than ours, and so I don't feel it's fair to judge them or their actions by modern standards."[14] That may be true, but it's never stopped writers from the seventeenth through twenty-first centuries from taking sides; why should it be any different now?

Despite the wife fights, the *Tudors Wiki* was Natalie Sweet's "sanity" during graduate school, and it taught her that she should "never discredit the research and knowledge of another just because she did not hold a history degree . . . and who made me a better historian for the perspectives they provided to me."[15] Undoubtedly the most convincing proof of that statement is *The Anne Boleyn Files*. Although it began as "just a blog" that Claire Ridgway was writing for herself—a "journal of my journey into finding out more about Anne Boleyn . . . people started finding me and commenting on the site. I was blown away! There were other people out there who were just as fascinated by Anne! My research became all consuming, a passion that had taken hold, and by the summer of 2009 I had given up my freelance writing career and was researching Tudor history on a full-time basis. I've never looked back!"[16] Today, 23,000 people visit the site each month, and in response to reader demand, it has become much more than "just a blog." *The Anne Boleyn Files* provides links to other sites where one can purchase books and Tudor-themed products, buy such items as replicas of Anne's famous "B" necklace and pajamas and hoodies with her image on them, and sign up for yearly events such as the Anne Boleyn Experience Tour. It is also a clearinghouse for every kind of Tudor resource. Claire's own "journey," too, has evolved. Just in the few years I've been following the site, I've seen her blossom from a respectful reporter of the theories of published authors to an investigative historical journalist whose blog—recently made available in book form—is more rigorous than that of many professional historians.

ℰ An International Community of Myth Busters, Inspired by a Television Show

It's not surprising that, with the exception of *Tudorhistory.org*, the Tudor websites and Facebook pages postdate the April 2007 premiere of *The Tudors* and that some of the most popular sites were begun after the record-breaking second-season finale in June 2008, in which Anne's execution drew 852,000 viewers—83 percent above the numbers for the season-one finale. Google Trends recorded a dramatic peak in surfers for "Anne Boleyn" during 2008. But even after the second-season finale, the numbers did not return to their pre-*Tudors* levels, and sites continued to flourish—among them Barb Alexander's delightfully "cheeky guide to the dynasty," *The Tudor Tutor*, and Natalie Grueninger's *On the Tudor Trail*, which began as a place to document surviving locations that Anne Boleyn had once visited and now has grown to include interviews with authors and historians, its own line of Anne-inspired greeting cards, and plans to lead a tour, In the Footsteps of Anne Boleyn.

The Tudor Facebook pages and websites constitute an international community of Tudor scholars, many of them disappointed by the lack of available materials and discussion in their home countries. Jessica Prestes, who is Brazilian, was introduced to the Tudors at the age of eleven, when her history teacher took the class to watch the movie *Elizabeth*. But at the time she knew nothing about the story of Anne Boleyn, only that Henry VIII was Elizabeth's father. After *The Tudors* premiered, however, Anne became her "obsession." She's now a graduate student in history who runs several Facebook pages and sites with an international following.[17] Sarah Bryson, in Australia, was having trouble finding people with an interest in Tudor history there; today, her Internet site and Facebook page is one of the most personally engaging, with reviews of the latest books alternating with warm conversations among members.[18] Sylwia Sobczak Zupanec has been fascinated by Anne since she was thirteen, but with little information available in Polish, she was frustrated. Noticing the historical inaccuracies of *The Tudors*, she started purchasing books in English about Anne and joined a Polish forum about the show. "And then I thought: why not start my own website, where I could write about Anne and the Tudor period in Polish language?"[19] Sylwia started her website—the only site about Anne Boleyn in Polish—in 2010. It ultimately led to Sylwia creating a sister site and a Facebook page in English.

The Tudor websites and Facebook pages are far from being just "fan pages." Because most of those who run them are not professional historians (although some are graduate students in history, and many are writing books), they are freer to allow curiosity and skepticism—rather than the demands of specialization or publication—to guide their thinking. Each new book, media presentation, or public controversy immediately becomes a subject of review and debate. And because the nature of the sites is collective exploration, particular issues are much more rapidly and thoroughly explored than they typically are in academic forums. Poked and prodded by members, who together constitute a phenomenally well-read critical commu-

252 · AN ANNE FOR ALL SEASONS

nity, these sites have become think tanks of Tudor research, questioning some of the most entrenched myths, raising serious issues about
documentation, and delving into issues that appear only as footnotes
in the scholarly literature. In many ways, they operate as the critical
conscience of published Tudor research. A few prominent examples:
Ridgway has exposed numerous scholarly soft spots in Alison Weir's
book about Mary Boleyn, Grueninger led a rigorous investigation
into the historical meaning of the color yellow (which sources have
claimed Anne and Henry wore after Katherine's death), Zupanec was
the first to notice that a famous quote about Anne attributed to Francis I and endlessly recyled in much of the literature has never actually
been documented in any of the books that cite it. She presented her
research and spearheaded a collective exploration that, despite the
efforts of many scholars in many fields, has yet to be able to validate
the quotation. These critical investigations are the stuff of scholarly
findings of significance and potential widespread interest.

"Third-Wave" Anne/"Postmodern" Anne

According to Princess Diana's close friend Simon Berry, Diana confided one day that she was going to marry Prince Charles. Teased
about how she could be so sure (she had met him just once), Diana
responded (not knowing, apparently, about Henry and Katherine),
"He's the one man on the planet who is not allowed to divorce me."[20]
Berry recalls their nocturnal drives. "One time we went past Bucking-
ham Palace," he says. "I remember her saying, just drive round a few
more times. It was late at night. She said, 'What do you think? What
do you think? Do you think I stand a chance? It could be quite fun.
It would be like Anne Boleyn or Guinevere.'"[21] Did Diana not know
how Boleyn met her end? Perhaps she did — and didn't care. Life with
Prince Charming, even if short, may have seemed worth it to her. More
likely, though, Diana — like Anne, centuries before — wasn't thinking
of the end, only of the beginning. Which we, ironically, imagine as the

end. "Happily ever after" — the fairy tales (including adult ones such as *Pretty Woman*) promise this perpetual bliss just at the point where, in real life, things often begin to go awry.

Few of the young women in the Boleyn Internet community are wistful Dianas, dreaming about snagging a prince or looking dazzling in royal jewels. They may have heard the same fairy tales as Diana did when she was a child, but few of them were old enough to have watched the royal wedding on television, and they all know how *that* fairy tale ended. Having watched *The Tudors,* many people — including me — were annoyed but addicted, and they knew how that one ended too. None of them see Anne as a tragic victim either. Yes, they felt that a huge injustice had been done to her; but "victim" is not a word in their vocabulary. Even the youngest interviewees (twelve to nineteen), when asked what made them an Anne fan, spoke of her intelligence, her independence, her refusal to be silenced, and her spunk. "I love her motto — 'This is how it's going to be; let them grumble'; it's basically an elegant way of sticking two fingers up to the people who hated her. She definitely had guts."[22] "For shy, soft-spoken girls, she is an inspiration to stand up and say something, and for not so soft-spoken girls, they can relate to her forwardness."[23] As someone who'd researched girls' pain and depression over their bodies, I was touched by how often the younger girls mentioned Anne's confidence in her own appearance, "even though she wasn't overly pretty,"[24] "not just a pretty face,"[25] even "the antithesis of the ideal beauty."[26] "She wasn't the conventional beauty and yet she showed that you didn't have to fit the norm and that it was good to be different."[27]

I hardly ever asked a question or posted a feature that "announced" itself as feminist or that suggested that label in connection with Anne. (The one time that I did — on another page — I was trounced for being "anachronistic" and "ahistorical.") Yet without the word itself — poison to many young women nowadays — quite a few of my interviewees came pretty close to a classically feminist view. Especially among my post-twenty-year-old interviewees, phrases such as "male-dominated world" began to show up, and the analysis of inequality in Anne's time went beyond "roles." One twenty-six-year-old, while admitting that "Anne had power" and "made a difference in the world," also saw her as representing "the struggle women can have with men. Some men cannot handle it when a woman is so intelligent."[28] On another website, a reader complained: "It makes me CRAZY when people place all the blame on the 'loose woman' who ruins a marriage. They did it in the sixteenth century and they still do it today. Where is the man's/husband's culpability? Why do we always fall back on the easily blamed 'whore'? Why must the man be 'led' astray? He has no mind or libido of his own? Please."[29] "Look at Jane's motto: 'Bound to obey and serve,'" said a thirty-year-old interviewee. "If Anne lived nowadays, she would have said: 'What the hell is that?! We're not meant to be a man's doormat!'"[30] Even my one twelve-year-old praised Anne for the fact that "she knew she wasn't a second-class citizen."[31]

But although these young women might complain about continuing sexual inequality, they, like their younger counterparts, put more emphasis on the degree to which Anne triumphed over her situation, making use of whatever resources were available to her. As Lynn Phillips brilliantly demonstrates in her study of young women's attitudes toward sexuality, *Flirting with Danger*, these are generations that have grown up believing that being seen as a "victim" is the worst fate one can suffer. "Contrary to right-wing claims that women are eager to go public and 'cry victimization,'" Phillips found that her subjects (they were undergraduates in college in the late 1990s when her study was conducted) went to great psychological lengths to "disqualify" themselves as victims.[32] "Young women recounted many detailed stories of pain, humiliation, manipulation, violence, and force in their hetero-relations . . . Yet they were largely unwilling to use such labels as 'rape,' 'acquaintance rape,' 'battering,' or 'abuse' to describe those experiences."[33] Phillips suggests that "the generation of young women currently coming into adulthood may have quite different understandings of gendered power than those of second-wave feminist activists and scholars, perhaps twenty to fifty years their senior . . . Whereas feminist scholars may speak of male domination and women's victimization as rather obvious phenomena, younger women, raised to believe in their own independence, invulnerability, and sexual entitlement, may not so readily embrace such concepts."[34]

My twenty-somethings, like their younger counterparts, praised

Anne's intelligence, independence, courage, determination, and strength. But they also applauded (what they saw as) Anne's forthright sexuality. "She came across as fiery, but also as sexy and desirable."[35] "She was a modern-day girl in the wrong time period and people weren't ready for that. We relate because we act that way today. We are outspoken, a little feisty, and do what it takes to get what we want by using sex."[36] Surveying my interview responses as well as material from other websites, it became clear to me that Anne's young fans have not followed any of the historical prototypes, but have created their own Anne, patched together out of those pieces of the media images that they find attractive (beauty, style — Anne's favorite magazines would be *Vogue*, *InStyle*, *Elle*, *Marie Claire*, and *Cosmopolitan*[37]), actual historical information from the "elders" on the sites (which debunks many of the most vicious myths the media images promulgate), and, most of all, what they see as the many-sidedness of Anne's personality, which resists definition as either flirt or "brain," "feminine" or feisty, mother or career woman, sexpot or "one of the guys," saint or sinner. They identify passionately with, or aspire to, this many-sidedness; it's what has made Anne a distinctly contemporary heroine for them.

So, when asked on another website to respond to the query "Anne Boleyn — Angel or Devil?"[38] most participants refused the terms of the question.

"She was human, she had her assets and her flaws, and she showed off both." "She was neither an angel nor a devil. She was human." "I don't believe that Anne Boleyn was either a 'witch,' a 'whore,' or a 'saint.' I believe she was an ambitious, intellectual woman who like all the others before or since are rounded up into one of those tidy categories. Categories that allow society to pigeonhole 'difficult' women whom they don't know what else to do with. Certainly, her life contained elements of all three, but this is a complex, multifaceted personality that was more than the sum total of all her parts." "It's far too simplistic to define her as either an 'angel' or a 'devil.' She was an intelligent, educated, highly sophisticated woman, who certainly possessed many flaws, significant among them being considerable arrogance, but who was also far too complex to be dismissed as simply a 'bad' or 'good' character . . . She really was a great deal more than a home-wrecking harlot who ran off with another woman's husband, but she also wasn't an innocent lamb who had no idea what she was getting herself into. She was hugely complicated, and not easy to dismiss." "In Anne we have intelligence, strength, coquettishness, vulnerability, outspokenness and culture. And that may only be scratching the surface." "Anne was an extraordinary woman, and can't be lassoed into a single category."[39]

One of my interviewees described Anne as "the original feminist."[40] If so, her feminism, for these girls, is clearly of the "third-wave" variety — a woman of contradictions who cannot be "lassoed" or "pigeonholed," who skillfully walks the line between sexuality and sluttiness, girliness and brass, playfulness and power. So, if Anne was alive today, she'd be "provocative but not slutty."[41] She'd wear business suits during the day, but "designer outfits from Milan for evenings."[42] At Oktoberfest, "she would be flirtatious, magnetic."[43] But then she'd leave the guys dumbfounded by going home alone.

Unlike those consumers of pop culture who simply love to see a bitch get what's coming to her, these young women have constructed an Anne who "empowers" them without asking that they relinquish their femininity or become a parody of it in the process. She's neither a "victim" nor a "power feminist," but she's not "postfeminist" or "antifeminist" either. Her very independence of mind and heart insists that it's her right, and her pleasure, to dance, and flirt, and thrill to beautiful clothes — and then, if she chooses, leave the party alone. This Anne winks at young women across the centuries and understands the challenges they face and the questions they ask. Can I be myself — fully myself, sexual and smart, serious and playful, sometimes demanding, sometimes jealous, sometimes too loud, sometimes wanting to leave the party alone — and still be loved? Can I be loved — fully loved, body, soul, and mind — and still remain myself? If forced to choose, what will I sacrifice and what will I hold fast to?

Where did this "third-wave" Anne come from? In no small part, the answer is Showtime's *The Tudors*. For many, born long after 1969, when the movie version of *Anne of the Thousand Days* — my generation's introduction to Anne — was released, the series was their first taste of the sexy, seamy side of British history, made all the more enticing by the gorgeous, stylishly updated leads who looked nothing like the characters in their high school texts. (In fact, most of the people I interviewed had learned virtually nothing about Henry VIII's wives — just "the Reformation" — in high school.) Without Natalie Dormer's contribution to the role, however, only the most avid young researchers would have had the material out of which to forge a "third-wave" Anne. To professional historians, it may seem as though her hard-won revisions amounted to little more than tweaking. But for young viewers of the show, the changes Dormer made went a long way. "She portrayed so many sides of Anne," said one of my seventeen-year-old interviewees, "strong, flirtatious, jealous, angry, intelligent, caring, loving . . . and she did so without ever losing the matchless allure that makes Anne so fascinating."[44] From an eighteen-year-old: "Natalie captured the signature 'I am no fool' aspect of Anne's personality. Her Anne demanded attention; she brought feistiness to the English court, and embodied curiosity, intellect and charm in a manner I have never seen."[45] A nineteen-year-old said, "She gave the good, the bad, the vulnerable, the mother, and a sense that Anne was a very strong woman. Especially at the end."[46] From a twenty-five-year-old: "She captured the different sides of Anne very well — the innocent, the proud, the unsure, the angry, the strong. Anne is an extremely multidimensional character, and Natalie showed her as such."[47]

Is this the "real" Anne? That's a question that is unanswerable. But she clearly is a new Anne — and she doesn't live only in the imaginations of young women and girls. British playwright Howard Brenton, without ever having watched *The Tudors* or visited an Anne Boleyn Internet site, arrived at a very similar conception in his critically acclaimed *Anne Boleyn*. Brenton didn't even begin from a particular interest in Anne. Asked to write a play for Shakespeare's Globe Theatre in London celebrating the 400th anniversary of the King James Bible, at first Brenton was stumped. "Then I remembered that Anne Boleyn had a Testament, a Tyndale Testament, and, of course, the King James Bible is largely based on Tyndale. I thought that was interesting, and then the play spun itself from that," he recalled.[48] If you begin with Anne the reformist rather than Anne the home wrecker you get a very different sort of story: "It is as if there were a Joan of Arc, driven by a religious vision, within the more familiar figure of Anne the dazzling sexual predator."[49] Working from Eric Ives's highly respected biography, *The Life and Death of Anne Boleyn* — but not limiting himself to the historical facts — Brenton "spins" the story of a fiercely dedicated Protestant with a wicked sense of humor who opens the play in her bloodstained execution dress, taunting the audience about the contents of an embroidered bag that looks suspiciously large enough to be carrying a head. "Do you want to see it? Who wants to see it? Do you? You?"[50] What she pulls out first — before the head — is Tyndale's Bible.

Judging from the reviews, for many in the audience — even the critics — Brenton's Anne was their first acquaintance with Anne the religious reformer, and with the now widely accepted explanation that her fall was engineered by Thomas Cromwell, with whom Anne fell out over the use of monastery monies. But although Brenton wanted to celebrate Anne's "life and legacy as a great English woman who helped change the course of our history," he didn't leave the dazzler entirely behind.[51] The artist in him, who eschews "message" and moralizing — and who admitted to me that he fell in love with Anne over the course of writing the play — couldn't see her as saintly. Like the "third-wave" Anne, Brenton's Anne is a flirt, and — as the play's Cromwell puts it — could "look straight at you and wasn't scared."[52] "What man," he goes on, "can deal with that?"[53]

Brenton didn't set out to create an Anne who challenged the duality of saint and sinner; in fact, writing the play was largely a matter of following his instincts.

"I don't think you can know," he told me, "whether something you're working on is going to resonate for an audience. And often later, if it does, you realize, 'Oh, that's why I was so obsessed with that at that time!' You can't ever have a message-driven play that tries to disrupt and so on. You just follow an instinct, something that you're obsessed with at the moment, and then only later do you realize why. It's very dangerous for writers to suddenly begin to think about their 'whys.' You can go bonkers; you turn into the label that you've created. We can't be moralists or ideologues. It's a different kind of truth we should be after. Dostoevsky was a great novelist, but if you read his political and religious tracts, they are awful. They're one dimensional, ranting, very little human feeling or insight to the human condition in them."[54]

When I asked Brenton what he realized about the "why" of it after writing the play, he replied, "I don't really know. Instability of regimes?"[55] This surprised me because what was clearly the most provocative and enjoyable dimension of the play for audiences was its mixture of the sacred and the profane, particularly in the character of Anne. Brenton's Anne can worship at the altar of "the word" one moment and wish, of Katherine, that "the bitch would piss off to a convent"[56] the next, be someone who can lecture King James (the play weaves back and forth through time between his reign and Henry's) about God's will, but when he asks if she was "such an insufferable holy cow" when she was alive, she replies, "Oh no, I had a lot of fun!"[57] Perhaps the key, both to Brenton's musing about the "instability of regimes" and his conception of Anne, is "instability" — not in the psychological sense (crazy Anne in the Tower, as in Donizetti's opera), but in the "postmodern" sense, in which everything that once seemed solid melts away, fixed truths are deconstructed, and rigid dualisms crumble. Brenton would never characterize himself as a postmodern, but then, very few of the women and girls who participate in the discussions on the Anne websites would characterize themselves as feminists. These things are not about the "positions" one takes but the cultural waves that flow through us. "We always write from our own time," Hilary Mantel told me — even when we try to swim against the tide.[58]

Anne, Susan, and Cassie

WE ALWAYS WRITE from our own time." And our own
lives. This book, for me, started as a kind of rescue fantasy. I have always been fascinated by girls and women
who began with great hope and promise and met tragic ends — Anne
Frank, Sylvia Plath, Marilyn Monroe, Princess Diana. And then, too,
the less famous but brilliant, troubled young women — the anorex-
ics, the cutters, the sexually abused — who have been drawn to me
as a teacher, writer, and friend. I have been adopting these girls all
my life, spellbound by the (almost always false) belief that if they just
had someone who truly understood, everything could be made right.
For them, of course, but also for me. As they sat in my office, sipping
their water, soothed and grateful, I would feel the capable, reassuring,
empathic Professor Bordo grow bigger and more real, until the sad,
fearful child that I had been, Susan Klein, would almost disappear.
Almost. Twenty-five years before, those feelings had led me to write
my first book, about cultural attitudes toward the female body and
their impact on girls and women; when I first began to research Anne
Boleyn, I felt I was being called to another maternal mission. I would
find the "real" Anne Boleyn and rescue her from the pile of mythology
that had built up around her. Presumptuous. Grandiose. But in the
end, isn't that why writers continue to add our puny words to the vast
pile? We want to save someone, something, some truth or other, from
oblivion, forgetfulness, stupidity, malice.

At an early stage in my research, I hung a postcard of a particular portrait of Anne on the whiteboard that sat next to my desk, decorated with other scraps of Tudoriana. Anonymous, undoubtedly a copy, and depicting a far younger Anne than the National Gallery portrait or any of the other later interpretations, the painting now hangs in Hever Castle, Anne's childhood home. I had surmised from the childishness of her plump cheeks and soft, dreamy eyes, and the fact that she is still wearing an English hood — starched, hair-concealing, with a gabled point similar to that of a nun's headdress — that she hadn't yet been sent abroad.[1] I figure her to be about twelve. It was a privilege, of course, to be "finished" abroad — and far less wrenching in the sixteenth century, when infant mortality was high and the affective bonds between parent and child were nothing like the norm today, when a middle-class child's leaving for college is a great drama for all concerned. Still, at twelve, Anne had known nothing but the secluded Hever countryside and an everyday life centered on learning and play with her mother, brother, and sister. It had to have been wrenching, if exciting, to leave this bucolic life behind.

I loved this dreamy portrait, whatever its origins. For me, it was a reminder that there was an Anne before Henry, before the divorce from Katherine, before the miscarriages, before the charges of adultery, before the Tower. An Anne who sat at a seventeen-foot table; laughing with her family; dining on roasts, olive pie, spiced custard, and the numerous fricassees and "quelque choses" that were the pride of every well-heeled Tudor housewife. An Anne who practiced her French with the diligence of a scholar. An Anne who slept in a tiny bedroom — snug, plain, and sweet, and among the few rooms at Hever that have not been plushly redecorated in Edwardian style — dreaming of . . . what? We really don't know. The Hever portrait reminds us that the archetypal temptress was once a real live child.

Looking at the portrait, I felt intensely protective. It was not unlike the feeling that sometimes floods me when I am talking to one of my eighteen-year-old students, and the nighttime cutter or purger is revealed to me behind the bravado of the belly-button piercing. And it called up my fears for my own daughter, Cassie, who from infancy was bolder, more independent, and more audacious than her peers. As

I watched with admiration as she resisted the pink police throughout elementary school, I had come to feel — in my heart, not in my head, which knew it was nonsense — that Cassie, whom we adopted, had been cosmically entrusted to me. I was relieved that neither the culture nor her DNA had given me a girl like Diana, dreaming of the day her prince might come. But I worried — and still do, of course — how her unconventional behavior would be met, as she grew older, by peers and teachers. The young Anne, as I imagine her, was once as sturdy and unafraid as my daughter. I see them both on horseback, sure and free, challenging each other. Faster! Faster! The countryside is hilly and difficult, but these are fearless girls, who take each turn and jump with ease, laughing, thrilled at their own expertise.

Cassie, then eight, was with me when I traveled to London during my first Boleyn-obsessed July, courtesy of a British conference invitation — ironically, on the topic of masculinity and pathology. By then, I had developed the spirit of an avenging mama. I was even angry at Hever Castle for devoting less space to Anne than to William Waldorf Astor's seventeenth- and eighteenth-century antiques. At that point, having spent several months obsessed with Anne, I was hoping to find something grippingly authentic there that I hadn't yet found in the books. But Astor and his wife, who had "combed the world" (through their agents) for paintings, furniture, carpets, and objets d'art "worthy" of the castle, had chased the ghosts of Anne and Henry from most of the house. Magnificent gardens, created in the early 1900s from marshland and rough meadows, frustrated my yearning to see and smell the natural surroundings of Anne's childhood. They were gorgeous, but I didn't want to see plush, satin-covered furniture and well-tended grounds; I wanted "Tudor" with everything wild and not-quite-civilized about it.

I was especially annoyed to find, on the second floor of the castle, elaborately costumed figures created by the costumiers Angels of London arranged in scenes commemorating "Henry VIII and His Six Wives" and "Scenes from the Life and Times of Anne Boleyn." Some of the figures are impressively lifelike and period appropriate, and the artist had lavished particular skill on the executioner. But Anne's face seems to have been modeled with Miss America 1959 (was it Mary

Ann Mobley?) in mind. Impossibly regular-featured and wide-eyed, she's a Breck Girl, a Junior Miss, a mannequin stolen from a fifties window display on "What the Modern Girl Will Wear to School This Fall" and redressed in Tudor garb. *And* the executioner had an ax, not a sword! To me, full of the passion of the newly converted, this was a travesty. My daughter, however, found the execution scene "awesome" and could only be dragged away by a reminder that there was a display of torture instruments on the second floor.

"What part of the body did they put those on?" my daughter asked excitedly, pointing to a particularly grisly pair of steel pincers. "How hard did they squeeze them? Did the person die, or could he live if they got him to a hospital in time?" She was pressed up against the glass, amazed that grown-ups had once been so creative with the nasty things that they did to one another's bodies. "I bet if they got him to a hospital right away, he could still live." Out of the corner of my eye I saw a pair of raised English eyebrows and pursed lips. "Historical education," I said, trying to elicit a laugh that never came and attempting to shift Cassie's interest to the suits of armor.

There are very few reminders at Hever of the real events that played out here. One is a room containing Anne's prayer books, under glass, where I stood spellbound for a few moments, staring at the inscription "*le temps viendra*" (the time will come) and indulging my belief in a mystical connection between Anne and me, which I now recognize as just the irrational mentality of the first stages of infatuation. Another is the room where Henry is said to have slept when he visited Hever. (He carried an enormous lock with him, which he had a locksmith affix to the bedroom door wherever he stayed during his progresses or as a visitor.) The massive bed is dated from about 1540 — four years after Anne's death — but it is easy to imagine Henry sleeping in one just like it. As I stared at Henry's bed, mentally trying Charles Laughton, Robert Shaw, Richard Burton, and Jonathan Rhys Meyers on for size, I suddenly remembered that Cassie was wandering alone through the rooms of the castle. "Cassie, where are you?" I kept my voice down, trying not to fulfill the "loud American" stereotype, but my daughter, as usual, had slipped out of my sight. "Cassie?" The rooms are maze-like and there were countless canes and walkers to negotiate. "Cassie?"

I finally found her searching, without any luck, for something interesting in a room with portraits. She was already chafing at the bit, eager to get to the gift shop, where we purchased a set of chocolates, seven in all, six wives and Bluff Hal in the middle.

Later that night, in our hotel room, Cassie immediately grabbed the chocolates and claimed the king — "I want Henry!" I was briefly annoyed that what she had taken away from our trip to Hever was a greater admiration for Henry, the big male boss. But after all, why shouldn't she want the centerpiece, the only one who was not, as the chocolates suggested, a part of a harem? I also knew that in her hands, Henry's reign wouldn't last very long. I secreted Anne away where no one could eat her. And Henry was devoured with dispatch by my daughter, the wrapper with his image crushed and discarded as soon as the chocolate was gone.

I returned to England in the summer of 2010, excited about planned interviews with Natalie Dormer and Howard Brenton, and hoping to see some of the sites I had missed the first time. Cassie wasn't with me this time (she was away at camp), so I wouldn't have to deal with her restless hand tugging me away from boring historical stuff. By then, too, my rescue fantasy had been informed by the recognition that Anne Boleyn didn't need me to save her. For what I had expected to be a steady historical onslaught of familiar stereotypes was, as I discovered in my years of research, a complex, varied, culturally revealing, and never-ending creation and re-creation. Yes, Henry had destroyed her fleshly life in real time, and many since had vilified her in the cultural "afterlife" that followed. But they didn't succeed — not in any permanent sense. Anne the real woman may have been silenced by Henry, but her restless spirit refuses to remain quiet, as she uses our shifting fancies, fantasies, and anxieties to write and rewrite her story over the centuries.

Still, there was a depressing gap between what I'd learned, digging deeply into things, and the more superficial, "official" representation. I loved Brenton's play, although I was annoyed that Miranda Raison hadn't been forced to dye her hair dark or wear a wig. ("Too uncomfortable," Brenton told me.[2]) But the official sites, for one obsessed with Anne, turned out to be disappointing. Hampton Court, apparently determined to make the site tourist and family friendly, is scrubbed of everything ugly about Henry's reign. "Bluff King Hal" rules — with Disney and Showtime cheering him on. In the gift shop, would-be warriors and princesses can buy plastic suits of armor and pink gowns available at any suburban mall. In the Information Centre, children can pick up activity booklets with titles such as *Henry's Palace* ("Ever wondered how the royals used to rock? Step this way and discover how Henry created England's most fabulous party venue") and borrow mock-velvet cloaks for their visit. There are themed, costumed enactments, in which talented actors stage merry moments in the life of Henry VIII. Nothing frightening or tragic is permitted.[3] And the guides don't know how many H's and A's were left on the ceiling and walls of the Great Hall. It seemed that five hundred years later, Henry had gotten his way at Hampton Court.

At the Tower of London[4], where things went very bad for Anne and where the "Beefeater" guides delight in telling visitors anecdotes associated with its famous prisoners, Anne is just one among many. On Tower Green she quietly shares a placid memorial with seven other men and women whose "jewelled names were broken from the vivid thread of life" on the Green, including her cousin Katherine Howard, Robert Devereux (Elizabeth's Earl of Essex), and Lady Jane Grey, who was beheaded when she was just sixteen. In the Chapel Royal of St. Peter ad Vincula, where Anne is buried, her name is listed on a bronze plaque along with all the other famous prisoners entombed within (including Thomas More, who opposed Henry's divorce from Katherine and would no doubt be squirming to know he shares a crypt with Anne). Anne's tomb itself bears no indication of who lies within beyond the name "Anne Boleyn" not very prominently etched in the stone. You can spend an entire day at the Tower of London and leave without ever learning that the first queen ever executed in Britain, not to mention under such explosive and suspect circumstances, is entombed in this altar. The day I was there, the chapel was virtually empty, while long lines gathered at the armory to see the Crown Jewels.

To add injury to insult, later that day I got hit by a bicycle while crossing a busy London street. Megadoses of Advil and the endorphin high from the pleasure of talking to Dormer and Brenton saw me through the interviews, but by the time we got to the National Portrait Gallery, I had used up my tolerance for pain and royal PR and was in a foul mood. I was determined, though, to see the one portrait of Anne that has the stamp of "official," so I limped along, making my way to the Tudor rooms where I searched for a half hour, unable to locate the painting. There was Holbein's famous towering sketch of Henry dominating all others. Many paintings of Elizabeth, showing the gradual emergence of the iconography of the Virgin Queen and her "golden age." A huge painting of Thomas More and all his descendants. A brilliantly colored oil of Katherine Parr, Henry's last wife. But no Anne. Finally, I turned to the two guides standing in the corner of the room, presumably available for expert information about the gallery. "Isn't the portrait of Anne Boleyn supposed to be here?" I asked. They look baffled for a moment, taken off guard. Hadn't anyone else asked this question?

"Hmmm. I think it's around somewhere."

"No. I've looked everywhere — several times."

"Oh, wait, I think . . . Wasn't she loaned out somewhere?"

"Yes, that's right!" said her partner. "She's on loan. But I'm not sure where. If you go online downstairs, you probably can find out."

I must have looked crestfallen, so the guide tried to cheer me up with a joke. "Well, you know, the wives have to take their turns!" I didn't find it funny. "*He* never has to take a turn, does he?" I said, pointing to the mammoth Holbein Henry.

Henry's effort to erase Anne seemed to have been successful, at least at the National Portrait Gallery. But later, after I returned to the United States, I found out that Anne's portrait, which had deteriorated badly, was not, in fact, loaned out, as the guides had said, but was down for restoration, and a massive fund-raising effort was being undertaken to finance the work. Natalie Grueninger had started a second Facebook page, with endorsements from Alison Weir and Natalie Dormer, devoted to "help save Anne's portrait," and the money was coming in. My daughter, picked up from camp, seemed to have grown several inches in height and immeasurably in stature, in her own eyes anyway. I longed for a melting hug. But that was one of the small sacrifices I have to pay for having such a formidable, strong-minded daughter.

In the British papers, which I now was reading regularly online, theatre reviewers, initially taken aback by Howard Brenton's complex "revisionist" Anne, were raving about the play. But, as throughout history, the old dualities were still irresistible to some. HARLOT OR HEROINE? WAS SHE A SCHEMING SEXUAL PREDATOR, OR A BRAVE REFORMER WHO CHANGED BRITAIN FOREVER? THE JURY'S BEEN OUT FOR THE PAST 500 YEARS — NOW A NEW PLAY AIMS TO SET THE RECORD STRAIGHT.[5] That was the *Daily Mail's* headline for its review of Brenton's play. The historical Anne, who was able to make bitter jokes even as she was hours away from death about the labels history would pin on her, would have laughed. So would have Brenton's Anne. At the very end of the play, she speaks to the audience, the godless "demons of the future." "You're so strange to me, as I must be strange to you," she says.[6] "Beware of love," she tells the audience as she says her good-byes.[7] But she doesn't mean it. "No, don't! We must all die, so die greatly, for a better world, for love."[8] But the preachy mood passes too. "Good-bye, demons. God bless you all," she says.[9] And then, ever the elusive flirt, she blows us a kiss.

Acknowledgments

In the spring of 2007, I was working on a novel when I got an e-mail from the British writer and journalist Matt Shoard with an idea for a collaborative project on famous female rebels. Although I didn't know it at the time, the intense, intimate, and incredibly enjoyable months of exchanged e-mails and trial-balloon proposals that followed were the beginnings of this book. As the original idea gradually changed from many female subjects to one and a collaborative project to a singly authored book, Matt remained a generous, creative adviser and friend. It's a noninflated fact to say that this book would not have happened without him.

Since my fascination with Anne emerged unexpectedly in the middle of another writing project (which immediately was put on hold), this book required more help "finding itself" than my others had. With the help of Matt, Marilyn Silverman, my amazing writing group — Janet Eldred, Kathi Kern, and Ellen Rosenman — and my agent, Sam Stoloff — a man who has brought intelligence, kindness, pragmatism, and sanity to every stage of this process — I went through at least a half-dozen different conceptualizations over the next four months.

I also talked to several editors, who were enthusiastic about my final proposal but uncertain about the broad appeal of a book about Anne Boleyn. (This was midway through the first season of *The Tudors*, and Tudormania was not yet in full flower.) Some were confused about what I planned to do in the book — understandably, because I still wasn't sure myself. Then, the cosmic matchmaker of authors and editors stepped in, and I had my first conversation with George Hodgman. From the moment he guessed my first idol (Pauline Kael) to the day, a year later, when he told me to stop thinking like an academic, to put my books down, and to call Geneviève Bujold for an interview, George was the editor I had dreamed of finding: brilliant, inspired, demanding, and — unexpected bonus — hilariously funny. I was blessed to have George Hodgman mentor this book; he wanted a lot from it; he wrestled with me until he got it — and I will be forever grateful for his guidance, humor, and wonderful mind.

Thanks to a generous endowed professorship from the University of Kentucky, I was lucky to have two splendid research assistants. Michelle Del Toro, my staff assistant and go-to for popular culture information and insight, also read through a draft of the manuscript and told me where more information and background was needed for the "general" reader. Natalie Sweet did endless hours of research into the original documents, delved fearlessly and knowledgeably into the thorniest of historical controversies, prepared the citations for the book, made sure that I had committed no huge historical blunders, and offered advice at every stage of the process. Natalie also came up with the inspired idea of creating a Facebook page for the book, a site that became home base for interviews and discussion with other Tudorphiles and scholars. She continues to co-manage this page with me, as well as a website that she designed and administers.

This project turned an important corner when, on George Hodgman's urging, I contacted Geneviève Bujold, Natalie Dormer, and Michael Hirst, all of whom, to my amazement and delight, granted me lengthy candid interviews — as did Howard Brenton, who met with me in the cafeteria of Shakespeare's Globe Theatre just after the opening of his acclaimed play, *Anne Boleyn*. I am also grateful to the novelists and historians who spoke to me on the phone or via e-mail — Robin Maxwell, Hilary Mantel, Margaret George, David Loades, Alison Weir, Suzannah Lipscomb, and Nell Gavin — and to those leading lights of the Tudor Facebook "community" who provided support, enthusiasm, and shared their stories with me: Sue Booth, Lara Eakins, Claire Ridgway, Barbara Conn Alexander, Natalie Grueninger, Sylwia Sobczak Zupanec, Jessica Prestes, Sarah Morris, and Sarah Bryson.

It's impossible to adequately describe or enumerate the contributions of the members of *The Creation of Anne Boleyn* Facebook page. Special thanks go to Rhys Tudor, Jéssica Prestes, and Cris Gomes, who helped me trace the beautiful portrait on the cover of this book and contact the artist, Alexandre Jubran. Many thanks also to the page members who responded to an e-mail questionnaire about the appeal of Anne Boleyn to younger women: Raven Allen, Karissa Baker, Iliana Begetis, Haven Carlson, Makenzie Case, Sara Compton, Jessica Crowley, Memory Michelle Gargiulo, Cris Gomez, Brittani Hall, Robyn Heisel, Cailin Humphrys, Kayla Johns, Michelle Kistler, Angel Marks, Ilana Redler, Helen Reeves, Chrystina Rice, Elizabeth Schulz, Lynn Seitadi, Simone Shahid, Katherine Stinson, Marlessa Stivala, Elle van Petersen, Sophie Walker, Nicole Wheeler, and Casey Wilson. With advance apologies for those I am certain to miss, I'd also like to single out some of the earliest supporters and most frequent contributors to the page: Jan Abraham, Valerie Abrams, Valerie Adams, Ingibjörg Ágústsdóttir, Tammy J. Banks, Toni Frazer Barber, Lois Bateson, Anne Barnhill, Courtney Beatty, Claire Biggs-Tandy, Charna Baronoffsky Blumberg, Felicity Kate Boardman, Bollie Smit-Bolhuis, Sue Booth, Sarah Bryson, Susan Buffano, Becky Bunsic, Sarah Butterfield, Daphnée Diane Callas, Marina Camp, Bess Chilver, Cate Clement, Jessica Crowley, Howard Dalton, Holly Davis, Lisa Davis, Adrienne Dillard, Cynthia Carlin Drake, Cheryl Esselman, Donna Fagan, Isabelle Fallon, Emma Fuery, Jilly Fullerton-Louth, Cris Gomes, Clare Hancock, Denise Hansen, Susan Higginbotham, Lesley Holmes-Gurney, Fran Jablway, Cynthia Jokela, Pamela Kapustka, Binnie Klein, Ralphine L. Lamonica, Karissa Larsen, Linda Lofaro, Angel Marks, Jasmine Marrero-Pratt, Clive Morgan, Samantha Morris, Sarah Morris, Joanna Moore, Vicki Munden, Eliza Na, Fiona Orr, Robert Parry, Opal Crews Phelps, Jéssica Prestes, Tiffany Reddy, Krystel Marie Rivera, Jessica Rodriguez, Gareth Russell, Sandi Teresa Salas, Jessica Scarlett, Libby Schofield, Heidi Smith, Danielle Stasko, Katherine Stinson, Matthew Sweet, Sara Thornton, Lisa Tecoulesco, Rhys Tudor, Elle van Petersen, Sophie Walker, Emma Watson (with special thanks for the beautiful Anne scrapbook), Samantha Weber, Hope Olivia Elizabeth Wells, and Jenny Zeek-Schmeidler.

Nicole Angeloro, who came to the project late but has been essential to its completion, read the entire manuscript with more care, editorial wisdom, and affection than I could have hoped for. The final book has benefited greatly from her guidance. David Hough was the most meticulous and knowledgeable copy editor I could have asked for. Thanks to him, I send this book into the world unafraid of source scrutinizers and punctuation police.

A project that takes as long as this one is never written uninterrupted or sheltered from personal difficulties, unexpected delays, and professional obligations of life outside the writer's cave (in my case, a tiny study — formerly a dining nook — next to the kitchen, where I can make five AM coffee without waking up the rest of the house). There were times when I seriously doubted whether "my life" would allow me to finish my book. For helping me through those times, I thank my husband, Edward Lee; my sisters, Binnie Klein and Marilyn Silverman; Cristina Alcalde; Kate Black; Michelle Del Toro; Donna DePenning; Janet Eldred; George Hodgman; Kathi Kern; Ellen Rosenman; Natalie Sweet; and Lee Ann Whites.

My little study is the only room on the first floor of our house that can be closed off to dogs and other people, thanks to a door I installed; to press the point home, I put a sign up: DO NOT DISTURB: WRITER AT WORK. The sign means nothing to my daughter, Cassie, who barges in as she pleases, to describe the latest gruesome episode of her favorite television show or insist that I watch how many push-ups she can do. She thinks I'm a relic of another era, finds it quaintly amusing that someone would voluntarily sit writing, surrounded by books, when there are horses to ride, hoops to shoot, friends to text. She finds it a symptom of my derangement ("Mom, you *concern* me") that I consider her the inspiration for a book about a sixteenth-century queen. She doesn't know yet that there are many ways to be fierce and strong, and that I find her push-ups less stirring than her insistence, day after day, on being herself in every way.

Susan Bordo
Lexington, Kentucky
September 2012

Notes

Introduction: The Erasure of Anne Boleyn and the Creation of "Anne Boleyn"

1. Lord Cromwell to Sir William Kingston, May 18, 1536, in Norton 2011, 248.
2. Sir William Kingston to Lord Cromwell, ibid. Modern spelling applied.
3. Actually, Katherine Howard was also beheaded for adultery. As with Anne (who was, in fact, Katherine's cousin), this marriage began with passionate infatuation on Henry's part and ended with his former beloved on the scaffold. Barely a year after the marriage, Katherine (who likely did have at least one adulterous relationship) was placed under house arrest at Hampton Court and accused of leading "an abominable, base, carnal, voluptuous, and vicious life, like a common harlot, with diverse persons." Katherine tried, unsuccessfully, to see Henry in person and talk him out of it. (Henry's policy, perhaps because he feared he would be vulnerable to in-person pleas, was always to make sure that those he wanted dispensed with remained "out of mind" by keeping them "out of sight.") She was executed on Tower Green in 1542.
4. Goodman 2005.
5. de Carles 1927, 234. Original: *En ce pays, elle fut retenue / Par Claude, qui Royne après succedda: / Ou tellement ses graces amenda / Que ne l'eussiez oncques jugee Anglise / En ses façon, mais nifve Françoise.*
6. She later became a passionate admirer and defender of William Tyndale's English-language Bible, at the time banned in England but smuggled in for Anne, who had her ladies-in-waiting read it daily.

1. Why You Shouldn't Believe Everything You've Heard About Anne Boleyn

1. Starkey 2004, 443.
2. Friedmann, vol. II, 1884, 297.

3. Froude 1891, 324.

4. Herbert 1855, 171.

5. Starkey 2004, 524.

6. Ibid., 421.

7. Ibid., 510.

8. Ibid., 361

9. Ibid., 527.

10. Bennett 2012.

11. Mattingly 1932, 178.

12. Ibid, 184.

13. Pascual de Gayangos (editor), "Spain: September 1529, 1–10," *Calendar of State Papers, Spain*, Volume 4, Part 1: Henry VIII, 1529–1530, British History Online, http://www.british-history.ac.uk/report.aspx?compid=87687.

14. Pascual de Gayangos (editor), "Spain: May 1536, 16–31," *Calendar of State Papers, Spain*, Volume 5, Part 2: 1536–1538, British History Online, http://www.british -history.ac.uk/report.aspx?compid=87961.

15. James Gairdner (editor), "Henry VIII: April 1533, 11–20," *Letters and Papers, Foreign and Domestic, Henry VIII*, Volume 6: 1533, British History Online, http:// www.british-history.ac.uk/report.aspx?compid=77546.

16. Adrienne Dillard, October 13, 2011, comment on *The Anne Boleyn Files* Facebook page, "Interesting Article on Eustace Chapuys by Susan Bordo," accessed October 15, 2011, www.facebook.com/theanneboleynfiles.

17. October 13, 2011, comment on *The Anne Boleyn Files* Facebook page, "Interesting Article on Eustace Chapuys by Susan Bordo," accessed October 15, 2011, www .facebook.com/theanneboleynfiles.

18. Ibid.

19. Deborah Kuzyk, October 13, 2011, comment on *The Anne Boleyn Files* Facebook page, "Interesting Article on Eustace Chapuys by Susan Bordo," accessed October 15, 2011, www.facebook.com/theanneboleynfiles.

20. Loades 2009, 52.

21. Ibid.

22. Tremlett 2010, 250–51.

23. Loades 2009, 16.

24. J. S. Brewer (editor), "Henry VIII: May 1529, 1–10," *Letters and Papers, Foreign and Domestic, Henry VIII*, Volume 4: 1524–1530, British History Online, http://www .british-history.ac.uk/report.aspx?compid=91361.

25. Strickland and Strickland 2010, 561.

26. Herbert 1856, 317.

27. One is Annette Crosbie's Katherine, in the first episode (written by Rosemary Sisson) of the 1970 BBC television series *The Six Wives of Henry VIII*.

28. James Gairdner (editor), "Henry VIII: July 1533, 26–31," *Letters and Papers, Foreign and Domestic, Henry VIII*, Volume 6: 1533, British History Online, http://www .british-history.ac.uk/report.aspx?compid=77563.

29. Rawdon Brown (editor), "Venice: November 1531," *Calendar of State Papers Relating to English Affairs in the Archives of Venice*, Volume 4: 1527–1533, British History Online, http://www.british-history.ac.uk/report.aspx?compid=94624.

30. James Gairdner (editor), "Henry VIII: June 1533, 1–5," *Letters and Papers, Foreign and Domestic, Henry VIII*, Volume 6: 1533, British History Online, http://www.british-history.ac.uk/report.aspx?compid=77553.

31. Pascual de Gayangos (editor), "Spain: December 1533, 26–31," *Calendar of State Papers, Spain*, Volume 4, Part 2: 1531–1533, British History Online, http://www.british-history.ac.uk/report.aspx?compid=87797.

32. Pascual de Gayangos (editor), "Spain: October 1533, 1–20," *Calendar of State Papers, Spain*, Volume 4, Part 2: 1531–1533, British History Online, http://www.british-history.ac.uk/report.aspx?compid=87791.

33. Pascual de Gayangos (editor), "Spain: December 1533, 26–31," *Calendar of State Papers, Spain*, Volume 4, Part 2: 1531–1533, British History Online, http://www.british-history.ac.uk/report.aspx?compid=87797.

34. Lundell 2001, 77.

35. James Gairdner (editor), "Henry VIII: May 1536, 1–10," *Letters and Papers, Foreign and Domestic, Henry VIII*, Volume 10: January–June 1536, British History Online, http://www.british-history.ac.uk/report.aspx?compid=75429.

36. Pascual de Gayangos (editor), "Spain: April 1533, 1–25," *Calendar of State Papers, Spain*, Volume 4, Part 2: 1531–1533, British History Online, http://www.british-history.ac.uk/report.aspx?compid=87778.

37. James Gairdner (editor), "Henry VIII: July 1533, 11–15," *Letters and Papers, Foreign and Domestic, Henry VIII*, Volume 6: 1533, British History Online, http://www.british-history.ac.uk/report.aspx?compid=77560.

38. Pascual de Gayangos (editor), "Spain: November 1535, 1–30," *Calendar of State Papers, Spain*, Volume 5, Part 1: 1534–1535, British History Online, http://www.british-history.ac.uk/report.aspx?compid=87926.

39. James Gairdner (editor), "Henry VIII: February 1534, 11–20," *Letters and Papers, Foreign and Domestic, Henry VIII*, Volume 7: 1534, British History Online, http://www.british-history.ac.uk/report.aspx?compid=79296.

40. Pascual de Gayangos (editor), "Spain: May 1534, 21–31," *Calendar of State Papers, Spain*, Volume 5, Part 1: 1534–1535, British History Online, http://www.british-history.ac.uk/report.aspx?compid=87897.

41. Pascual de Gayangos (editor), "Spain: June 1534, 16–30," *Calendar of State Papers, Spain*, Volume 5, Part 1: 1534–1535, British History Online, http://www.british-history.ac.uk/report.aspx?compid=87899.

42. James Gairdner (editor), "Henry VIII: February 1534, 11–20," *Letters and Papers, Foreign and Domestic, Henry VIII*, Volume 7: 1534, British History Online, http://www.british-history.ac.uk/report.aspx?compid=79296.

43. Loades 2009, 71.

44. Froude 1891, 316; Friedmann, vol. II, 1884, 10.

45. Froude 1891, 280.

46. Friedmann 1884, 10.

47. Pollard 1919, 304.

48. Pascual de Gayangos (editor), "Spain: September 1533, 1–15," *Calendar of State Papers, Spain*, Volume 4, Part 2: 1531–1533, British History Online, http://www .british-history.ac.uk/report.aspx?compid=87789.

49. Ibid.

50. Starkey 2004, 420.

51. Weir 2010, 36.

52. Ibid., 30.

53. Ibid.

54. Ibid.

55. Ibid., 10.

56. Pascual de Gayangos (editor), "Spain: May 1536, 16–31," *Calendar of State Papers, Spain*, Volume 5, Part 2: 1536–1538, British History Online, http://www.british -history.ac.uk/report.aspx?compid=87961.

57. Weir 2011, 82.

2. Why Anne?

1. The exact passage is Leviticus 20:21: "And if a man shall take his brother's wife, it is an unclean thing: he has uncovered his brother's nakedness; they shall be childless." (KJV)

2. Letter 4, Henry VIII to Anne Boleyn, in Norton 2011, 42.

3. J. S. Brewer (editor), "Henry VIII: February 1528, 11–20," *Letters and Papers, Foreign and Domestic, Henry VIII*, Volume 4: 1524–1530, British History Online, http://www.british-history.ac.uk/report.aspx?compid=91312.

4. J. S. Brewer (editor), "Henry VIII: February 1528, 11–20," *Letters and Papers, Foreign and Domestic, Henry VIII*, Volume 4: 1524–1530, British History Online, http://www.british-history.ac.uk/report.aspx?compid=91312. An almost word-for-word description of Anne also occurs in James Gairdner (editor), "Henry VIII: January 1534, 1–5," *Letters and Papers, Foreign and Domestic, Henry VIII*, Volume 7: 1534, British History Online, http://www.british-history.ac.uk/report .aspx?compid=79289. The repetition suggests that Wolsey's early description of Anne had become official governmentspeak.

5. Pollard 1919, 176.

6. J. S. Brewer (editor), "Henry VIII: February 1516, 16–29," *Letters and Papers, Foreign and Domestic, Henry VIII*, Volume 2: 1515–1518, British History Online, http://www.british-history.ac.uk/report.aspx?compid=90899.

7. J. S. Brewer (editor), "Henry VIII: December 1527, 1–9," *Letters and Papers, Foreign and Domestic, Henry VIII*, Volume 4: 1524–1530, British History Online, http:// www.british-history.ac.uk/report.aspx?compid=91303.

8. Froude 1891, 23.

9. Ibid., 32.

10. Cavendish 1905, 12.

11. Strickland and Strickland 2010, 575.

12. Ibid., 576.

13. The exact nature and number of Anne's pre-Henry relationships are fuzzy, but virtually all historians believe that she had some sort of serious romantic entanglement with Henry Percy, heir of the fifth Earl of Northumberland.

14. Cavendish 1905, 15.

15. Ibid., 16.

16. Dixon 1874, 107.

17. Anderson 1977, 30.

18. Hirst 2007, 161.

19. Ibid., 163.

20. Ives 2005, 40.

21. Rawdon Brown (editor), "Venice: October 1532," *Calendar of State Papers Relating to English Affairs in the Archives of Venice*, Volume 4: 1527–1533, British History Online, http://www.british-history.ac.uk/report.aspx?compid=94635.

22. George Wyatt's *Life of Queen Anne Boleigne*, in Norton 2011, 17.

23. Ibid.

24. Vincent 2009, 149.

25. Pitman 2003, 61–62.

26. Pointer 2005, 78–79.

27. If you happened to have been born with less than shining gold tresses, there were many recipes for curing that. You could take the scrapings from rhubarb, steep them in white wine or clear lye, and wet your hair with the solution, leaving it to dry in the sun (repeat if necessary). Sulphur and lead were also useful and could bleach freckles too. But the most successful procedures depended on lye — a great deal of it. (The success was temporary; golden tresses, tortured by lye, usually fell out over time.) Other formulas were employed to achieve the "whitely" complexion that was most admired. You can soak wheat in water for fifteen days, then grind it and blend it with water, strain it through a cloth, and let it crystallize through evaporation. You then mix it with rosewater, which "will obtain a make-up which will be as white as snow." White ceruse (containing lead carbonate, lead oxide, and lead hydroxide) could also be smeared on the face to simulate a pale matte complexion. (It was poisonous, but other popular recipes — such as egg whites — left the face shiny and stiff.)

28. Actually, the sociobiological arguments fall apart against the historical and geographical spectacle of human diversity.

29. Connor 2004, 97.

30. Daneau 1575.

31. Sander 1877, 25.

32. James Gairdner (editor), "Henry VIII: June 1533, 1–5," *Letters and Papers, Foreign and Domestic, Henry VIII*, Volume 6: 1533, British History Online, http://www .british-history.ac.uk/report.aspx?compid=77553.

33. Norton 2011, 19.

34. Loades 1968, 22. Modern spelling applied.

35. Wyatt 1817, 424.

36. The third nipple, too, is reported as fact (or is described as "widely rumored" or as she "was said to have," a characterization that tends to perpetuate itself) on numerous websites, many of which cite the popular *The Book of Lists*, first published in 1977, as their source. This book, which the authors admit was written "for fun," quickly became a source for schoolchildren "to spice up their schoolwork."

37. Bailey 2010.

38. Chapman 1974, 28.

39. Smith 1973, 119.

40. When I asked Howard Brenton in an interview why the blonde Anne — I thought that perhaps he was making some point by going against archetype — he said it was simply because a wig would have been too uncomfortable for the blonde actress to wear. Of course, Raison could have dyed her hair, as Natalie Dormer did, and I wonder if Brenton would have given up so easily if other historical facts had collided with his cast's preferences. My suspicion is that our own lingering blonde fetishism, still asserting itself even in an era of multiracial aesthetics, played a role.

41. Drew 1912, 14.

42. Wyatt 1817, 424.

43. de Carles 1927, 234.

44. Wyatt 1858, 3.

45. The history of the mole is a case in point. Between the sixteenth and seventeenth centuries, a mole's "disruption" of the skin changed from being the devil's handiwork to nature's accentuation of especially pretty features (such as the lips or the eyes). Men and women alike began to put false spots (beauty patches) on areas of their faces they wished to draw attention to. (Or they might use them to hide scars or pockmarks.) Like actual moles, these mimic moles developed a code, but the meanings were far less menacing than the medieval interpretation: A spot on the forehead showed majesty, on the nose sauciness, on the midcheek gaiety, and near the corner of the eye passion. A patch on the lips invited a kiss. "It is a Riddle," mused Robert Codrington in his seventeenth-century conduct manual, "that a Blemish should appear a Grace, and that a Deformity should adde unto Beauty." (Vincent 2009, 150.) But that is often the way ideals of beauty change.

46. Meyer 2004, 19.

47. Ives 2005, 18.

48. Margaret of Austria to Sir Thomas Boleyn, in Norton 2011, 25.

49. Cholakian and Cholakian 2006, 4.

50. Erasmus 1995, 292.

51. Starkey 2004, 258.

52. Pizan 1997, 119–20.

53. Knecht 2008, 227.

54. Benger 1821, 137.

55. Singer 1827, 120.

56. Pollard 1919, 191.

57. Ibid., 191–92.

58. James Gairdner (editor), "Henry VIII: September 1535, 11–20," *Letters and Papers, Foreign and Domestic, Henry VIII*, Volume 9: August–December 1535, British History Online, http://www.british-history.ac.uk/report.aspx?compid=75668.

59. Ives 2005, 33.

60. Only Aristophanes, as depicted in Plato's *Symposium,* had up until then come close to providing a model of the kind of love that Shakespeare — and *we* — think of as "romantic": two personalities who find their wholeness, power, and peace in coming together. And Socrates, not Aristophanes, won that debate in Plato — and thus in medieval culture, which was strongly shaped by neo-Platonism.

61. From Sharon Jansen's introduction to France 2004, 8.

62. France 2004, 51.

63. Vives 2000, 127.

64. Ibid., 105.

65. Ibid., 55, 57.

66. Ibid., 131.

67. Ibid, 132.

68. Ibid., 178–9.

69. Ibid., 245, 255.

70. Castiglione 1903, 176–77.

71. Ibid., 177.

72. Ibid., 179.

73. Ibid., 180.

74. Ibid., 179.

75. This was important not just to fulfill ideals of feminine conduct, but because her official function was to serve as a lady-in-waiting to a princess or queen.

76. A. Jones 1987, 45.

77. Cavendish 1905, 35.

78. Tyndale 2000, 184.

79. Lorenzo Campeggio wrote Rome that Henry knew more about the Bible than a great theologian, and the French ambassador Guillaume du Bellay reported to France that the king needed no lawyer since he understood the case so well. Henry more than once tried to persuade Thomas More, pointing out the key texts in the Bible from which he had concluded that his marriage to Katherine was unlawful.

80. Starkey 2004, 285.
81. Ibid., 285–86.

3. In Love (or Something Like It)

1. http://www.telegraph.co.uk/culture/culturenews/5194183/Love-letter-from
   -Henry-VIII-to-Anne-Boleyn-on-display-for-first-time.html.
2. Letter 16, Henry VIII to Anne Boleyn, in Norton 2011, 45.
3. Letter 5, Henry VIII to Anne Boleyn, in Norton 2011, 42.
4. Ibid.
5. Hirst 2007, 304.
6. Ibid., 307.
7. Ibid., 199.
8. Weir 1991, 173–74.
9. Ibid.
10. Ibid., 174.
11. Letter 5, Henry VIII to Anne Boleyn, in Norton 2011, 42.
12. Letter 14, Henry VIII to Anne Boleyn, in Norton 2011, 45.
13. Michael Hirst, interview with author, telephone, Lexington, KY, April 28, 2011.
14. Letter 16, Henry VIII to Anne Boleyn, in Norton 2011, 45.
15. It's not known just how rapacious Henry was. Kelly Hart's recent *The Mistresses of Henry VIII* says we can be certain of Lady Anne Stafford, Bessie Blount (who provided Henry with a son), Mary Boleyn, and Mary Shelton, and we "can confidently add" Jane Popincourt, Elizabeth Carew, Etiennette de la Baume, Elizabeth Amandas, and Mary Skipforth, and "there were undoubtedly many, many more" (199). Other historians argue that we can only really be sure of Bessie Blount and Mary Boleyn, and that Henry's sexual antics never approached those of Francis I.
16. James Gairdner (editor), "Henry VIII: April 1533, 11–20," *Letters and Papers, Foreign and Domestic, Henry VIII*, Volume 6: 1533, British History Online, http://www.british-history.ac.uk/report.aspx?compid=77546.
17. Ibid.
18. Pascual de Gayangos (editor), "Spain: April 1536, 1–20," *Calendar of State Papers, Spain*, Volume 5, Part 2: 1536–1538, British History Online, http://www.british-history.ac.uk/report.aspx?compid=87958.
19. Stone 1979, 78.
20. From *Henry VIII: Mind of a Tyrant* (2009), directed by David Sington.
21. Hutchinson 2011, 133–34.
22. Bordo 1987, 49–53, from Stephen Toulmin, "The Inwardness of Mental Life," *Critical Inquiry* 6: 1–16.
23. Ibid., 53, from Owen Barfield, *Saving the Appearances: A Study in Idolatry* (New York: Harcourt Brace Jovanovich, 1965).
24. Smith 1971, 57.

25. Letter 1, Henry VIII to Anne Boleyn, in Norton 2011, 41.

26. Even in his letters to Anne, Henry frequently cuts it short, claiming it's "for lack of time," "for fear of tiring you," "for want of room," etc.

27. Mattingly 1960, 121.

28. Wilson 2003, 71.

29. Rawdon Brown (editor), "Venice: July 1517," *Calendar of State Papers Relating to English Affairs in the Archives of Venice*, Volume 2: 1509–1519, British History Online, http://www.british-history.ac.uk/report.aspx?compid=94239.

30. Castiglione 1903, 217.

31. Capellanus 1960, 185–6.

32. Malory 2001, 458.

33. Wyatt 1858, 174–5.

34. "*Circa Regna Tonat,*" in Norton 2011, 237.

35. Letter 4, Henry VIII to Anne Boleyn in Norton 2011, 42.

36. Henry VIII to Ferdinand of Aragon, July 26, 1509, in Byrne 1968, 11.

37. Ridley 1985, 176.

38. Letter 10, Henry VIII to Anne Boleyn, in Norton 2011, 44.

39. Anne Boleyn to Cardinal Wolsey, in Norton 2011, 47–8.

40. Henry VIII to Cardinal Wolsey, in Norton 2011, 48.

41. Weir 1991, 207.

42. David Loades, breaking with the Anne-blaming posture of most histories, writes: "Anne had no incentive to undermine Wolsey's position with the King as long as he seemed to be the most likely person to secure the annulment of Henry's marriage. Once he had demonstrated his inability to deliver that prize, the King's indignation scarcely needed stimulation . . . The idea that [Anne] was masterminding a powerful anti-Wolsey coalition, including the Dukes of Norfolk and Suffolk, seems to have originated in the fertile mind of Inigo de Mendoza, the imperial ambassador, although Cavendish also believed it many years later." (Loades 2009, 51.)

43. Henry VIII to Cardinal Wolsey, in Norton 2011, 48.

4. A Perfect Storm

1. James Gairdner (editor), "Henry VIII: October 1532, 1–10," *Letters and Papers, Foreign and Domestic, Henry VIII*, Volume 5: 1531–1532, British History Online, http://www.british-history.ac.uk/report.aspx?compid=77494.

2. Ives 2005, 159–60.

3. Ibid., 160.

4. Weir 1991, 151. According to Weir, Francis wrote of Anne: "*Venus était blonde, on m'a dit: / L'on voit bien, qu'elle est brunette.*" I have not been able to substantiate this quote, however.

5. Massie 2008, 68.

6. Ibid.

7. Ives 2005, 160. *The Manner of the Triumph at Calais and Boulogne* was printed by Wynkyn de Worde.

8. Ibid., 182.

9. Ibid., 183.

10. Fraser 1993, 220.

11. Weir 1991, 303.

12. James Gairdner (editor), "Henry VIII: September 1533, 1–10," *Letters and Papers, Foreign and Domestic, Henry VIII*, Volume 6: 1533, British History Online, http://www.british-history.ac.uk/report.aspx?compid=77567.

13. Rival 1971, 116.

14. Lofts 1963, 279.

15. Gregory 2007, 487.

16. Fraser 1993, 199.

17. Starkey 2004, 508.

18. Ives 2005, 184.

19. Borman 2009, 21.

20. Loades 2009, 66.

21. Borman 2009, 25.

22. Perry 1999, 5.

23. Ibid.

24. Starkey 2004, 511.

25. Ibid.

26. Strickland and Strickland 1864, 652.

27. Leti 2010, 97.

28. James Gairdner (editor), "Henry VIII: September 1533, 1–10," *Letters and Papers, Foreign and Domestic, Henry VIII*, Volume 6: 1533, British History Online, http://www.british-history.ac.uk/report.aspx?compid=77567.

29. Ibid.

30. Ibid.

31. Wilson 2003, 384.

32. Pascual de Gayangos (editor), "Spain: December 1533, 16–25," *Calendar of State Papers, Spain*, Volume 4, Part 2: 1531–1533, British History Online, http://www.british-history.ac.uk/report.aspx?compid=87796.

33. Pascual de Gayangos (editor), "Spain: September 1534, 1–30," *Calendar of State Papers, Spain*, Volume 5, Part 1: 1534–1535, British History Online, http://www.british-history.ac.uk/report.aspx?compid=87904.

34. Pascual de Gayangos (editor), "Spain: October 1534, 1–15," *Calendar of State Papers, Spain*, Volume 5, Part 1: 1534–1535, British History Online, http://www.british-history.ac.uk/report.aspx?compid=87905.

35. Pascual de Gayangos (editor), "Spain: October 1534, 16–20," *Calendar of State Papers, Spain*, Volume 5, Part 1: 1534–1535, British History Online, http://www.british-history.ac.uk/report.aspx?compid=87906.

36. Ives 2005, 194.

37. Weir 2010, 230.
38. Ives 2005, 196.
39. Starkey 2008, 330.
40. Stjerna 2009, 152.
41. Carley 2004, 8.
42. Freeman 1995, 819.
43. Bordo 1987, 128–29.
44. Knecht 2008, 231.
45. Jansen 2002, 1.
46. Jansen 2008, 15.
47. For more on this famous stance taken by Elizabeth I, see Levine 1994.
48. Pascual de Gayangos (editor), "Spain: April 1536, 1–20," *Calendar of State Papers, Spain*, Volume 5, Part 2: 1536–1538, British History Online, http://www.british-history.ac.uk/report.aspx?compid=87958.
49. Froude 1891, 384.
50. Loades 2009, 69.
51. Weir 2010, 230.
52. Jordan 1990, 122.
53. Ibid., 123.
54. Weir 2010, 230.
55. Pascual de Gayangos (editor), "Spain: October 1534, 21–31," *Calendar of State Papers, Spain*, Volume 5, Part 1: 1534–1535, British History Online, http://www.british-history.ac.uk/report.aspx?compid=87907.
56. Pascual de Gayangos (editor), "Spain: October 1534, 21–31," *Calendar of State Papers, Spain*, Volume 5, Part 1: 1534–1535, British History Online, http://www.british-history.ac.uk/report.aspx?compid=87907.
57. de Carles 1927, 234; Pascual de Gayangos (editor), "Spain: October 1534, 21–31," *Calendar of State Papers, Spain*, Volume 5, Part 1: 1534–1535, British History Online, http://www.british-history.ac.uk/report.aspx?compid=87907.
58. Pascual de Gayangos (editor), "Spain: October 1534, 21–31," *Calendar of State Papers, Spain*, Volume 5, Part 1: 1534–1535, British History Online, http://www.british-history.ac.uk/report.aspx?compid=87907.
59. Pascual de Gayangos (editor), "Spain: June 1535, 1–15," *Calendar of State Papers, Spain*, Volume 5, Part 1: 1534–1535, British History Online, http://www.british-history.ac.uk/report.aspx?compid=87920.
60. Fraser 1993, 219.
61. Hutchinson 2007, 42.
62. Pascual de Gayangos (editor), "Spain: June 1535, 1–15," *Calendar of State Papers, Spain*, Volume 5, Part 1: 1534–1535, British History Online, http://www.british-history.ac.uk/report.aspx?compid=87920.
63. Wilson 2003, 386.
64. Ibid., 385.
65. Ives 2005, 295.

66. Pascual de Gayangos (editor), "Spain: January 1536, 21–31," *Calendar of State Papers, Spain*, Volume 5, Part 2: 1536–1538, British History Online, http://www .british-history.ac.uk/report.aspx?compid=87953.

67. Pascual de Gayangos (editor), "Spain: April 1536, 1–20," *Calendar of State Papers, Spain*, Volume 5, Part 2: 1536–1538, British History Online, http://www.british -history.ac.uk/report.aspx?compid=87958.

68. Ibid.

69. Ives 2005, 298.

70. Pascual de Gayangos (editor), "Spain: February 1536, 21–29," *Calendar of State Papers, Spain*, Volume 5, Part 2: 1536–1538, British History Online, http://www .british-history.ac.uk/report.aspx?compid=87956.

71. Pascual de Gayangos (editor), "Spain: February 1536, 16–20," *Calendar of State Papers, Spain*, Volume 5, Part 2: 1536–1538, British History Online, http://www .british-history.ac.uk/report.aspx?compid=87955.

72. Ives 2005, 302.

73. Pascual de Gayangos (editor), "Spain: April 1536, 1–20," *Calendar of State Papers, Spain*, Volume 5, Part 2: 1536–1538, British History Online, http://www.british -history.ac.uk/report.aspx?compid=87958.

74. Pascual de Gayangos (editor), "Spain: December 1533, 16–25," *Calendar of State Papers, Spain*, Volume 4, Part 2: 1531–1533, British History Online, http://www .british-history.ac.uk/report.aspx?compid=87796.

75. Weir 1991, 309.

76. Ives 2005, 312.

77. Ibid., 315.

78. James Gairdner (editor), "Henry VIII: April 1536, 21–25," *Letters and Papers, Foreign and Domestic, Henry VIII*, Volume 10: January–June 1536, British History Online, http://www.british-history.ac.uk/report.aspx?compid=75427.

79. Weir 2010, 95.

80. Pascual de Gayangos (editor), "Spain: May 1536, 1–15," *Calendar of State Papers, Spain*, Volume 5, Part 2: 1536–1538, British History Online, http://www.british -history.ac.uk/report.aspx?compid=87960.

81. Pascual de Gayangos (editor), "Spain: May 1536, 1–15," *Calendar of State Papers, Spain*, Volume 5, Part 2: 1536–1538, British History Online, http://www.british -history.ac.uk/report.aspx?compid=87960.

82. Weir 2010, 123.

5. The Tower and the Scaffold

1. Pascual de Gayangos (editor), "Spain: May 1536, 1–15," *Calendar of State Papers, Spain*, Volume 5, Part 2: 1536–1538, British History Online, http://www.british -history.ac.uk/report.aspx?compid=87960.

2. Ibid.

3. James Gairdner (editor), "Henry VIII: May 1536, 1–10," *Letters and Papers, Foreign and Domestic, Henry VIII*, Volume 10: January–June 1536, British History Online, http://www.british-history.ac.uk/report.aspx?compid=75429.

4. James Gairdner (editor), "Henry VIII: May 1536, 26–31," *Letters and Papers, Foreign and Domestic, Henry VIII*, Volume 10: January–June 1536, British History Online, http://www.british-history.ac.uk/report.aspx?compid=75433.

5. Ibid.

6. William Kingston to Lord Cromwell, in Norton 2011, 245.

7. Ibid., 246. Modern spelling applied.

8. Ibid. Modern spelling applied.

9. Wilson 2003, 375.

10. Sir William Kingston to Lord Cromwell, in Norton 2011, 246.

11. Lindsey 1995, 122.

12. Lipscomb 2009, 82.

13. James Gairdner (editor), "Henry VIII: May 1536, 11–15," *Letters and Papers, Foreign and Domestic, Henry VIII*, Volume 10: January–June 1536, British History Online, http://www.british-history.ac.uk/report.aspx?compid=75430.

14. Weir 2010, 235.

15. Wyatt 1817, 446.

16. James Gairdner (editor), "Henry VIII: June 1536, 1–5," *Letters and Papers, Foreign and Domestic, Henry VIII*, Volume 10: January–June 1536, British History Online, http://www.british-history.ac.uk/report.aspx?compid=75435.

17. James Gairdner (editor), "Henry VIII: May 1536, 1–10," *Letters and Papers, Foreign and Domestic, Henry VIII*, Volume 10: January–June 1536, British History Online, http://www.british-history.ac.uk/report.aspx?compid=75429.

18. Ibid.

19. Ibid.

20. Norton 2011, 34.

21. James Gairdner (editor), "Henry VIII: May 1536, 11–15," *Letters and Papers, Foreign and Domestic, Henry VIII*, Volume 10: January–June 1536, British History Online, http://www.british-history.ac.uk/report.aspx?compid=75430.

22. Weir 2010, 203.

23. Contributed by Natalie Sweet, "May 12, 1536," http://thecreationofanneboleyn.wordpress.com/2011/06/27/may-12-1536-the-trial-of-mark-smeaton-henry-norris-francis-weston-and-william-brereton/ (accessed June 27, 2011).

24. James Gairdner (editor), "Henry VIII: May 1536, 16–20," *Letters and Papers, Foreign and Domestic, Henry VIII*, Volume 10: January–June 1536, British History Online, http://www.british-history.ac.uk/report.aspx?compid=75431.

25. Ibid.

26. Pascual de Gayangos (editor), "Spain: May 1536, 16–31," *Calendar of State Papers, Spain*, Volume 5, Part 2: 1536–1538, British History Online, http://www.british-history.ac.uk/report.aspx?compid=87961.

27. Lipscomb 2009, 88–89.

28. Ibid., 89.

29. Weir 2010, 212.

30. Ibid., 219.

31. Ibid., 121.

32. Sir William Kingston to Lord Cromwell, in Norton 2011, 246. Modern spelling applied.

33. Ibid. Modern spelling applied.

34. Weir 2010, 223. Note that John Guy, in his review of Weir's book (*The Lady in the Tower: The Fall of Anne Boleyn*, November 1, 2009, http://www.thesundaytimes .co.uk/sto/culture/books/non_fiction/article188852.ece), claims that de Milherve and Lancelot de Carles have been shown by French scholars to be the same person.

35. Ibid.

36. Weir 2010, 225. Weir is quoting here from Jane Dunn, *Elizabeth and Mary: Cousins, Rivals, Queens*, London: HarperCollins, 2003.

37. James Gairdner (editor), "Henry VIII: May 1536, 16–20," *Letters and Papers, Foreign and Domestic, Henry VIII*, Volume 10: January–June 1536, British History Online, http://www.british-history.ac.uk/report.aspx?compid=75431.

38. Weir 2010, 230.

39. Sir William Kingston to Lord Cromwell, in Norton 2011, 246. Modern spelling applied.

40. Ibid.

41. Norton 2011, 256–7.

42. Ives 2005, 58.

43. Ibid.

44. Ellis 1824, 53.

45. Pascual de Gayangos (editor), "Spain: May 1536, 16–31," *Calendar of State Papers, Spain*, Volume 5, Part 2: 1536–1538, British History Online, http://www.british -history.ac.uk/report.aspx?compid=87961.

46. Sir William Kingston to Lord Cromwell, in Norton 2011, 248. Modern spelling applied.

47. Ibid. Modern spelling applied.

48. Ibid. Modern spelling applied.

49. Ibid. Modern spelling applied.

50. Ibid., 249. Modern spelling applied.

51. Weir 2010, 267.

52. Norton 2011, 225.

53. D'Aubigné 1869, 193.

54. Norton 2011, 267.

55. Norton 2011, 261. Modern spelling applied.

56. Ibid., 265.

57. Weir 2010, 285.

58. James Gairdner (editor), "Henry VIII: June 1536, 1–5," *Letters and Papers, Foreign*

and Domestic, Henry VIII, Volume 10: January–June 1536, British History Online, http://www.british-history.ac.uk/report.aspx?compid=75435.

59. Thomas 1995, 105.
60. Ibid.
61. Dostoevsky 2008.

6. Henry: How Could He Do It?

1. Weir, 2010, 121.
2. Elton 1977, 71.
3. Lipscomb 2009, 87.
4. "Henry VIII and Miscarriage" 2011. Note that all but the first pregnancy between a Kell positive man and a Kell negative woman — which Anne Boleyn and Katherine of Aragon *might* have been — are vulnerable to miscarriages.
5. Cressy 2002, 46.
6. Sohn 2011.
7. Ibid.
8. Michael Hirst, interview with author, telephone, Lexington, KY, April 28, 2011.
9. Wilson 2003, 53.
10. Walker 2005, 7.
11. Ibid., 6.
12. Ibid., 11.
13. Ibid., 13.
14. Tremlett 2010, 357.
15. Wilson 2003, 217.
16. Boker 1850, 133.
17. Smith 1971, 25.
18. Erickson 1980, 287.
19. Longford 1989, 210.
20. Howard Brenton, interview with author, London, England, July 30, 2010.
21. Kreisman and Straus 1989, 10.
22. Smith 1971, 68.
23. Wilson 2003, 256.
24. Smith 1971, 82.
25. Hutchinson 2011, 15.
26. Erickson 1980, 50.
27. Ibid., 51.
28. Withrow 2009, 45.
29. Hackett 1945, 181. When doubts about his actions did arise (as they often did with Henry, whom Lacey Baldwin Smith describes as something of a "spiritual hypochondriac" who was constantly taking the temperature of the state of his soul), his tendency was to wall them out by placing the blame on others. If Katherine could not produce a male heir, that was her fault, not his. Although

Henry may have genuinely believed the "sin" (of marrying one's brother's wife) was shared, he felt the remedy did not require any contrition on his part; he just got rid of the wife.

30. Anderson 1977, 8–9.

7. Basic Historical Ingredients

1. Pascual de Gayangos (editor), "Spain: May 1536, 16–31," *Calendar of State Papers, Spain*, Volume 5, Part 2: 1536–1538, British History Online, http://www.british-history.ac.uk/report.aspx?compid=87961.
2. Ibid.
3. Ibid.
4. Ibid.
5. Ibid.
6. Ibid.
7. Pascual de Gayangos (editor), "Spain: May 1536, 16–31," *Calendar of State Papers, Spain*, Volume 5, Part 2: 1536–1538, British History Online, http://www.british-history.ac.uk/report.aspx?compid=87961.
8. James Gairdner (editor), "Henry VIII: June 1536, 6–10," *Letters and Papers, Foreign and Domestic, Henry VIII*, Volume 10: January–June 1536, British History Online, http://www.british-history.ac.uk/report.aspx?compid=75436.
9. Ibid.
10. Ibid.
11. James Gairdner (editor), "Henry VIII: December 1536, 1–5," *Letters and Papers, Foreign and Domestic, Henry VIII*, Volume 11: July–December 1536, British History Online, http://www.british-history.ac.uk/report.aspx?compid=75489.
12. Norton 2011, 241. Ales had a terrifying dream the night before Anne's execution, in which he saw Anne's severed head, with all the veins, nerves, and arteries exposed. He didn't know that Anne was to be executed that day, but shortly found out from the Archbishop of Canterbury, who—according to Ales—burst into tears: "She who has been the Queen of England upon earth will today become a Queen in heaven."
13. Anne had encouraged Henry to send a delegation to seek the support of Lutheran Germany for the divorce.
14. Norton 2011, 242.
15. Ibid., 243.
16. Ibid., 239.
17. Weir 2010, 330.
18. Edward and Dudley's motives differed, but fell in line with each other. Edward was worried that Mary would bring Catholicism back as the religion of the realm, and it was impossible to make a legal argument for Elizabeth but not Mary. Edward passed over both of them to name the sons of his remaining female relatives. None of those sons were born yet, however, so Dudley, to serve his

own personal ambitions, had Jane Grey — who stood second in Edward's line of succession — marry his own son. The plan: Jane and Guilford Dudley's eventual son would be the next ruler of England. Unfortunately for Dudley (and hapless Jane Grey), he did not reckon on Mary's huge popular support among the people. Her "rebel" army ultimately numbered nearly twenty thousand, and Dudley's own garrison of sailors defected to her cause — a mutiny that dramatically showed which way the wind was blowing and led to the Privy Council shifting allegiance and proclaiming Mary queen.

19. Norton 2011, 239–45.
20. Freeman 1995, 799.
21. Foxe 1857, 58.
22. Lee 1909, 750.
23. Highley 2006, 158–59.
24. Hirst 2007, 161.
25. Levin 2008, 115.
26. Norton 2011, 16–24.
27. Ibid.
28. Wyatt tells virtually the same anecdote that Foxe does about Anne's showing Henry *Supplication for the Beggars,* but in Wyatt, it is Tyndale's *The Obedience of a Christian Man,* not Fish's book, that Anne shows Henry. They were both "hot" reformist tracts, so it's not surprising that in retrospective books written on the basis of the accounts of others, they may have gotten mixed up.
29. Norton 2011, 16–24.
30. Cavendish 1905, 34–35.
31. Ibid., 34.
32. Norton 2011, 17.
33. Ibid., 18.
34. Ibid.
35. Ibid.
36. Ibid.
37. Miller-Tomlinson 2008.
38. Banks 1981, 74. Modern spelling applied.
39. Ibid., 68.
40. Ibid.

8. Anne's Afterlives, from She-Tragedy to Historical Romance

1. Banks 1981, 9. Modern spelling applied.
2. Ibid., 38.
3. Hutchinson 2011, ix.
4. Allen 2009.
5. Ibid.
6. Austen 1993, 12–14.

7. Benger 1821, 21–22.
8. Ibid., 98.
9. Ibid., 98–99.
10. Ibid., 99.
11. Ibid.
12. Ibid., 45–46.
13. Ibid., 198–99.
14. Ibid., 201–2.
15. Starkey 2004, 585.
16. Macaulay 1849, 3.
17. Women historians willingly accepted, and even promoted, the idea that they were doing something different from "general history" — writing "memoirs" or "lives" to create a place for themselves that would not be seen as "encroaching upon the province" male historians had carved out for themselves and were unwilling to share. See, for example, the Stricklands' insistence that their own "unambitious pages" "will not admit of launching into the broad stream of general history." (Maitzen 1998, 36.)
18. Maitzen 1998, 33.
19. Oliphant 1855, 437.
20. Strickland and Strickland 1864, 198.
21. Ibid.
22. Hunter 2002, 71.
23. Ibid.
24. Taylor 1877, 402.
25. Ibid., 373.
26. Goldsmith 1771, 353–54, 377–78, 384–85. Modern spelling applied.
27. Dickens 1854, 20–21, 59, 37.
28. Callcott 1856, 133.
29. Gardiner 1881, 142, 149.
30. Farmer 1887, 154–55.
31. Herbert 1856, vi, 310.
32. Ibid., 336.
33. Ibid., 317.
34. Ibid., 323–24.
35. Ibid., 324.
36. Worn, Herbert claims elsewhere, because it is "the color which best becomes a brunette"! (Ibid., 217.)
37. Ibid., 300–301.
38. See, for example, William Hepworth Dixon (*History of Two Queens: Catharine of Aragon and Anne Boleyn,* 1873) and James Anthony Froude (*The Divorce of Catherine of Aragon,* 1862) for critical discussions of Chapuys.
39. Weir 2010, 334.
40. Froude 1891, 324, 167.

41. Ibid., 280.
42. Ibid., 277.
43. Friedmann 1884, 265.
44. Pollard 1919, 345–46.
45. Ibid., 192.
46. Bradley 1912, 246–48.
47. Ibid, viii. Bradley met her husband, a lawyer, big-game hunter, traveler, and explorer, while doing research in England for *The Favor of Kings*. They traveled the world together, collecting specimens for zoos and museums. In addition to writing many books and short stories, Bradley also was a war correspondent for *Collier's* magazine and wrote a series of articles on the Holocaust.
48. Ibid., viii.
49. Ibid., viii–ix.
50. Ibid., 22–23.
51. Drew 1912, 14.
52. Hunter 2002, 392.
53. Bradley 1912, 220.
54. Ibid., 26.
55. It's her pride, too, in Bradley's version, that is behind her antipapalism. "What is a priest to tell me what I must and must not read? A priest is but a petticoated man whom you would not trust with your kitchen wench. Have I not a soul as clean and a brain as shrewd as a priest? Can I not see with as good eyes, think with as keen wits, feel with as fine sensibilities?" And even as Anne is escorted into the Tower, Bradley provides her with a defiant spin on her famous remark to Kingston, when he informs her she will be lodged in the same room she stayed in the night before her coronation: "A bitter smile parted Anne's lips. 'It is too good for me, is it not?'" The "is it not?" added by Bradley turns a wail of despair into a mocking, sardonic one-up on the hypocrisy of her accusers.
56. Bradley 1912, 68.
57. Ibid., 79.
58. Ibid., 111.
59. Ibid.
60. Hackett 1939, 446.
61. Barrington 1934, 281–82.
62. Ibid., 156.
63. Barrington also slips a bit of fairly militant feminism into her critique of marriage: "Who cared for women? What were they on the throne?" she has Anne thinking, but then inserts her own comment: "It was true that Anne herself with others were unconsciously building a far different world where women would set their feet on men's necks and rule. But that was in the future." (Ibid.)
64. Rival 1971, 105.
65. Ibid., 141.
66. Hackett 1939, 118.

67. At the end of the book, Hackett included an essay called "History in This Novel" in which he enumerates what he has invented in the novel, where his Anne departs from "the tradition," why that tradition requires revision, and why he chose to write a novel rather than a history.

68. Greco 2004, 61.

9. Postwar: Domestic Trouble in the House of Tudor

1. *All About Eve* is another notable example.

2. Barnes 2008, 5–6.

3. Ibid., 100.

4. Ibid., 101.

5. Ibid.

6. Ibid., 157.

7. This alienation becomes fatal after Anne tells him, in a fit of fury over Jane Seymour, that she had never loved him and that she was no virgin when she met him.

8. Barnes 2008, 296–98.

9. Ibid., 335.

10. Lofts 1963, 81.

11. Ibid., 233.

12. Ibid., 236.

13. Ibid.

14. Ibid., 237.

15. Ibid.

16. Ibid., 374.

17. Atkinson 1948.

18. The scene immediately became a cultural icon, and newspapers published tips on "how to eat à la Charles Laughton."

19. Anderson 1977, 12.

20. Eventually, after he moved to Hollywood, Ernst Lubitsch became famous for his own glamorous "touch." But when he made *Anna Boleyn,* he was still in Germany under the influence of the dark, anxiety-soaked Expressionist movement in German film. The cover of the DVD captures the mood of the film precisely, as a predatory Henry (Emil Jannings) has a terrified deerlike Anne in his clutches, both of them starkly shadowed.

21. Korda hired Oberon, who was later to become his wife, to fill the role of the "exotic" in his stable of starlets.

22. Hackett 1945, x.

23. And Hackett, in my opinion, succeeds. A well-known journalist and book reviewer who wrote for the *New Republic* from 1914 to 1922, he spent more than six years in England researching "Henry the man," resulting in a book that is both psychologically astute and historically quite (which is to say mostly)

accurate. Although it has now regrettably disappeared from the corpus of Henry biographies, it was extremely successful at the time it was published; translated into fourteen foreign editions, it had sold more than 650,000 copies by 1949.

24. Hackett 1945, 167.

25. Hackett planned to turn his *Queen Anne Boleyn* into a play, and apparently a script was written and circulated. But the play was never produced. When *Anne of the Thousand Days* opened on Broadway nine years later, Hackett claimed in the *New York Times* that Anderson had plagiarized his books. Having read both his books as well as Anderson's play, I can see why Hackett was angry. His conceptions of the personalities of Henry and Anne — as well as his "personal" approach to history — are strongly echoed in the play. But "humanizing" historical figures is not exactly an approach that one can copyright. Anderson filed a libel suit, which was settled out of court.

26. Anderson 1977, 23. She hasn't slept with him yet. Her knowledge of his sexual style comes from the fact that it was her "doubtful pleasure once to sleep in Mary's room — or to lie awake when you thought me asleep, and observe the royal porpoise at play."

27. Ibid., 30.

28. Ibid., 47.

29. Ibid., 48.

30. Ibid., 48–49.

31. Plato was the first to "theorize" this kind of dilemma, as illustrated in *The Symposium*, in which every relationship consists of a passionate, pursuing "lover" and a more emotionally detached "beloved." The instability inherent in these roles is that while the fierce desire of the lover is to conquer the beloved and he does everything he can to achieve this — for love wants what it doesn't have — the moment the beloved is conquered, she is no longer as desirable. So for Plato, the only way to achieve any constancy in life is to transfer the desire for a mortal person to the pursuit of immortal, timeless Beauty, which always tantalizes and enchants, and never gives itself over entirely. But Anne and Henry, in Anderson's play, are not about to elevate their love in that way.

32. Lofts 1963, 233.

33. Ibid.

34. Krutch 1948.

35. Anderson 1977, 70.

36. Ibid.

10. It's the Anne That Makes the Movie:
Anne of the Thousand Days

1. Wallis and Higham 1980, 171.

2. Ibid., 163.

3. Ibid.

4. Munn 2008, 174–75.
5. Wallis and Higham 1980, 167.
6. Ibid.
7. Ibid.
8. Ibid., 168.
9. He brought less concern for historical detail to the casting of Irene Papas, who was Greek and very, very dark (the universal movie code, it seems, for "Spanish").
10. Geneviève Bujold, interview with author, telephone, Lexington, KY, June 21, 2010.
11. Ibid.
12. Hackett 1945, 248.
13. Walker 2003, 71. Laughton maintained, incredibly, that the film, whose liberties with history run rampant (and rollicking), was true to historical fact. When the film was lambasted by some of the British press for presenting a "disrespectful" view of imperial history, Laughton insisted on its authenticity. "Most of the dialogue was copied straight from contemporary records of Henry's actual words," he claimed, a bald-faced lie that mattered little to viewers or most critics, most of whom were swept away not by the film's accuracy, but by the entertaining life it breathed into Henry as a personality.
14. Hackett 1945, 248.
15. Anderson 1977, 74.
16. Ibid.
17. Ibid.
18. Ibid.
19. Although nowadays pop culture tends to call the shots on "reality," it used to be that it took awhile for movies to catch up with events in the real world. In 1969, Women's Liberation groups were forming all over the country. But it would be another five years or so before films such as Martin Scorsese's *Alice Doesn't Live Here Anymore* and Paul Mazursky's *An Unmarried Woman* would bow, gently, in the direction of a "new woman." It wouldn't be until *Thelma & Louise* (1991) that the deepest gender conventions would be challenged. In *Alice Doesn't Live Here Anymore* and *An Unmarried Woman*, the independence of the heroines (Ellen Burstyn and Jill Clayburgh) is tempered by the presence of two gorgeous, really nice guys (Kris Kristofferson and Alan Bates, each at the height of his appeal) who, it is implied, will remain in the women's lives, providing support and great sex while the heroines pursue their careers. In *Thelma & Louise*, in contrast, even the nicest male characters are impotent; despite every attempt, they cannot alter the tragic course of events. The women have chosen, and they — like the rebel males of the earlier films — will have to pay the price.
20. Comment on *The Creation of Anne Boleyn* Facebook page, August 2, 2011, www .facebook.com/thecreationofanneboleyn. Bujold admits that she was also "telling off" Elizabeth Taylor when she filmed that scene. After hearing rumors about Burton's interest in Bujold, Liz had unexpectedly shown up on the set that day. "It

was all rubbish," Burton told his biographer, Michael Munn, but it was a "problem for Gin, because she had Elizabeth training her sights on her." (Munn 2008, 177.) When Taylor showed up on the set, Bujold, as Wallis relates in his autobiography, "was fighting mad" and "flung herself into the scene with a display of acting skill I have seldom seen equaled in my career. Then she stormed off the set." (Wallis and Higham 1980, 169.)

21. Cate Clement, interview with author, e-mail, Lexington, KY, 2011.
22. Sir William Kingston to Lord Cromwell, in Norton 2011, 245. Modern spelling applied.
23. Ibid. Modern spelling applied.
24. Ibid., 246. Modern Spelling applied.
25. Ibid., 248-49. Modern spelling applied.
26. Canby 1970.
27. Ibid.
28. Simon 1970.
29. "Cinema: The Lion in Autumn," 1970.
30. Ibid.
31. Harmetz 1970.
32. Solanas 2005, 175.
33. Anne — played by Vanessa Redgrave — is on screen for just a moment, to give Henry a breathless, adoring kiss.
34. Geneviève Bujold, interview with author, telephone, Lexington, KY, June 21, 2010.
35. Ibid.
36. Internet Movie Database n.d.
37. Holleran 2007.
38. Ibid.
39. Geneviève Bujold, interview with author, telephone, Lexington, KY, June 21, 2010.
40. Ibid.
41. Ibid.
42. Sue Booth, July 31, 2011, comment on *The Creation of Anne Boleyn* Facebook page, www.facebook.com/thecreationofanneboleyn.
43. Ginger James, July 31, 2011, comment on *The Creation of Anne Boleyn* Facebook page, www.facebook.com/thecreationofanneboleyn.
44. Ralphine Lamonica, July 31, 2011, comment on *The Creation of Anne Boleyn* Facebook page, www.facebook.com/thecreationofanneboleyn.
45. Isabelle Fallon, July 31, 2011, comment on *The Creation of Anne Boleyn* Facebook page, www.facebook.com/thecreationofanneboleyn.
46. Donna Fagan, August 1, 2011, comment on *The Creation of Anne Boleyn* Facebook page, www.facebook.com/thecreationofanneboleyn.
47. Lindsey Nicholls, August 1, 2011, comment on *The Creation of Anne Boleyn* Facebook page, www.facebook.com/thecreationofanneboleyn.
48. Jerry Watkins, July 31, 2011, comment on *The Creation of Anne Boleyn* Facebook page, www.facebook.com/thecreationofanneboleyn.

49. Lindsey Nicholls, August 2, 2011, comment on *The Creation of Anne Boleyn* Facebook page, www.facebook.com/thecreationofanneboleyn.
50. Geneviève Bujold, interview with author, telephone, Lexington, KY, June 21, 2010.

11. *The Tudors*

1. Fulkerson 1973.
2. Marcus 2004.
3. Wallenstein 2010.
4. Hohenadel 2007.
5. Stuttaford 2007.
6. Hohenadel 2007.
7. Michael Hirst, interview with author, telephone, Lexington, KY, April 28, 2011.
8. Ibid.
9. Ibid.
10. "When Royals Become Rock Stars," 2007.
11. Das 2007.
12. Deggans 2007.
13. Moore 2007.
14. Ibid.
15. Whitelock 2007.
16. Brand 2008.
17. Michael Hirst, interview with author, telephone, Lexington, KY, April 28, 2011.
18. Ibid.
19. Hohenadel 2007.
20. Das 2011.
21. Natalie Dormer, interview with author, Richmond upon Thames, England, July 31, 2010.
22. Ibid.
23. Ibid.
24. Ibid.
25. Ibid.
26. Ibid.
27. Ibid.
28. Ibid.
29. Ibid.
30. Michael Hirst, interview with author, telephone, Lexington, KY, April 28, 2011.
31. Ibid.
32. Hohenadel 2007.
33. Michael Hirst, interview with author, telephone, Lexington, KY, April 28, 2011.
34. Das 2007.
35. Michael Hirst, interview with author, telephone, Lexington, KY, April 28, 2011.

36. This all takes place in a dream of Henry's, sidestepping any charges of historical inaccuracy.
37. Stanley 2007.
38. Cox 2007.
39. Bellafante 2008.
40. Mirror.co.uk 2008.
41. Fienberg 2007.
42. Moodie 2007.
43. Ibid.
44. Das 2007.
45. Cox 2011.
46. Das 2007.
47. Moodie 2007.
48. Marikar 2008.
49. Martin 2008.
50. Hough 2009.
51. Guy 2008.
52. Zobo, April 1, 2011, comment on Dugdale 2011.
53. Michael Hirst, interview with author, telephone, Lexington, KY, April 28, 2011.
54. Mantel 2013, 409.
55. Ibid., 159.
56. Michael Hirst, interview with author, telephone, Lexington, KY, April 28, 2011.
57. Natalie Dormer, interview with author, Richmond upon Thames, England, July 31, 2010.
58. Ibid.
59. Michael Hirst, interview with author, telephone, Lexington, KY, April 28, 2011.
60. Natalie Dormer, interview with author, Richmond upon Thames, England, July 31, 2010.
61. Ibid.
62. Michael Hirst, interview with author, telephone, Lexington, KY, April 28, 2011.
63. Natalie Dormer, interview with author, Richmond upon Thames, England, July 31, 2010.
64. Ibid.
65. Michael Hirst, interview with author, telephone, Lexington, KY, April 28, 2011.
66. Nordyke 2008.
67. Jenny Zeek-Schmeidler, September 10, 2011, comment on *The Creation of Anne Boleyn* Facebook page, www.facebook.com/thecreationofanneboleyn.
68. Bernadette Boddin, September 10, 2011, comment on *The Creation of Anne Boleyn* Facebook page, www.facebook.com/thecreationofanneboleyn.
69. Taken from promotional material found on *The Tudors*, Season 3, DVD case.
70. Gilbert 2011.
71. Natalie Dormer, interview with author, Richmond upon Thames, England, July 31, 2010.

12. Chapuys' Revenge

1. Maxwell 1997, 279.
2. Plaidy 1986, 1.
3. Robin Maxwell, interview with author, telephone, Lexington, KY, August 19, 2011.
4. Gregory 2007, 655.
5. Reaves 2008.
6. "Philippa Gregory watches as her bestseller 'The Other Boleyn Girl' gets the Hollywood treatment," 2008.
7. Rich 2008.
8. Purdon 2009.
9. Hilary Mantel, interview with author, e-mail, Lexington, KY, October 5, 2011.
10. Robin Maxwell, interview with author, telephone, Lexington, KY, August 19, 2011.
11. Michael Hirst, interview with author, telephone, Lexington, KY, April 28, 2011.
12. Hanks 2007.
13. Jones 2011. But this is nothing new. In the acclaimed PBS series on Henry as well as in *Anne of the Thousand Days*, Anne is never seen reading a book, let alone conversing with Henry — as the actual Anne often did — about the religious debates of the day. Her role in Henry's break from Rome is purely as the tantalizing object of his desire, his history-launching Helen, for whom he was willing to defy the pope, suffer excommunication, have old friends such as More executed, and create a poisonous schism in his kingdom. One of the innovations of *The Tudors* is its break with this convention, largely due to the intervention of Natalie Dormer.
14. Carbone 2008.
15. Stephenson 2010.
16. Driscoll 2008.
17. Flynn n.d.
18. Passafuime 2008.
19. Russell n.d.
20. Reed 2008.
21. Alexander 2008.
22. Rocchi 2008.
23. Gregory, *Washington Post*, 2008.
24. Ibid.
25. Ibid.
26. Gregory 2003, 668.
27. Gregory, *Washington Post*, 2008.
28. Gregory, *Telegraph*, 2008.
29. Ibid.
30. Alison Weir: "It really annoys me when historical novelists present themselves — or are publicized — as reliable historians when they know only the outline of a

story and have no real understanding of the period or the social setting." (Alison Weir, interview with author, e-mail, Lexington, KY, August 24, 2011.) David Loades: "What is important is that the author should be honest and not claim a historical basis that does not, in fact, exist. It would have been safer if Philippa Gregory had claimed to be writing fiction, because that is what she was doing." (David Loades, interview with author, e-mail, Lexington, KY, August 29, 2011.)

31. Margaret George, interview with author, e-mail, Lexington, KY, August 15, 2011.

32. "My Cromwell," she writes, "shakes hands with the Cromwell of the *Book of Martyrs*, and with the trickster Cromwell of the truly awful but funny Elizabethan play about him. I am conscious of all his later, if fugitive, incarnations in fiction and drama. I am conscious on every page of hard choices to be made, and I make sure I never believe my own story." (Hilary Mantel, interview with author, e-mail, Lexington, KY, October 5, 2011.)

33. Mantel 2012, 409.

34. Philippa Gregory official website n.d.

35. Kosman 2008.

36. Gareth Russell, October 10, 2011, comment on *The Creation of Anne Boleyn* Facebook page, accessed October 15, 2011, www.facebook.com/thecreationof anneboleyn.

37. Katherine Stinson, October 10, 2011, comment on *The Creation of Anne Boleyn* Facebook page, accessed October 15, 2011, www.facebook.com/ thecreationofanneboleyn.

38. Michael, February 28, 2011, comment on "What are the differences between history and historical fiction?" accessed March 21, 2011. http://www .philippagregory.com/debates/what-are-the-differences-between-history -and-historical-fiction.

39. Gregory 2005, 241.

40. Ibid.

41. Hanks 2007.

42. Margaret George, interview with author, e-mail, Lexington, KY, August 15, 2011.

43. Marche 2011.

44. Hilary Mantel, interview with author, e-mail, Lexington, KY, October 2011.

45. Ibid.

46. Weir 1991, 3.

47. Ibid., 173.

48. Ibid., 3.

49. Weir 2010, 150.

50. Raz 2010.

51. Ibid.

52. Pascual de Gayangos (editor), "Spain: May 1536, 16–31," *Calendar of State Papers, Spain*, Volume 5, Part 2: 1536–1538, British History Online, http://www.british -history.ac.uk/report.aspx?compid=87961.

53. Weir 2011, 73.
54. The works from which I quote in this chapter are all "popular" histories and novels. Among more scholarly works, there are many that are more sensitive to the social context — including gender inequities — that constrained and condemned Anne. Among these are (in publication order) Retha Warnicke's *The Rise and Fall of Anne Boleyn* (1989), Antonia Fraser's *The Wives of Henry VIII* (1994), Eric Ives's *The Life and Death of Anne Boleyn* (2004), Joanna Denny's *Anne Boleyn* (2004), David Loades's *The Six Wives of Henry VIII* (2009; revised from 2004), and Suzannah Lipscomb's *The Year That Changed Henry VIII* (2009).
55. Bernard 2010, 192.
56. Ibid., 185. Bernard also cites all those who had called Anne a "whore" during her lifetime and suggests it would be unreasonable to suppose that all of this was pure slander, based only on hostility toward Anne. "Would any woman who had won the king . . . have been dismissed as a whore?" (Bernard 2010, 184.) The answer to that — and it's hardly as preposterous as Bernard makes it out to be, given Anne's nonroyal status and the popularity of Katherine of Aragon — seems to have been a resounding yes. Anne did not have many genuflectors to her queenly status (except on formal occasions, when Henry was watching, or in the coerced signatures to her oaths and decrees); up until the end, there was a critical mass who didn't even see her as a legitimate queen. But Bernard chooses instead to take the "where there's smoke, there's fire" approach to the gossip about Anne via a series of "suppose that"s and "could have"s, beginning with the unfounded premise ("for the sake of argument," he says) that the dates given, at her trial, for the adulteries, were "broadly correct."

> Anne would then have committed adultery with Henry Norris in October/November 1533 and with William Brereton in November 1533, just after what was for Henry the disappointment that Anne's child born in September was a daughter rather than the hoped-for son and heir, and just after Henry's interest in another lady had provoked Anne, if Chapuys is to be believed. Anne was then accused of having committed adultery with Mark Smeaton in April/May 1534 and with Sir Francis Weston in May/June 1534. If Anne was indeed pregnant in those months, that would be highly improbable; but suppose Anne knew that she was not pregnant, but experiencing a phantom pregnancy, then maybe such affairs could be seen as an attempt to become pregnant by someone else. And Anne's alleged incest with her brother in November/December 1535 could just be seen as an ever more desperate attempt at pregnancy: and an early miscarriage in January could be seen as her body's swift rejection of an unnatural pregnancy. (Bernard 2010, 188)

All these "could have"s and "maybe"s — some of them, such as the phantom pregnancy and the desire for intercourse with another so shortly after Elizabeth's birth (out of jealous vengeance, Bernard suggests), seemingly pulled out of thin air — make Bernard's purportedly scholarly study sound more like the closing statements of a particularly sleazy lawyer.

57. Hull and Alberge 2010.

58. Marshall n.d.

59. Hull and Alberge 2010.

60. Erickson 2011.

61. Mantel 2009, 317.

62. Ibid., 287.

63. Ibid., 137.

64. Ibid., 317.

65. Mantel 2013, 304.

66. Ibid., 345.

67. Ibid., 409.

68. See page 101 for discussion of this incident.

69. Clapp 2010.

70. Billington 2010.

71. Bermingham 2011.

72. Dowell 2010.

73. Ridgway 2011.

74. Broadbent 2010.

75. Billington 2010.

76. Letts 2010.

77. Williams 2011.

78. Howard Brenton, interview with author, London, England, July 30, 2010.

79. Ibid.

80. Paglia 1991, 13.

81. Melissa Mazza, October 10, 2011, comment on *The Creation of Anne Boleyn* Facebook page, accessed October 15, 2011, www.facebook.com/thecreationof anneboleyn.

82. *The Real Housewives of Atlanta*, season 1.

83. *The Real Housewives of Orange County*, season 3.

84. *The Real Housewives of Atlanta*, season 1.

85. Stevens 2011. Stevens here is actually talking about prime-time sitcoms. But reality television, clearly, is the nastiest and — judging from its dominance as a genre — broadest platform for the bitch to perform on. Whether they are competing with their nails out on *The Bachelor* or hurling insults at one another (and sometimes threatening physical violence) on the "reunion" shows of *The Real Housewives,* the women of reality television, apparently, have no impulse control whatsoever. And those impulses are generally envious, narcissistic, knee-jerk defensive, and brutally catty. They seem incapable of seeing another person's point of view, which is why their fights inevitably escalate into increasingly juvenile rants. They goad one another: "Bring it on!" is their favorite mantra. (Or what amounts to the same thing — "You don't want to go there!" — which virtually ensures that they will.)

Are these people for real? Yes and no. Many of the housewives seem to have been chosen on the basis of the size of their houses and the ostentation of their decorating, pretty much ensuring that the shows won't be about the lifestyles of the modest and self-restraining. The most attention-getting reality-show participants get rewarded with fame, book deals, record contracts — talent is irrelevant — so bad behavior pays off. (One of the housewives of the Miami franchise complained that their show wasn't as popular as the others because the women weren't being outrageous enough.) The footage is "real," reality-TV execs emphasize, and captures nothing that didn't actually happen. But psychological manipulation on shows such as *The Bachelor* (constant surveillance, feeding misinformation to participants, abundant alcohol, and isolation) and skillful editing ensures that the worst comes out, often in the mode of various regional and ethnic stereotypes.

86. Herbst 2010, 133.
87. Eades 2007.
88. Stepp 2011.
89. Ibid.
90. Denby 2009.
91. Douglas 2009.
92. N. Wolf 1994, xxvii.
93. Ibid.
94. Ibid., xxvii–xxviii.
95. Roiphe 1994.
96. Paglia 1992, 62.
97. Argov 2002.
98. Dargis 2008.
99. Emerson 2008.
100. LaSalle 2008.
101. Burr 2008.
102. Kosman 2008.
103. Merin n.d.

13. Anne Gets the Last Word (for Now)

1. Phyllis Wolf, 2011, comment on *The Creation of Anne Boleyn* Facebook page, www.facebook.com/thecreationofanneboleyn.
2. Connie Panzariello, 2011, comment on *The Creation of Anne Boleyn* Facebook page, www.facebook.com/thecreationofanneboleyn.
3. Lara Eakins, interview with author, e-mail, Lexington, KY, November 25, 2011.
4. Ibid.
5. Ibid.
6. Ibid.
7. Ibid.

8. Ibid.
9. *The Tudors Wiki* 2008.
10. Claire Ridgway, interview with author, e-mail, Lexington, KY, October 24, 2011.
11. Sue Booth, interview with author, e-mail, Lexington, KY, October 24, 2011.
12. Ibid.
13. Natalie Sweet, interview with author, e-mail, Lexington, KY, October 24, 2011.
14. Barb Alexander, interview with author, e-mail, Lexington, KY, October 24, 2011.
15. Natalie Sweet, interview with author, e-mail, Lexington, KY, October 24, 2011.
16. Claire Ridgway, interview with author, e-mail, Lexington, KY, October 24, 2011.
17. Jessica Prestes, interview with author, e-mail, Lexington, KY, October 24, 2011.
18. Sarah Bryson, interview with author, e-mail, Lexington, KY, October 24, 2011.
19. Sylwia Sobczak Zupanec, interview with author, e-mail, Lexington, KY, October 24, 2011.
20. Brown 2007, 75.
21. Ibid.
22. Marlessa Stivala, interview with author and Natalie Sweet, e-mail, Lexington, KY, April 2011.
23. Karissa Baker, interview with author and Natalie Sweet, e-mail, Lexington, KY, April 2011.
24. Sara Compton, interview with author and Natalie Sweet, e-mail, Lexington, KY, April 2011.
25. Sophie Walker, interview with author and Natalie Sweet, e-mail, Lexington, KY, April 2011.
26. Michelle Kistler, interview with author and Natalie Sweet, e-mail, Lexington, KY, April 2011.
27. Makenzie Case, interview with author and Natalie Sweet, e-mail, Lexington, KY, April 2011.
28. Jessica Crowley, interview with author and Natalie Sweet, e-mail, Lexington, KY, April 2011.
29. Kristian, 2011, comment on *The Anne Boleyn Files* Facebook page, http://www.theanneboleynfiles.com/1142/anne-boleyn-the-great-whore.
30. Cris Gomez, interview with author and Natalie Sweet, e-mail, Lexington, KY, April 2011.
31. Sara Compton, interview with author and Natalie Sweet, e-mail, Lexington, KY, April 2011.
32. Phillips 2000, 150.
33. Ibid.
34. Ibid., 10.
35. Robyn, interview with author and Natalie Sweet, e-mail, Lexington, KY, April 2011.
36. Brittani Hall, interview with author and Natalie Sweet, e-mail, Lexington, KY, April 2011.

37. *The Tudors Wiki* 2008.
38. Ibid., 2009.
39. Ibid.
40. Ilana Redler, interview with author and Natalie Sweet, e-mail, Lexington, KY, April 2011.
41. *The Tudors Wiki* 2008.
42. Ibid.
43. Ibid.
44. Marlessa Stivala, interview with author and Natalie Sweet, e-mail, Lexington, KY, April 2011.
45. Michelle Kistler, interview with author and Natalie Sweet, e-mail, Lexington, KY, April 2011.
46. Makenzie Case, interview with author and Natalie Sweet, e-mail, Lexington, KY, April 2011.
47. Ilana Redler, interview with author and Natalie Sweet, e-mail, Lexington, KY, April 2011.
48. Howard Brenton, interview with author, London, England, July 30, 2010.
49. Ibid.
50. Brenton 2010, 11.
51. Howard Brenton, interview with author, London, England, July 30, 2010.
52. Brenton 2010, 113.
53. Ibid.
54. Howard Brenton, interview with author, London, England, July 30, 2010.
55. Ibid.
56. Brenton 2010, 35.
57. Ibid., 115.
58. Hilary Mantel, interview with author, e-mail, Lexington, KY, October 5, 2011.

Afterword: Anne, Susan, and Cassie

1. In France, fashionable women wore a different kind of hood than the British: rounded and set farther back on the head so a woman's hair, parted down the middle and drawn to the sides, was visible. Anne is credited with having brought the style to England, which was far more of a transformation than it first appears, as over the years the hood itself became smaller and smaller, as well as placed farther back on the head, so that by Elizabeth's time, the nunlike gabled hood had given way to highly decorative headbands that called attention to a woman's hair as her "glory" rather than a vanity to be imprisoned and effaced.

2. Howard Brenton, interview with author, London, England, July 30, 2010.

3. I enjoyed these little enactments, which frequently made knowing "winks" to more sobering events and to the religious politics always at play in the Tudor court. The day I visited, the marriage of Henry and Katherine Parr was being celebrated. Katherine's aunt, preparing her for the wedding, enthused over the

fact that Henry was marrying "a good, decent woman . . . unlike some of her predecessors . . . and best of all, a Protestant!" Katherine herself made continual references to the things she daren't talk about in Henry's previous marriages. ("But we won't linger on that on this joyous day.") If you knew your Tudor history, the presentation was loaded with unspoken subtext about the dangers of a marriage to Henry. (Even "kind and loving" Katherine was almost taken to the Tower for her subversive Protestantism. Unlike Anne Boleyn and Katherine Howard, she was able to see Henry and talk him out of it.) The enactment's oblique references, unfortunately, only carried irony if you came to Hampton Court with some knowledge of history. Judging from their whispered questions to one another, few visitors had. And beyond learning how 600 people were fed twice a day in an average year (8,200 sheep, 2,300 deer, 1,870 pigs, 1,240 oxen, 760 calves, and 53 wild boar), they wouldn't get it from Hampton Court.

4. From the singular grammar ("The" Tower of London) and old Boris Karloff movies, U.S. visitors probably expect one dark, creepy building full of dungeons and torture chambers. In fact, the Tower of London is a complex of towers, built up over the centuries, that have served a variety of individual purposes, from medieval fortresses and places of royal refuge from outside attack, to strongholds for official papers and valuables, to royal residences and sites of important state ceremonies such as coronations (and trials), to prisons for high-status offenders such as Thomas More, Anne, Sir Walter Raleigh, and, for a time, Elizabeth I.

5. Rennell 2010.

6. Brenton 2010, 115.

7. Ibid.

8. Ibid.

9. Ibid.

Sources

Books, Periodicals, and Websites

Alexander, Victoria. "Film Reviews: The Other Boleyn Girl." *Films in Review.* February 29, 2008. http://www.filmsinreview.com/2008/02/29/the-other-boleyn-girl (accessed March 25, 2012).

Allen, Vanessa. "Women turn history into a bizarre soap opera, says Starkey." *Mail Online.* March 31, 2009. http://www.dailymail.co.uk/news/article-1166125 /Women-turn-history-bizarre-soap-opera-says-Starkey.html (accessed March 15, 2012).

Anderson, Maxwell. *Anne of the Thousand Days.* New York: Dramatists Play Service, Inc., 1977.

Argov, Sherry. "Releasing Your Inner Bitch," http://scallywagandvagabond .com/2011/04/releasing-your-inner-bitch-may-help-you-land-the-right-male/.

Atkinson, Brooks. "Anne and Henry: Maxwell Anderson Chronicles a Stormy Love Affair in a Historical Play." *New York Times,* December 19, 1948.

Armstrong, Jessie. *My Friend Anne: A Story of the Sixteenth Century.* London: F. Warne, 1935.

Austen, Jane. *The History of England: By a partial, prejudiced, & ignorant Historian (Note: There will be very few Dates in this History).* Chapel Hill, NC: Algonquin Books, 1993.

Bailey, Alyssa. "I might have a third nipple." *Girls' Life.* December 7, 2010. http://www .girlslife.com/post/2010/12/07/I-might-have-a-third-nipple.aspx (accessed February 20, 2012).

Banks, John. *Vertue Betray'd: or Anna Bullen.* Los Angeles: The Augustan Reprint Society, 1981.

Bannet, Eve Tavor. "Secret History: Or Telling Tales Inside and Outside the Secretorie." *Huntington Library Quarterly* 68, no. 1–2 (March 2005): 375–96.

Barnes, Margaret Campbell. *Brief Gaudy Hour: A Novel of Anne Boleyn.* Naperville, IL: Sourcebooks, Inc., 2008.

Barrington, E. *Anne Boleyn*. Garden City: Doubleday, Doran & Company, Inc., 1934.

BBC Two. "Production Notes." *The Other Boleyn Girl*.

Bellafante, Gina. "Nasty, but Not So Brutish and Short." *New York Times*. March 28, 2008. http://tv.nytimes.com/2008/03/28/arts/television/28tudo.html?_r=1 (accessed January 15, 2012).

Benger, Elizabeth. *Memoirs of the Life of Anne Boleyn, Queen of Henry VIII*. London: A. & R. Spottiswoode, 1821.

Bennett, Vanora. "Dreamer or schemer? Step forward the real Anne Boleyn." *Mail Online*. March 3, 2012. http://www.dailymail.co.uk/home/you/article-2108838 /Dreamer-schemer-Step-forward-real-Anne-Boleyn.html (accessed March 25, 2012).

Bermingham, Ciaran. "Anne Boleyn." *Morning Star*. July 27, 2011. http://www. morningstaronline.co.uk/news/content/view/full/107553 (accessed March 25, 2012).

Bernard, G. W. *Anne Boleyn: Fatal Attractions*. New Haven, CT: Yale University Press, 2010.

———. "Anne Boleyn's Religion." *The Historical Journal* 36, no. 1 (March 1993): 1–20.

———. "The Fall of Anne Boleyn." *The English Historical Review* 106, no. 420 (July 1991): 584–610.

———. "The Fall of Anne Boleyn: A Rejoinder." *The English Historical Review* 107, no. 424 (1992): 665–74.

———. *The King's Reformation: Henry VIII and the Remaking of the English Church*. New Haven, CT: Yale University Press, 2007.

Billington, Michael. "Anne Boleyn." *The Guardian*. July 29, 2010. http://www.guardian .co.uk/stage/2010/jul/29/anne-boleyn-review (accessed March 25, 2012).

Blessington, Marguerite, editor. *The Book of Beauty, or Regal Gallery*. London: D. Bogue, 1848.

Bloom, Allan. *The Closing of the American Mind: How Higher Education Has Failed Democracy and Impoverished the Souls of Today's Students*. New York: Simon & Schuster Inc., 1987.

Boker, George H. *Anne Boleyn, A Tragedy*. Philadelphia: A. Hart, 1850.

Bordo, Susan. *The Flight to Objectivity: Essays on Cartesianism and Culture*. Albany, NY: State University of New York Press, 1987.

———, and Natalie Sweet. *The Creation of Anne Boleyn*. Facebook page. 2011–2012.

Borman, Tracy. *Elizabeth's Women: Friends, Rivals, and Foes Who Shaped the Virgin Queen*. New York: Bantam Books, 2009.

Bradley, Mary Hastings. *The Favor of Kings*. New York and London: D. Appleton and Company, 1912.

Brand, Madeleine. "'The Tudors' Battles with the Truth." *Day to Day (NPR)*, March 28, 2008.

Brenton, Howard. *Anne Boleyn*. London: Nick Hern Books, 2010.

British History Online. n.d. http://www.british-history.ac.uk/ (accessed February 13, 2012).

Broadbent, Giles. "Review: Anne Boleyn, Shakespeare's Globe." *The Wharf.* August 4, 2010. http://www.wharf.co.uk/2010/08/review-anne-boleyn-shakespeare.html (accessed March 15, 2012).

Brown, Tina. *The Diana Chronicles.* New York: Broadway Books, 2007.

Burr, Ty. "'Boleyn Girl' is a royal pity." *boston.com.* February 29, 2008. http://articles .boston.com/2008-02-29/ae/29274755_1_boleyn-sisters-boleyn-girl-justin -chadwick (accessed March 25, 2012).

Burstein, Miriam Elizabeth. "The Fictional Afterlife of Anne Boleyn: How to Do Things with the Queen, 1901–2006." *CLIO* 37 (2007).

——. "The Reduced Pretensions of the Historic Muse: Agnes Strickland and the Commerce of Women's History." *The Journal of Narrative Technique* 28, no. 3 (Fall 1998): 219–42.

Bush, Annie Forbes. *Memoirs of the Queens of France.* Philadelphia: A. Hart, late Carey & Hart, 1851.

Byrne, M. St. Clare, editor. *The Letters of King Henry VIII: A Selection, with a Few Other Documents.* New York: Funk & Wagnalls, 1968.

Callcott, Lady Maria. *Little Arthur's History of England.* London: John Murray, 1856.

Canby, Vincent. "Anne of the Thousand Days (1969)." *New York Times.* January 21, 1970. http://movies.nytimes.com/movie/review?res= 9907EFDA1F39EF34BC4951DFB766838B669EDE (accessed February 17, 2012).

Capellanus, Andreas. *The Art of Courtly Love.* Translated by John Jay Parry. New York: Columbia University Press, 1960.

Carbone, Gina. "'Other Boleyn Girl': It's a bust." *Seacoast Online.* March 1, 2008. http://www.seacoastonline.com/apps/pbcs.dll/article?AID=/20080301 /ENTERTAIN04/80301008 (accessed March 30, 2012).

Carley, James P. *The Books of King Henry VIII and His Wives.* London: The British Library, 2004.

Castiglione, Baldassarre. *The Book of the Courtier.* Translated by Leonard Eckstein Opdycke. New York: Charles Scribner's Sons, 1903.

Castiglione, Count Baldesar. *The Book of the Courtier.* Translated by Leonard Eckstein Opdycke. New York: Charles Scribner's Sons, 1901.

Cavendish, George. *The Life and Death of Cardinal Wolsey.* Boston and New York: Houghton Mifflin and Company, 1905.

Chapman, Hester W. *The Challenge of Anne Boleyn.* New York: Coward, McCann & Geoghegan, 1974.

Cholakian, Patricia F., and Rouben C. Cholakian. *Marguerite de Navarre: Mother of the Renaissance.* New York: Columbia University Press, 2006.

"Cinema: The Lion in Autumn." *Time.* February 2, 1970. http://www.time.com/time /magazine/article/0,9171,878191,00.html (accessed March 15, 2012).

Clapp, Susannah. "Anne Boleyn; Danton's Death; The Prince of Homburg." *Guardian.* July 31, 2010. http://www.guardian.co.uk/stage/2010/aug/01/anne-boleyn -danton-death-prince-homberg (accessed March 25, 2012).

Cohen, Alex. "'The Tudors' Battles with the Truth." *NPR.* March 28, 2008. http://www

.npr.org/templates/story/story.php?storyId=89182466 (accessed February 15, 2012).

Connor, Steven. *The Book of Skin.* Ithaca, NY: Cornell University Press, 2004.

"Corpus Christi." *Castilla-La Mancha.* n.d. http://www.visitclm.com/art-culture /festivities/toledo/corpus-christi/ (accessed April 9, 2009).

Cox, Ted. "History goes down easy on Showtime: 'The Tudors' sees Henry VIII as a royal Tony Soprano." *Daily Herald,* March 29, 2007: Page 1, Section 4.

Cox, Tom. "These Tudors are all sex and soundbites." *Mail on Sunday,* April 24, 2011.

Cressy, David. *Birth, Marriage & Death: Ritual, Religion, and the Life-Cycle in Tudor and Stuart England.* Oxford, UK: Oxford University Press, 2002.

Daneau, Lambert. *A Dialogue of Witches in foretime commonly called Sorcerers.* English Translation. Rev. EP, 1575.

Dargis, Manohla. "Rival Sisters Duke It Out for the Passion of a King." *New York Times.* February 29, 2008. http://movies.nytimes.com/2008/02/29/movies/29bole.html (accessed March 25, 2012).

Das, Lina. "How horrible can Henry get? It's the last ever series of historical romp The Tudors, and the King's at his ghastly worst." *Mail Online.* January 28, 2011. http:// www.dailymail.co.uk/femail/article-1351379/How-horrible-Henry-Its-series -historical-romp-The-Tudors-Kings-ghastly-worst.html (accessed January 15, 2012).

——. "Lie back and think of Olde England! Is this TV's sexiest historical romp?" *Mail Online.* September 7, 2007. http://www.dailymail.co.uk/tvshowbiz/reviews /article-480475/Lie-think-Olde-England-Is-TVs-sexiest-historical-romp.html (accessed January 15, 2012).

d'Aubigné, Jean Henri Merle. *History of the Reformation in Europe in the Time of Calvin.* Vol. V. London: Longmans, Green, and Co., 1869.

d'Aulnoy, Marie-Catherine. *The novels of Elizabeth, Queen of England containing the history of Queen Ann of Bullen.* London: Mark Pardoe, 1680.

de Carles, Lancelot. "Poèm Sur La Mort D'Anne Boleyn, par Lancelot de Carles." In *La Grande-Bretagne Devant L'opinion Française au XVIIe siècl,* by Georges Ascoli. Paris: J. Gamber, 1927.

Deggans, Eric. "Meet Henry VIII, rock star." *Tampa Bay Times.* March 31, 2007. http:// www.sptimes.com/2007/03/31/news_pf/Floridian/Meet_Henry_VIII__rock .shtml (accessed February 15, 2012).

de Navarre, Marguerite. *Selected Writings: A Bilingual Edition.* Chicago: University of Chicago Press, 2008.

Denby, David. *Snark: It's Mean, It's Personal, and It's Ruining Our Conversation.* New York: Simon & Schuster, 2009.

Denny, Joanna. *Anne Boleyn: A New Life of England's Tragic Queen.* Philadelphia: Da Capo Press, 2007.

Dickens, Charles. *A Child's History of England: England from the Reign of Henry the Seventh to the Revolution of 1688.* London: Bradbury and Evans, 1854.

Dixon, William H. *History of Two Queens: I. Catherine of Aragon. II. Anne Boleyn.* Leipzig: Bernhard, 1874.

Donizetti, Gaetano. *Anne Boleyn; Opera in 2 Acts and 6 Scenes.* Translated by Chester Kallman. New York: G. Ricordi, 1959.

Dostoevsky, Fyodor. *The Idiot.* MobileReference, 2008.

Douglas, Susan J. "Where Have You Gone, Roseanne Barr?" *Shriver Report.* October 2009. http://www.shriverreport.com/awn/media.php (accessed March 25, 2012).

Dowell, Ben. "Anne Boleyn." *Stage Reviews.* July 29, 2010. http://www.thestage .co.uk/reviews/review.php/29073/anne-boleyn (accessed March 25, 2012).

Drew, Reginald. *Anne Boleyn.* Boston: Sherman, French & Company, 1912.

Driscoll, Rob. "The Movies: Sister Act." *Western Mail,* March 7, 2008: 14.

Dugdale, John. "What The Tudors has taught us." *Guardian.* April 1, 2011. http://www .guardian.co.uk/tv-and-radio/tvandradioblog/2011/apr/01/the-tudors-history -revelations (accessed March 26, 2012).

Eades, Mark. "Producer gets real about the real housewives." *Orange County Register.* January 10, 2007. http://www.ocregister.com/news/people-180668-think-coto .html (accessed March 15, 2012).

Ellis, Henry. *Original Letters, Illustrative of English History; Including Numerous Royal Letters: From Autographs in the British Museum, and One or Two Other Collections. With Notes and Illustrations.* Vol. II. London: Harding, Triphook, and Lepard, 1824.

Elton, Geoffrey Rudolph. *England Under the Tudors.* London: Methuen, 1977.

Elyot, Thomas. *The Defence of Good Women.* London: In aedibus T. Bertheleti, 1545.

Emerson, Jim. "The Other Boleyn Girl: Catfight in the House of Tudor." *Chicago Sun-Times.* February 29, 2008. http://rogerebert.suntimes.com/apps/pbcs.dll /article?AID=/20080228/REVIEWS/52204881&template=printart (accessed March 15, 2012).

Erasmus, Desiderius. "The Praise of Folly." In *Readings in Western Religious Thought, II: The Middle Ages Through the Reformation,* by Patrick V. Reid, 283–297. New York/Mahwah, NJ: Paulist Press, 1995.

———. *The Education of a Christian Prince with the Panegyric for Archduke Philip of Austria.* Cambridge, UK: Cambridge University Press, 2003.

Erickson, Carolly. *The Favored Queen.* New York: St. Martin's Press, 2011.

———. *Great Harry.* New York: St. Martin's Griffin, 1980.

Farmer, Lydia Hoyt. *The Girl's Book of Famous Queens.* New York: Thomas Y. Crowell & Co., 1887.

Fielding, Helen. *Bridget Jones's Diary.* New York: Penguin Books, 1996.

Fienberg, Daniel. "Review: 'The Tudors' on Showtime." *Zap 2 it.* March 30, 2007. http:// blog.zap2it.com/frominsidethebox/2007/03/review-the-tudors-on-showtime .html (accessed January 15, 2012).

Fish, Simon. *A Supplication for the Beggars.* Edited by Edward Arber. London, 1529.

Flynn, Gaynor. "Natalie Portman The Other Boleyn Girl Interview." *girl.com.au.* n.d.

http://www.girl.com.au/natalie-portman-the-other-boleyn-girl-interview.htm (accessed March 1, 2012).

Foxe, John. *The Acts and Monuments of John Foxe.* The Church Historians of England. Vol. V. London: Beeleys, 1857.

France, Anne of. *Anne of France: Lessons for My Daughter.* Edited by Sharon L. Jansen. Cambridge: D. S. Brewer, 2004.

Fraser, Antonia. *The Six Wives of Henry VIII.* London: Mandarin Publishing, 1993.

Freeman, Thomas S. "Research, Rumour and Propaganda: Anne Boleyn in Foxe's 'Book of Martyrs'." *The Historical Journal* 38, no. 4 (1995): 797–819.

Friedmann, Paul. *Anne Boleyn: A Chapter of English History 1527–1536.* Vol. I. London: MacMillan and Co., 1884.

———. *Anne Boleyn: A Chapter of English History 1527–1536.* Vol. II. London: MacMillan and Co., 1884.

Froude, James A. *The Divorce of Catherine of Aragon: The Story as Told by the Imperial Ambassadors Resident at the Court of Henry VIII.* London: Longmans, Green and Co., 1891.

Fulkerson, Perry. "Henry VIII: Who Needs Wives?" *Evening Independent,* November 5, 1973: 10-B.

Gairdner, James. *The Reign of Henry VIII from His Accession to the Death of Wolsey.* Vol. II. London: John Murray, 1884.

Gardiner, S. R. *English History for Students.* New York: Henry Holt and Company, 1881.

Gardner, Laurien. *A Lady Raised High: A Novel of Anne Boleyn.* New York: Berkley Publishing Group, 2006.

Gavin, Nell. *Threads: The Reincarnation of Anne Boleyn.* Book and Quill Press, 2001.

George, Margaret. *The Autobiography of Henry VIII: With Notes by His Fool, Will Somers.* New York: St. Martin's Press, 1986.

Gilbert, Gerard. "Golden girl: How Natalie Dormer became the new queen of the screen." *Independent.* September 17, 2011. http://www.independent.co.uk/news/people/profiles/golden-girl-how-natalie-dormer-became-the-new-queen-of-the-screen-2354626.html (accessed January 15, 2012).

Goldsmith, Oliver. *The History of England, From the Earliest Times to the Death of George II.* Vol. II. London: T. Davies, 1771.

Goodman, Irene. "Why Anne Boleyn Is the Poster Girl of Historical Fiction." *The Historical Novel Society.* November 2005. http://www.historicalnovelsociety.org/solander/anne_boleyn.htm (accessed February 1, 2012).

Gregory, Philippa. "Book World Live: Historical Novelist Philippa Gregory." *Washington Post.* October 9, 2008. http://www.washingtonpost.com/wp-dyn/content/discussion/2008/10/02/DI2008100202254.html (accessed April 13, 2012).

———. "Historic Passion Born a Writer: Forged as a Historian." *History Workshop Journal,* no. 59 (2005): 237–242.

———. "KING SIZE! As Jonathan Rhys Meyers Returns to Our Screens in The Tudors, Research Shows That the Real Henry VIII Had a 52in Waist and Paid a High Price for Being a Rotund Royal." *Daily Mail.* April 10, 2009, p. 13.

———. *The Other Boleyn Girl*. New York: Pocket Star Books, 2007.

———. *The Other Boleyn Girl*. New York: Touchstone, 2003.

———. "The Other Boleyn Girl: History in the making." *Telegraph*. February 23, 2008. http://www.telegraph.co.uk/culture/film/3671391/The-Other-Boleyn-Girl-History-in-the-making.html (accessed March 25, 2008).

———. Philippa Gregory official website. *http://www.philippagregory.com/* (accessed 2011).

———. "What happened when the retiring author of The Other Boleyn Girl collided with greedy Hollywood?" *Mail Online*. February 23, 2008. http://www.dailymail.co.uk/femail/article-517758/What-happened-retiring-author-The-Other-Boleyn-Girl-collided-greedy-Hollywood.html (accessed March 25, 2012).

Grueninger, Natalie. *On the Tudor Trail*. http://onthetudortrail.com/Blog/ (accessed March 15, 2012).

Guy, John. "Why The Tudors is hilarious historical bunk." *Telegraph*. August 1, 2008. http://www.telegraph.co.uk/culture/tvandradio/3557583/Why-The-Tudors-is-hilarious-historical-bunk.html (accessed January 15, 2012).

Hackett, Francis. *Anne Boleyn*. New York: Popular Library, 1939.

———. *Henry the Eighth: The Personal History of a Dynasty and His Six Wives*. New York: Liveright Publishing Corporation, 1945.

Harmetz, Aljean. "How to Win an Oscar Nomination, From 'Anne' to 'Z'." *New York Times*, April 5, 1970.

Hanks, Robert. "Peter Morgan: Drama King." *Independent*, February 24, 2007.

Hart, Kelly. *The Mistresses of Henry VIII*. Charleston, SC: The History Press, 2011.

"Henry VIII and Miscarriage; Was It the Kell Antigen?" *Science 2.0*. March 3, 2011. http://www.science20.com/news_articles/henry_viii_and_miscarriages_was_it_kell_antigen-76877 (accessed February 22, 2012).

"Henry VIII reveals his softer side in never-before-seen gushing love letter to Anne Boleyn." *Mail Online*. February 14, 2009. http://www.dailymail.co.uk/news/article-1145429/Henry-VIII-reveals-softer-seen-gushing-love-letter-Anne-Boleyn.html (accessed February 15, 2012).

Herbert, William Henry. *Frank Forester's Fish and Fishing in the United States and British Provinces of North America*. New York: Arno Press, 1970.

———. *Memoirs of Henry VIII of England: With the Fortunes, Fates, and Characters of His Six Wives*. New York and Auburn: Miller, Orton & Mulligan, 1856.

Herbst, Susan. *Rude Democracy: Civility and Incivility in American Politics*. Philadelphia: Temple University Press, 2010.

Hester, Nathalie. "Travel and the Art of Telling the Truth: Marie-Catherine d'Aulnoy's Travels to Spain." *Huntington Library Quarterly* 70, no. 1 (March 2007): 87–102.

Highley, Christopher. "A Pestilent and Seditious Book: Nicholas Sander's *Schismatis Anglicani* and Catholic Histories." In *The Uses of History in Early Modern England*, edited by Paulina Kewes. San Marino, CA: Henry E. Huntington Library and Art Gallery, 2006.

Hirst, Michael. *The Tudors: It's Good to Be King — Final shooting scripts 1–5 for The

Tudors *from Showtime Network, Inc.* New York: Simon Spotlight Entertainment, 2007.

Hohenadel, Kristin. "The King Goes A-courting." *Sun Sentinel.* April 1, 2007. http://articles.sun-sentinel.com/2007-04-01/news/0703280572_1_tudors-rhys-meyers-henry-s-father/2 (accessed January 15, 2012).

———. "He's Henry the Eighth, he is." *Sunday Times,* April 8, 2007.

Holleran, Scott. "Close-Up: Actress Geneviève Bujold." *Box Office Mojo.* April 13, 2007. http://boxofficemojo.com/features/?id=2290&p=.htm (accessed February 17, 2012).

Hough, Andrew. "BBC period show, The Tudors, is 'historically inaccurate', leading historian says." *Telegraph.* August 10, 2009. http://www.telegraph.co.uk/culture/tvandradio/6005582/BBC-period-show-The-Tudors-is-historically-inaccurate-leading-historian-says.html (accessed January 15, 2012).

Hull, Liz, and Dalya Alberge. "Anne Boleyn DID have an affair with her brother: The poem that 'proves' the adultery of Henry VIII's queen." *Mail Online.* February 23, 2010. http://www.dailymail.co.uk/news/article-1252993/Poem-backs-claims-Anne-Boleyn-lovers—brother.html (accessed March 25, 2012).

Hunter, Jane H. *How Young Ladies Became Girls: The Victorian Origins of American Girlhood.* New Haven, CT: Yale University Press, 2002.

Hutchinson, Robert. *Thomas Cromwell: The Rise and Fall of Henry VIII's Most Notorious Minister.* New York: St. Martin's Press, 2007.

———. *Young Henry: The Rise of Henry VIII.* London: Weidenfeld & Nicholson, 2011.

Internet Movie Database. n.d. http://www.imdb.com/name/nm0000991/bio#quotes (accessed February 17, 2012).

Ives, Eric. "Anne Boleyn and the Early Reformation in England: The Contemporary Evidence." *The Historical Journal* 37, no. 2 (June 1994): 389–400.

———. "The Fall of Anne Boleyn Reconsidered." *The English Historical Review* 107, no. 424 (July 1992): 651–64.

———. *The Life and Death of Anne Boleyn.* Malden, MA: Blackwell Publishing, 2005.

Jansen, Sharon L. *Debating Women, Politics, and Power in Early Modern Europe.* New York: Palgrave Macmillan, 2008.

———.*The Monstrous Regiment of Women: Female Rulers in Early Modern Europe.* New York: Palgrave Macmillan, 2002.

Jones, Ann Rosalind. "Nets and bridles: early modern conduct books and sixteenth-century women's lyrics." In *The Ideology of Conduct: Essays in Literature and the History of Sexuality,* edited by Nancy Armstrong and Leonard Tennenhouse. New York: Methuen, 1987.

Jones, Christine A. "Madame d'Aulnoy Charms the British." *The Romantic Review* 99, no. 3–4 (2008): 239–56.

Jones, Jonathan. "Do artists need to be accurate to recreate history?" *Guardian.* February 28, 2011. http://www.guardian.co.uk/artanddesign/jonathanjonesblog/2011/feb/28/artists-accurate-history-robin-hood (accessed March 1, 2012).

Jordan, Constance. *Renaissance Feminism: Literary Texts and Political Models*. Ithaca, NY: Cornell University Press, 1990.

Klausner, Julie. "The comic geniuses of 'Real Housewives.'" *Salon.com*. October 4, 2010. http://www.salon.com/2010/10/04/real_housewives_klausner/ (accessed April 13, 2012).

Knecht, Robert. *The French Renaissance Court*. New Haven, CT: Yale University Press, 2008.

Knox, John. *Political Writings of John Knox: The First Blast of the Trumpet Against the Monstrous Regiment of Women and Other Selected Works*. Washington, D.C.: Folger Books, 1985.

Kosman, Joshua. "Queen of Tudor Novels." *SFGate*. March 2, 2008. http://www.sfgate.com/cgi-bin/article.cgi?f=/c/a/2008/02/29/PKGFV5UIP.DTL (accessed March 25, 2012).

Kreisman, Jerold J., and Hal Straus. *I Hate You — Don't Leave Me: Understanding the Borderline Personality*. New York: Avon Books, 1989.

Krutch, Joseph Wood. "Mr. Anderson's New Venture Into Poetic Drama." *New York Times*, December 12, 1948.

Kucich, Greg. "Women's Historiography and the (Dis)embodiment of Law: Ann Yearsley, Mary Hays, Elizabeth Benger." *Wordsworth Circle* 33, no. 1 (2002).

LaSalle, Mick. "Review: Sisters face off in 'Other Boleyn Girl.'" *SFGate*. February 29, 2008. http://www.sfgate.com/cgi-bin/article.cgi?f=/c/a/2008/02/28/DD29V9PFR.DTL (accessed March 25, 2012).

Lee, Sidney, editor. *Dictionary of National Biography*. Vol. XVII. New York: The Macmillan Company, 1909.

Leti, Gregorio. *La Vie d'Elizabeth Reine d'Angleterre*. Translated by Louis Antoine Le Peletier. Charleston, SC: Nabu Press, 2010.

Letts, Quentin. "Anne Boleyn: Miranda Raison blooms as a Tudor rose." *Mail Online*. July 29, 2010. http://www.dailymail.co.uk/tvshowbiz/article-1298770/Anne-Boleyn-Miranda-Raison-blooms-Tudor-rose.html (accessed March 25, 2012).

Levin, Carole. *Dreaming the English Renaissance: Politics and Desire in Court and Culture*. New York: Palgrave Macmillan, 2008.

———. *The Heart and Stomach of a King: Elizabeth I and the Politics of Sex and Power*. Philadelphia: University of Pennsylvania Press, 1994.

Lindsey, Karen. *Divorced, Beheaded, Survived: A Feminist Reinterpretation of the Wives of Henry VIII*. Cambridge, MA: Da Capo Press, 1995.

Lipscomb, Suzannah. *1536: The Year That Changed Henry VIII*. Oxford: Lion, 2009.

Loades, David. *The Six Wives of Henry VIII*. Gloucestershire, UK: Amberley Publishing Plc, 2009.

———, editor. *The Papers of George Wyatt Esquire of Boxley Abbey in the County of Kent Son and Heir of Sir Thomas Wyatt the Younger*. Vol. 5. London: Butler and Tanner Ltd., 1968.

Lofts, Norah. *The Concubine: A Novel*. New York: Touchstone, 2008.

Longford, Elizabeth, editor. *The Oxford Book of Royal Anecdotes*. Oxford, UK: Oxford University Press, 1989.

Lundell, Richard Edward. "The Mask of Dissimulation: Eustace Chapuys and Early Modern Diplomatic Technique, 1536–1545." Dissertation, Urbana-Champaign: University of Illinois at Urbana-Champaign, 2001.

Macaulay, Thomas Babington. *The History of England from the Accession of James II.* Vol. I. Boston: Phillips, Sampson and Company, 1849.

Maitzen, Rohan Amanda. "'The Feminine Preserve': Historical Biographies by Victorian Women." *Victorian Studies* 38, no. 3 (Spring 1995): 371–93.

——— . *Gender, Genre, and Victorian Historical Writing*. New York: Garland Publishing, Inc., 1998.

Malory, Thomas. *Malory's Le Morte d'Arthur: King Arthur and the Legends of the Round Table.* Translated by Keith Baines. New York: Penguin Group Inc., 2001.

The Manner of the Triumph at Calais and Boulogne. The second printing. With additions. London, 1532.

Mantel, Hilary. *Wolf Hall: A Novel.* New York: Henry Holt and Company, LLC, 2009.

——— . *Bring Up the Bodies*. New York: Henry Holt and Company, LLC, 2012.

Marche, Stephen. "Wouldn't It Be Cool if Shakespeare Wasn't Shakespeare?" *New York Times.* October 21, 2011. http://www.nytimes.com/2011/10/23/magazine /wouldnt-it-be-cool-if-shakespeare-wasnt-shakespeare.html?pagewanted=all (accessed March 25, 2012).

Marcus, Laurence. "The Six Wives of Henry VIII." *Television Heaven.* 2004. http:// www.televisionheaven.co.uk/henry.htm (accessed March 26, 2012).

Marikar, Sheila. "'Tudors': History Stripped Down, Sexed Up." ABC News. March 29, 2008. http://abcnews.go.com/Entertainment/story?id=4545935&page=1 #.TzvdQLKaJ8E (accessed February 15, 2012).

Marshall, Peter. "Married to a Monster." *Literary Review.* n.d. http://www .literaryreview.co.uk/marshall_04_10.html (accessed March 25, 2012).

Martin, Nicole. "BBC period drama The Tudors is 'gratuitously awful' says Dr David Starkey." *Telegraph.* October 16, 2008. http://www.telegraph.co.uk/news /celebritynews/3210142/BBC-period-drama-The-Tudors-is-gratuitously-awful -says-Dr-David-Starkey.html (accessed January 15, 2012).

Massie, Elizabeth. *The Tudors: King Takes Queen.* New York: Simon Spotlight Entertainment, 2008.

Matthews, Kristin L. "A Mad Proposition in Postwar America." *The Journal of American Culture* 30, no. 2 (2007).

Mattingly, Garrett. "A Humanist Ambassador." *The Journal of Modern History*, Vol. 4, no. 2 (June 1932): 175–85.

Maxwell, Robin. *Mademoiselle Boleyn.* New York: New American Library, 2007.

——— . *The Secret Diary of Anne Boleyn*. New York: Scribner Paperback Fiction, 1997.

Merin, Jennifer. "Philippa Gregory — Jennifer Merin Interview re 'The Other Boleyn Girl.'" *Alliance of Women Film Journalists.* n.d. http://awfj.org/2008/03/01

/philippa-gregory-discusses-the-other-boleyn-girl-with-jennifer-merin
/ (accessed March 25, 2012).

Meyer, Carolyn. *Doomed Queen Anne.* Orlando: Gulliver Books, 2004.

Miller, Arthur. *Death of a Salesman: Certain Private Conversations in Two Acts and a Requiem.* New York: Viking Press, 1949.

Miller-Tomlinson, Tracey. "Pathos and Politics in John Banks' Vertue Betray'd, or Anna Bullen (1682)." *Restoration and 18th Century Theatre* 23, no. 1 (2008): 22.

Mirror.co.uk. "'Tudors' glossy style of history is plots of fun." *Mirror.* August 11, 2008. http://www.mirror.co.uk/news/uk-news/tudors-glossy-style-of-history-is -plots-325944 (accessed March 26, 2012).

Moodie, Clemmie. "Henry VIII: The glaring errors in BBC's sexed-up, dumbed-down Tudors." *Mail Online.* October 24, 2007. http://www.dailymail.co.uk/tvshowbiz /article-489336/Henry-VIII-The-glaring-errors-BBCs-sexed-dumbed-Tudors .html (accessed January 1, 2012).

Moore, Victoria. "The troubling truth about Jonathan Rhys Meyers." *Mail Online.* November 24, 2007. http://www.dailymail.co.uk/tvshowbiz/article-496104/The -troubling-truth-Jonathan-Rhys-Meyers.html (accessed January 15, 2012).

Munn, Michael. *Richard Burton: Prince of Players.* New York: Skyhorse Publishing, 2008.

Neigher, Julie. "Emmy-nominated costume designers on dressing characters with success." *Los Angeles Times.* 2010. http://www.latimes.com/features/image/la-ig -fidm-20100815,0,4709221.story?page=2 (accessed February 20, 2012).

Nettesheim, Heinrich Cornelius Agrippa von. *Of the Nobilitie and Excellencye of Womankynde.* Translated by David Clapam. London, 1542.

Nordyke, Kimberly. "'Tudors' finale doubles its first-season ratings." *Hollywood Reporter.* June 4, 2008. http://www.hollywoodreporter.com/news/tudors-finale -doubles-first-season-113105 (accessed January 15, 2012).

Norton, Elizabeth. *Anne Boleyn: In Her Own Words & in the Words of Those Who Knew Her.* Gloucestershire, UK: Amberley Publishing Plc, 2011.

Oakley-Brown, Liz, and Louise J. Wilkinson. *The Rituals and Rhetoric of Queenship: Medieval to Early Modern.* Dublin: Four Courts Press, 2009.

Oliphant, Margaret. "Modern Light Literature — History." *Blackwood's Edinburgh Magazine* (William Blackwood & Sons) LXXVIII, no. CCCCLXXVII (July 1855).

Paglia, Camille. *Sex, Art, and American Culture: Essays.* New York: Vintage Books, 1992.

———. *Sexual Personae: Art and Decadence from Nefertiti to Emily Dickinson.* Vintage Books: New York, 1991.

Palmer, Melvin D. "Madame d'Aulnoy in England." *Comparative Literature* 27, no. 3 (Summer 1975): 237–253.

Passafuime, Rocco. "Eric Bana interview for The Other Boleyn Girl." *The Cinema Source.* March 14, 2008. http://www.thecinemasource.com/blog/interviews/eric -bana-interview-for-the-other-boleyn-girl/ (accessed April 1, 2012).

Patterson, Annabel. *Early Modern Liberalism.* Cambridge, UK: Cambridge University Press, 1997.

Perry, Maria. *The Word of a Prince: A Life of Elizabeth I.* Woodbridge: Boydell Press, 1999.

"Philippa Gregory watches as her bestseller 'The Other Boleyn Girl' gets the Hollywood treatment." *Times.* February 15, 2008. http://entertainment .timesonline.co.uk/tol/arts_and_entertainment/books/fiction/article3377094.ece (accessed April 13, 2009).

Phillips, Lynn M. *Flirting with Danger: Young Women's Reflections on Sexuality and Domination.* New York: New York University Press, 2000.

Pitman, Joanna. *On Blondes.* New York and London: Bloomsbury, 2003.

Pizan, Christine de. "From *The Book of the City of Ladies.*" In *The Selected Writings of Christine de Pizan.* Edited by Renate Blumenfeld-Kosinski, translated by Renate Blumenfeld-Kosinski and Kevin Brownlee, 116–55. New York: W. W. Norton & Company, 1997.

Plaidy, Jean. *Murder Most Royal: The Story of Anne Boleyn and Catherine Howard.* New York: Three Rivers Press, 2006.

——— . *The Lady in the Tower.* New York: Three Rivers Press, 1986.

Plato. *Plato's Symposium: A Translation by Seth Bernardete with Commentaries by Allan Bloom and Seth Bernardete.* Translated by Seth Bernardete. Chicago: The University of Chicago Press, 2001.

Pointer, Sally. *The Artifice of Beauty: A History and Practical Guide to Perfumes and Cosmetics.* Stroud, UK: Sutton Publishing, 2005.

Pollard, Albert F. *Henry VIII.* London: Longmans, Green and Co., 1919.

Pozner, Jennifer L. "The Surreal Life . . . Reality TV: Harmful fluff or a humorous escape?" *Reality Bites Back Book.* November 2010. http://www .realitybitesbackbook.com/wp-content/uploads/2010/07/Elle-Canada-Surreal -Life.pdf (accessed April 13, 2012).

Purdon, Fiona. "Philippa Gregory found a passion for history turned into the perfect career." *Perth Now.* August 21, 2009. http://www.perthnow.com.au /entertainment/philippa-gregory-found-a-passion-for-history-turned-into-the -perfect-career/story-e6frg3j3-1225765161945 (accessed March 1, 2012).

Raz, Guy. "Alison Weir, Arguing the Case for Anne Boleyn." *All Things Considered.* January 24, 2010. http://www.npr.org/templates/story/story. php?storyId=122872854 (accessed March 25, 2012).

Reaves, Jessica. "Hollywood is no mystery to Gregory." *Chicago Tribune.* March 2, 2008. http://articles.chicagotribune.com/2008-03-02/news/0802290394_1_boleyn-girl -tudor-era-henry-viii (accessed April 13, 2012).

Reed, Rex. "Hot Tudors! Portman, Johansson Are the Boleyn Babes." *New York Observer.* February 26, 2008. http://www.observer.com/2008/02/hot-tudors -portman-johansson-are-the-boleyn-babes/ (accessed March 25, 2012).

Reinke, Rachel. "Catfight: A Feminist Analysis." In *Chrestomathy: Annual Review* of Undergraduate Research, School of Humanities and Social Sciences, School of Languages, Cultures, and World Affairs, College of Charleston (College of Charleston) 9 (2010): 162–85.

Rennell, Tony. "Anne Boleyn, harlot or heroine? Was she a scheming sexual predator, or a brave reformer who changed Britain forever?" *Mail Online.* July 24, 2010. http://www.dailymail.co.uk/femail/article-1296826/Anne-Boleyn-harlot -heroine-Was-scheming-sexual-predator-brave-reformer-changed-Britain-ever .html (accessed March 15, 2012).

Rich, Katey. "Exclusive Interview: Phillippa Gregory, Author of The Other Boleyn Girl." *CinemaBlend.com.* February 28, 2008. http://www.cinemablend.com /new/Exclusive-Interview-Phillippa-Gregory-Author-Of-The-Other-Boleyn -Girl-7994.html (accessed March 1, 2012).

Richardson, R. C. "Historians, History Brokers, Consumers, and English Historical Culture 1800–1970." *CLIO* 37, no. 1 (2007).

Ridgway, Claire. "Anne Boleyn at Shakespeare's Globe — Review." *The Anne Boleyn Files.* August 12, 2011. http://www.theanneboleynfiles.com/10498/anne-boleyn -at-shakespeares-globe-review/ (accessed March 15, 2012).

Ridley, Jasper. *Henry VIII: The Politics of Tyranny.* New York: Viking, 1985.

Rival, Paul. *The Six Wives of Henry VIII.* New York: Berkley Medallion Books, 1971.

Rocchi, James. "Review: The Other Boleyn Girl." *Moviefone.* February 29, 2008. http:// blog.moviefone.com/2008/02/29/review-the-other-boleyn-girl/ (accessed March 25, 2012).

Rodgers, Richard, Oscar Hammerstein, and Joshua Logan. *South Pacific: A Musical Play.* New York: Random House, 1949.

Roiphe, Katie. *The Morning After: Sex, Fear, and Feminism.* New York: Back Bay Books, 1994.

Russell, Gareth. "The Other Boleyn Girl" (review). *Popular.* http://garethrussellpopular .blogspot.com/2011/02/other-boleyn-girl-review.html (accessed March 15, 2012).

Sander, Nicholas. *The Rise and Growth of the Anglican Schism.* London: Burns and Oates, 1877.

Shakespeare, William. *King Henry VIII.* Cambridge, UK: Cambridge University Press, 2012.

——. *The Tragedy of Hamlet, Prince of Denmark.* New Folger. Edited by Barbara A. Mowat and Paul Werstine. New York: Washington Square Press, 1992.

Simon, John. "The Oscars: They Shun the Best, Don't They?" *New York Times,* March 1, 1970.

Singer, S. W. In *The Life of Cardinal Wolsey,* by George Cavendish. London: Harding and Lepard, 1827.

Smith, Lacey Baldwin. "Christ, What a Fright: The Tudor Portrait As an Icon." *Journal of Interdisciplinary History* IV, no. I (Summer 1973): 119–27.

——. *Henry VIII: The Mask of Royalty.* London: Jonathan Cape, 1971.

Sohn, Emily. "King Henry VIII's Madness Explained." *Discovery News.* March 11,

2011. http://news.discovery.com/history/henry-viii-blood-disorder-110311.html (accessed February 22, 2012).

Solanas, Valerie. *SCUM Manifest (1967)*. Vol. III: 1960 to the Present, in *Public Women, Public Words: A Documentary History of American Feminism*, edited by Dawn Keetley and John Pettegrew. Lanham, MD: Rowman & Littlefield Publishers, Inc., 2005.

Solotaroff, Ted. "The Paperbacking of Publishing." *The Nation* 253, no. 11 (October 1991).

Stanley, Alessandra. "Renaissance Romping With Henry and His Rat Pack." *New York Times*. March 30, 2007. http://tv.nytimes.com/2007/03/30/arts /television/30tudo.html?adxnnl=1&pagewanted=all&adxnnlx=1329321911 -kfUxGL6f+8Fx3NXQitmyYg (accessed January 15, 2012).

Starkey, David. *Six Wives: The Queens of Henry VIII*. New York: HarperCollins Publishers, 2004.

———. *Henry: Virtuous Prince*. London: Harper Press, 2008.

Stephenson, Hannah. "The Female Struggle through History; Philippa Gregory Talks to Hannah Stephenson about Translating Her Tales on the Historical Plight of Women for the Screen." *Birmingham Post*. August 27, 2010. www .birminghampost.net (accessed August 30, 2010).

Stepp, Laura. "'Mean Girls' Myth: Why Can't Some Women Let It Go?" *Huffington Post*. February 23, 2011. http://www.huffingtonpost.com/laura-stepp/mean-girls -myth_b_825800.html (accessed March 25, 2012).

Stevens, Hampton. "Fall TV's mean women, milquetoast men." *Washington Times*. September 21, 2011. http://www.washingtontimes.com/news/2011/sep/21/mean -women-milquetoast-men/ (accessed March 25, 2012).

Stjerna, Kirsi. *Women and the Reformation*. Malden, MA: Blackwell Publishing, 2009.

Stone, Lawrence. *The Family, Sex and Marriage in England 1500–1800*. New York: Penguin Books, 1979.

Strickland, Agnes, and Elizabeth Strickland. *Lives of the Queens of England from the Norman Conquest*. Cambridge, UK: Cambridge University Press, 2010.

Stuttaford, Andrew. "Ohhh, Henry: The wickedly entertaining *Tudors*." *National Review Online*. April 2, 2007. http://www.nationalreview.com/articles/220492 /ohhh-henry/andrew-stuttaford (accessed January 15, 2012).

Sweet, Natalie. *Semper Eadem: An Elizabeth I Blog*. sempereademelizabeth.wordpress .com.

Taylor, Tom. "Anne Boleyn." In *Historical Dramas*, by Tom Taylor, 343–414. London: Chatto & Windus, 1877.

Thelander, Dorothy R. "Mother Goose and Her Goslings: The France of Louis XIV as Seen Through the Fairy Tale." *The Journal of Modern History* 54, no. 3 (September 1982): 467–96.

Thomas, Lewis. *The Medusa and the Snail: More Notes of a Biology Watcher*. New York: Penguin Books, 1995.

"Timeless heroines." *Press and Journal*. August 21, 2010. http://www.pressandjournal
.co.uk/Article.aspx/1881239 (accessed March 25, 2010).

Tremlett, Giles. *Catherine of Aragon: The Spanish Queen of Henry VIII*. New York:
Walker Publishing, 2010.

The Tudors Wiki. 2008. http://www.thetudorswiki.com/thread (accessed July 1, 2009).

Tyndale, William. *The Obedience of a Christian Man*. Edited by David Daniell. London:
Penguin Books, 2000.

Vincent, Susan J. *The Anatomy of Fashion: Dressing the Body from the Renaissance to
Today*. Oxford, UK: Berg, 2009.

Vives, Juan Luis. *The Education of a Christian Woman: A Sixteenth-Century Manual*.
Translated by Charles Fantazzi. Chicago: The University of Chicago Press, 2000.

Walker, Greg. *The Private Life of Henry VIII*. The British Film Guide 8. London: I. B.
Tauris & Co. Ltd., 2003.

———. "Rethinking the Fall of Anne Boleyn." *The Historical Journal* 45, no. 1 (March
2002): 1–29.

———. *Writing Under Tyranny: English Literature and the Henrician Reformation*.
Oxford, UK: Oxford University Press, 2005.

Wallechinsky, David, Irving Wallace, and Amy Wallace. *The People's Almanac Presents
The Book of Lists*. New York: William Morrow & Co, 1977.

Wallenstein, Andrew. "Robert Greenblatt's Showtime legacy." *Hollywood Reporter*.
June 27, 2010. http://www.hollywoodreporter.com/news/robert-greenblatts
-showtime-legacy-25016 (accessed March 26, 2012).

Wallis, Hal B., and Charles Higham. *Starmaker: The Autobiography of Hal Wallis*. New
York: Macmillan Publishing Co., 1980.

Warnicke, Retha M. "Anne Boleyn's Childhood and Adolescence." *The Historical
Journal* 28, no. 4 (December 1985): 939–952.

———. "Anne Boleyn Revisited." *The Historical Journal* 34, no. 4 (December 1991):
953–954.

———. "The Fall of Anne Boleyn Revisited." *The English Historical Review* 108, no. 428
(July 1993): 653–665.

———. *The Rise and Fall of Anne Boleyn*. Cambridge, UK: Cambridge University Press,
2002.

Weir, Alison. *Mary Boleyn: The Mistress of Kings*. New York: Ballantine Books, 2011.

———. *The Lady in the Tower: The Fall of Anne Boleyn*. New York: Ballantine Books,
2010.

———. *The Six Wives of Henry VIII*. New York: Grove Press, 1991.

"When Royals Become Rock Stars." *Time*. March 22, 2007. http://www.time.com/time
/magazine/article/0,9171,1601865-1,00.html (accessed January 15, 2012).

Whitelock, Anna. "Was Henry VIII really an oaf in leather trousers?" *Guardian*.
October 4, 2007. http://www.guardian.co.uk/theguardian/2007/oct/05
/features11.g2 (accessed January 15, 2007).

Windling, Terri. "*Les Contes des Fées*: The Literary Fairy Tales of France." *The Journal*

of Mythic Arts: Archived Articles. 2000. http://www.endicott-studio.com/rdrm
/forconte.html (accessed April 18, 2011).

Williams, Hattie. "Anne Boleyn — Globe Theatre, London." *Public Reviews*. July 19,
2011. http://www.thepublicreviews.com/anne-boleyn-%E2%80%93-globe
-theatre-london/ (accessed March 25, 2012).

Wilson, Derek. *In the Lion's Court: Power, Ambition, and Sudden Death in the Reign of
Henry VIII*. New York: St. Martin's, 2003.

Withrow, Brandon G. *Katherine Parr: A Guided Tour of the Life and Thought of a
Reformation Queen*. Phillipsburg, NJ: P & R Publishing, 2009.

Wolf, Jeanne. "Jonathan Rhys Meyers: 'I'm Glad to Say Goodbye' to Tudors." *Parade*.
April 6, 2010. http://www.parade.com/celebrity/celebrity-parade/2010/0406
-jonathan-rhys-meyers-tudors.html (accessed January 15, 2012).

Wolf, Naomi. *Fire with Fire: The New Female Power and How to Use It*. New York:
Vintage, 1994.

Woolf, D. R. "A Feminine Past? Gender, Genre, and Historical Knowledge in
England, 1500–1800." *The American Historical Review* 102, no. 3 (June 1997):
645–79.

Wyatt, George. *Extracts from the Life of the Virtuous Christian and Renowned Queen
Anne Boleigne*. Isle of Thanet: Rev. John Lewis, 1817.

Wyatt, Thomas. "Of the Courtier's Life." In *The Poetical Works of Sir Thomas Wyatt
With Memoir and Critical Dissertation by the Rev. George Gilfillan*. Edinburgh:
James Nichol, 1858.

———. "The Love Describeth His Being Stricken With Sight of His Love." In *The
Poetical Works of Sir Thomas Wyatt With Memoir and Critical Dissertation by
the Rev. George Gilfillan*. Edinburgh: James Nichol, 1858.

Films and Television Series

Adam's Rib. Directed by George Cukor. Performed by Spencer Tracy, Katharine
Hepburn, and Judy Holliday. 1949.

The Adventures of Robin Hood. Directed by Michael Curtiz and William Keighley.
Performed by Olivia de Havilland, Basil Rathbone, and Errol Flynn. 1938.

Alice Doesn't Live Here Anymore. Directed by Martin Scorsese. Performed by Kris
Kristofferson, Mia Bendixsen, and Ellen Burstyn. 1974.

Ally McBeal. Directed by Mel Damski, et al. Performed by Calista Flockhart, Greg
Germann, and Jane Krakowski. 1997–2002.

America's Next Top Model. Directed by Tony Croll, et al. Performed by Tyra Banks, Jay
Manuel, and Nigel Barker. 2003–2012.

Anna Boleyn. Directed by Ernst Lubitsch. Performed by Henny Porten, Emil Jannings,
and Paul Hartmann. 1920.

Anne of the Thousand Days. Directed by Charles Jarrott. Performed by Geneviève
Bujold and Richard Burton. 1969.

Anonymous. Directed by Roland Emmerich. Performed by Rhys Ifans, Vanessa Redgrave, and David Thewlis. 2011.

The Bachelor. Directed by Ken Fuchs, et al. Performed by Brad Womack, Ali Fedotowsky, and Chris Harrison. 2002–2012.

Barefoot in the Park. Directed by Gene Saks. Performed by Robert Redford, Jane Fonda, and Charles Boyer. 1967.

Becket. Directed by Peter Glenville. Performed by Richard Burton, Peter O'Toole, and John Gielgud. 1964.

Beverly Hills, 90210. Directed by Daniel Attias, et al. Performed by Jason Priestley, Shannen Doherty, and Luke Perry. 1990–2000.

Bonnie and Clyde. Directed by Arthur Penn. Performed by Warren Beatty, Faye Dunaway, and Michael J. Pollard. 1967.

Brideshead Revisited. Directed by Michael Lindsay-Hogg and Charles Sturridge. Performed by Jeremy Irons, Diana Quick, and Roger Milner. 1981.

Butch Cassidy and the Sundance Kid. Directed by George Roy Hill. Performed by Paul Newman, Robert Redford, and Katharine Ross. 1969.

Camelot. Directed by Joshua Logan. Performed by Richard Harris, Vanessa Redgrave, and Franco Nero. 1967.

Casablanca. Directed by Michael Curtiz. Performed by Humphrey Bogart, Ingrid Bergman, and Paul Henreid. 1942.

Dallas. Directed by Leonard Katzman, et. al. Performed by Ken Kercheval, Patrick Duffy, and Larry Hagman. 1978–1991.

Danger UXB. Directed by Ferdinand Fairfax, et. al. Performed by Maurice Roëves, George Innes, and Anthony Andrews. 1979.

Dawson's Creek. Directed by Gregory Prange, et al. Performed by James Van Der Beek, Katie Holmes, and Michelle Williams. 1998–2003.

Desperate Housewives. Directed by David Grossman, et al. Performed by Teri Hatcher, Felicity Huffman, and Marcia Cross. 2004–2012.

Dexter. Directed by John Dahl, et al. Performed by Michael C. Hall, Jennifer Carpenter, and Lauren Vélez. 2006–2012.

Dynasty. Directed by Irving J. Moore, et al. Performed by Linda Evans, Joan Collins, and John Forsythe. 1981–1989.

Easy Rider. Directed by Dennis Hopper. Performed by Peter Fonda, Dennis Hopper, and Jack Nicholson. 1969.

Elizabeth: The Golden Age. Directed by Shekhar Kapur. Performed by Cate Blanchett, Geoffrey Rush, and Clive Owen. 1998.

Elizabeth R. Directed by Roderick Graham, et al. Performed by Glenda Jackson, Ronald Hines, and Stephen Murray. 1971.

Fatal Attraction. Directed by Adrian Lyne. Performed by Michael Douglas, Glenn Close, and Anne Archer. 1987.

Father of the Bride. Directed by Vincente Minnelli. Performed by Spencer Tracy, Joan Bennett, and Elizabeth Taylor. 1950.

The Forsyte Saga. Directed by James Cellan Jones and David Giles. Performed by
 Margaret Tyzack, Nyree Dawn Porter, and Eric Porter. 1967.

Frost/Nixon. Directed by Ron Howard. Performed by Frank Langella, Michael Sheen,
 and Kevin Bacon. 2008.

The Graduate. Directed by Mike Nichols. Performed by Dustin Hoffman, Anne
 Bancroft, and Katharine Ross. 1967.

La Guerre Est Finie. Directed by Alain Resnais. Performed by Yves Montand, Ingrid
 Thulin, and Geneviève Bujold. 1966.

The Hand That Rocks the Cradle. Directed by Curtis Hanson. Performed by Annabella
 Sciorra, Rebecca De Mornay, and Matt McCoy. 1992.

Henry VIII. Directed by Pete Travis. Performed by Ray Winstone, Joss Ackland, and
 Sid Mitchell. 2003.

Henry VIII: Mind of a Tyrant. Directed by David Sington. Performed by Roger Aston-
 Griffiths, Laurence Spellman, and David Starkey. 2009.

House M.D. Directed by Greg Yaitanes, et al. Performed by Hugh Laurie, Omar Epps,
 and Robert Sean Leonard. 2004–2012.

I, Claudius. Directed by Herbert Wise. Performed by Derek Jacobi, John Hurt, and Siân
 Phillips. 1976.

In the Heat of the Night. Directed by Norman Jewison. Performed by Sidney Poitier,
 Rod Steiger, and Warren Oates. 1967.

Isabel. Directed by Paul Almond. Performed by Geneviève Bujold, Lynden Bechervaise,
 and Therese Cadorette. 1968.

JFK. Directed by Oliver Stone. Performed by Gary Oldman, Jack Lemmon, and Kevin
 Costner. 1991.

King of the Hill. Directed by Klay Hall, et al. Performed by Mike Judge, Kathy Najimy,
 and Pamela Adlon. 1997–2010.

The L Word. Directed by Rose Troche, et al. Performed by Leisha Hailey, Laurel
 Holloman, and Jennifer Beals. 2004–2012.

The Last King of Scotland. Directed by Kevin Macdonald. Performed by James McAvoy,
 Forest Whitaker, and Gillian Anderson. 2006.

Little Caesar. Directed by Mervyn LeRoy. Performed by Douglas Fairbanks Jr., Glenda
 Farrell, and Edward G. Robinson. 1931.

Lonesome Dove. Directed by Simon Wincer. Performed by Robert Duvall, Tommy Lee
 Jones, and Danny Glover. 1989.

A Man for All Seasons. Directed by Fred Zinnemann. Performed by Robert Shaw, Paul
 Scofield, and Wendy Hiller. 1966.

Mean Girls. Directed by Mark Waters. Performed by Lindsay Lohan, Jonathan Bennett,
 and Rachel McAdams. 2004.

Melrose Place. Directed by Charles Correll, et al. Performed by Heather Locklear,
 Andrew Shue, and Courtney Thorne-Smith. 1992–1999.

Midnight Cowboy. Directed by John Schlesinger. Performed by Jon Voight, Sylvia Miles,
 and Dustin Hoffman. 1969.

The Other Boleyn Girl. Directed by Justin Chadwick. Performed by Natalie Portman, Scarlett Johansson, and Eric Bana. 2008.

The Other Boleyn Girl. Directed by Philippa Lowthorpe. Performed by Natascha McElhone, Jodhi May, and Jared Harris. 2003.

Party of Five. Directed by Daniel Attias, et al. Performed by Scott Wolf, Neve Campbell, and Matthew Fox. 1994–2000.

Pretty Woman. Directed by Garry Marshall. Performed by Richard Gere, Julia Roberts, and Jason Alexander. 1990.

The Prime of Miss Jean Brodie. Directed by Ronald Neame. Performed by Maggie Smith, Gordon Jackson, and Robert Stephens. 1969.

The Private Life of Henry VIII. Directed by Alexander Korda. Performed by Charles Laughton, Robert Donat, and Franklin Dyall. 1933.

The Private Lives of Elizabeth and Essex. Directed by Michael Curtiz. Performed by Bette Davis, Errol Flynn, and Olivia de Havilland. 1939.

The Queen. Directed by Stephen Frears. Performed by Michael Sheen, James Cromwell, and Helen Mirren. 2006.

The Real Housewives of Atlanta. Directed by Carlos P. Sanchez, et al. Performed by NeNe Leakes, Sheree Whitfield, and Kim Zolciak. 2008–2012.

The Real Housewives of Orange County. Directed by Michael Dimich, et al. Performed by Vicki Gunvalson, Tamra Barney, and Gretchen Rossi. 2006–2010.

Roots. Directed by David Greene, et al. Performed by LeVar Burton, Olivia Cole, and Ben Vereen. 1977.

Sex and the City. Directed by Michael Patrick King, et al. Performed by Sarah Jessica Parker, Kim Cattrall, and Kristin Davis. 1998–2004.

Six Feet Under. Directed by Alan Ball, et al. Performed by Peter Krause, Michael C. Hall, and Frances Conroy. 2001–2005.

The Six Wives of Henry VIII. Directed by Naomi Capon and John Glenister. Performed by Keith Michell, Anthony Quayle, and Patrick Troughton. 1970.

The Sopranos. Directed by Timothy Van Patten, et al. Performed by James Gandolfini, Lorraine Bracco, and Edie Falco. 1999–2007.

Steel Magnolias. Directed by Herbert Ross. Performed by Shirley MacLaine, Olympia Dukakis, and Sally Field. 1989.

Thelma & Louise. Directed by Ridley Scott. Performed by Susan Sarandon, Geena Davis, and Harvey Keitel. 1991.

True Confessions. Directed by Ulu Grosbard. Performed by Robert De Niro, Robert Duvall, and Charles Durning. 1981.

True Grit. Directed by Henry Hathaway. Performed by John Wayne, Kim Darby, and Glen Campbell. 1969.

The Tudors. Directed by Ciaran Donnelly, et al. Performed by Jonathan Rhys Meyers, Henry Cavill, and Anthony Brophy. 2007–2010.

An Unmarried Woman. Directed by Paul Mazursky. Performed by Alan Bates, Michael Murphy, and Jill Clayburgh. 1978.

Weeds. Directed by Craig Zisk, et al. Performed by Mary-Louise Parker, Hunter Parrish, and Alexander Gould. 2005–2012.

The West Wing. Directed by Alex Graves, et al. Performed by Martin Sheen, Rob Lowe, and Allison Janney. 1999–2006.

Who's Afraid of Virginia Woolf? Directed by Mike Nichols. Performed by Elizabeth Taylor, Richard Burton, and George Segal. 1966.

The Wild Bunch. Directed by Sam Peckinpah. Performed by William Holden, Ernest Borgnine, and Robert Ryan. 1969.

The Winds of War. Directed by Dan Curtis. Performed by Robert Mitchum, Ali MacGraw, and Jan-Michael Vincent. 1983.

The X-Files. Directed by Kim Manners, et al. Performed by Gillian Anderson, Mitch Pileggi, and David Duchovny. 1993–2002.

Yankee Doodle Dandy. Directed by Michael Curtiz. Performed by Joan Leslie, Walter Huston, and James Cagney. 1942.

Interviews

Alexander, Barb. Interview with author, e-mail, Lexington, KY, October 24, 2011.

Baker, Karissa. Interview with author and Natalie Sweet, e-mail, Lexington, KY, April 2011.

Booth, Sue. Interview with author, e-mail, Lexington, KY, October 24, 2011.

Brenton, Howard. Interview with author, London, England, July 30, 2010.

Bryson, Sarah. Interview with author, e-mail, Lexington, KY, October 2011.

Bujold, Geneviève. Interview with author, telephone, Lexington, KY, June 21, 2010.

Case, Makenzie. Interview with author and Natalie Sweet, e-mail, Lexington, KY, April 2011.

Clement, Cate. Interview with author, e-mail, Lexington, KY, 2011.

Compton, Sara. Interview with author and Natalie Sweet, e-mail, Lexington, KY, April 2011.

Crowley, Jessica. Interview with author and Natalie Sweet, e-mail, Lexington, KY, April 2011.

Dormer, Natalie. Interview with author, Richmond upon Thames, England, July 31, 2010.

Eakins, Lara. Interview with author, e-mail, Lexington, KY, November 25, 2011.

George, Margaret. Interview with author, e-mail, Lexington, KY, August 15, 2011.

Gomez, Cris. Interview with author and Natalie Sweet, e-mail, Lexington, KY, April 2011.

Hall, Brittani. Interview with author and Natalie Sweet, e-mail, Lexington, KY, April 2011.

Hirst, Michael. Interview with author, telephone, Lexington, KY, April 28, 2011.

Kistler, Michelle. Interview with author and Natalie Sweet, e-mail, Lexington, KY, April 2011.

Loades, David. Interview with author, e-mail, Lexington, KY, August 29, 2011.

Mantel, Hilary. Interview with author, e-mail, Lexington, KY, October 5, 2011.

Maxwell, Robin. Interview with author, telephone, Lexington, KY, August 19, 2011.

Prestes, Jessica. Interview with author, e-mail, Lexington, KY, October 2011.

Redler, Ilana. Interview with author and Natalie Sweet, e-mail, Lexington, KY, April 2011.

Ridgway, Claire. Interview with author, e-mail, Lexington, KY, October 24, 2011.

Robyn. Interview with author and Natalie Sweet, e-mail, Lexington, KY, April 2011.

Stivala, Marlessa. Interview with author and Natalie Sweet, e-mail, Lexington, KY, April 2011.

Sweet, Natalie. Interview with author, e-mail, Lexington, KY, October 24, 2011.

Walker, Sophie. Interview with author and Natalie Sweet, e-mail, Lexington, KY, April 2011.

Weir, Alison. Interview with author, e-mail, Lexington, KY, August 24, 2011.

Zupanec, Sylwia Sobczak. Interview with author, e-mail, Lexington, KY, October 24, 2011.

Index